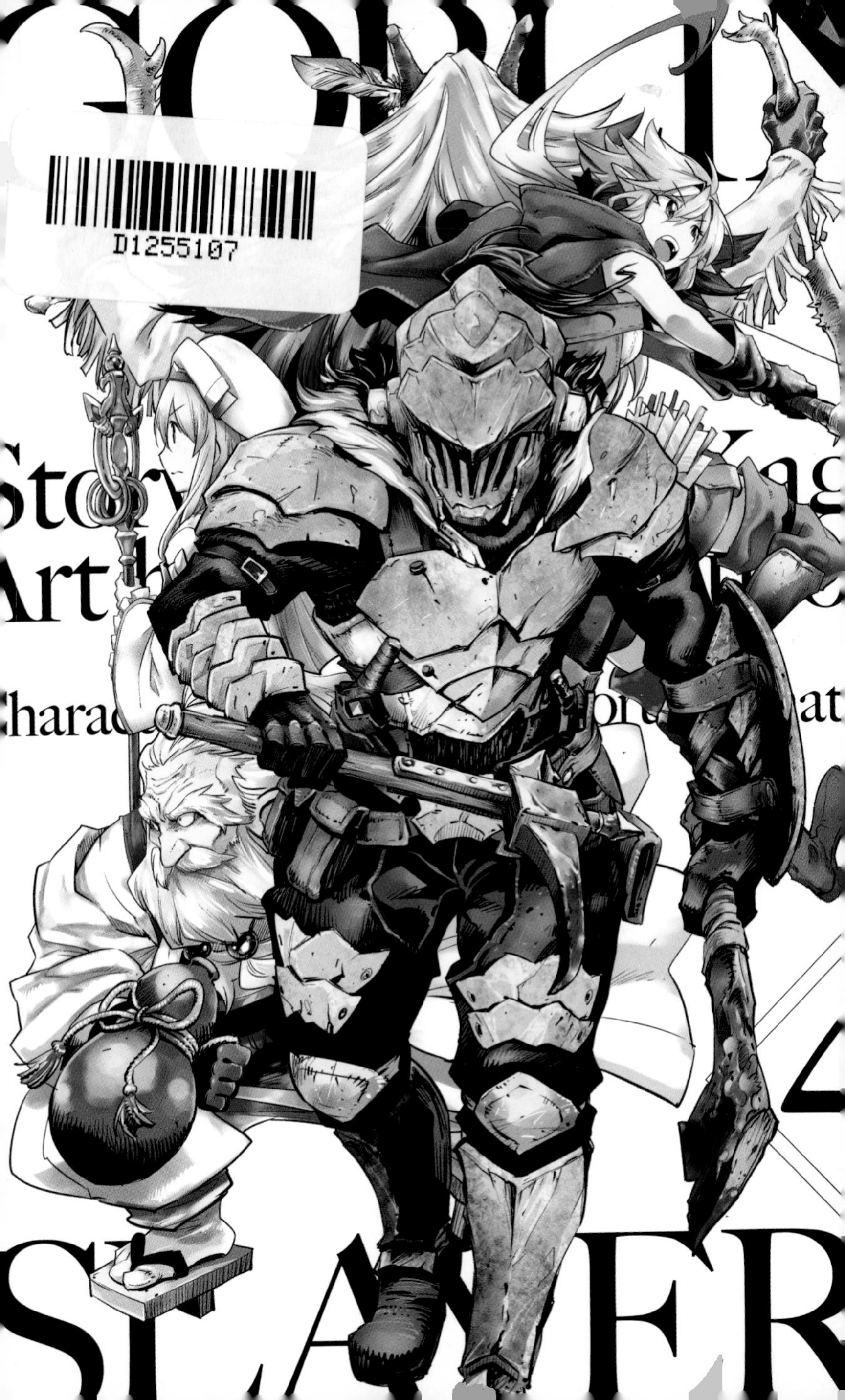

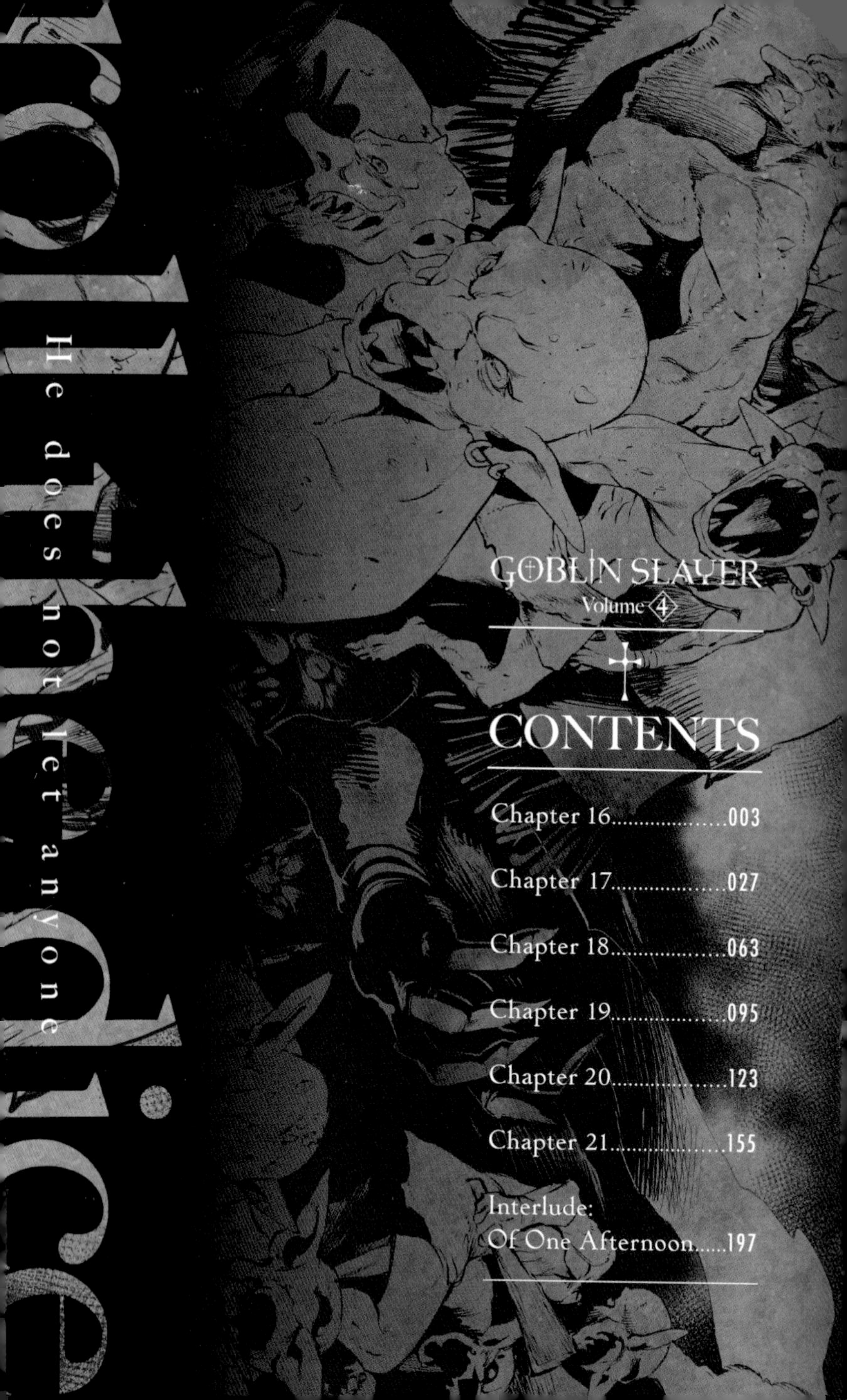
He does not let anyone
roll the dice

GOBLIN SLAYER
Volume 4

CONTENTS

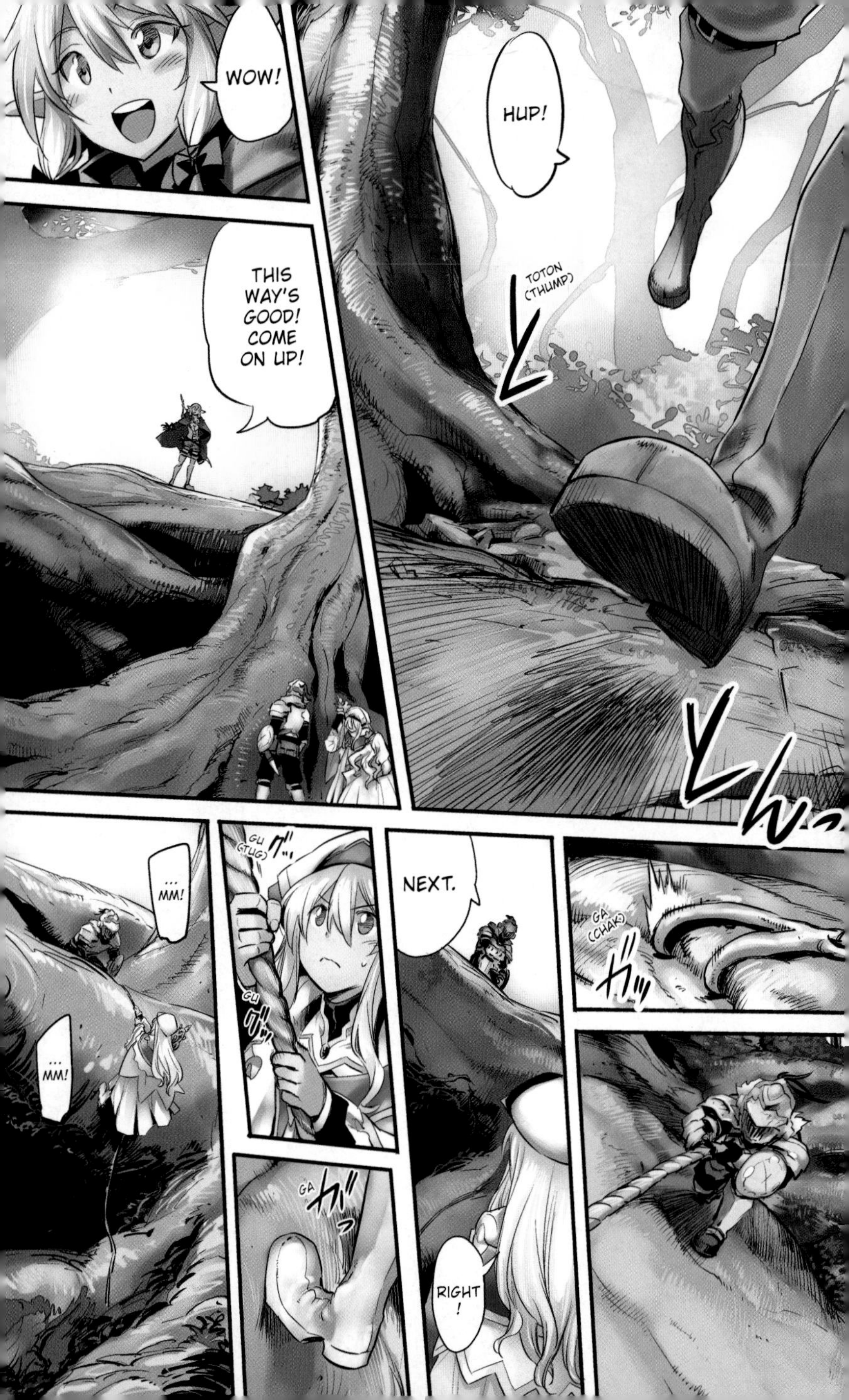
HUP!
TOTON (THUMP)
WOW!
THIS WAY'S GOOD! COME ON UP!
GA (CHAK)
NEXT.
GU (TUG)
GU
RIGHT!
GA
... MM!
... MM!

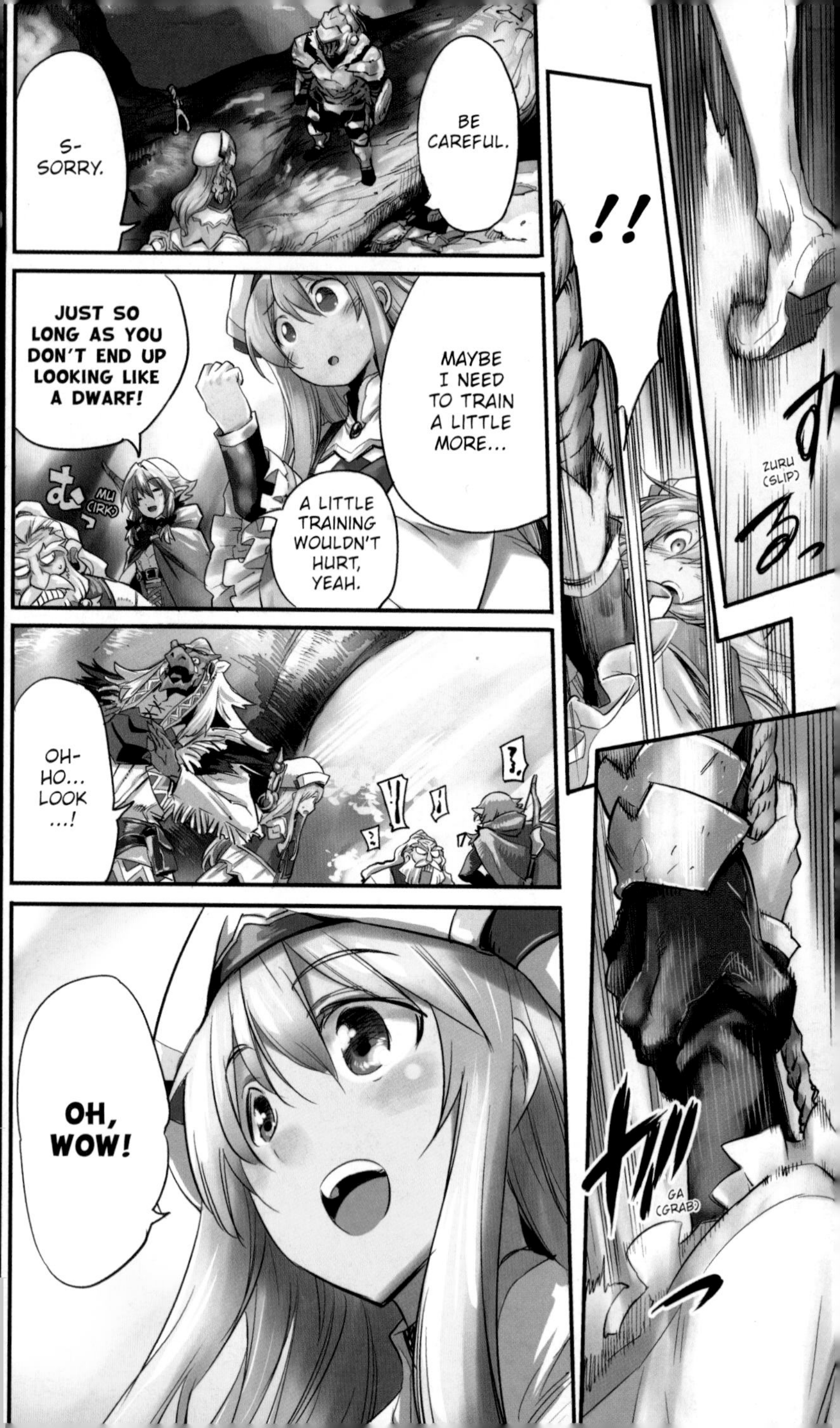
ZURU (SLIP)
!!
GA (GRAB)
BE CAREFUL.
S- SORRY.
MAYBE I NEED TO TRAIN A LITTLE MORE...
JUST SO LONG AS YOU DON'T END UP LOOKING LIKE A DWARF!
A LITTLE TRAINING WOULDN'T HURT, YEAH.
MU (IRK)
OH-HO... LOOK...!
OH, WOW!

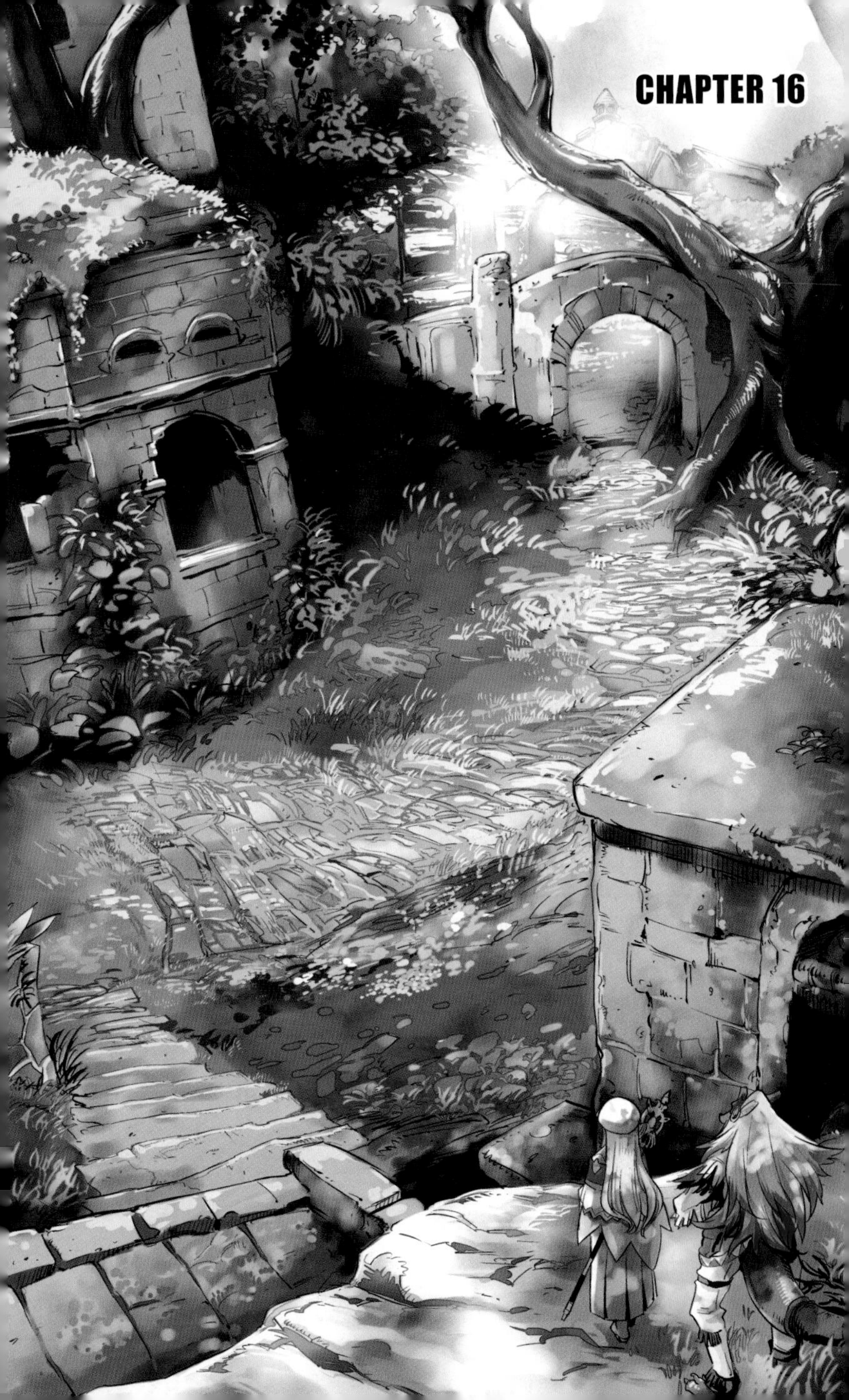
CHAPTER 16

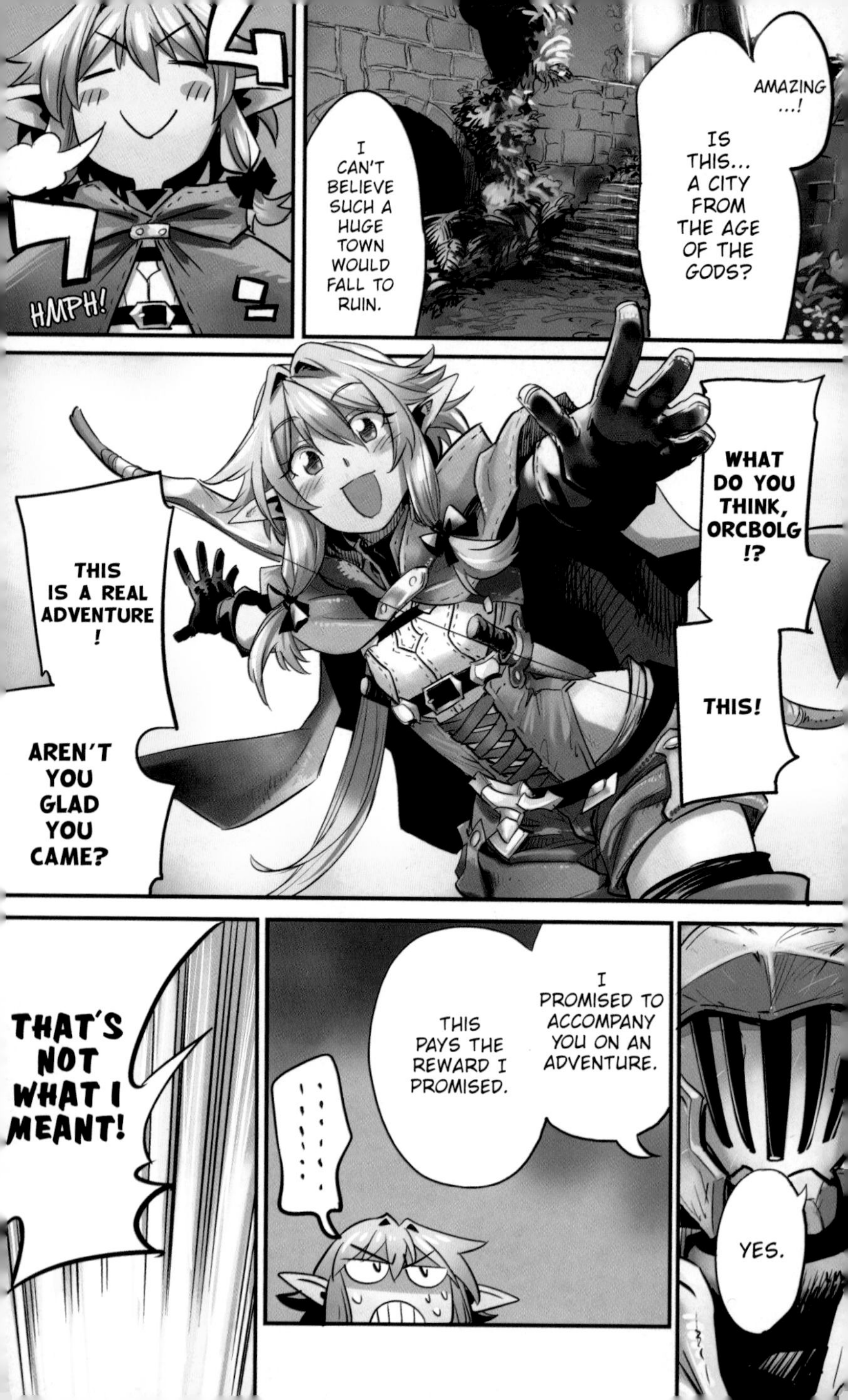
AMAZING...!
IS THIS... A CITY FROM THE AGE OF THE GODS?
I CAN'T BELIEVE SUCH A HUGE TOWN WOULD FALL TO RUIN.
HMPH!
WHAT DO YOU THINK, ORCBOLG!?
THIS!
THIS IS A REAL ADVENTURE!
AREN'T YOU GLAD YOU CAME?
YES.
I PROMISED TO ACCOMPANY YOU ON AN ADVENTURE.
THIS PAYS THE REWARD I PROMISED.
......
THAT'S NOT WHAT I MEANT!

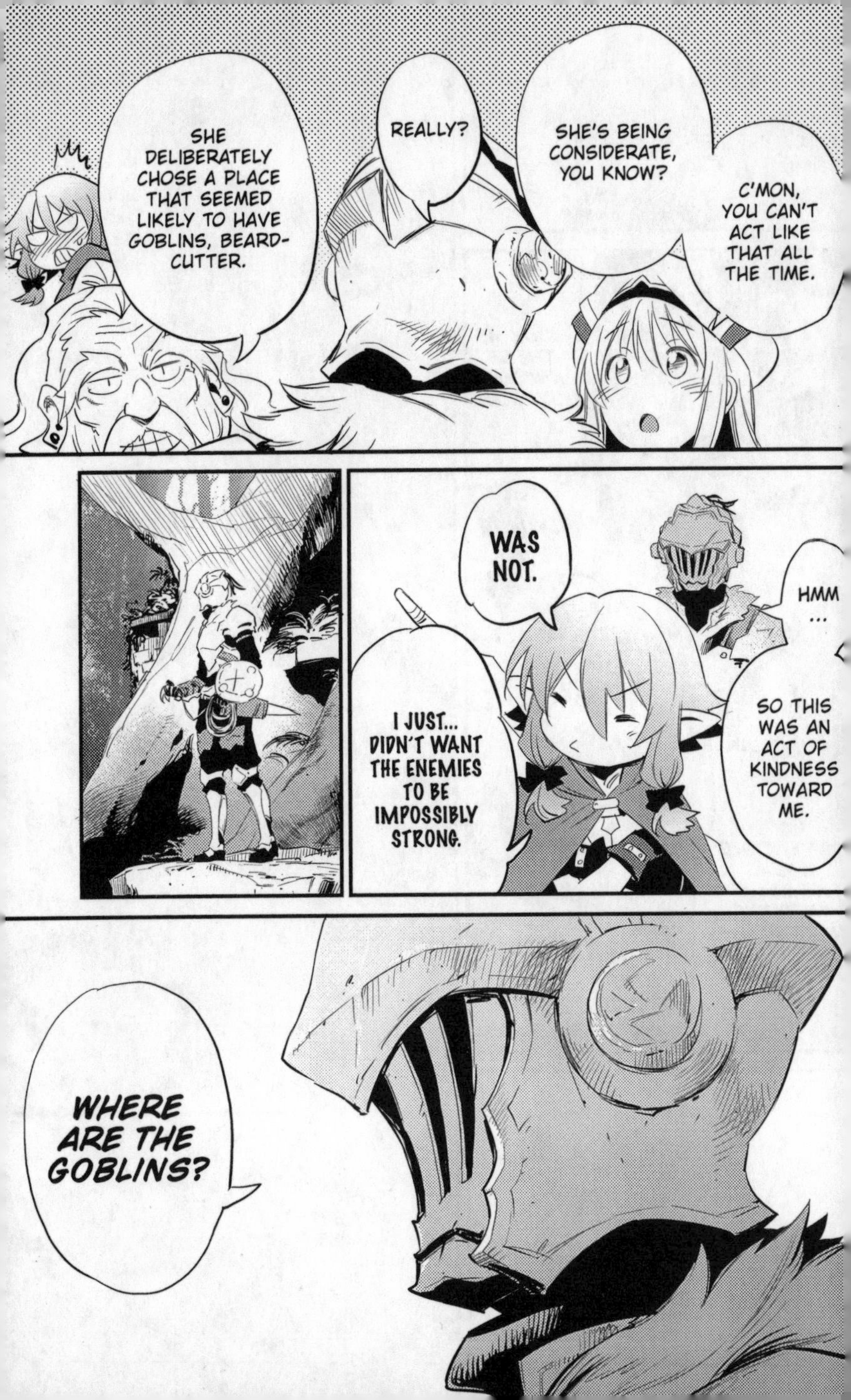
SHE'S BEING CONSIDERATE, YOU KNOW?
C'MON, YOU CAN'T ACT LIKE THAT ALL THE TIME.
REALLY?
SHE DELIBERATELY CHOSE A PLACE THAT SEEMED LIKELY TO HAVE GOBLINS, BEARD-CUTTER.
HMM ...
SO THIS WAS AN ACT OF KINDNESS TOWARD ME.
WAS NOT.
I JUST... DIDN'T WANT THE ENEMIES TO BE IMPOSSIBLY STRONG.
WHERE ARE THE GOBLINS?

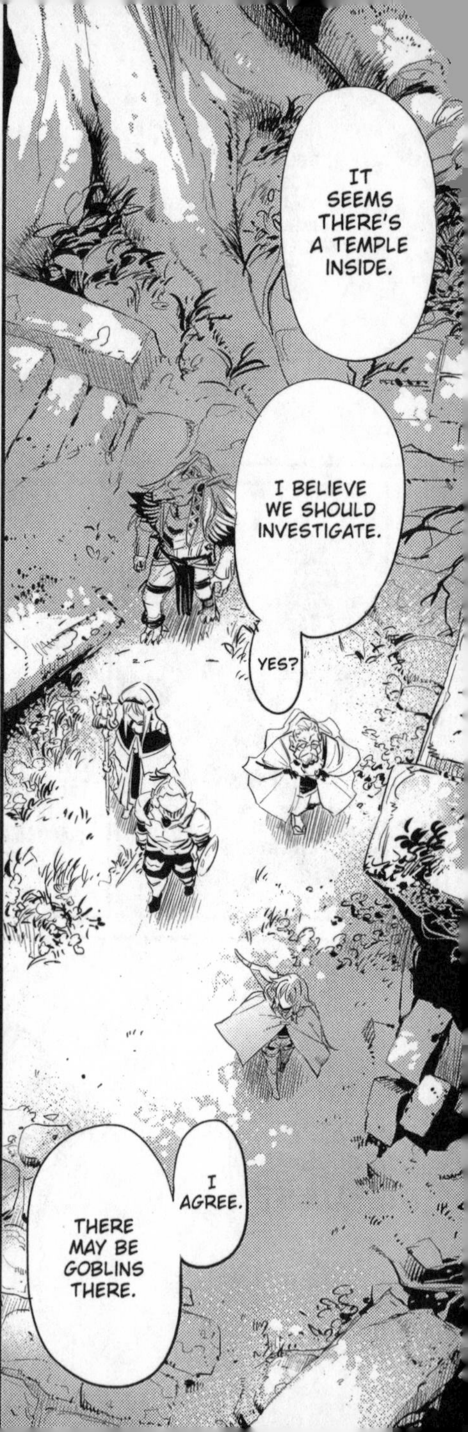
IT SEEMS THERE'S A TEMPLE INSIDE.
I BELIEVE WE SHOULD INVESTIGATE.
YES?
I AGREE.
THERE MAY BE GOBLINS THERE.

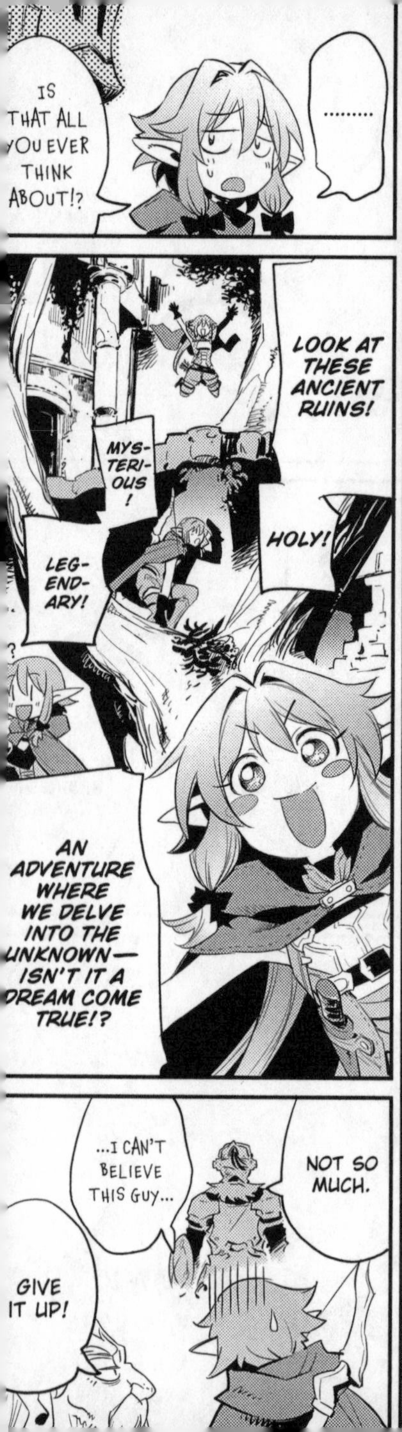
....
IS THAT ALL YOU EVER THINK ABOUT!?
LOOK AT THESE ANCIENT RUINS!
HOLY!
MYS-TERI-OUS!
LEG-END-ARY!
?
AN ADVENTURE WHERE WE DELVE INTO THE UNKNOWN—ISN'T IT A DREAM COME TRUE!?
NOT SO MUCH.
...I CAN'T BELIEVE THIS GUY...
GIVE IT UP!

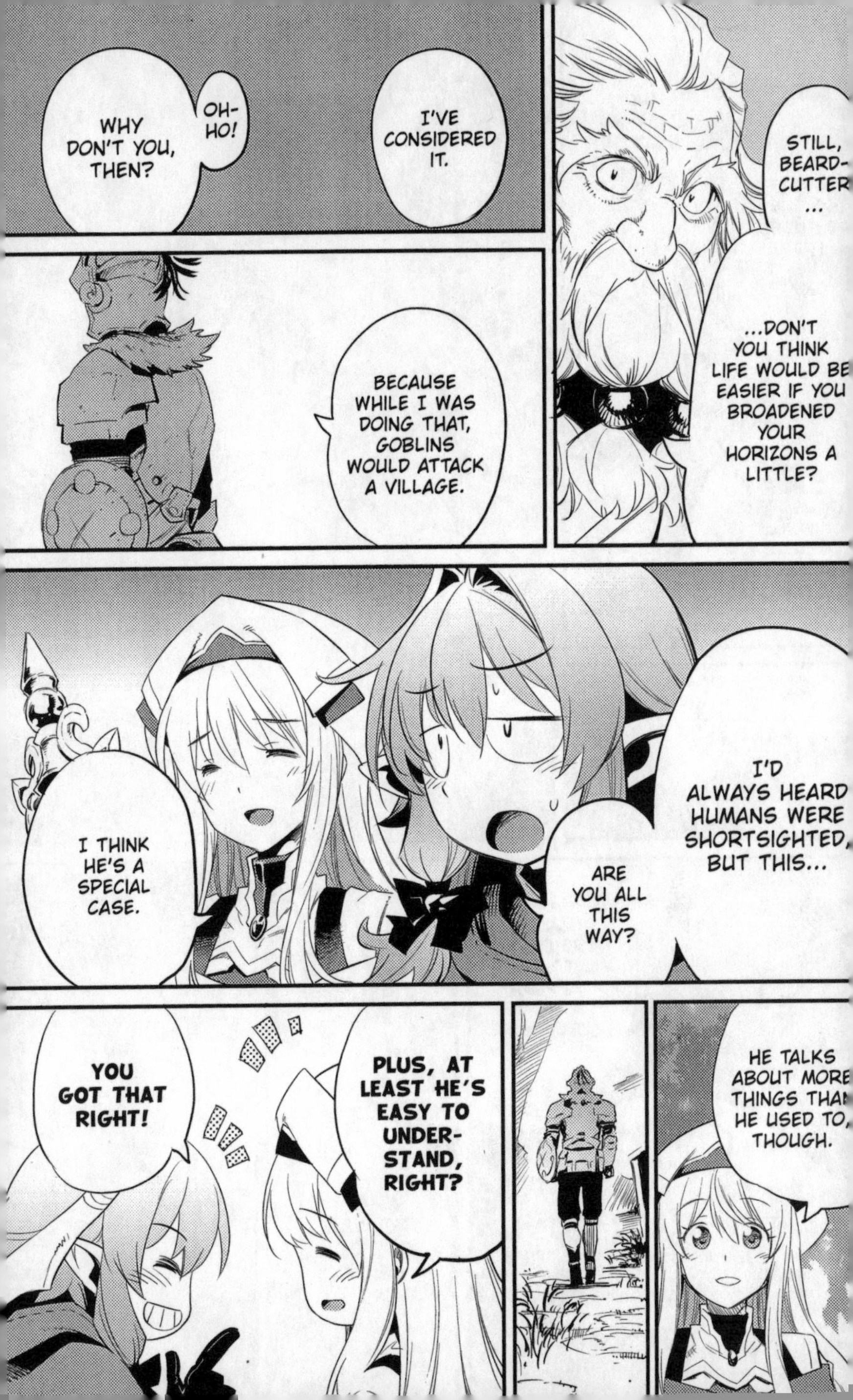
STILL, BEARD-CUTTER...
...DON'T YOU THINK LIFE WOULD BE EASIER IF YOU BROADENED YOUR HORIZONS A LITTLE?
I'VE CONSIDERED IT.
OH-HO!
WHY DON'T YOU, THEN?
BECAUSE WHILE I WAS DOING THAT, GOBLINS WOULD ATTACK A VILLAGE.
I'D ALWAYS HEARD HUMANS WERE SHORTSIGHTED, BUT THIS...
ARE YOU ALL THIS WAY?
I THINK HE'S A SPECIAL CASE.
HE TALKS ABOUT MORE THINGS THAN HE USED TO, THOUGH.
PLUS, AT LEAST HE'S EASY TO UNDERSTAND, RIGHT?
YOU GOT THAT RIGHT!

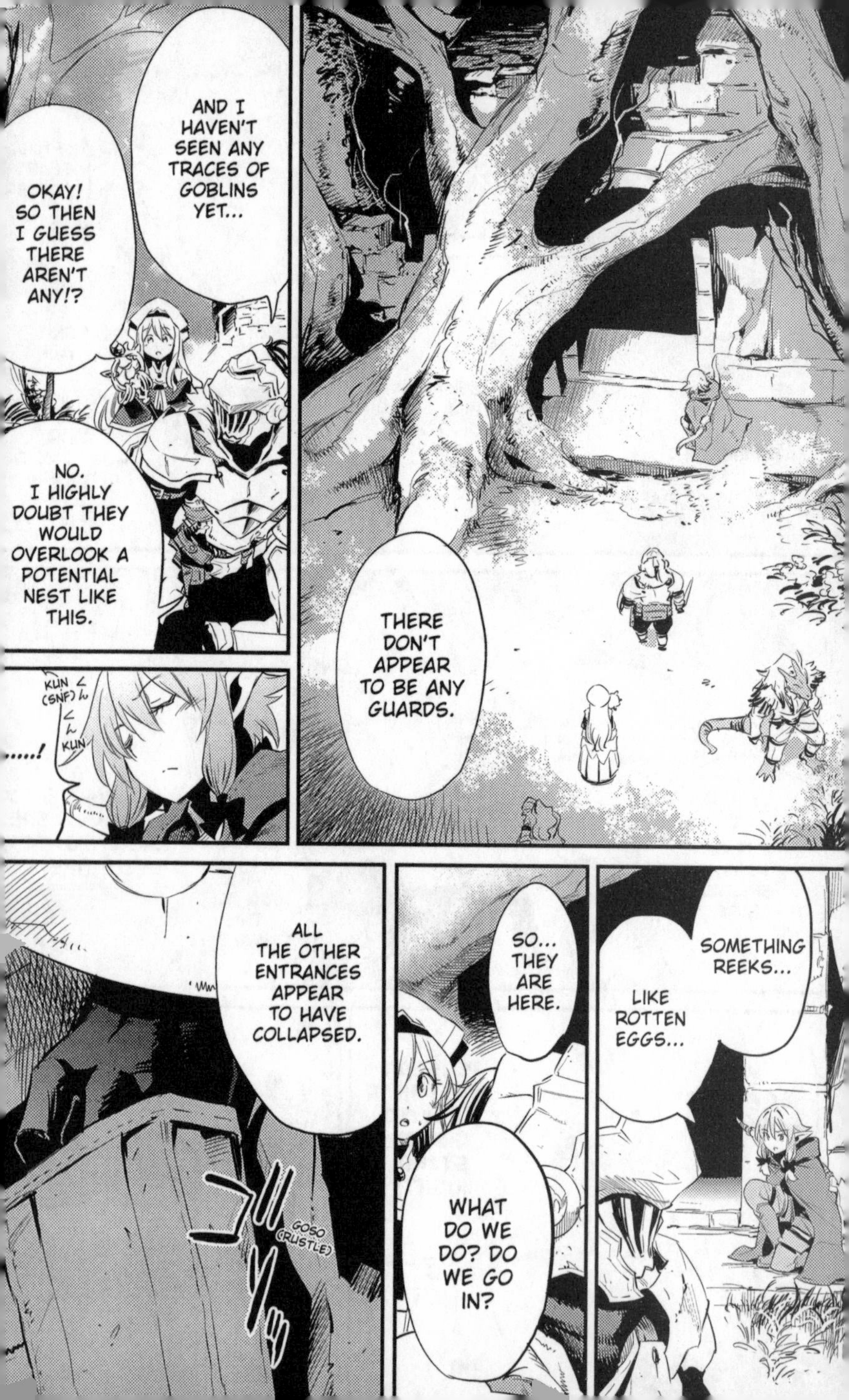
THERE DON'T APPEAR TO BE ANY GUARDS.
AND I HAVEN'T SEEN ANY TRACES OF GOBLINS YET...
OKAY! SO THEN I GUESS THERE AREN'T ANY!?
NO. I HIGHLY DOUBT THEY WOULD OVERLOOK A POTENTIAL NEST LIKE THIS.
KUN (SNF) KUN
.....!
SOMETHING REEKS...
LIKE ROTTEN EGGS...
SO... THEY ARE HERE.
WHAT DO WE DO? DO WE GO IN?
ALL THE OTHER ENTRANCES APPEAR TO HAVE COLLAPSED.
GOSO (RUSTLE)

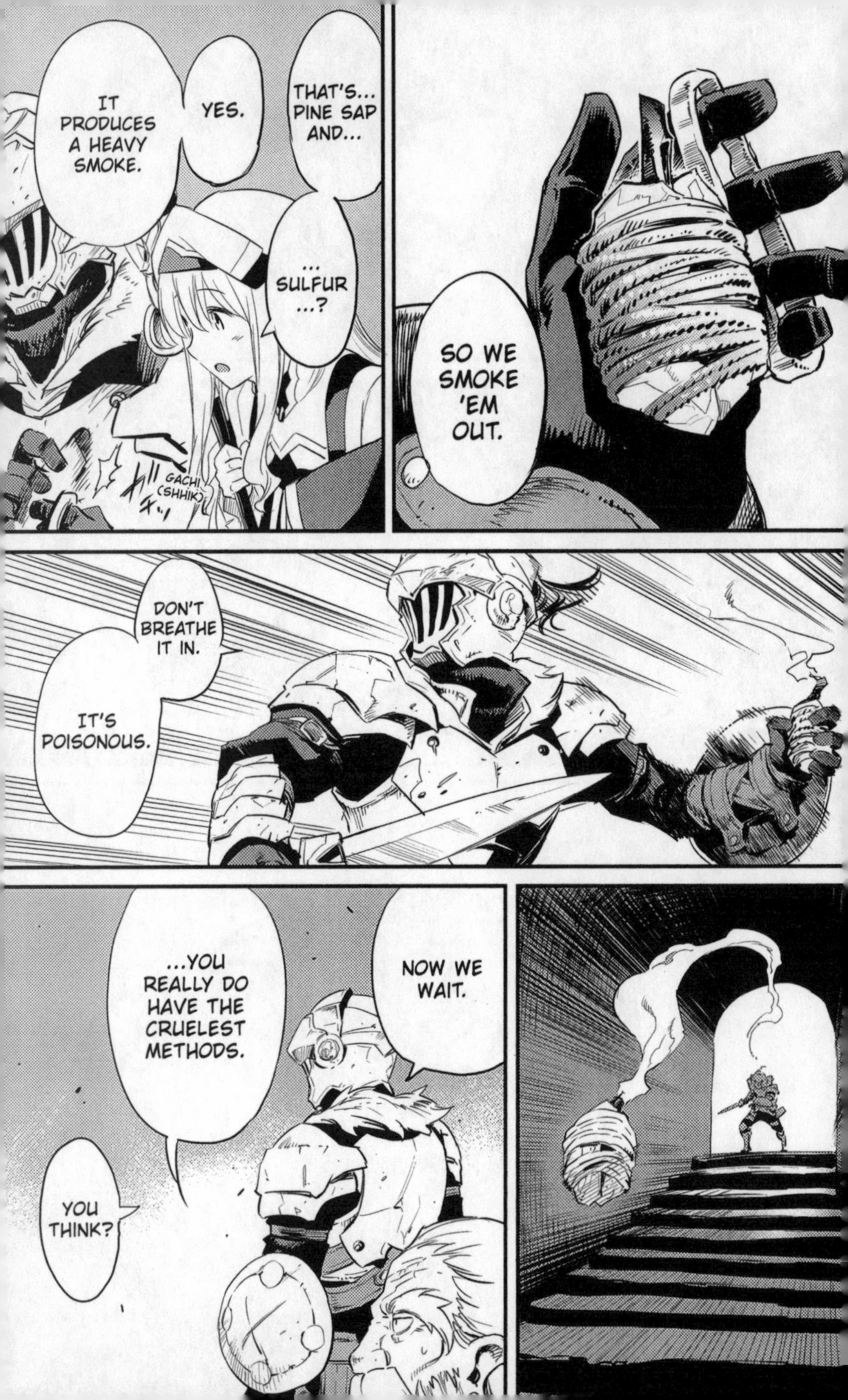
SO WE SMOKE 'EM OUT.
THAT'S... PINE SAP AND...
... SULFUR ...?
YES.
IT PRODUCES A HEAVY SMOKE.
GACHI (SHHIK)
DON'T BREATHE IT IN.
IT'S POISONOUS.
NOW WE WAIT.
...YOU REALLY DO HAVE THE CRUELEST METHODS.
YOU THINK?

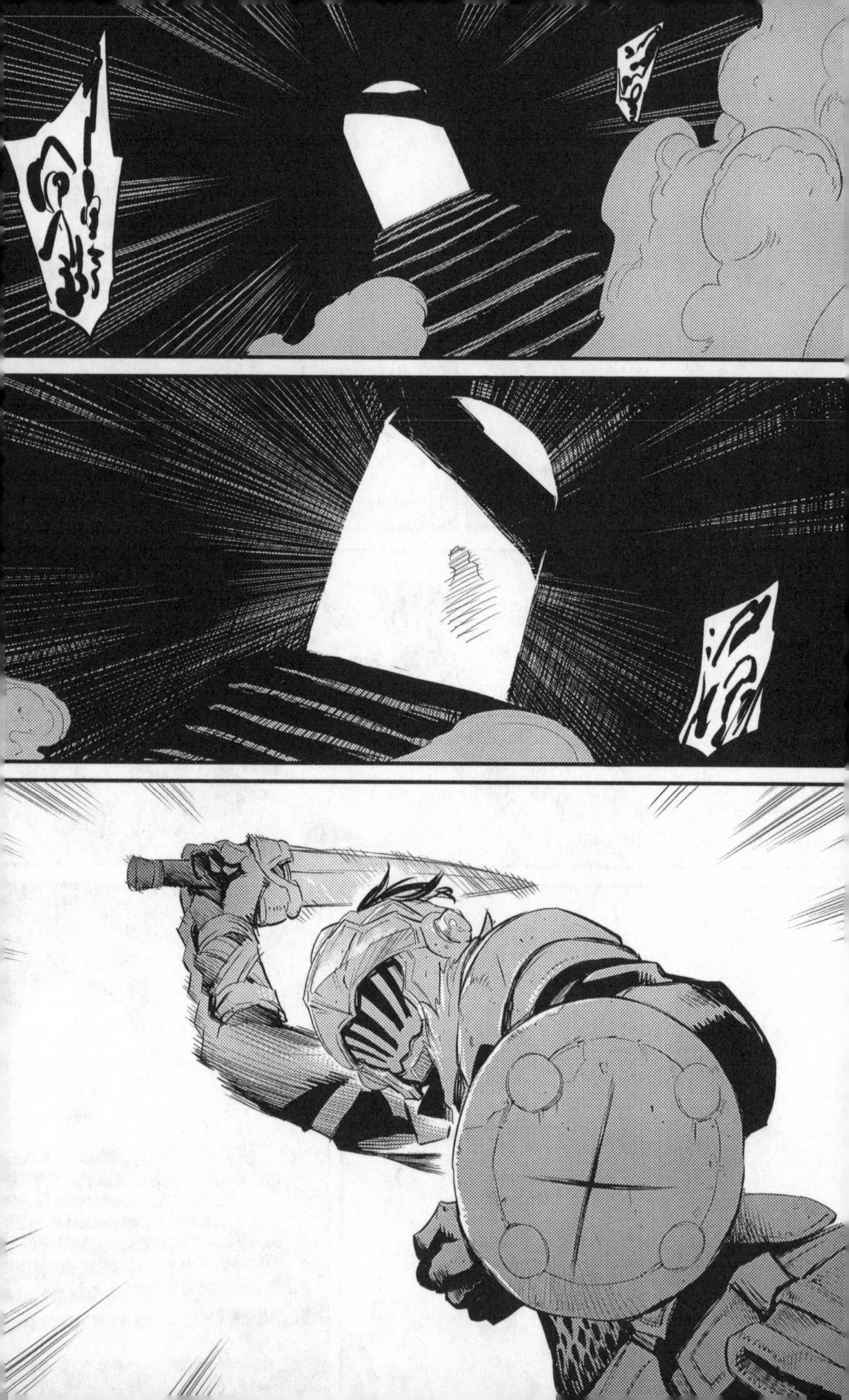

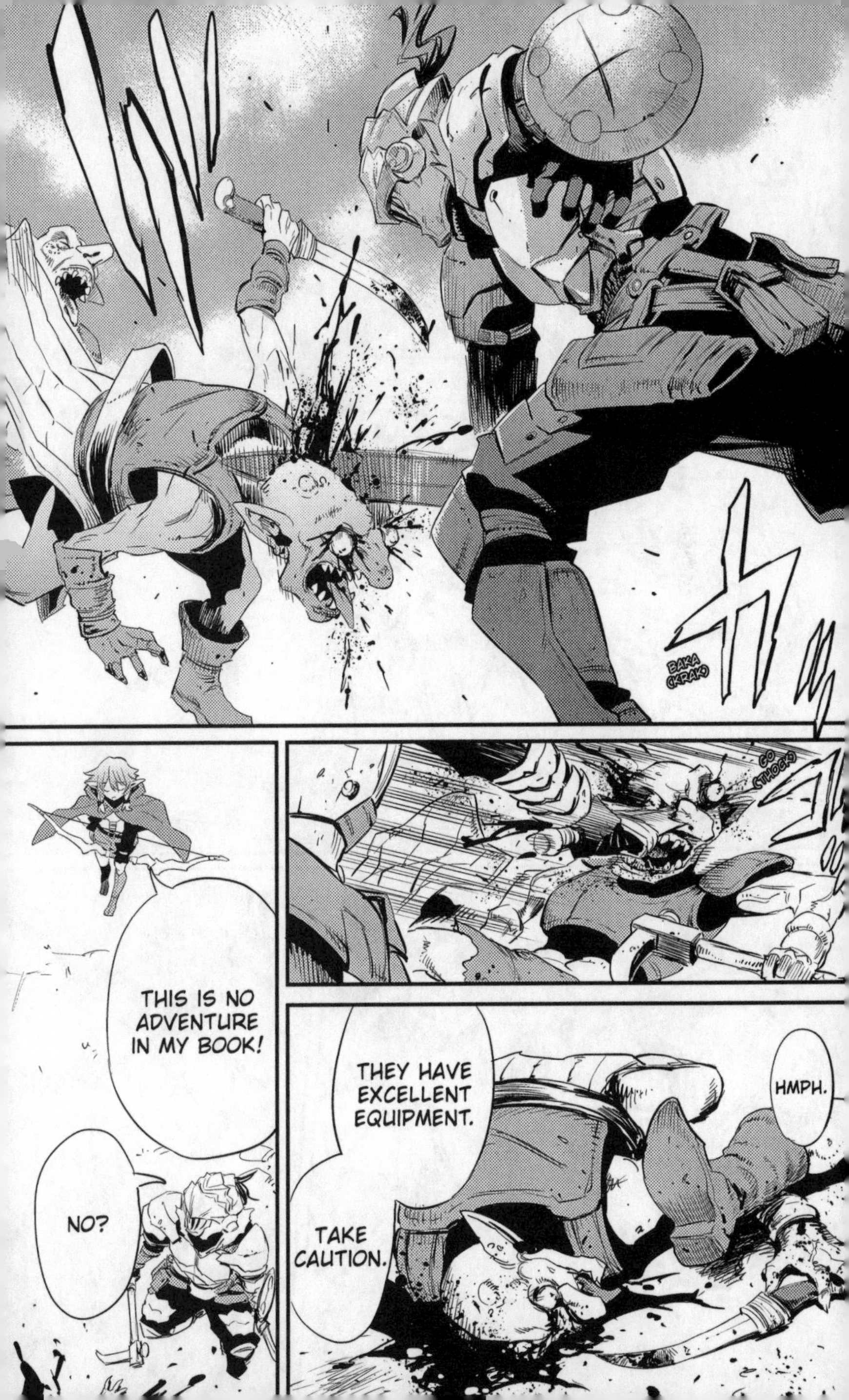
BAKA (KRAK)
GO (THOCK)
HMPH.
THEY HAVE EXCELLENT EQUIPMENT.
TAKE CAUTION.
THIS IS NO ADVENTURE IN MY BOOK!
NO?

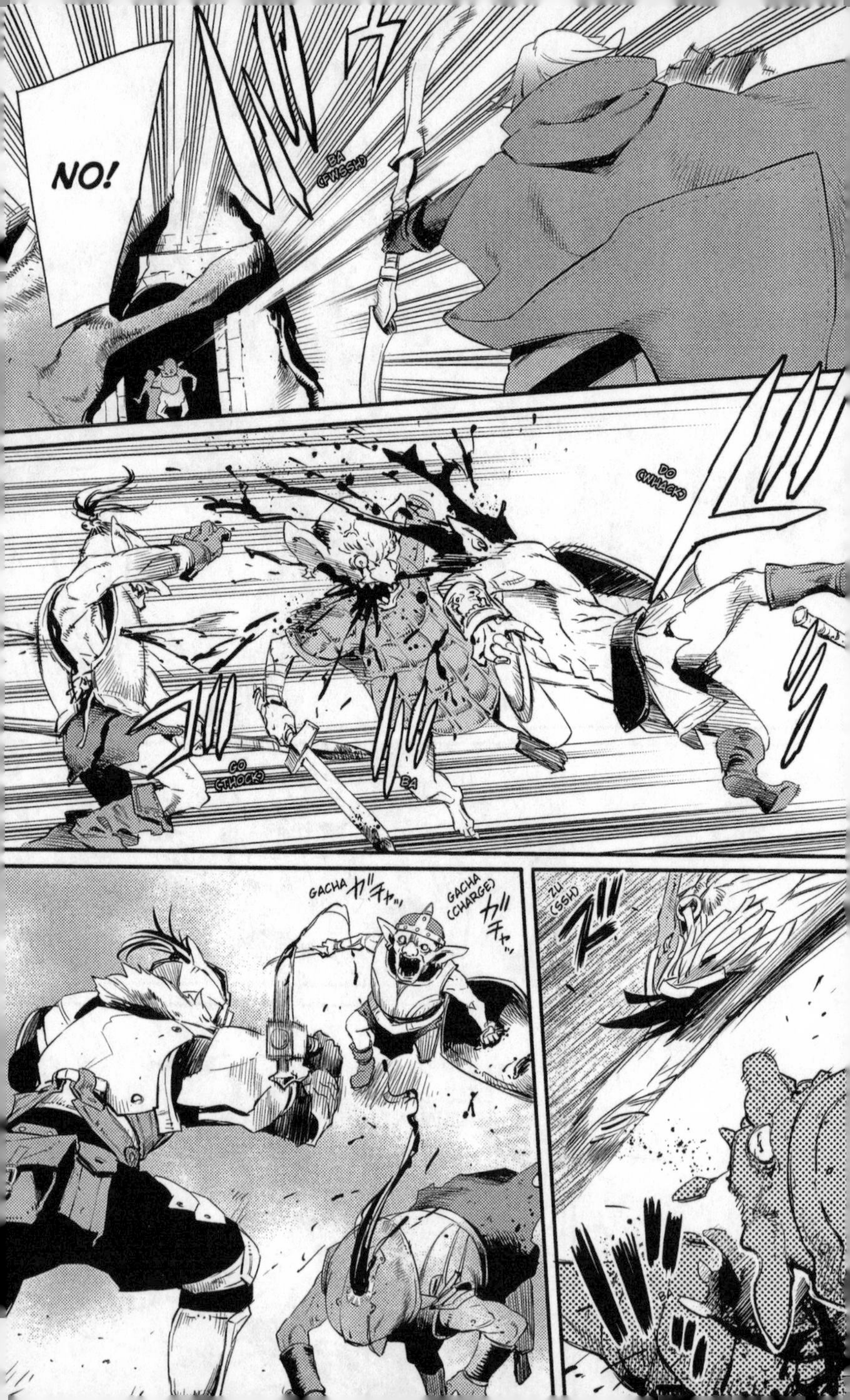
BA (FWSSH)
NO!
DO (WHACK)
BA
GO (THOCK)
ZU (SSH)
BA
GACHA (CHARGE)
GACHA

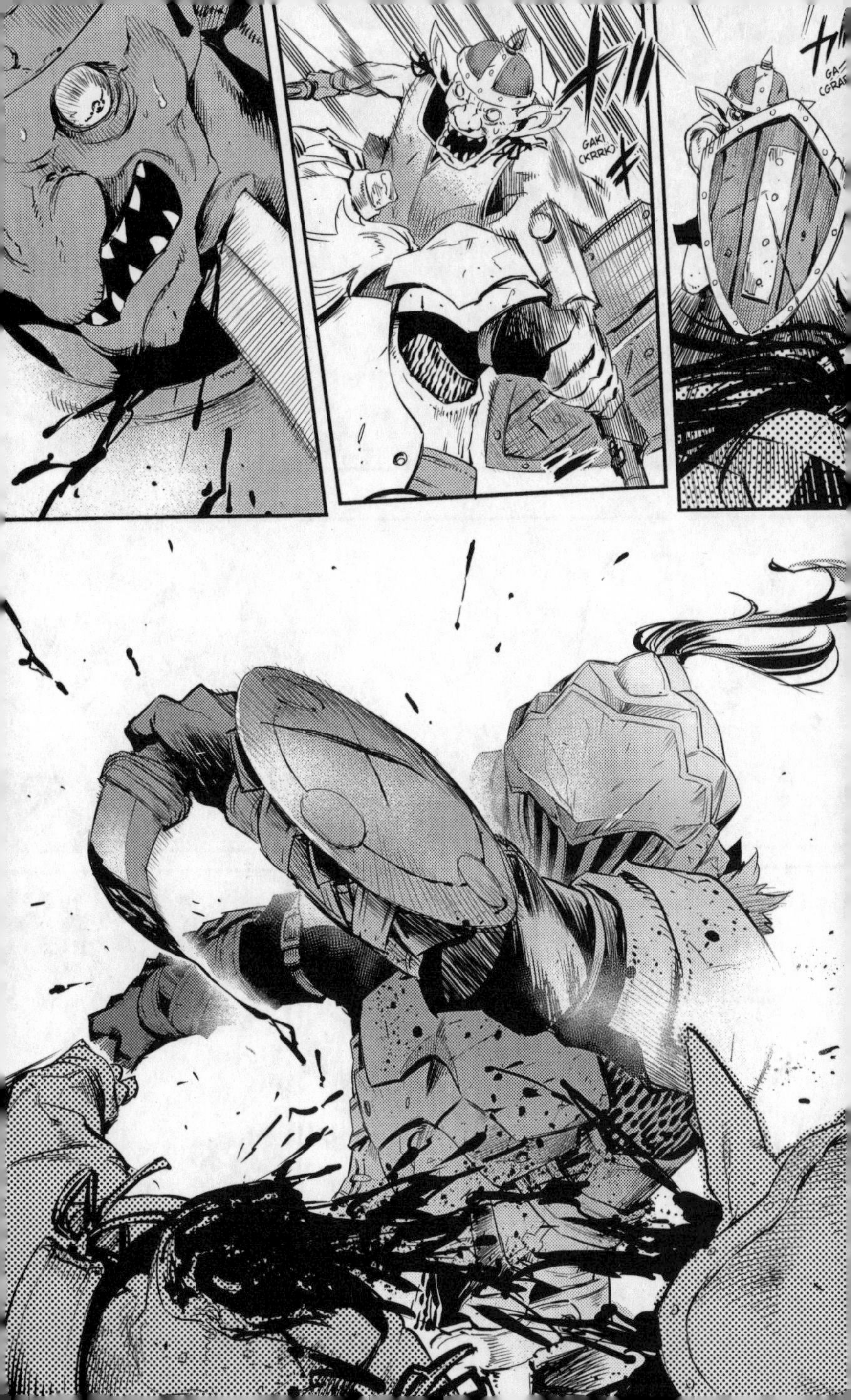

ガ
GA—
(GRAB
ガキ
GAKI
(KRRK)

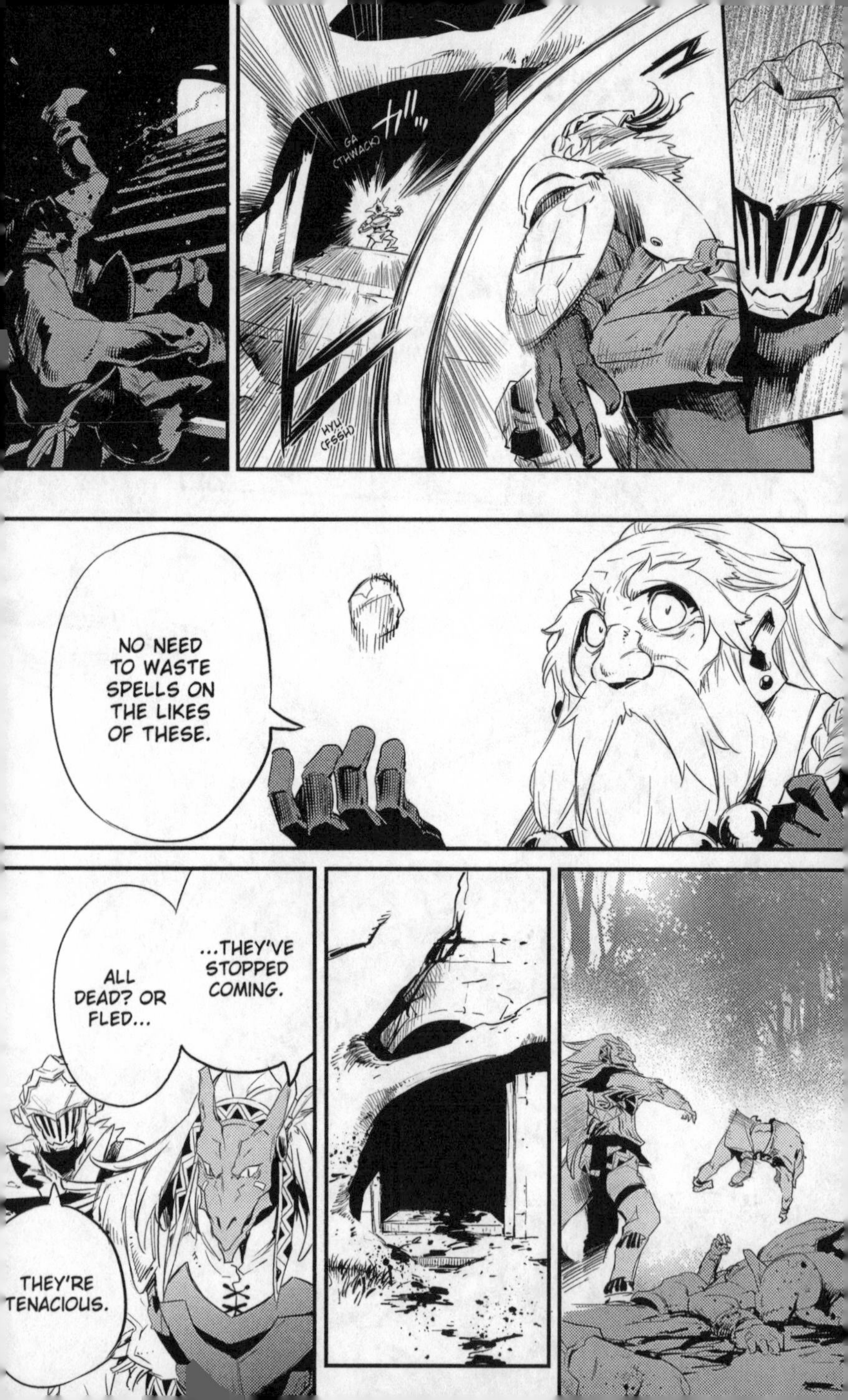
GA (THWACK)
HYU (FSSH)
NO NEED TO WASTE SPELLS ON THE LIKES OF THESE.
...THEY'VE STOPPED COMING.
ALL DEAD? OR FLED...
THEY'RE TENACIOUS.

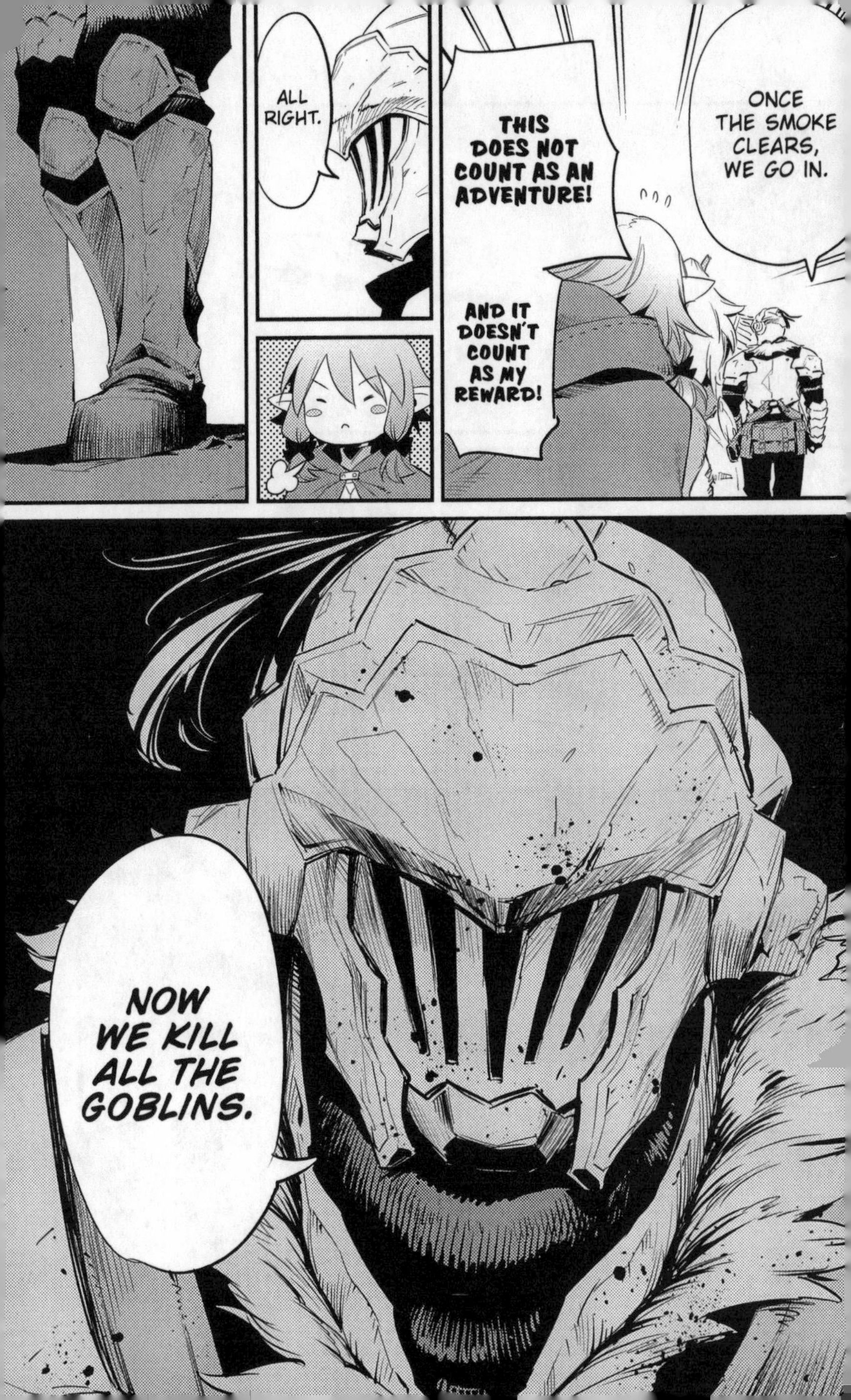

ONCE THE SMOKE CLEARS, WE GO IN.
THIS DOES NOT COUNT AS AN ADVENTURE!
AND IT DOESN'T COUNT AS MY REWARD!
ALL RIGHT.
NOW WE KILL ALL THE GOBLINS.

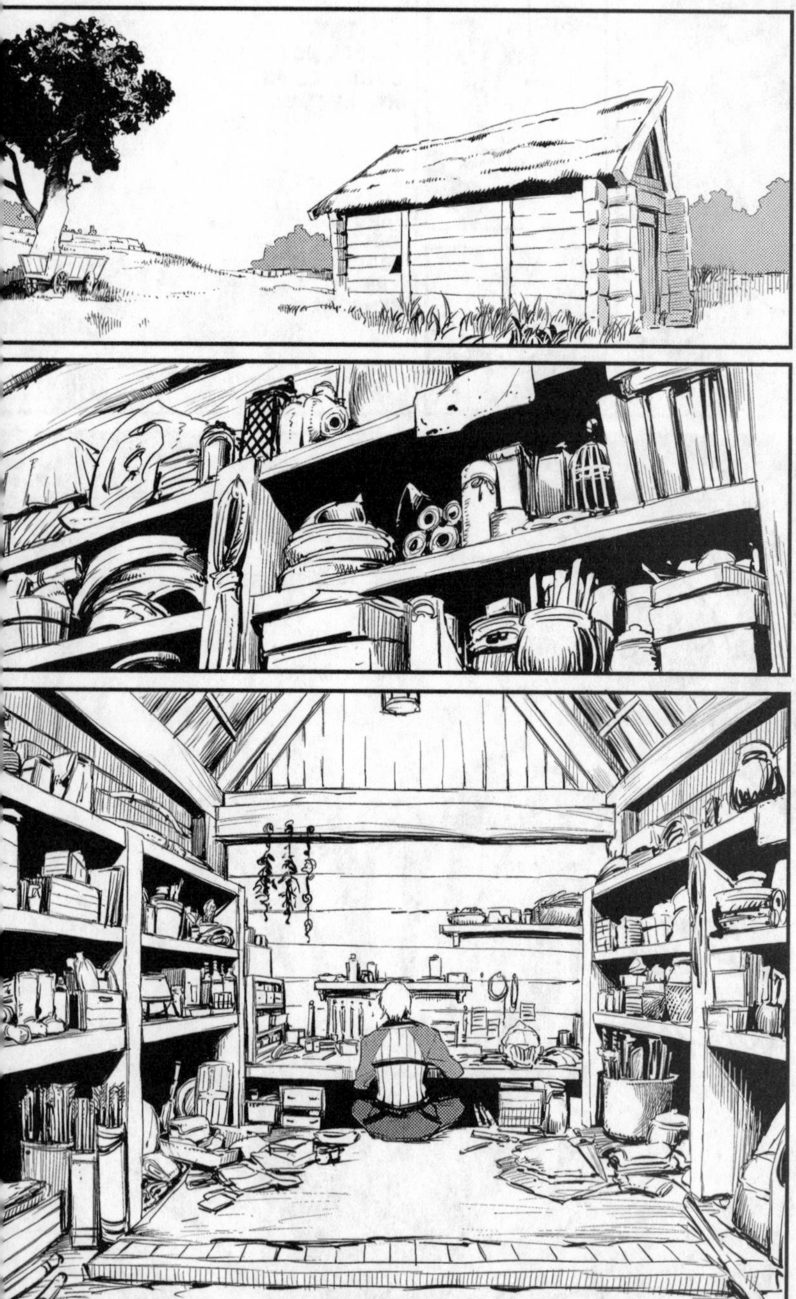

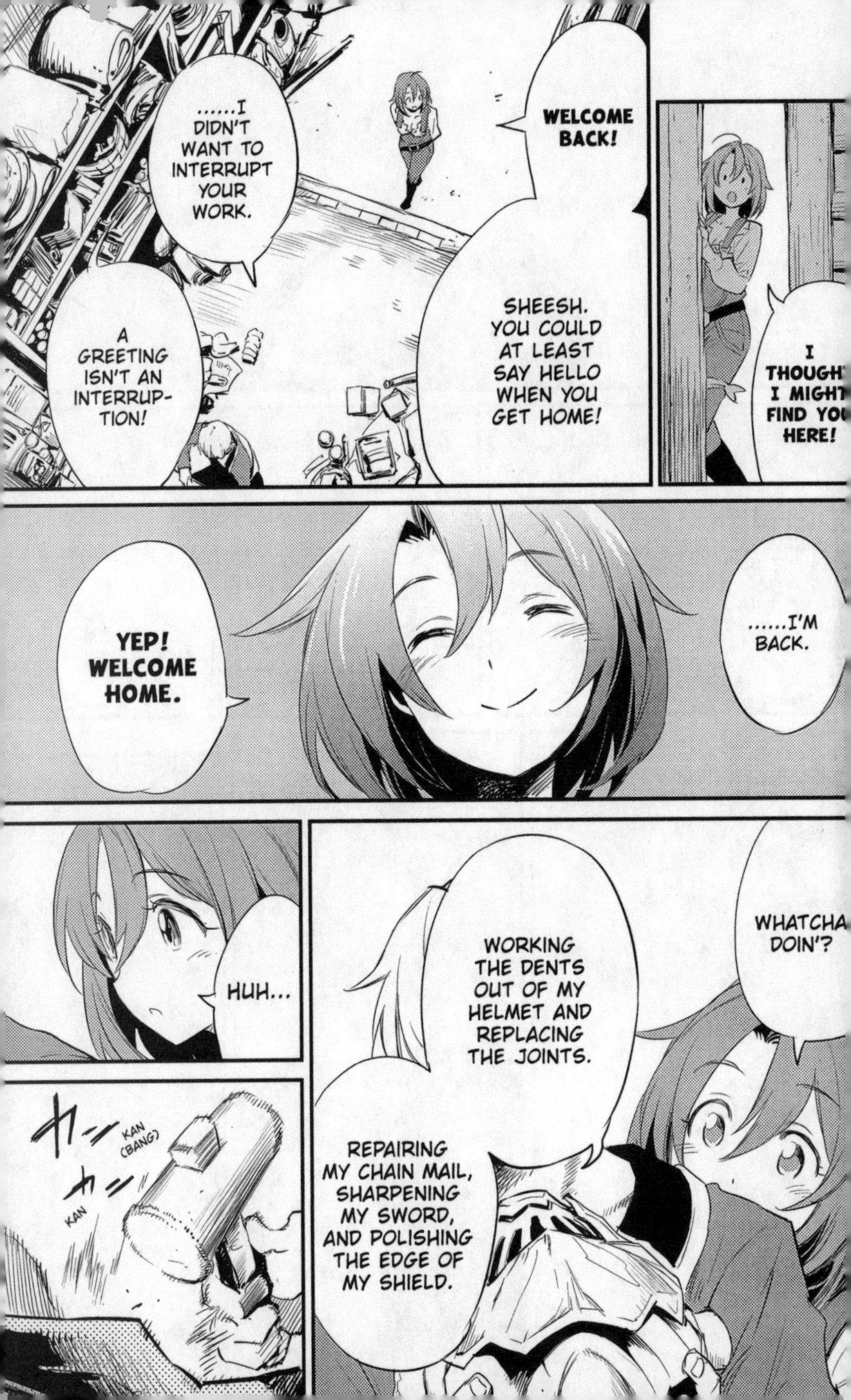
I THOUGHT I MIGHT FIND YOU HERE!
WELCOME BACK!
SHEESH. YOU COULD AT LEAST SAY HELLO WHEN YOU GET HOME!
......I DIDN'T WANT TO INTERRUPT YOUR WORK.
A GREETING ISN'T AN INTERRUP-TION!
......I'M BACK.
YEP! WELCOME HOME.
WHATCHA DOIN'?
WORKING THE DENTS OUT OF MY HELMET AND REPLACING THE JOINTS.
REPAIRING MY CHAIN MAIL, SHARPENING MY SWORD, AND POLISHING THE EDGE OF MY SHIELD.
HUH...
KAN (BANG)
KAN

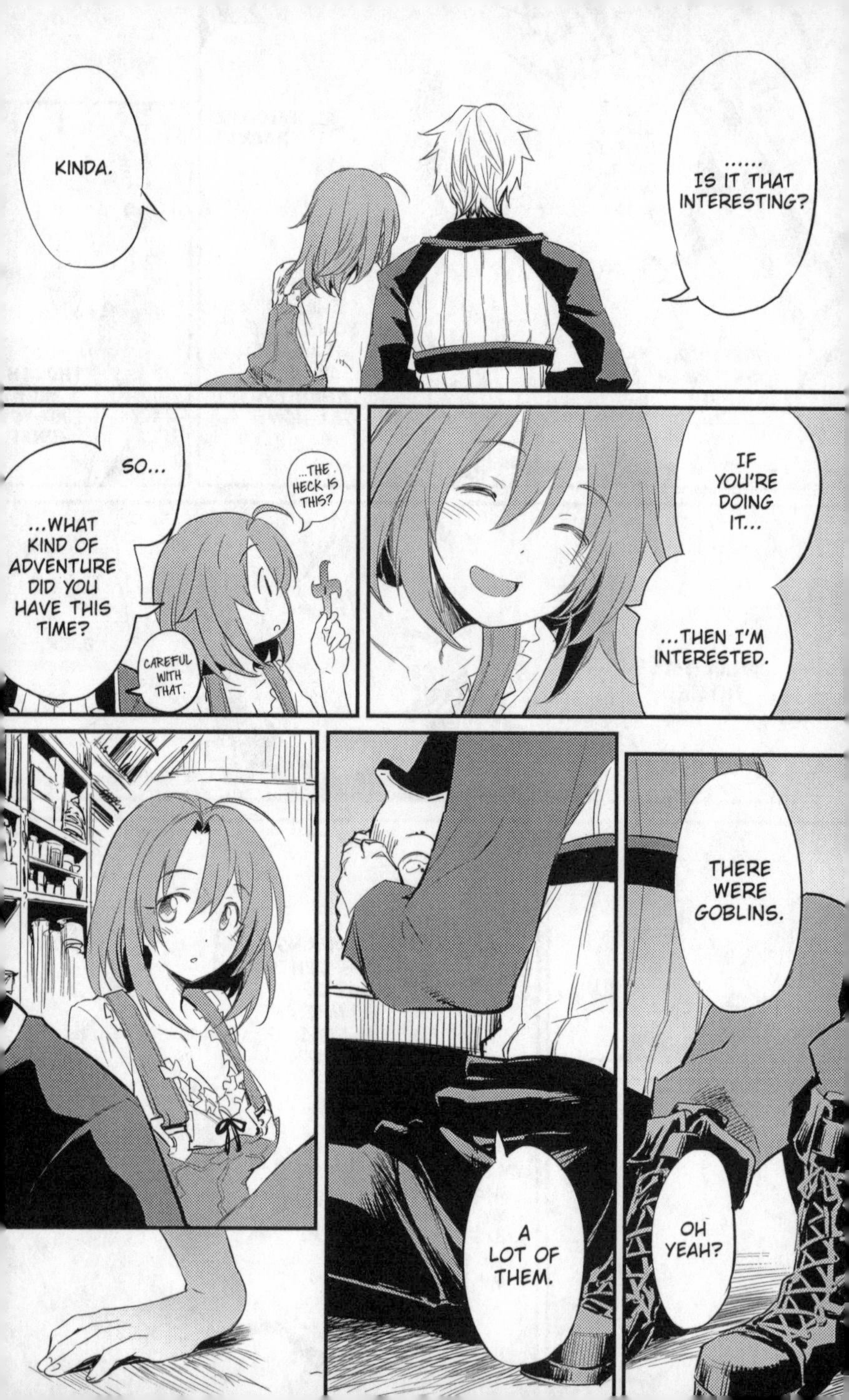
......
IS IT THAT INTERESTING?
KINDA.
IF YOU'RE DOING IT...
...THEN I'M INTERESTED.
SO...
...WHAT KIND OF ADVENTURE DID YOU HAVE THIS TIME?
...THE HECK IS THIS?
CAREFUL WITH THAT.
THERE WERE GOBLINS.
OH YEAH?
A LOT OF THEM.

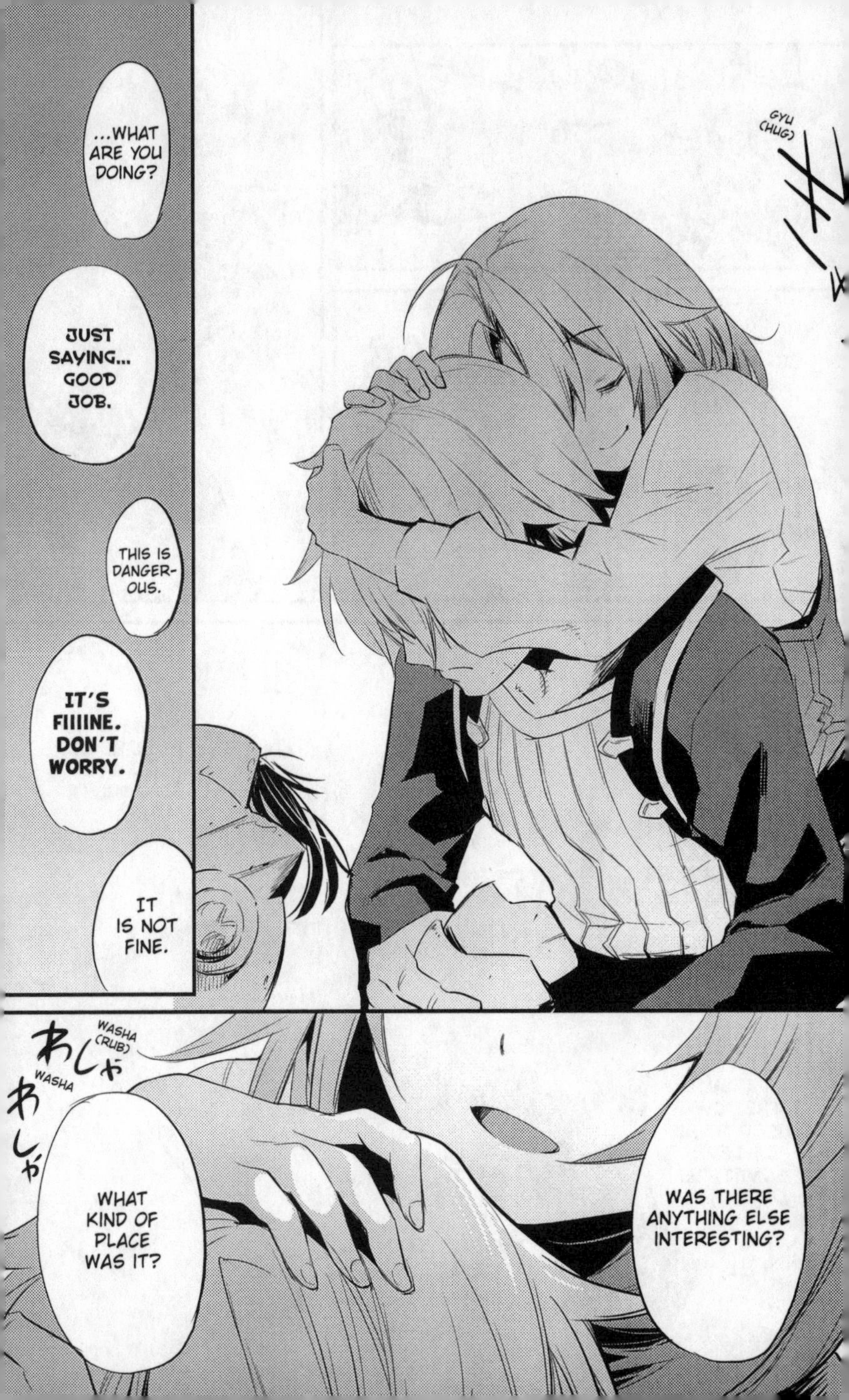
GYU (HUG)
...WHAT ARE YOU DOING?
JUST SAYING... GOOD JOB.
THIS IS DANGEROUS.
IT'S FIIIINE. DON'T WORRY.
IT IS NOT FINE.
WASHA (RUB) WASHA
WAS THERE ANYTHING ELSE INTERESTING?
WHAT KIND OF PLACE WAS IT?

GACHA
(CLATTER)

GYU
(TUG)

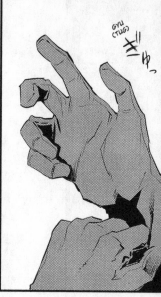

KARA

DON'T
TOUCH
THEM.
YOU'LL
GET A
RASH.

DON'T
WORRY.
I
WON'T.

KARA
(SHAKE)

WE
WENT TO
SOME OLD
RUINS IN A
FOREST.

TO SLAY
GOBLINS
THERE?

NO.
SOMEONE
INVITED
ME.

APPARENTLY,
THE TOWN
USED TO BE
CALLED...
SOMETHING
OR OTHER.

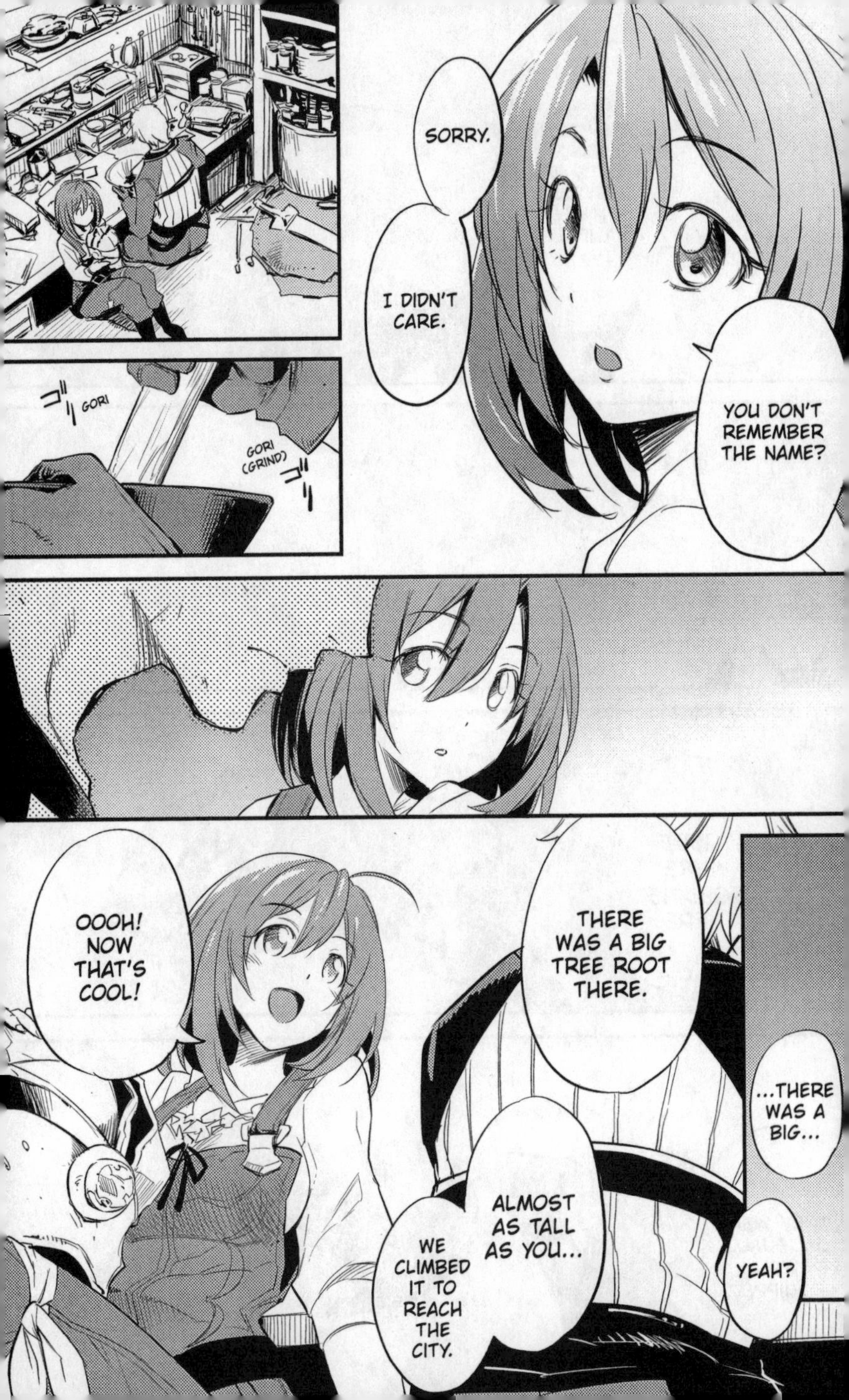
YOU DON'T REMEMBER THE NAME?
SORRY.
I DIDN'T CARE.
ゴリ GORI
GORI (GRIND) ゴリ
...THERE WAS A BIG...
YEAH?
THERE WAS A BIG TREE ROOT THERE.
ALMOST AS TALL AS YOU...
WE CLIMBED IT TO REACH THE CITY.
OOOH! NOW THAT'S COOL!

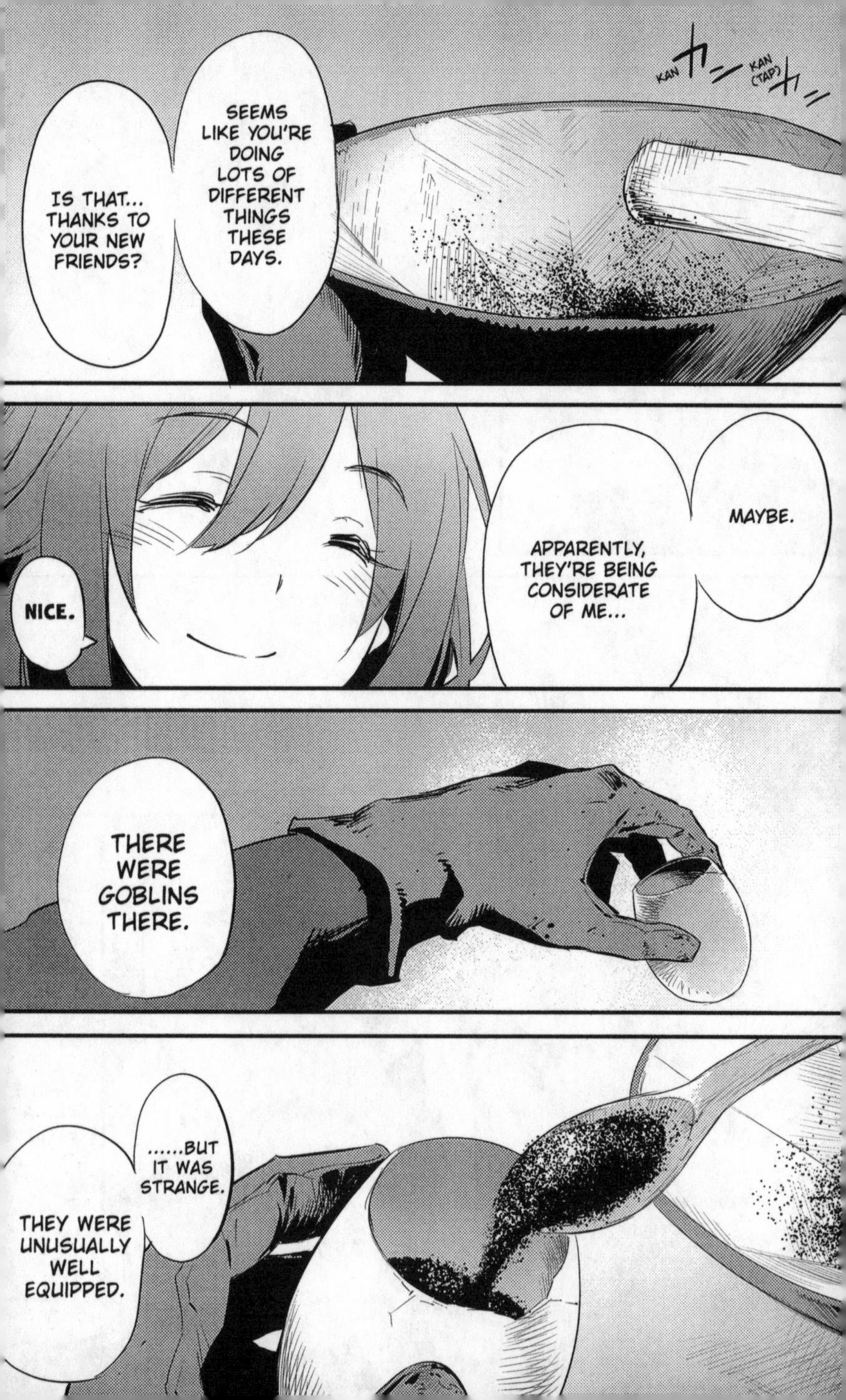
KAN
KAN (TAP)
SEEMS LIKE YOU'RE DOING LOTS OF DIFFERENT THINGS THESE DAYS.
IS THAT... THANKS TO YOUR NEW FRIENDS?
MAYBE.
APPARENTLY, THEY'RE BEING CONSIDERATE OF ME...
NICE.
THERE WERE GOBLINS THERE.
......BUT IT WAS STRANGE.
THEY WERE UNUSUALLY WELL EQUIPPED.

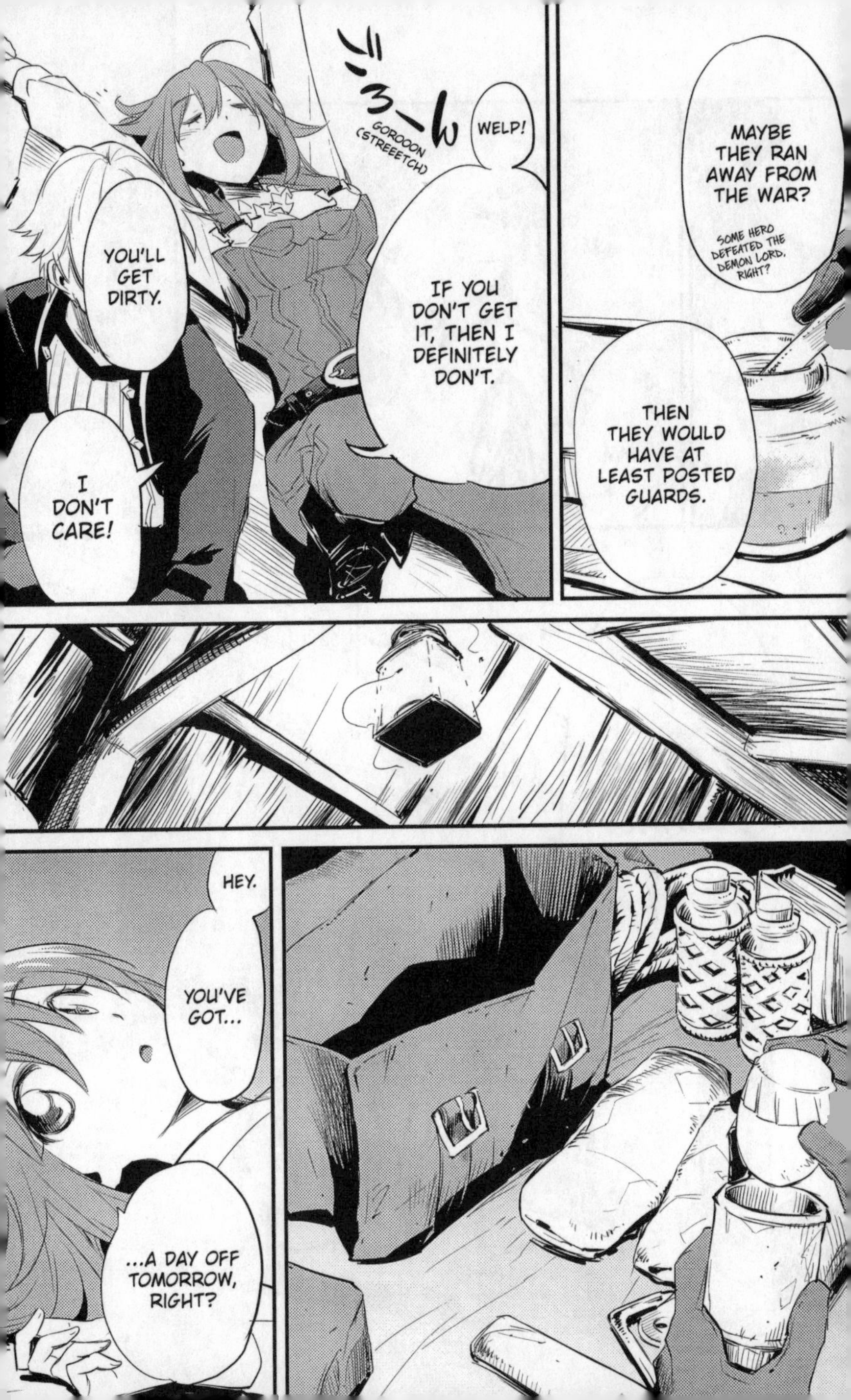
MAYBE THEY RAN AWAY FROM THE WAR?
SOME HERO DEFEATED THE DEMON LORD, RIGHT?
THEN THEY WOULD HAVE AT LEAST POSTED GUARDS.
ごろ〜ん
GOROOON (STREEETCH)
WELP!
IF YOU DON'T GET IT, THEN I DEFINITELY DON'T.
YOU'LL GET DIRTY.
I DON'T CARE!
HEY.
YOU'VE GOT...
...A DAY OFF TOMORROW, RIGHT?

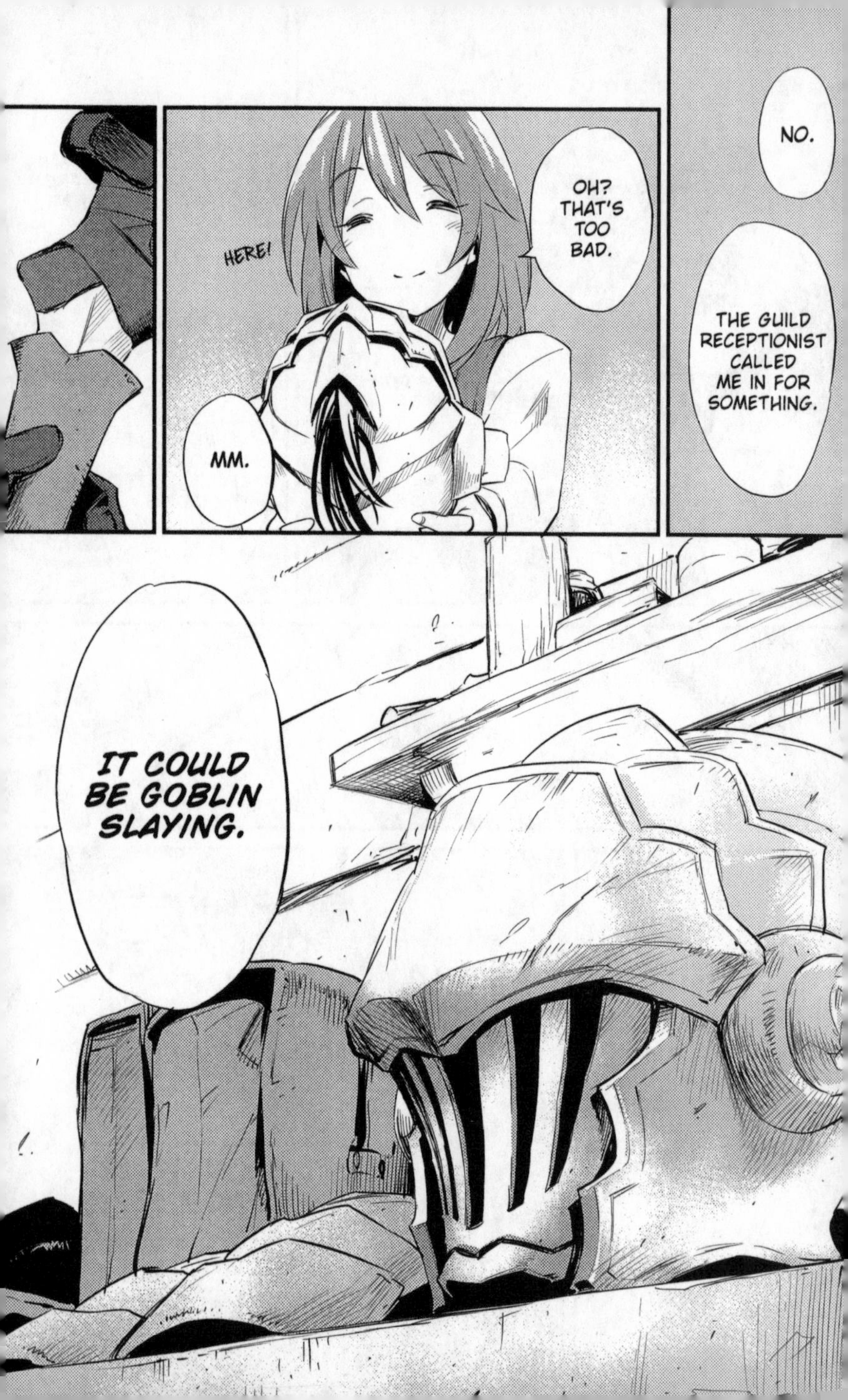
NO.
THE GUILD RECEPTIONIST CALLED ME IN FOR SOMETHING.
OH? THAT'S TOO BAD.
HERE!
MM.
IT COULD BE GOBLIN SLAYING.

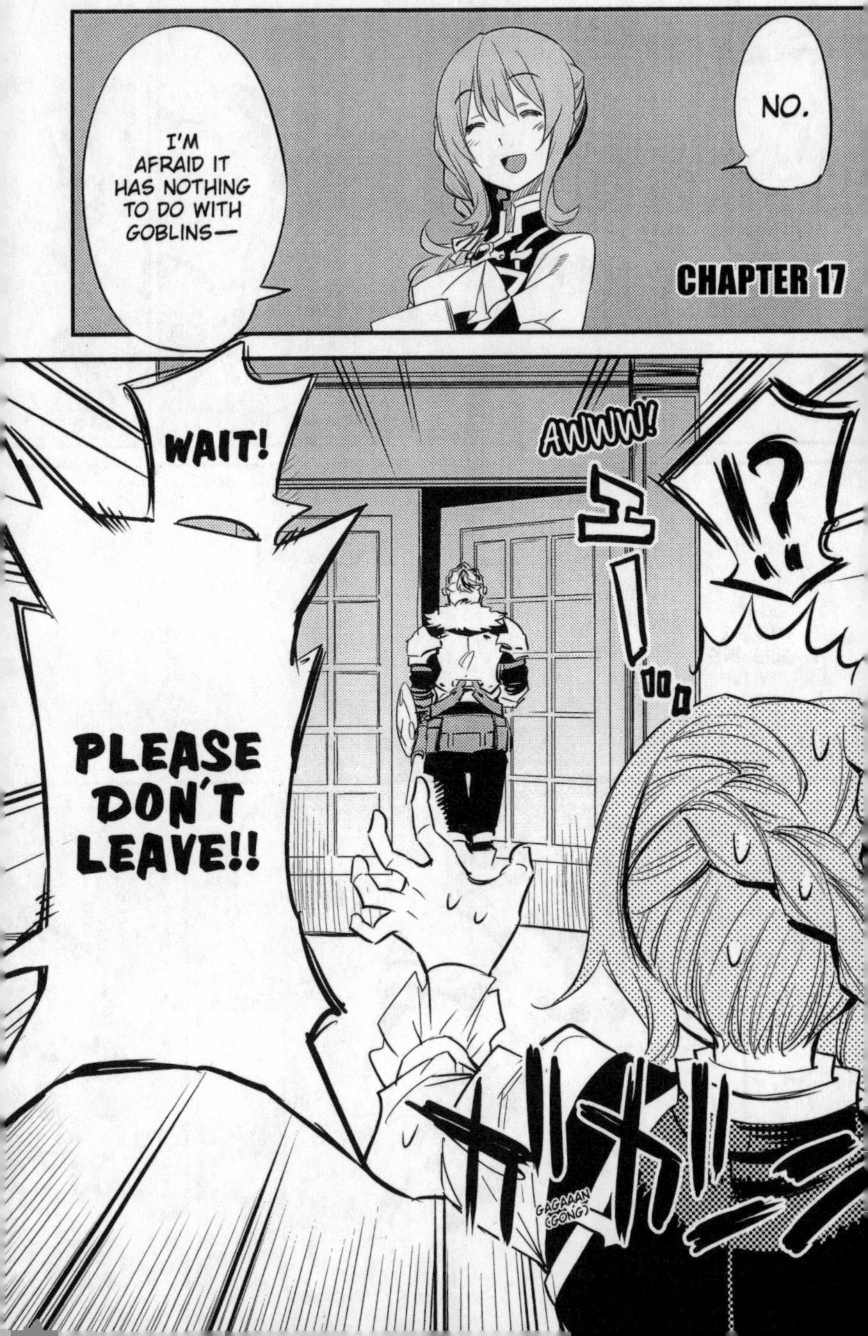
NO.
I'M AFRAID IT HAS NOTHING TO DO WITH GOBLINS—
CHAPTER 17
AWWW!
!?
WAIT!
PLEASE DON'T LEAVE!!
GAGAAAN (GONG)

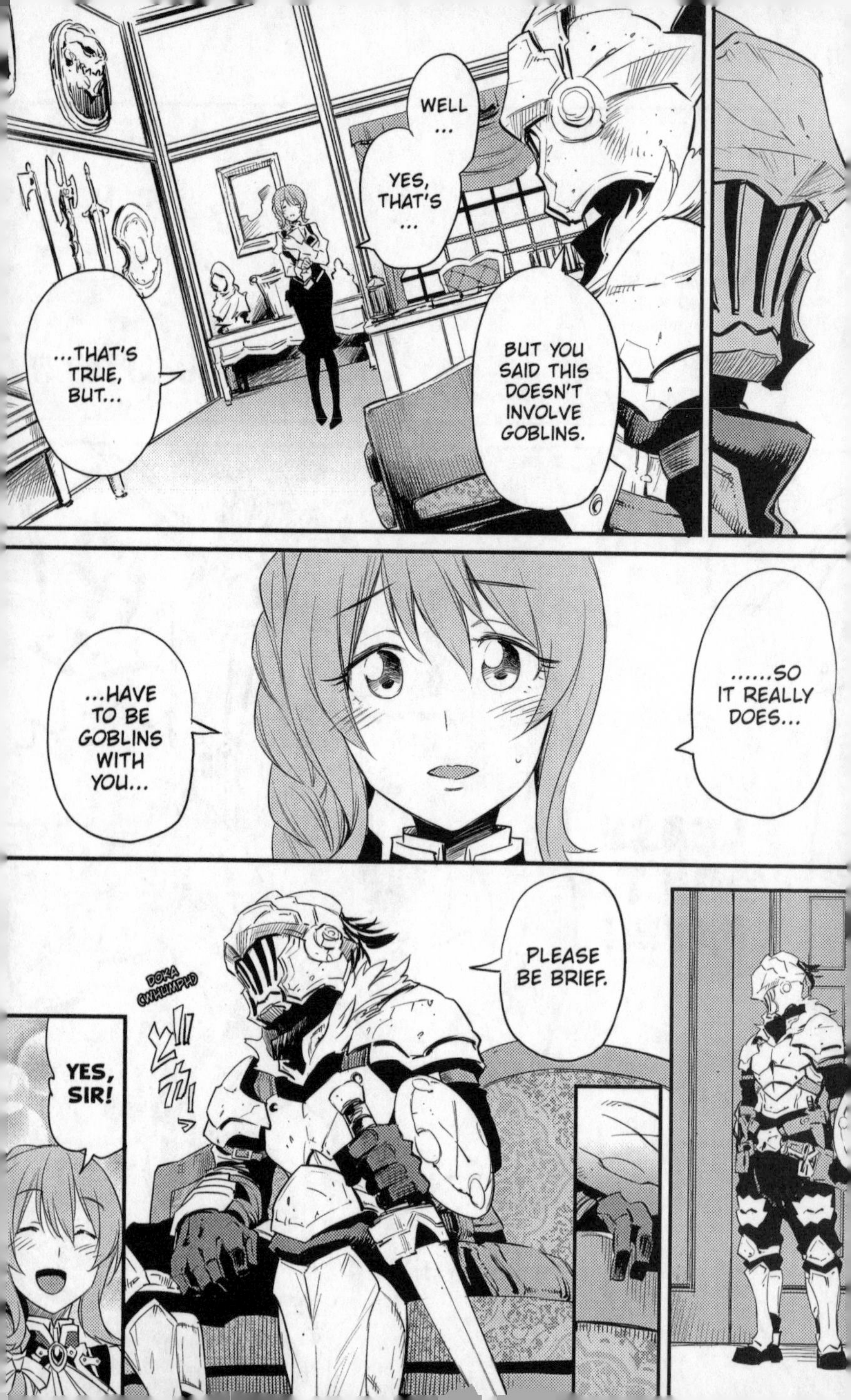
WELL... YES, THAT'S...
BUT YOU SAID THIS DOESN'T INVOLVE GOBLINS.
...THAT'S TRUE, BUT...
......SO IT REALLY DOES...
...HAVE TO BE GOBLINS WITH YOU...
PLEASE BE BRIEF.
DOKA (WHUMPH)
YES, SIR!

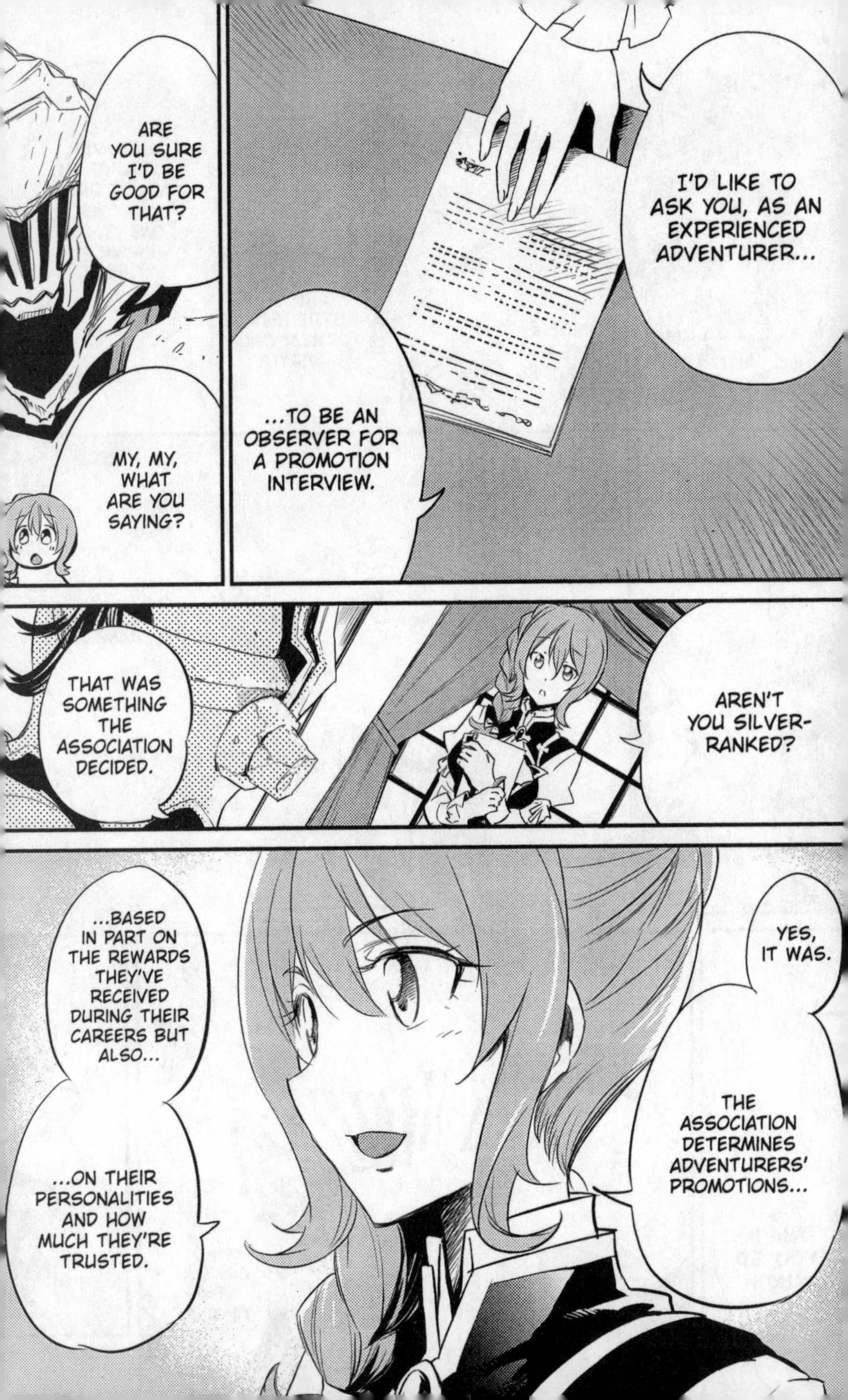
I'D LIKE TO ASK YOU, AS AN EXPERIENCED ADVENTURER...
...TO BE AN OBSERVER FOR A PROMOTION INTERVIEW.
ARE YOU SURE I'D BE GOOD FOR THAT?
MY, MY, WHAT ARE YOU SAYING?
AREN'T YOU SILVER-RANKED?
THAT WAS SOMETHING THE ASSOCIATION DECIDED.
YES, IT WAS.
THE ASSOCIATION DETERMINES ADVENTURERS' PROMOTIONS...
...BASED IN PART ON THE REWARDS THEY'VE RECEIVED DURING THEIR CAREERS BUT ALSO...
...ON THEIR PERSONALITIES AND HOW MUCH THEY'RE TRUSTED.

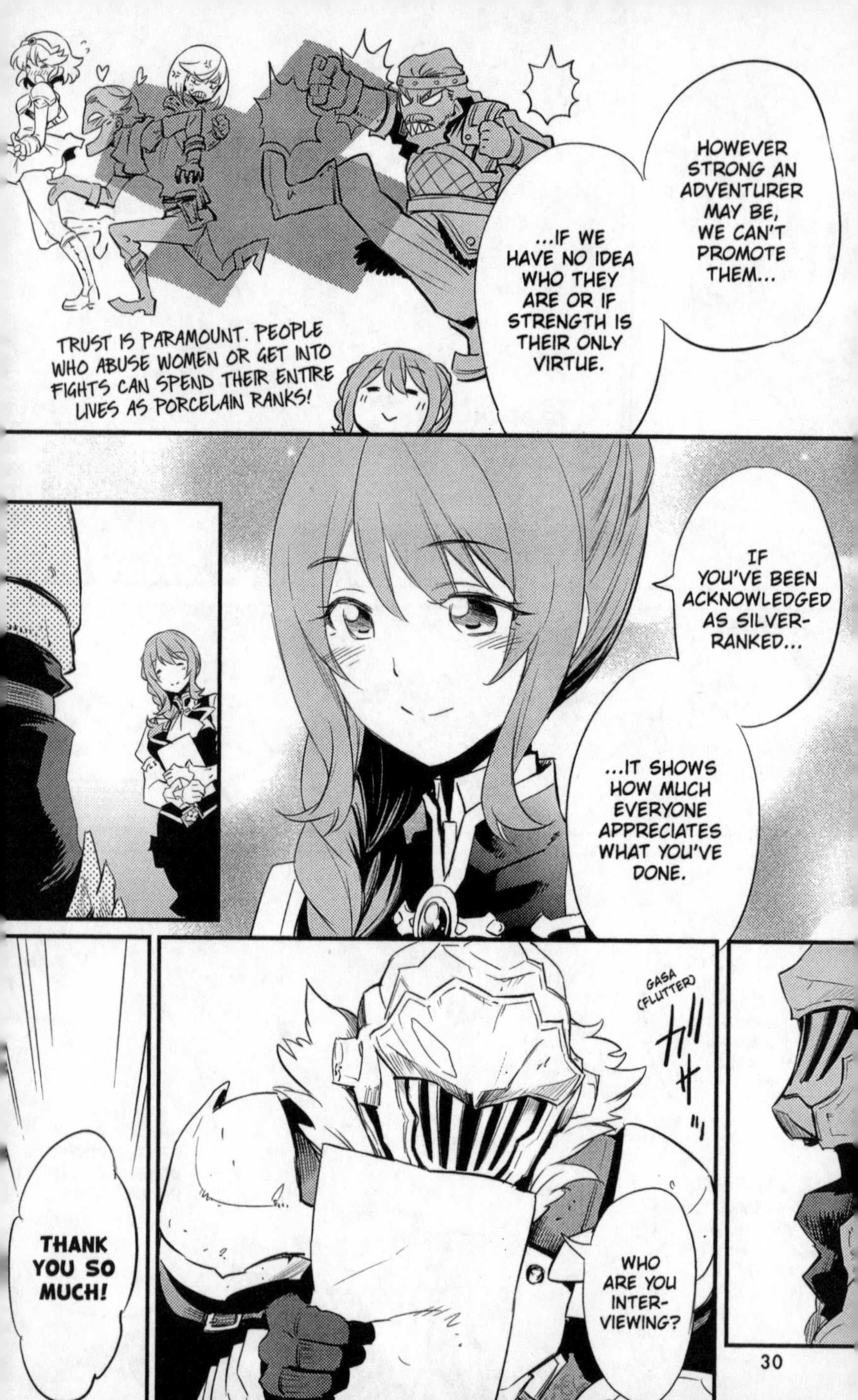
HOWEVER STRONG AN ADVENTURER MAY BE, WE CAN'T PROMOTE THEM...
...IF WE HAVE NO IDEA WHO THEY ARE OR IF STRENGTH IS THEIR ONLY VIRTUE.
TRUST IS PARAMOUNT. PEOPLE WHO ABUSE WOMEN OR GET INTO FIGHTS CAN SPEND THEIR ENTIRE LIVES AS PORCELAIN RANKS!
IF YOU'VE BEEN ACKNOWLEDGED AS SILVER-RANKED...
...IT SHOWS HOW MUCH EVERYONE APPRECIATES WHAT YOU'VE DONE.
GASA (FLUTTER)
WHO ARE YOU INTER-VIEWING?
THANK YOU SO MUCH!

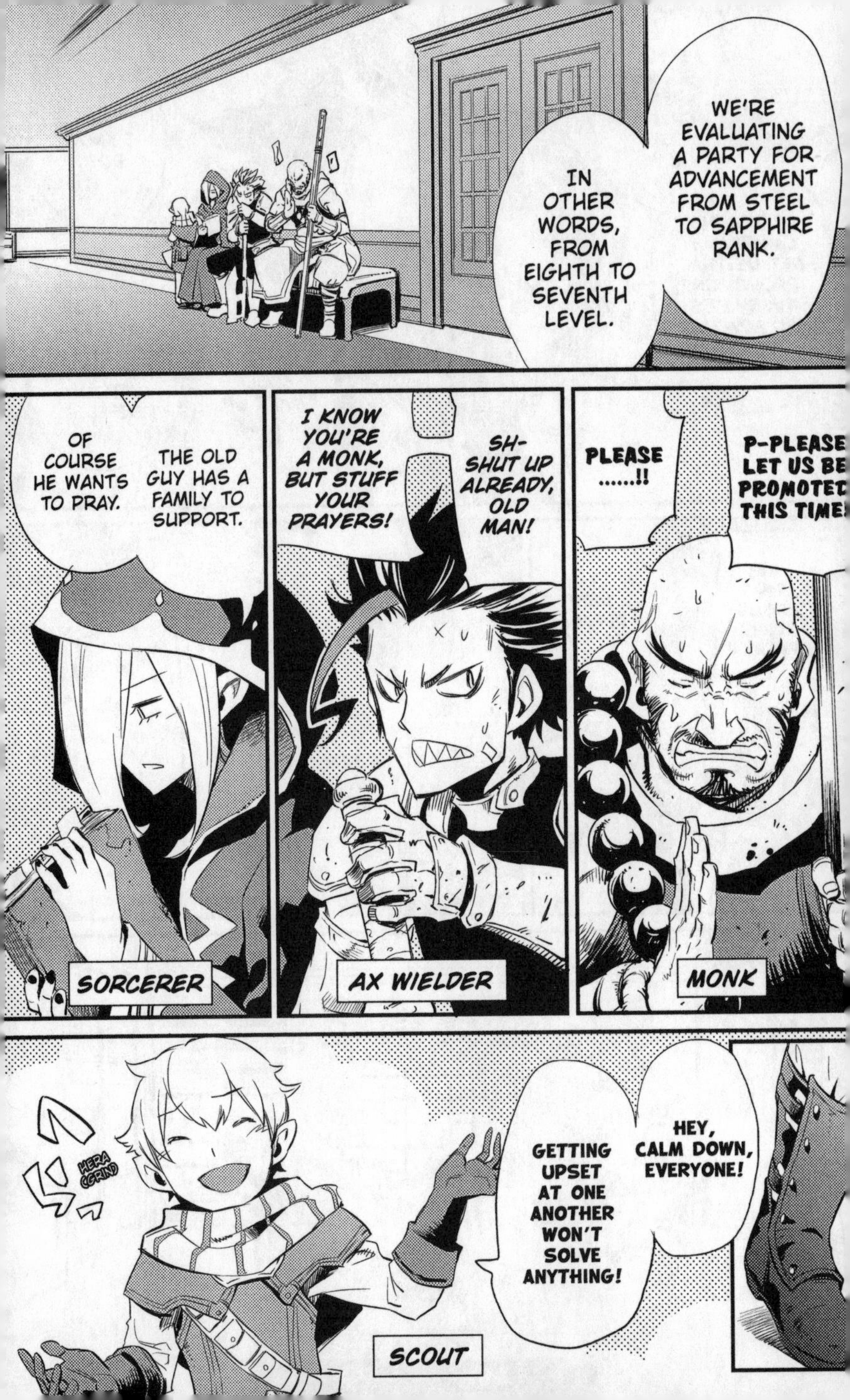
WE'RE EVALUATING A PARTY FOR ADVANCEMENT FROM STEEL TO SAPPHIRE RANK.
IN OTHER WORDS, FROM EIGHTH TO SEVENTH LEVEL.
P-PLEASE LET US BE PROMOTED THIS TIME!
PLEASE ......!!
MONK
SH-SHUT UP ALREADY, OLD MAN!
I KNOW YOU'RE A MONK, BUT STUFF YOUR PRAYERS!
AX WIELDER
THE OLD GUY HAS A FAMILY TO SUPPORT.
OF COURSE HE WANTS TO PRAY.
SORCERER
HEY, CALM DOWN, EVERYONE!
GETTING UPSET AT ONE ANOTHER WON'T SOLVE ANYTHING!
HERA (GRIN)
SCOUT

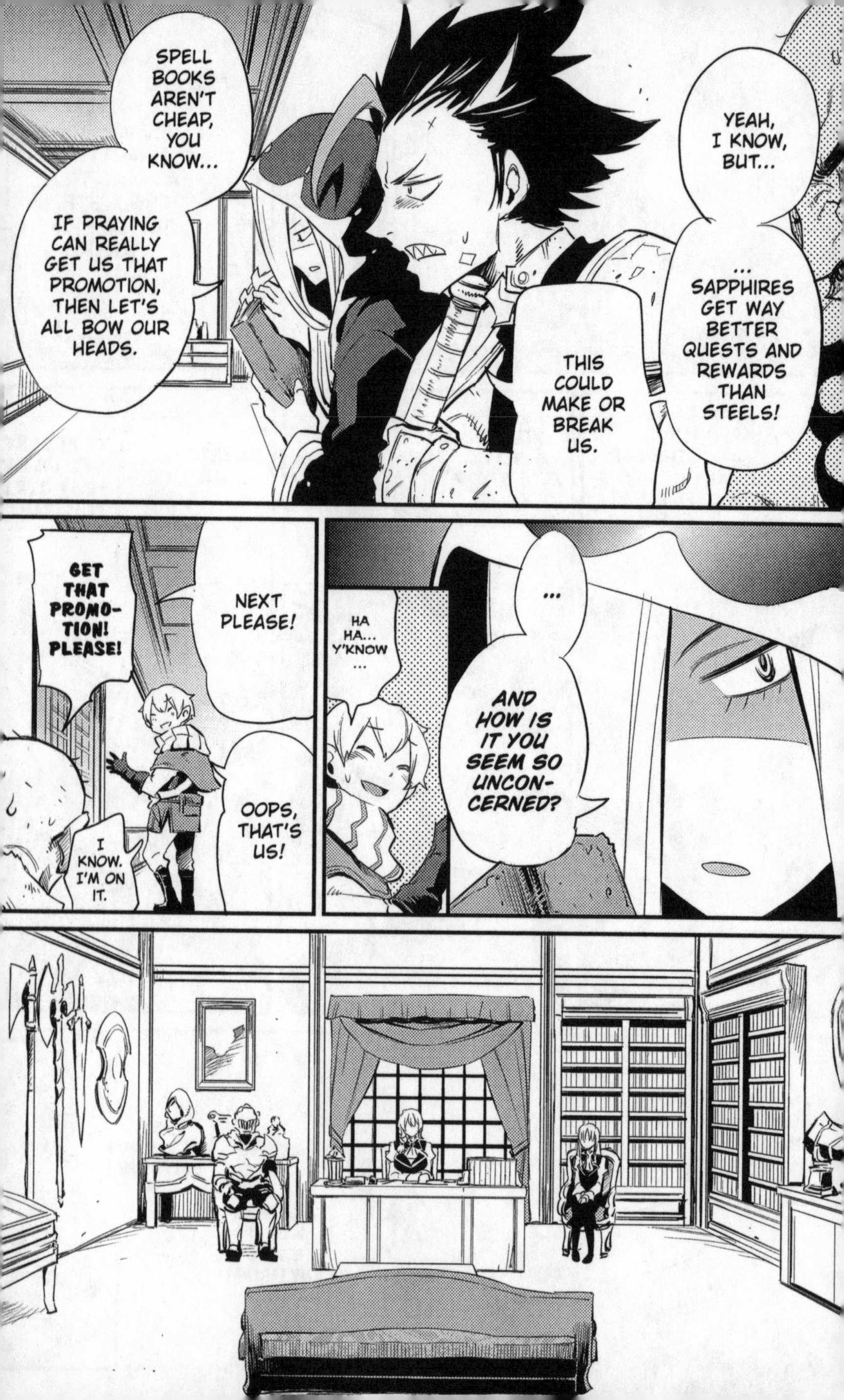
YEAH, I KNOW, BUT...
... SAPPHIRES GET WAY BETTER QUESTS AND REWARDS THAN STEELS!
THIS COULD MAKE OR BREAK US.
SPELL BOOKS AREN'T CHEAP, YOU KNOW...
IF PRAYING CAN REALLY GET US THAT PROMOTION, THEN LET'S ALL BOW OUR HEADS.
...
AND HOW IS IT YOU SEEM SO UNCONCERNED?
HA HA... Y'KNOW ...
NEXT PLEASE!
OOPS, THAT'S US!
GET THAT PROMOTION! PLEASE!
I KNOW. I'M ON IT.

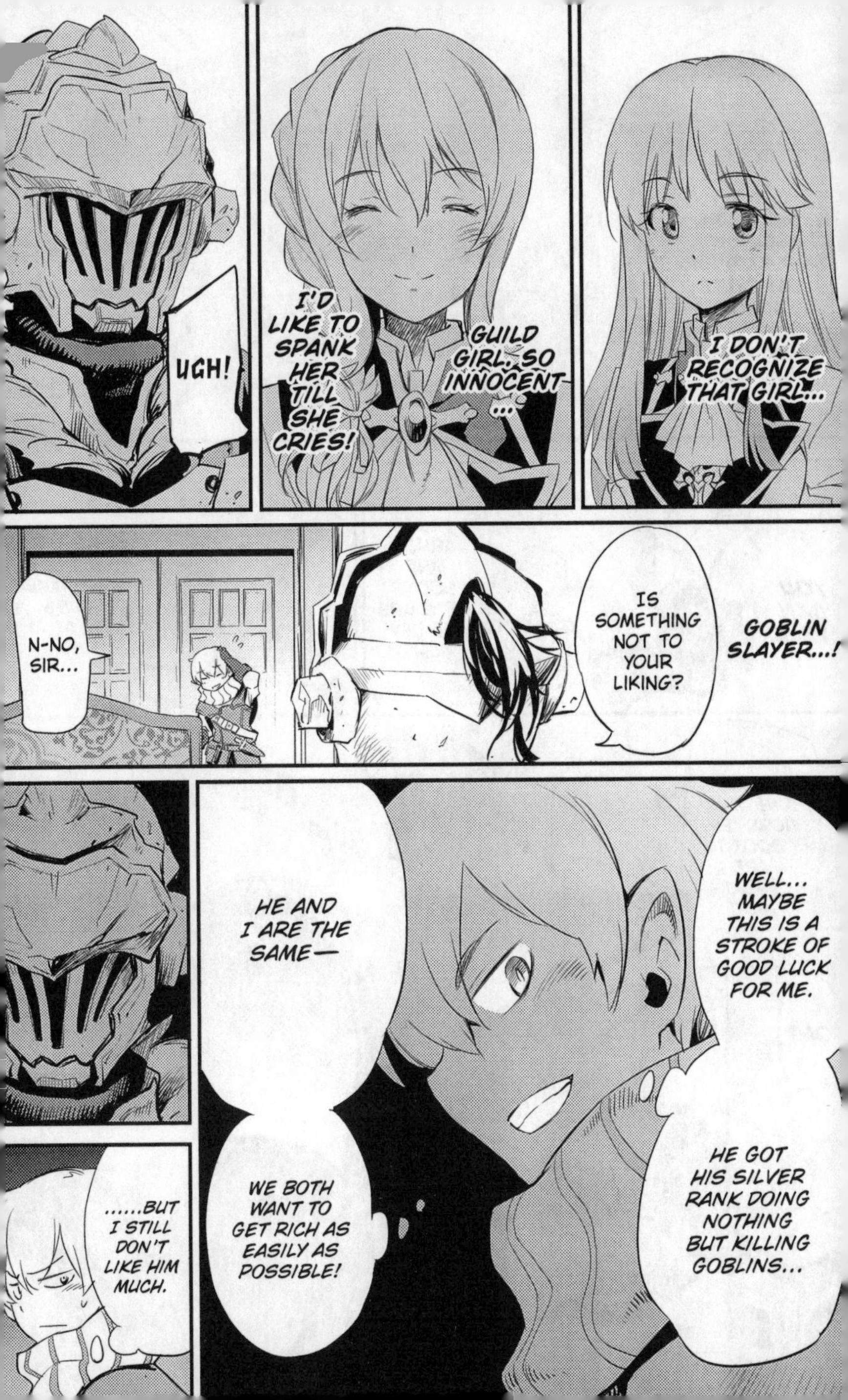
I DON'T RECOGNIZE THAT GIRL...
GUILD GIRL, SO INNOCENT...
I'D LIKE TO SPANK HER TILL SHE CRIES!
UGH!
GOBLIN SLAYER...!
IS SOMETHING NOT TO YOUR LIKING?
N-NO, SIR...
WELL... MAYBE THIS IS A STROKE OF GOOD LUCK FOR ME.
HE GOT HIS SILVER RANK DOING NOTHING BUT KILLING GOBLINS...
HE AND I ARE THE SAME—
WE BOTH WANT TO GET RICH AS EASILY AS POSSIBLE!
......BUT I STILL DON'T LIKE HIM MUCH.

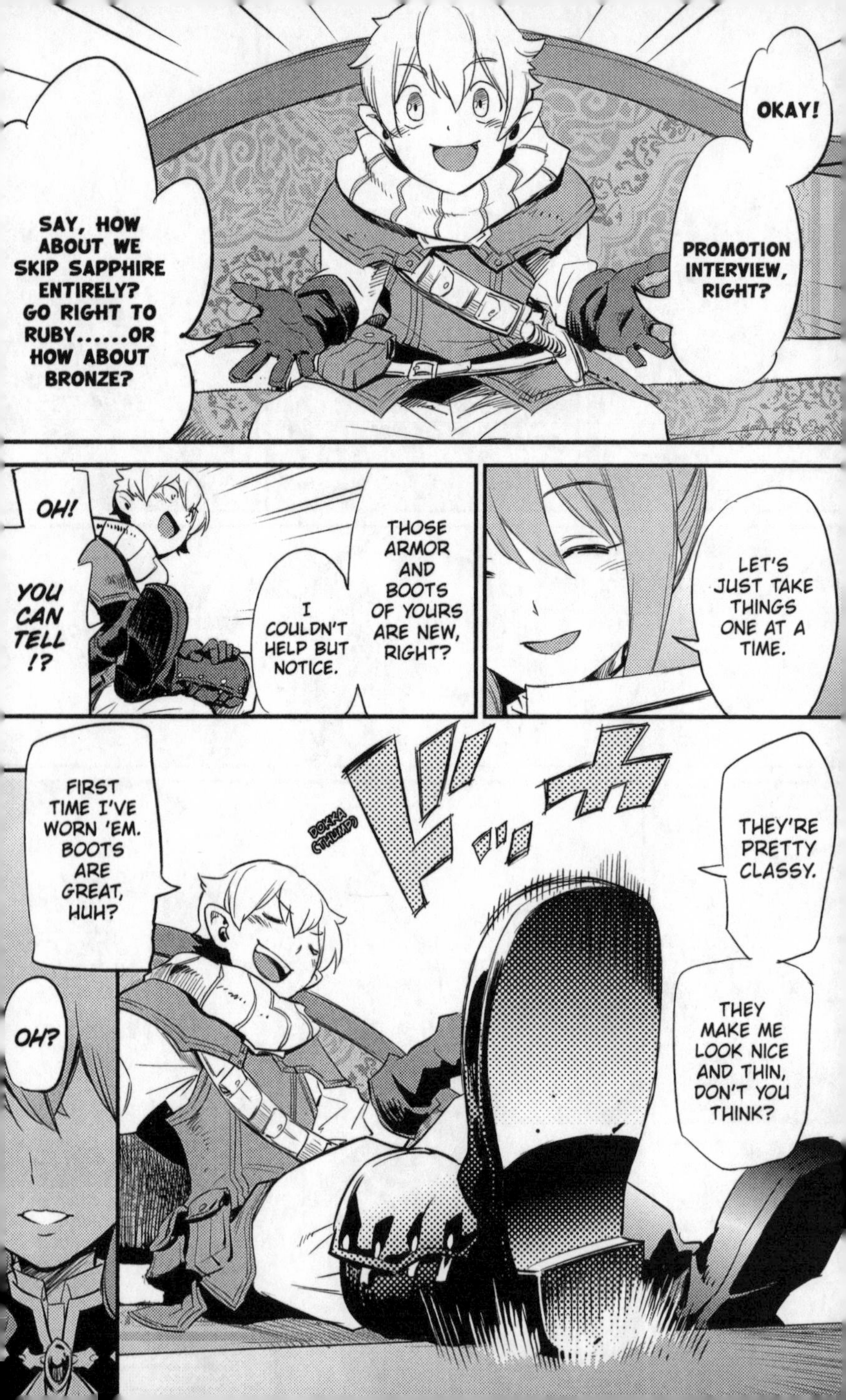
OKAY!
PROMOTION INTERVIEW, RIGHT?
SAY, HOW ABOUT WE SKIP SAPPHIRE ENTIRELY? GO RIGHT TO RUBY......OR HOW ABOUT BRONZE?
LET'S JUST TAKE THINGS ONE AT A TIME.
THOSE ARMOR AND BOOTS OF YOURS ARE NEW, RIGHT?
I COULDN'T HELP BUT NOTICE.
OH!
YOU CAN TELL!?
THEY'RE PRETTY CLASSY.
DOKKA (THUMP)
FIRST TIME I'VE WORN 'EM. BOOTS ARE GREAT, HUH?
THEY MAKE ME LOOK NICE AND THIN, DON'T YOU THINK?
OH?

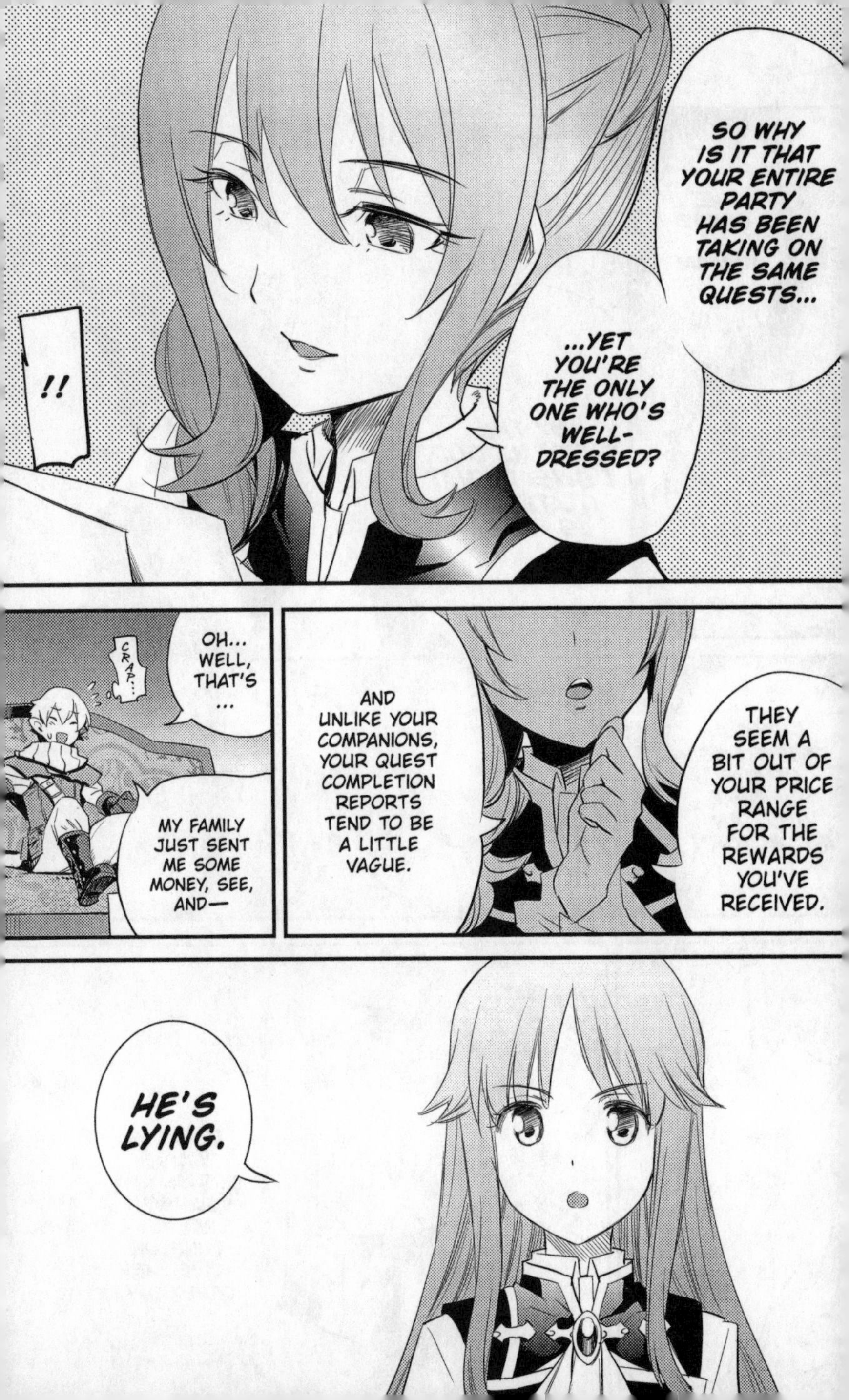
SO WHY IS IT THAT YOUR ENTIRE PARTY HAS BEEN TAKING ON THE SAME QUESTS...
...YET YOU'RE THE ONLY ONE WHO'S WELL-DRESSED?
!!
THEY SEEM A BIT OUT OF YOUR PRICE RANGE FOR THE REWARDS YOU'VE RECEIVED.
AND UNLIKE YOUR COMPANIONS, YOUR QUEST COMPLETION REPORTS TEND TO BE A LITTLE VAGUE.
OH... WELL, THAT'S ...
CRAP...
MY FAMILY JUST SENT ME SOME MONEY, SEE, AND—
HE'S LYING.

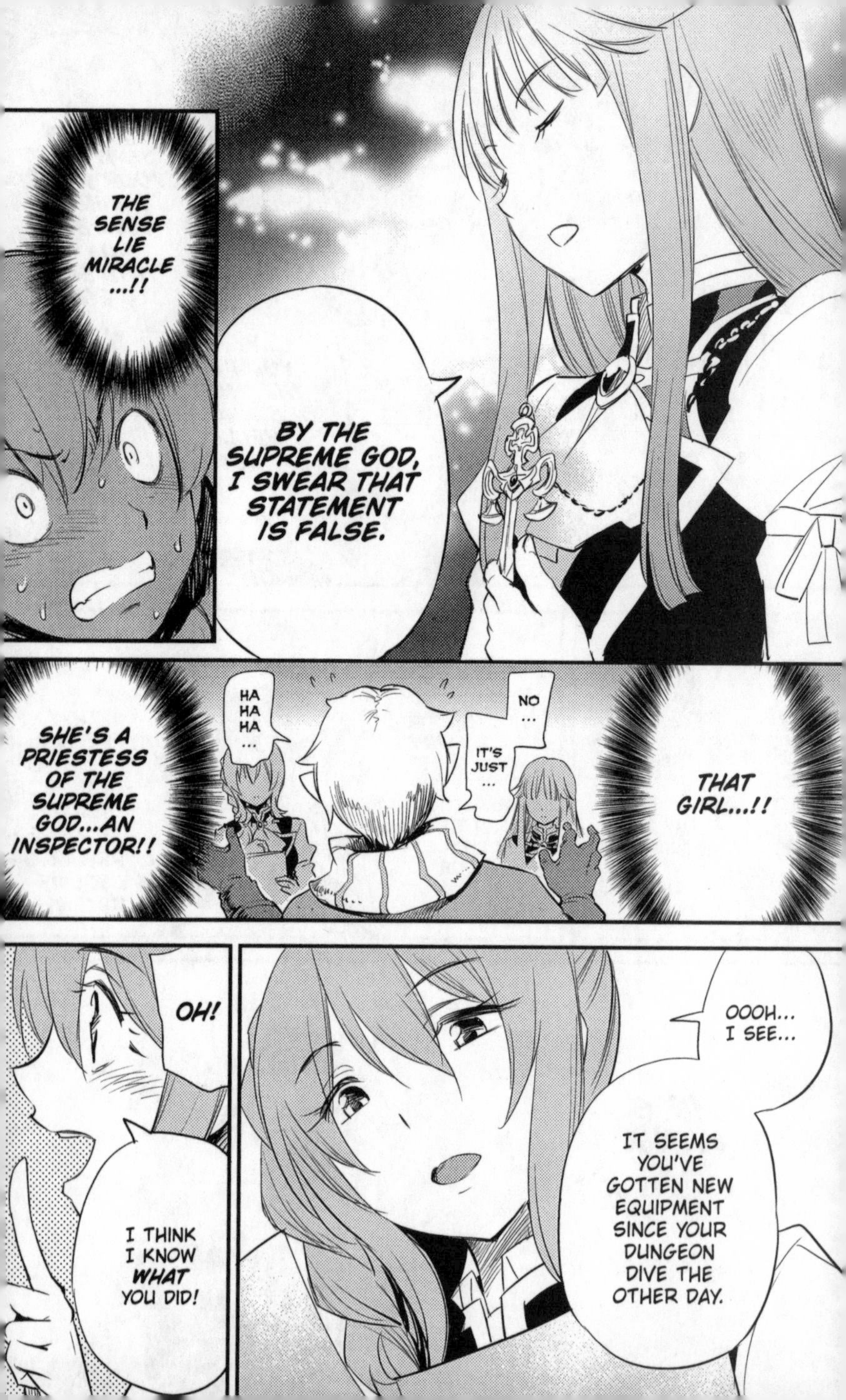
BY THE SUPREME GOD, I SWEAR THAT STATEMENT IS FALSE.
THE SENSE LIE MIRACLE...!!
THAT GIRL...!!
NO... IT'S JUST...
HA HA HA...
SHE'S A PRIESTESS OF THE SUPREME GOD...AN INSPECTOR!!
OOOH... I SEE...
IT SEEMS YOU'VE GOTTEN NEW EQUIPMENT SINCE YOUR DUNGEON DIVE THE OTHER DAY.
OH!
I THINK I KNOW WHAT YOU DID!

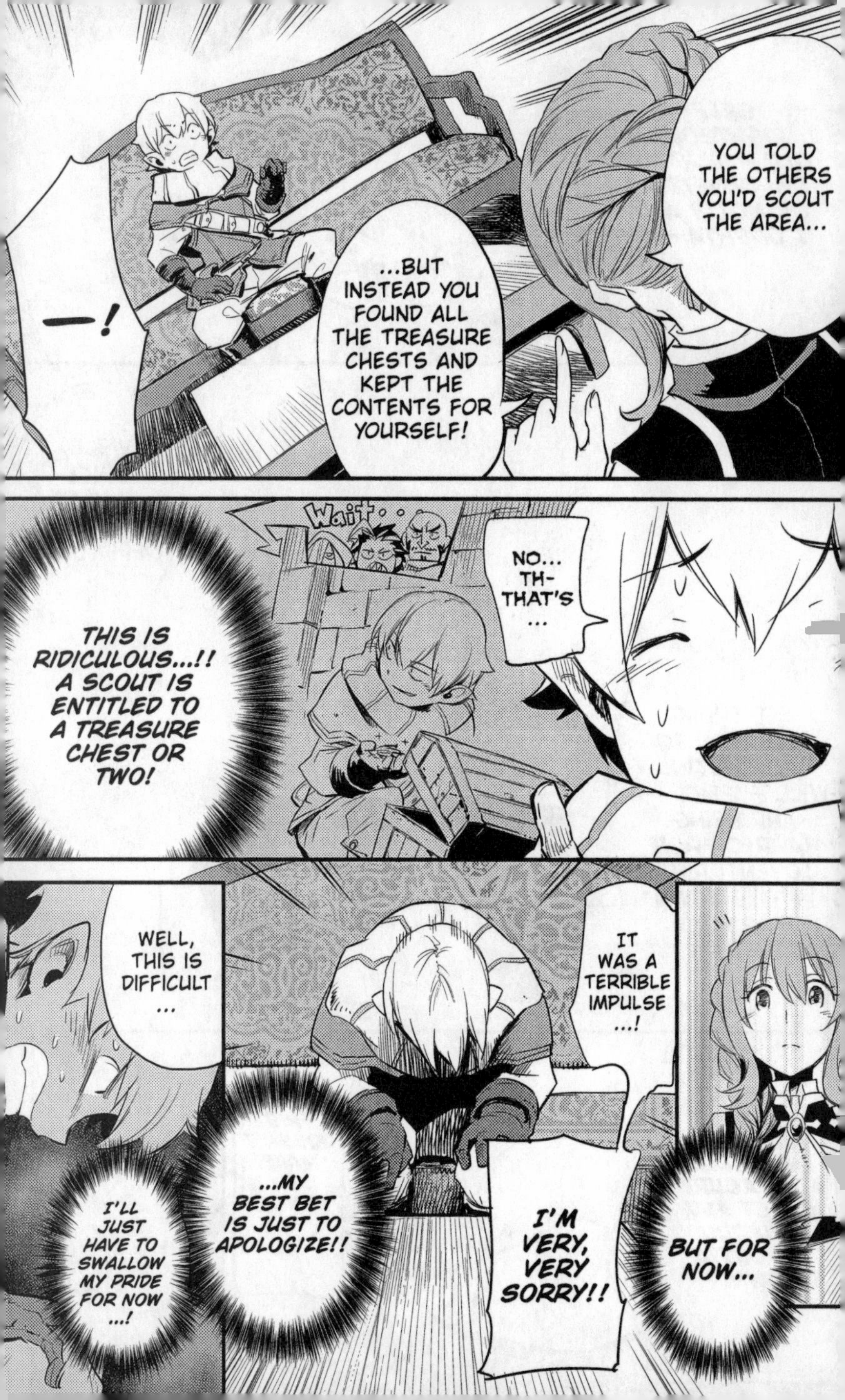

YOU TOLD THE OTHERS YOU'D SCOUT THE AREA...
...BUT INSTEAD YOU FOUND ALL THE TREASURE CHESTS AND KEPT THE CONTENTS FOR YOURSELF!
—!
NO... TH-THAT'S ...
Wait...
THIS IS RIDICULOUS...!! A SCOUT IS ENTITLED TO A TREASURE CHEST OR TWO!
BUT FOR NOW...
IT WAS A TERRIBLE IMPULSE ...!
I'M VERY, VERY SORRY!!
WELL, THIS IS DIFFICULT ...
...MY BEST BET IS JUST TO APOLOGIZE!!
I'LL JUST HAVE TO SWALLOW MY PRIDE FOR NOW ...!

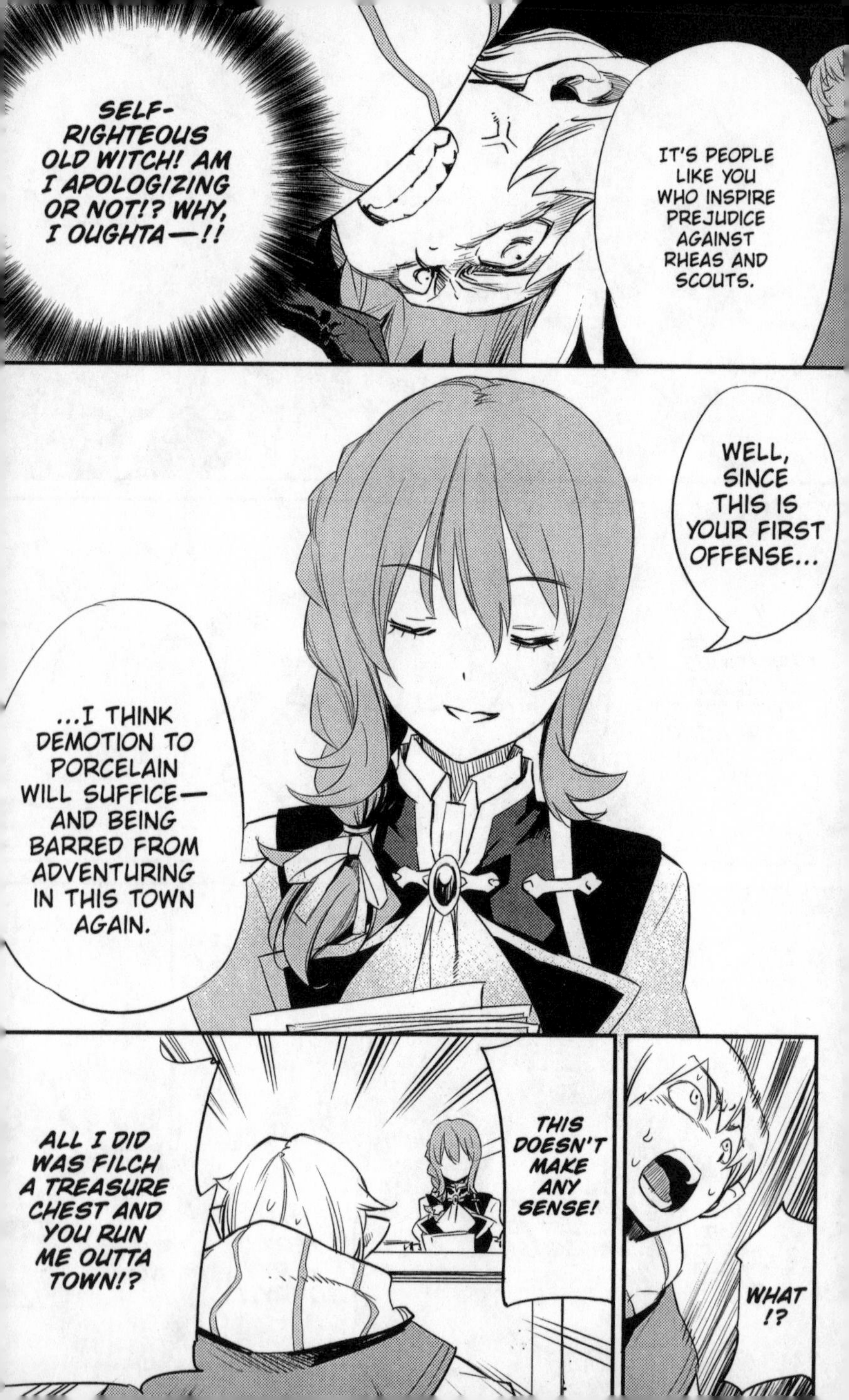
IT'S PEOPLE LIKE YOU WHO INSPIRE PREJUDICE AGAINST RHEAS AND SCOUTS.
SELF-RIGHTEOUS OLD WITCH! AM I APOLOGIZING OR NOT!? WHY, I OUGHTA—!!
WELL, SINCE THIS IS YOUR FIRST OFFENSE...
...I THINK DEMOTION TO PORCELAIN WILL SUFFICE—AND BEING BARRED FROM ADVENTURING IN THIS TOWN AGAIN.
WHAT!?
THIS DOESN'T MAKE ANY SENSE!
ALL I DID WAS FILCH A TREASURE CHEST AND YOU RUN ME OUTTA TOWN!?

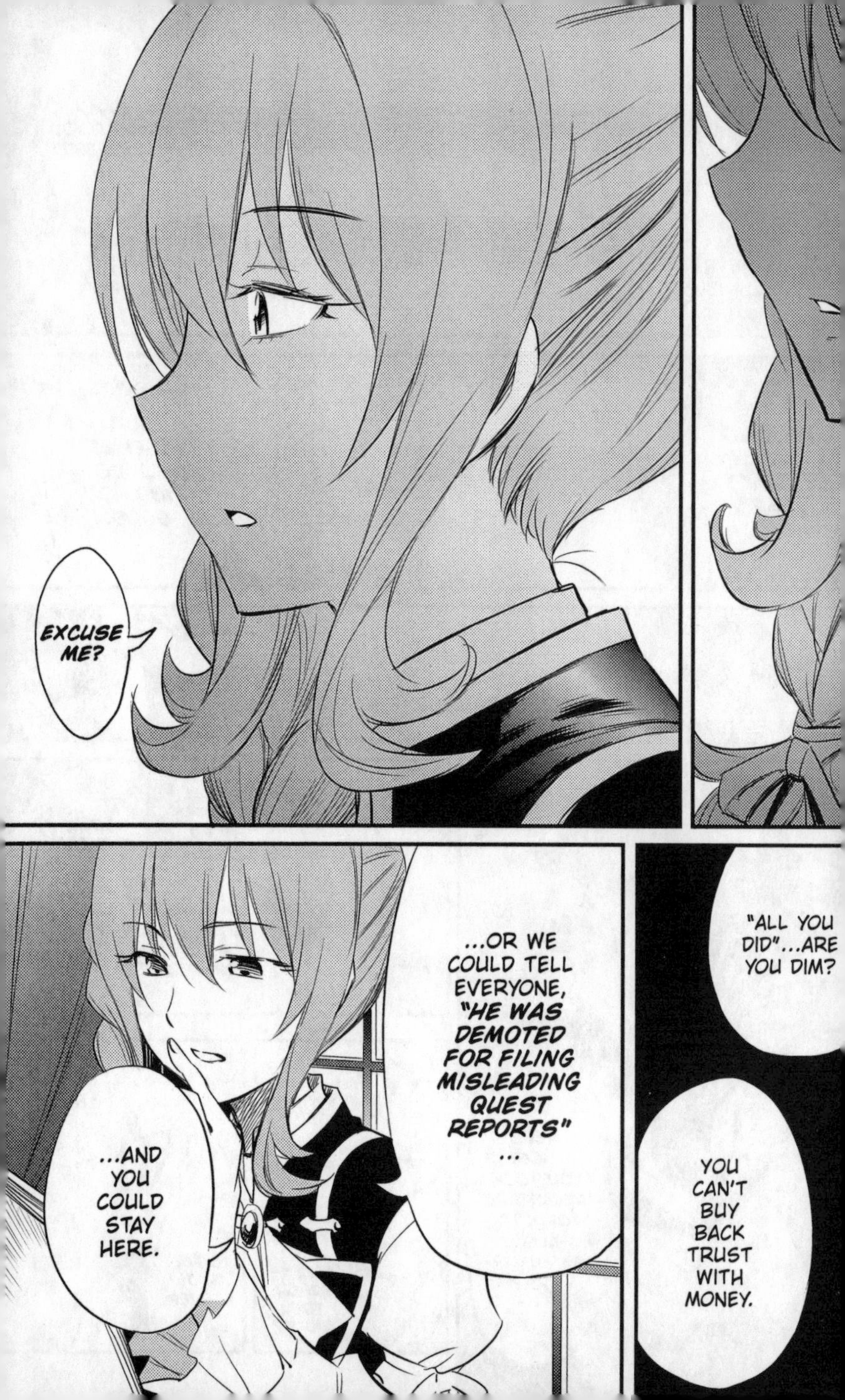
EXCUSE ME?
"ALL YOU DID"...ARE YOU DIM?
YOU CAN'T BUY BACK TRUST WITH MONEY.
...OR WE COULD TELL EVERYONE, "HE WAS DEMOTED FOR FILING MISLEADING QUEST REPORTS"...
...AND YOU COULD STAY HERE.

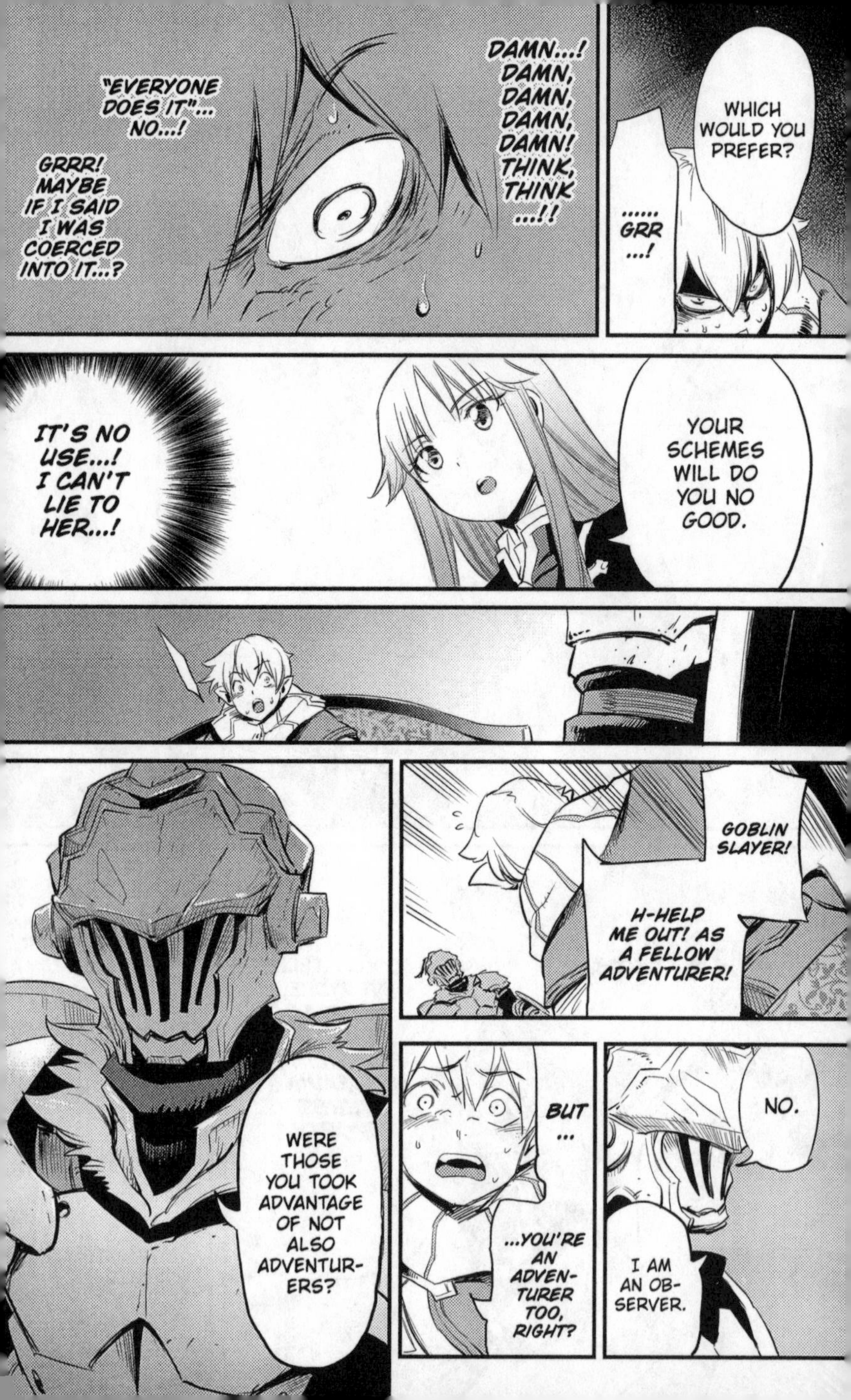
WHICH WOULD YOU PREFER?
......GRR...!
DAMN...! DAMN, DAMN, DAMN, DAMN! THINK, THINK...!!
"EVERYONE DOES IT"... NO...!
GRRR! MAYBE IF I SAID I WAS COERCED INTO IT...?
YOUR SCHEMES WILL DO YOU NO GOOD.
IT'S NO USE...! I CAN'T LIE TO HER...!
GOBLIN SLAYER!
H-HELP ME OUT! AS A FELLOW ADVENTURER!
NO.
I AM AN OBSERVER.
BUT...
...YOU'RE AN ADVENTURER TOO, RIGHT?
WERE THOSE YOU TOOK ADVANTAGE OF NOT ALSO ADVENTURERS?

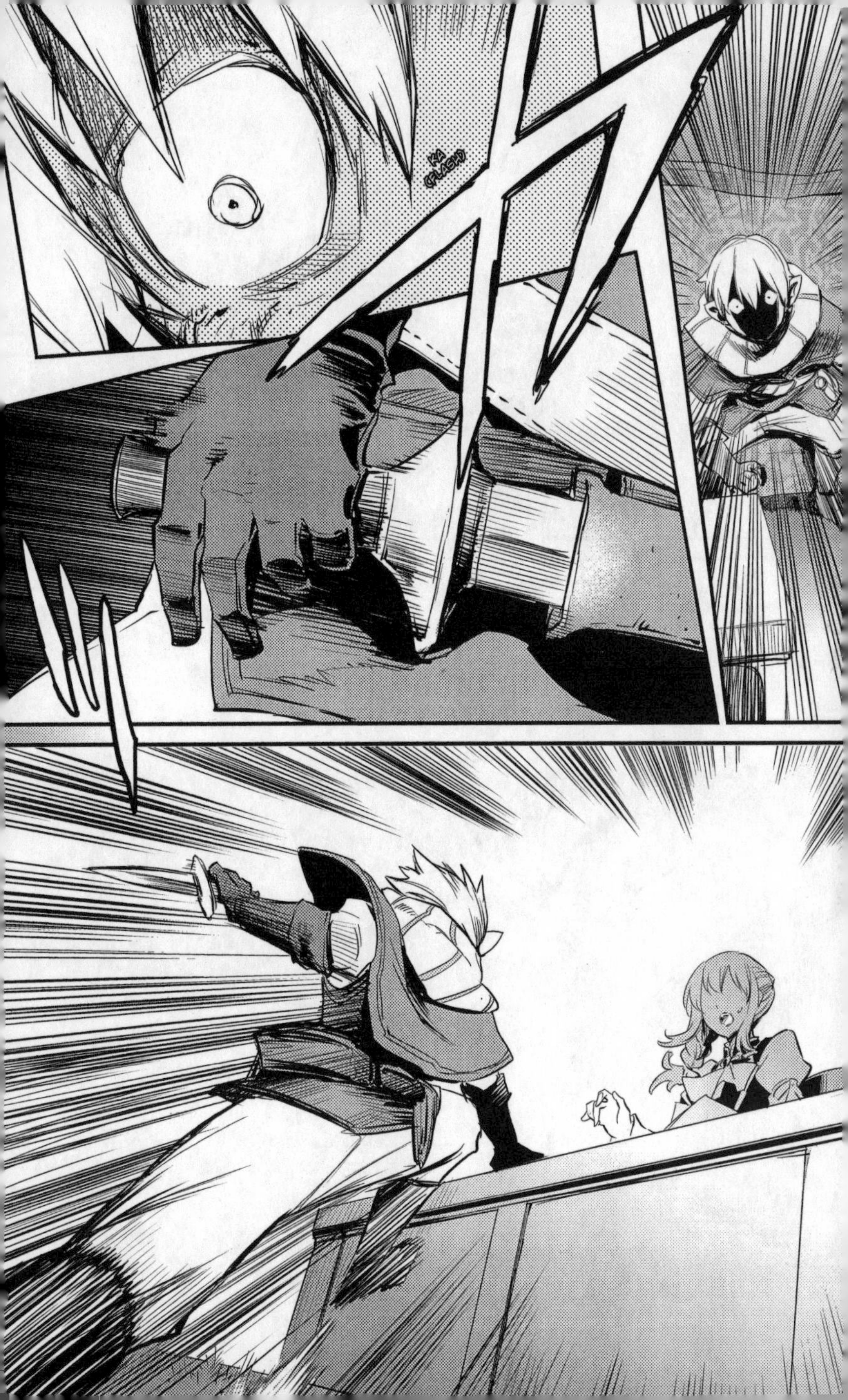
KA (FLASH)

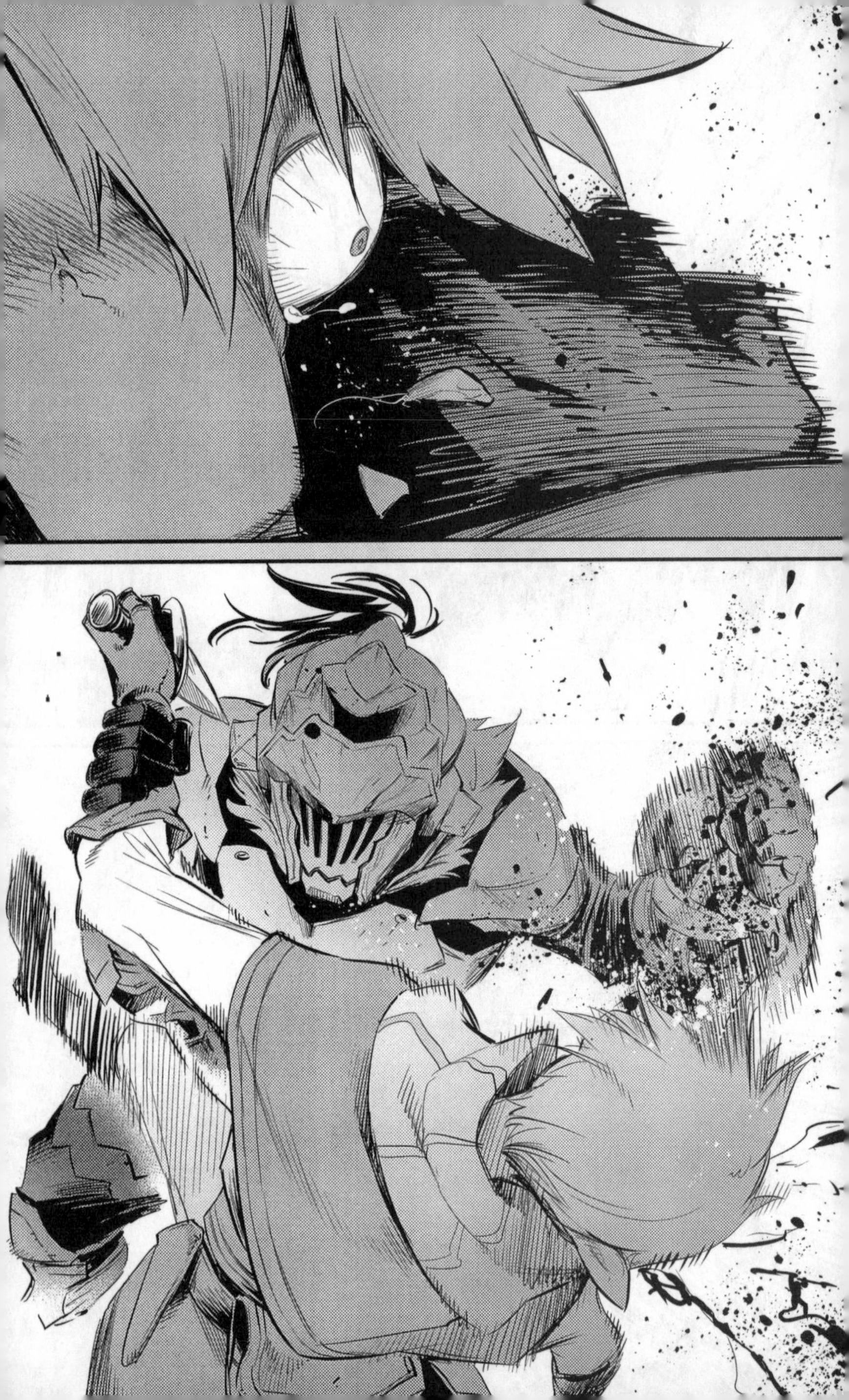

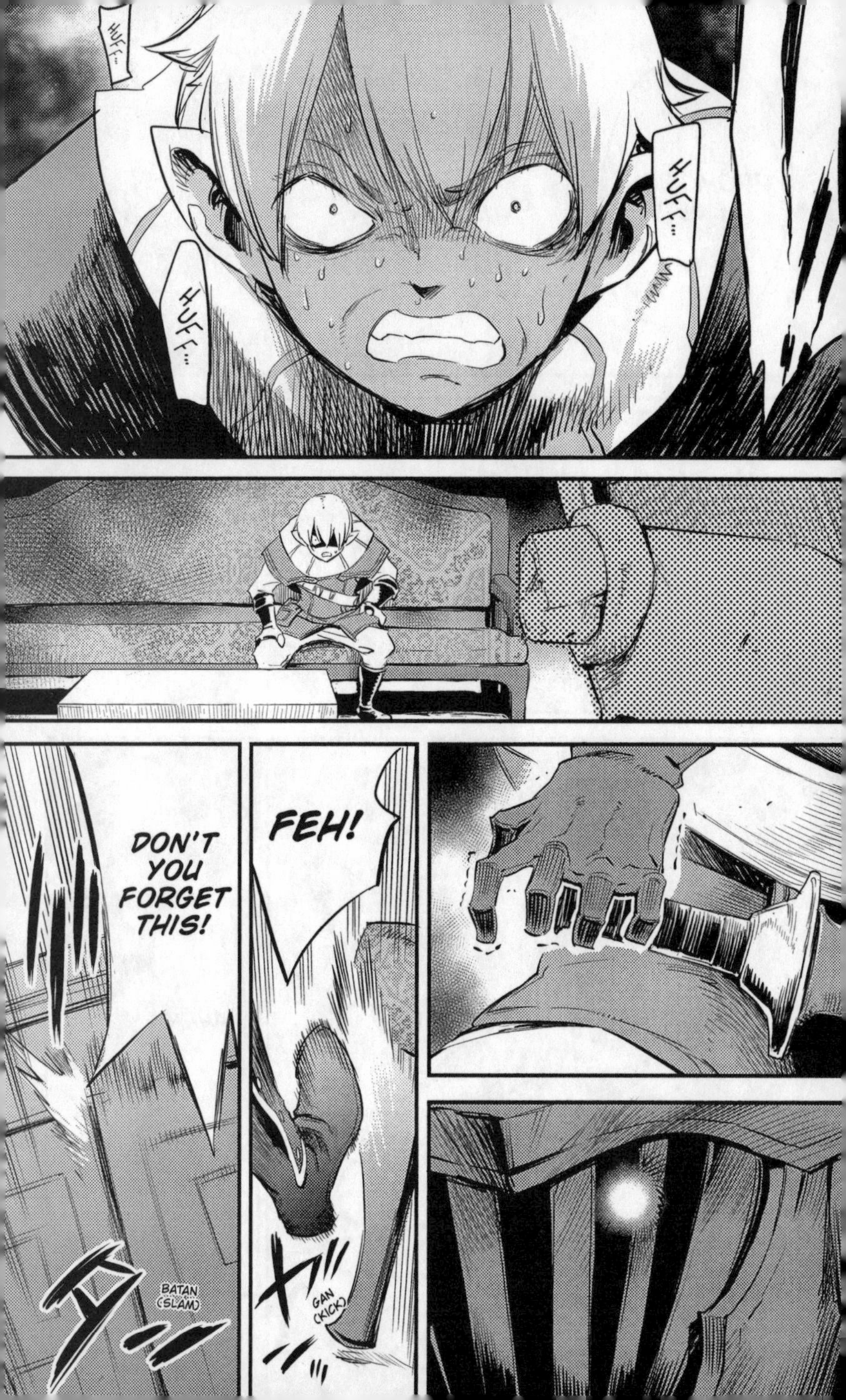
HUFF...
HUFF...
HUFF...
FEH!
GAN (KICK)
DON'T YOU FORGET THIS!
BATAN (SLAM)

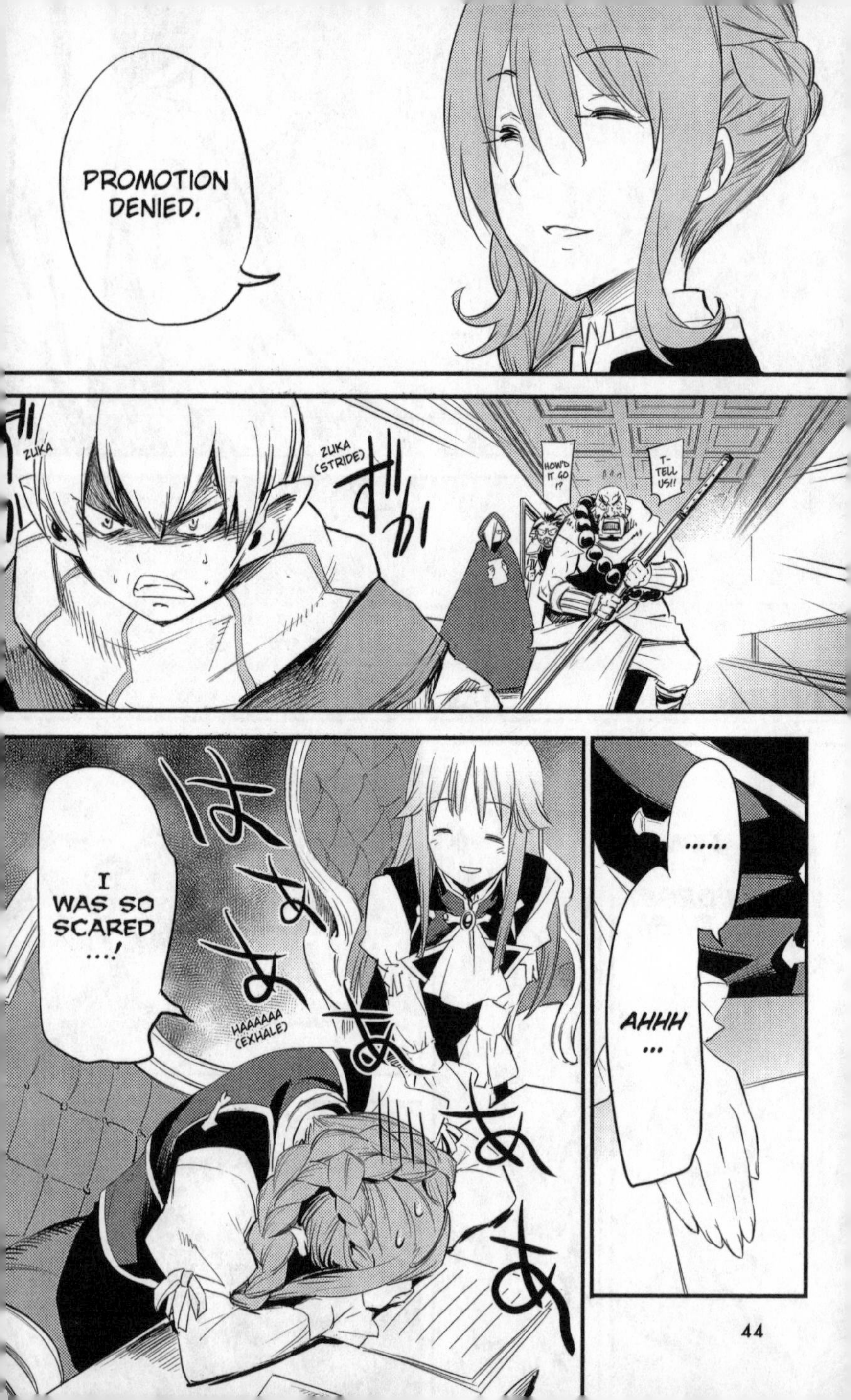
PROMOTION DENIED.
T- TELL US!!
HOW'D IT GO !?
ZUKA (STRIDE)
ZUKA
......
AHHH ...
I WAS SO SCARED ....!
HAAAAAA (EXHALE)

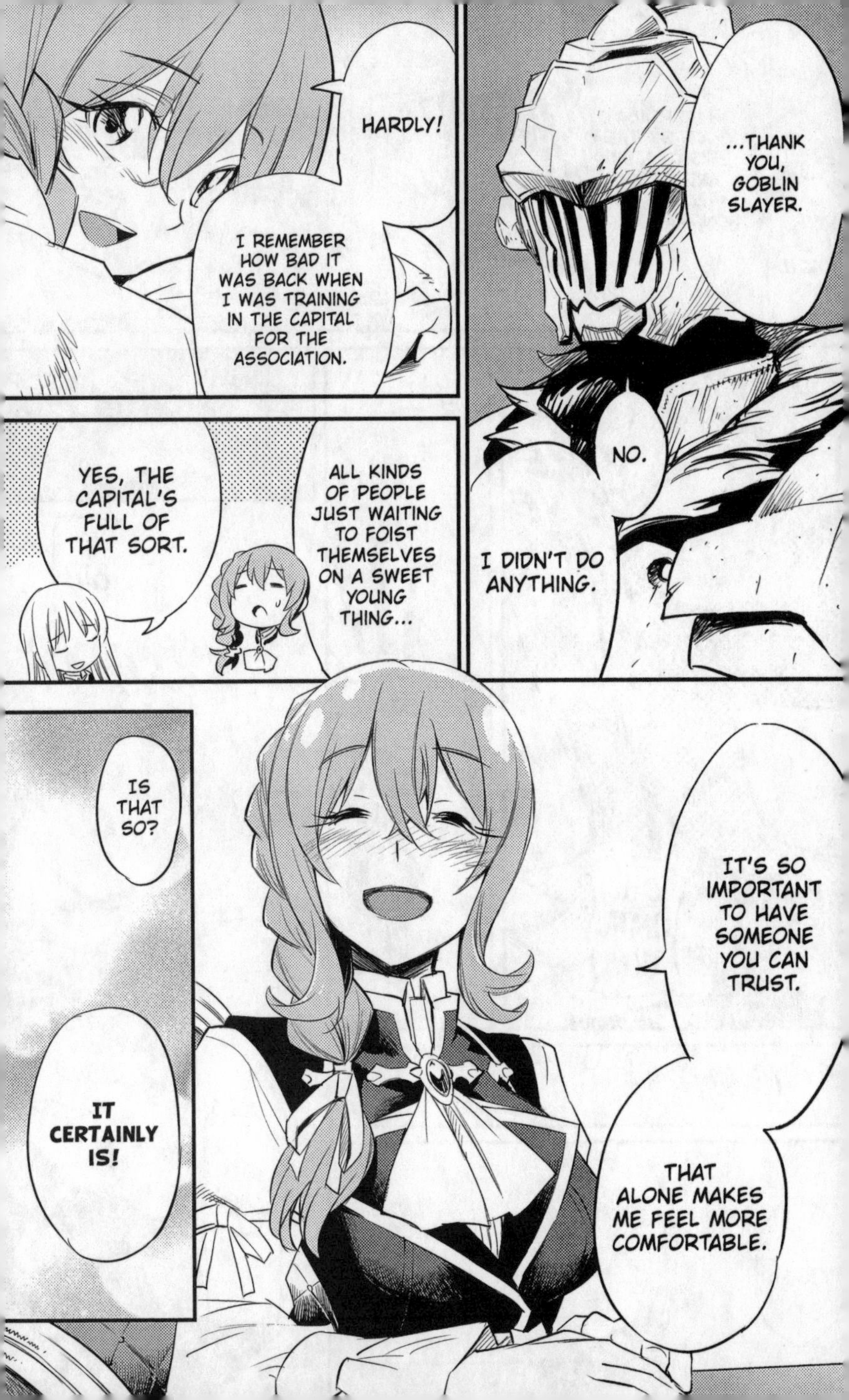

...THANK YOU, GOBLIN SLAYER.
NO.
I DIDN'T DO ANYTHING.
HARDLY!
I REMEMBER HOW BAD IT WAS BACK WHEN I WAS TRAINING IN THE CAPITAL FOR THE ASSOCIATION.
ALL KINDS OF PEOPLE JUST WAITING TO FOIST THEMSELVES ON A SWEET YOUNG THING...
YES, THE CAPITAL'S FULL OF THAT SORT.
IT'S SO IMPORTANT TO HAVE SOMEONE YOU CAN TRUST.
THAT ALONE MAKES ME FEEL MORE COMFORTABLE.
IS THAT SO?
IT CERTAINLY IS!

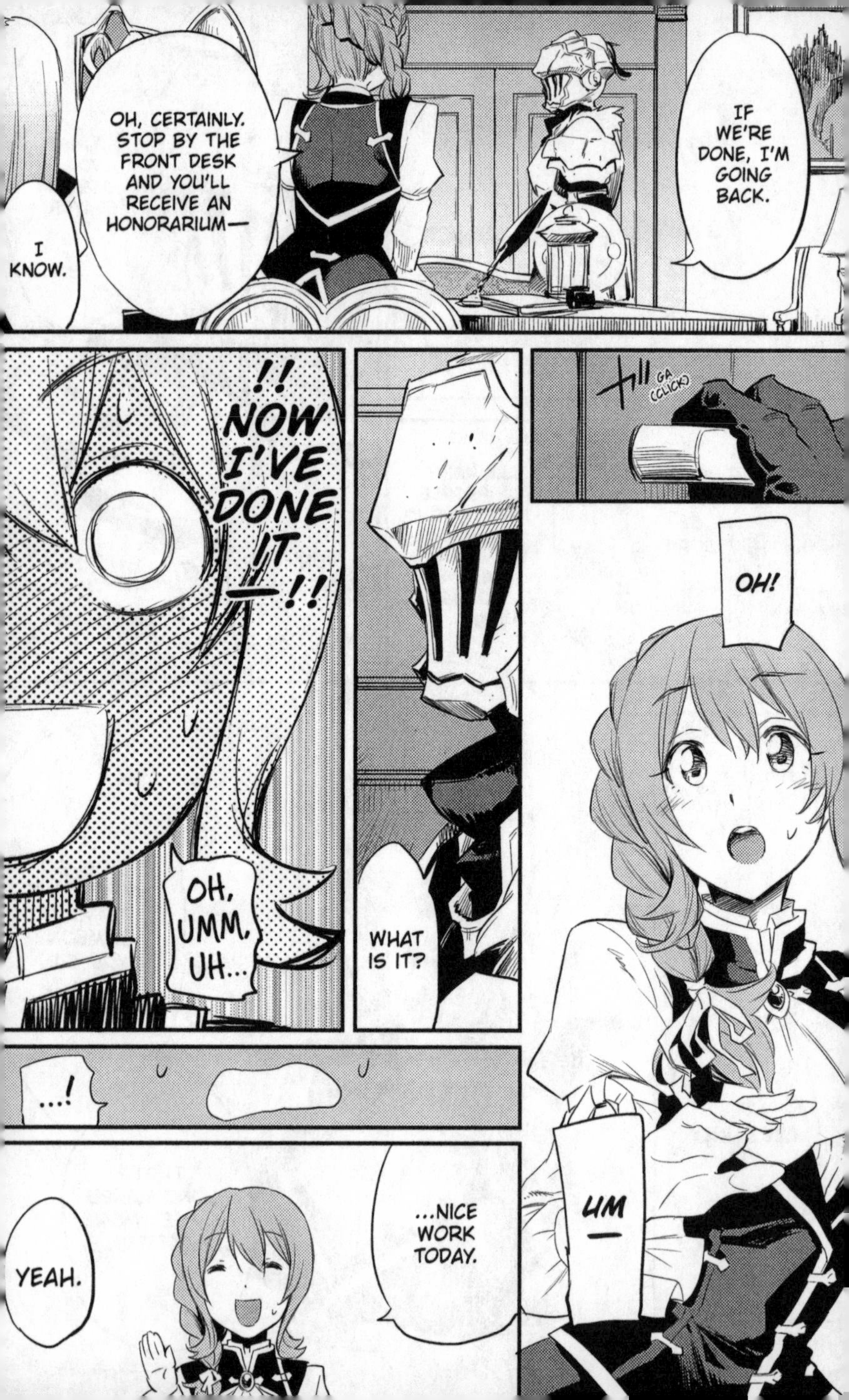
IF WE'RE DONE, I'M GOING BACK.
OH, CERTAINLY. STOP BY THE FRONT DESK AND YOU'LL RECEIVE AN HONORARIUM—
I KNOW.
GA (CLICK)
OH!
UM—
WHAT IS IT?
!! NOW I'VE DONE IT—!!
OH, UMM, UH...
...!
...NICE WORK TODAY.
YEAH.

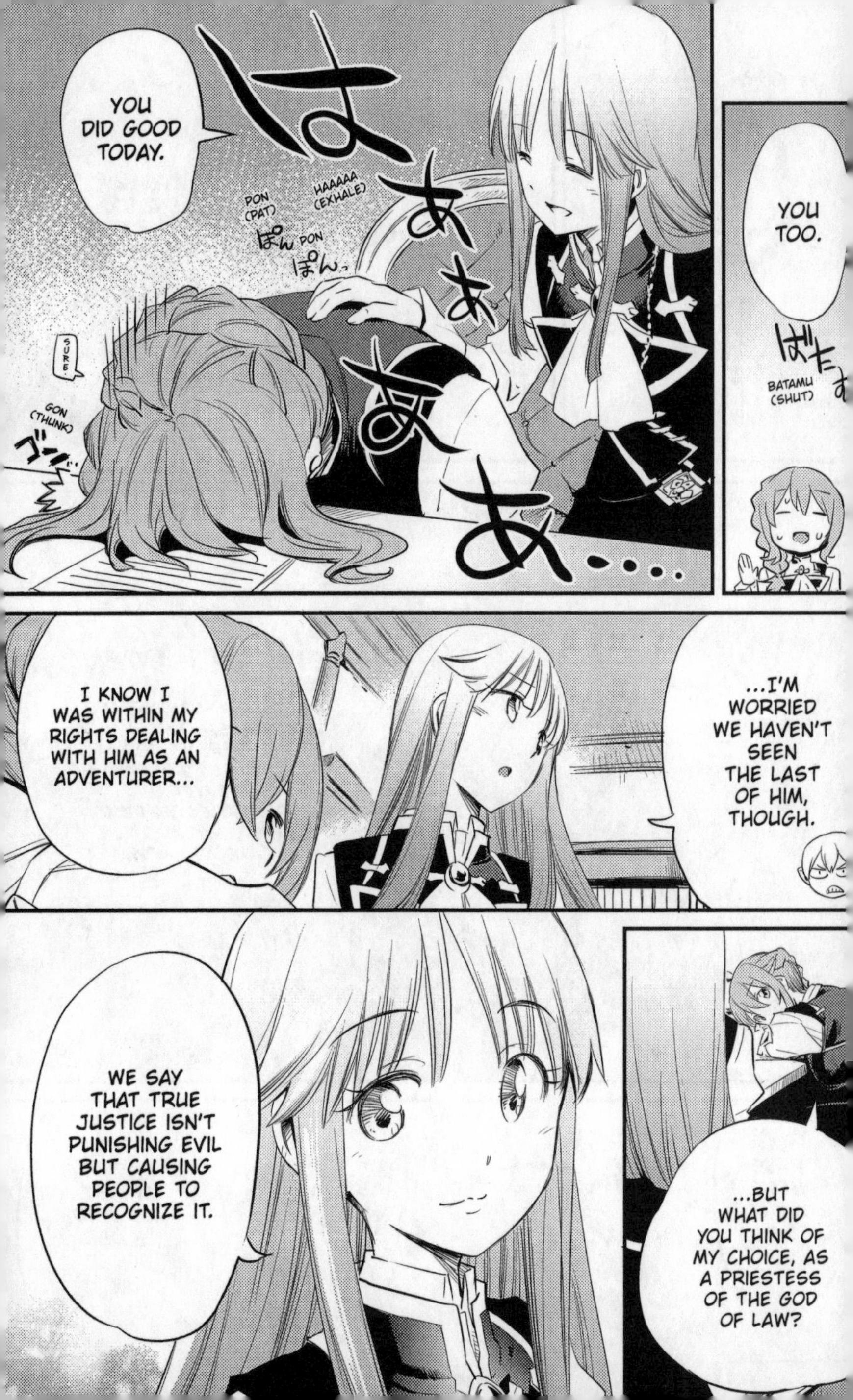
YOU TOO.
ばたむ
BATAMU (SHUT)
はあああ…
HAAAAA (EXHALE)
YOU DID GOOD TODAY.
PON (PAT)
ぽん PON
ぽんっ
SURE.
GON (THUNK)
…I'M WORRIED WE HAVEN'T SEEN THE LAST OF HIM, THOUGH.
I KNOW I WAS WITHIN MY RIGHTS DEALING WITH HIM AS AN ADVENTURER…
…BUT WHAT DID YOU THINK OF MY CHOICE, AS A PRIESTESS OF THE GOD OF LAW?
WE SAY THAT TRUE JUSTICE ISN'T PUNISHING EVIL BUT CAUSING PEOPLE TO RECOGNIZE IT.

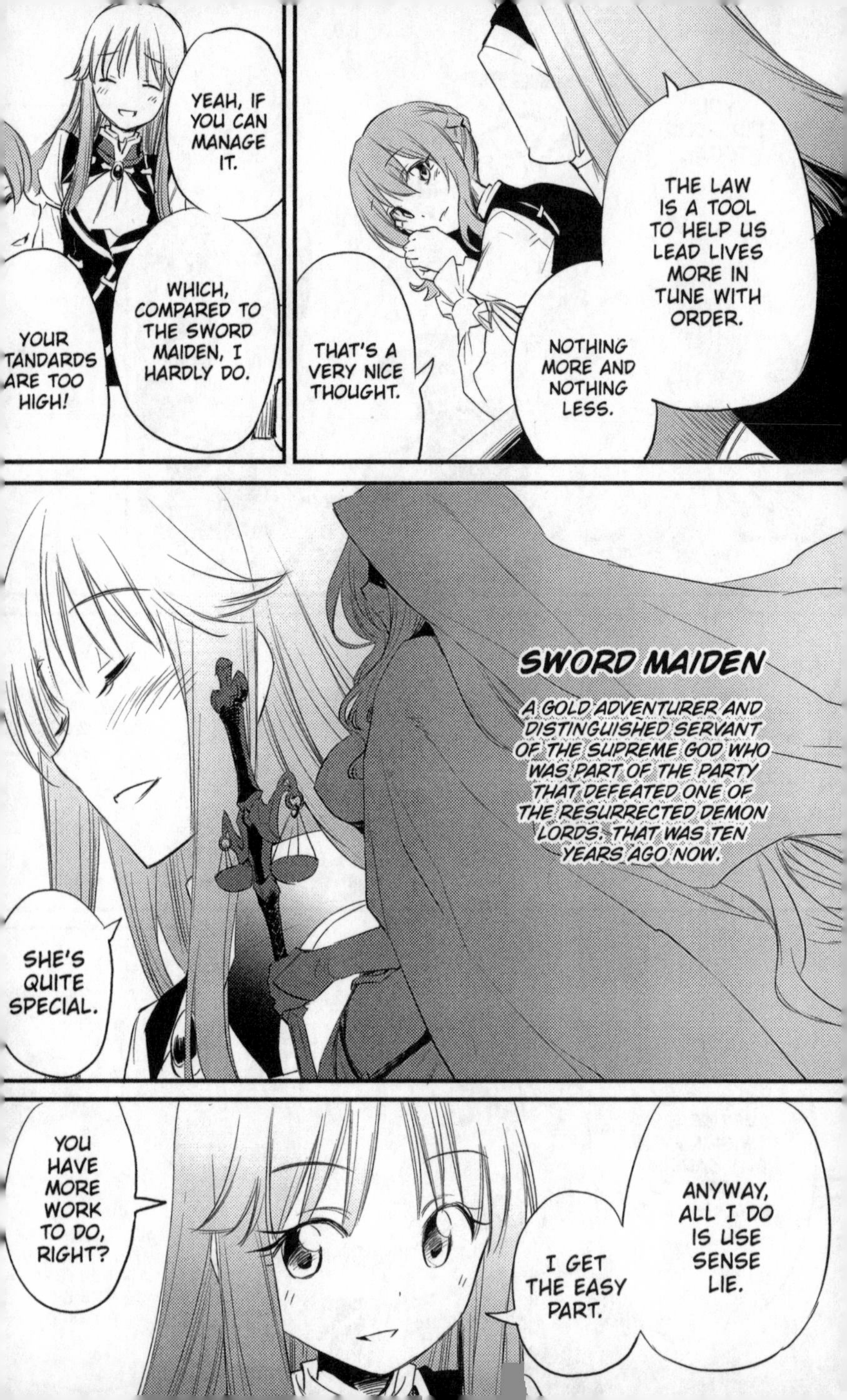
THE LAW IS A TOOL TO HELP US LEAD LIVES MORE IN TUNE WITH ORDER.
NOTHING MORE AND NOTHING LESS.
THAT'S A VERY NICE THOUGHT.
YEAH, IF YOU CAN MANAGE IT.
WHICH, COMPARED TO THE SWORD MAIDEN, I HARDLY DO.
YOUR TANDARDS ARE TOO HIGH!
SWORD MAIDEN
A GOLD ADVENTURER AND DISTINGUISHED SERVANT OF THE SUPREME GOD WHO WAS PART OF THE PARTY THAT DEFEATED ONE OF THE RESURRECTED DEMON LORDS. THAT WAS TEN YEARS AGO NOW.
SHE'S QUITE SPECIAL.
ANYWAY, ALL I DO IS USE SENSE LIE.
I GET THE EASY PART.
YOU HAVE MORE WORK TO DO, RIGHT?

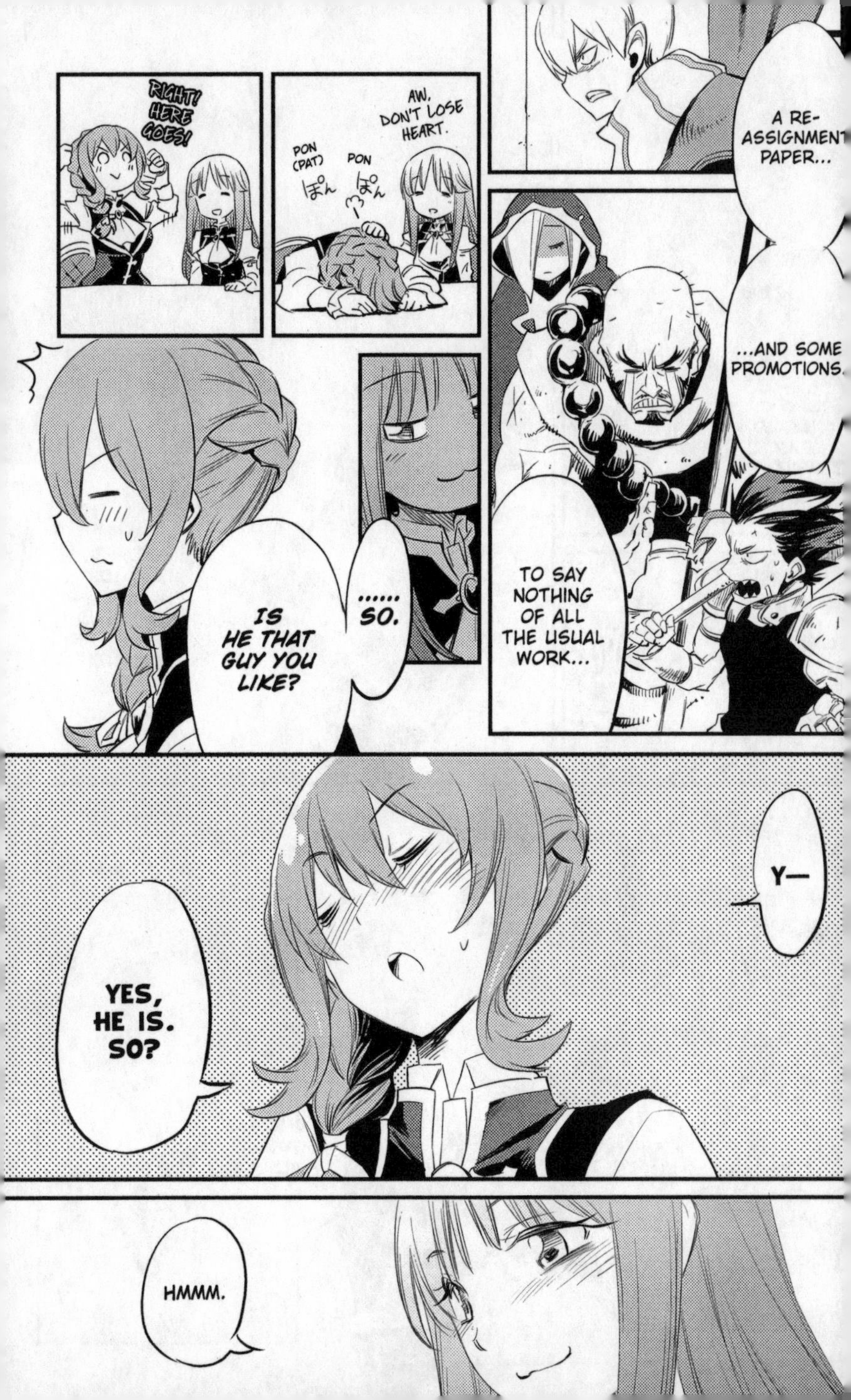
A RE-ASSIGNMENT PAPER...
...AND SOME PROMOTIONS.
TO SAY NOTHING OF ALL THE USUAL WORK...
AW, DON'T LOSE HEART.
PON (PAT) ぽん
PON ぽん
RIGHT! HERE GOES!
......SO.
IS HE THAT GUY YOU LIKE?
Y—
YES, HE IS. SO?
HMMM.

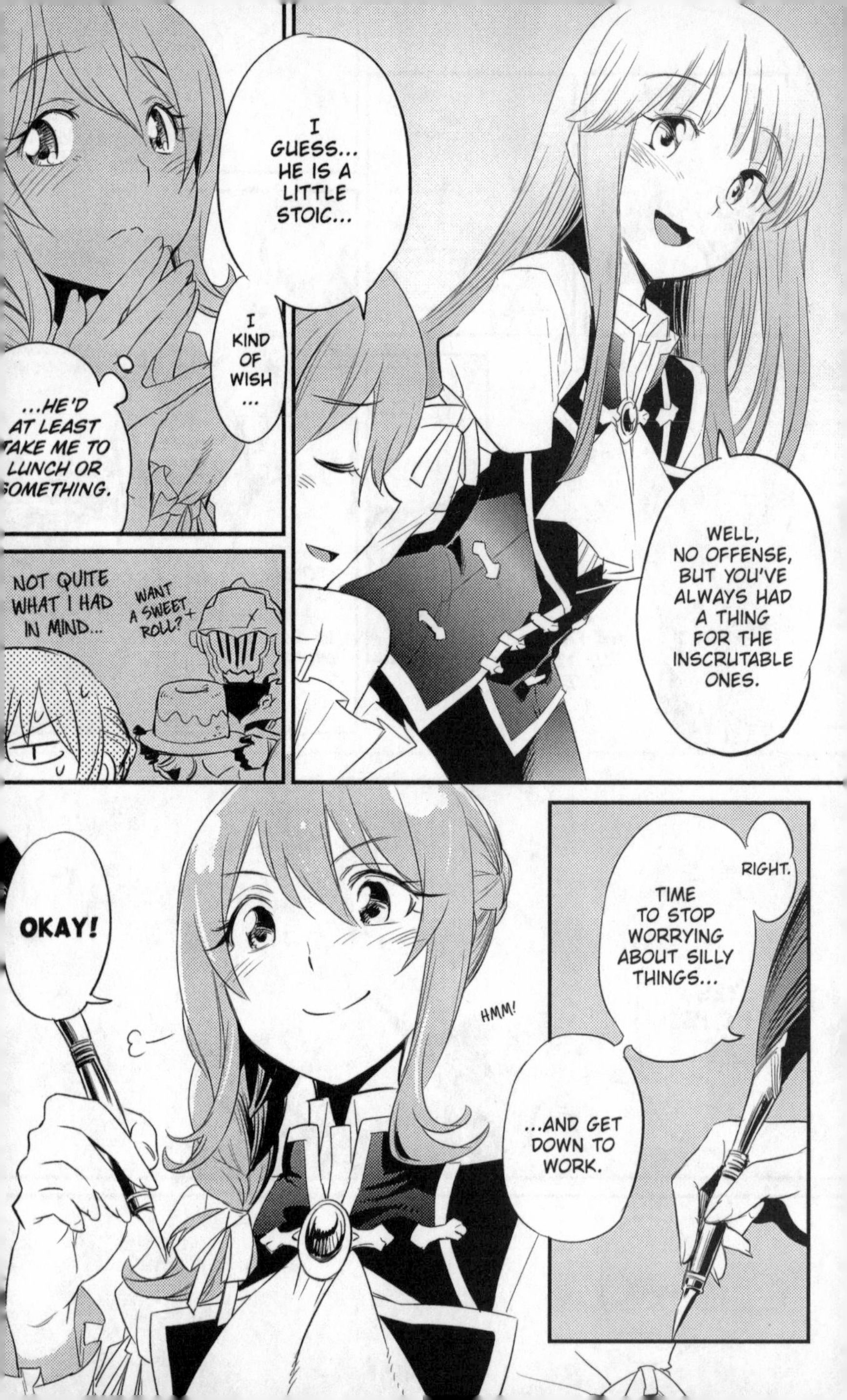

WELL, NO OFFENSE, BUT YOU'VE ALWAYS HAD A THING FOR THE INSCRUTABLE ONES.
I GUESS... HE IS A LITTLE STOIC...
I KIND OF WISH...
...HE'D AT LEAST TAKE ME TO LUNCH OR SOMETHING.
WANT A SWEET ROLL?
NOT QUITE WHAT I HAD IN MIND...
RIGHT.
TIME TO STOP WORRYING ABOUT SILLY THINGS...
...AND GET DOWN TO WORK.
HMM!
OKAY!

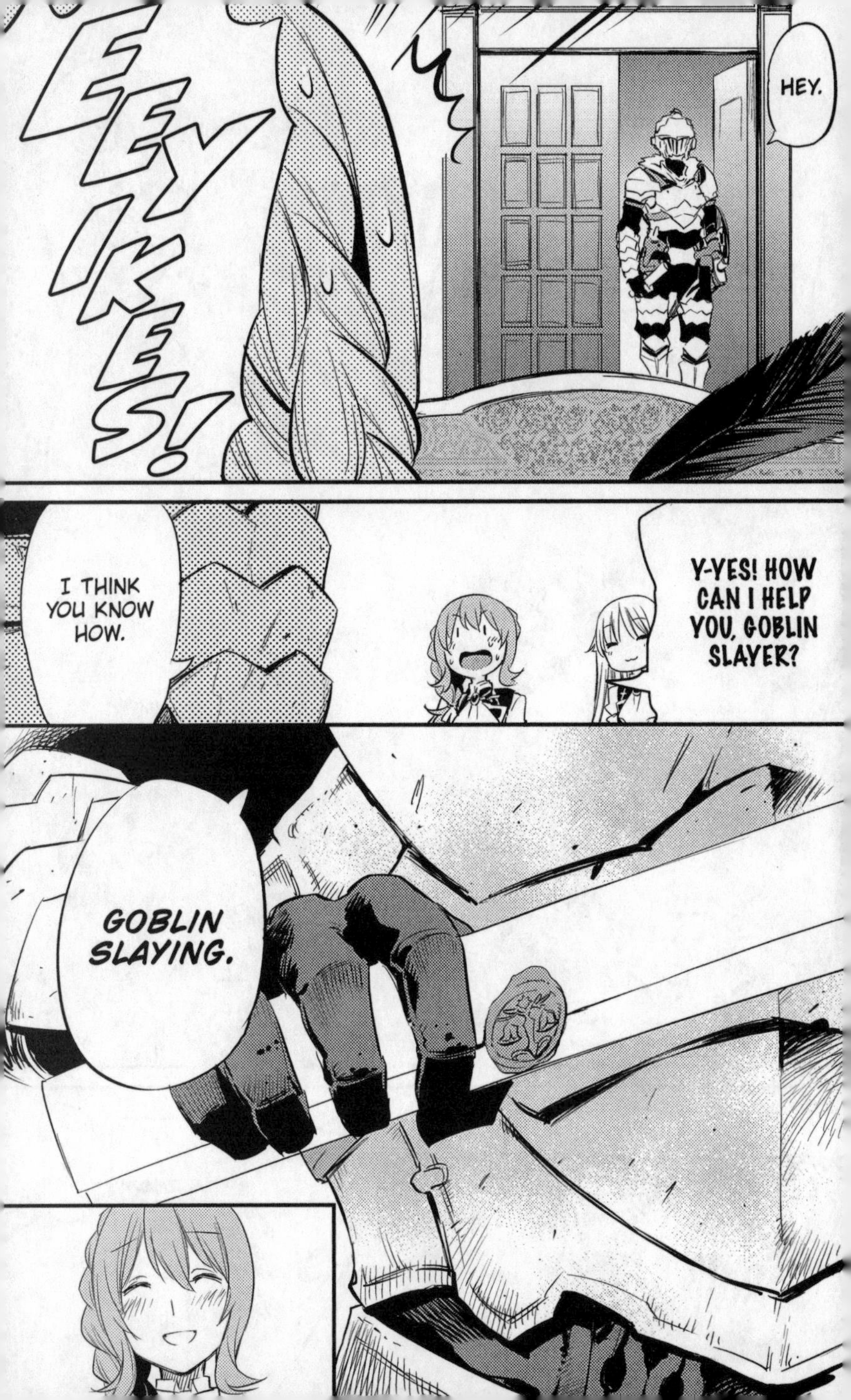
HEY.
EEYIKES!
Y-YES! HOW CAN I HELP YOU, GOBLIN SLAYER?
I THINK YOU KNOW HOW.
GOBLIN SLAYING.

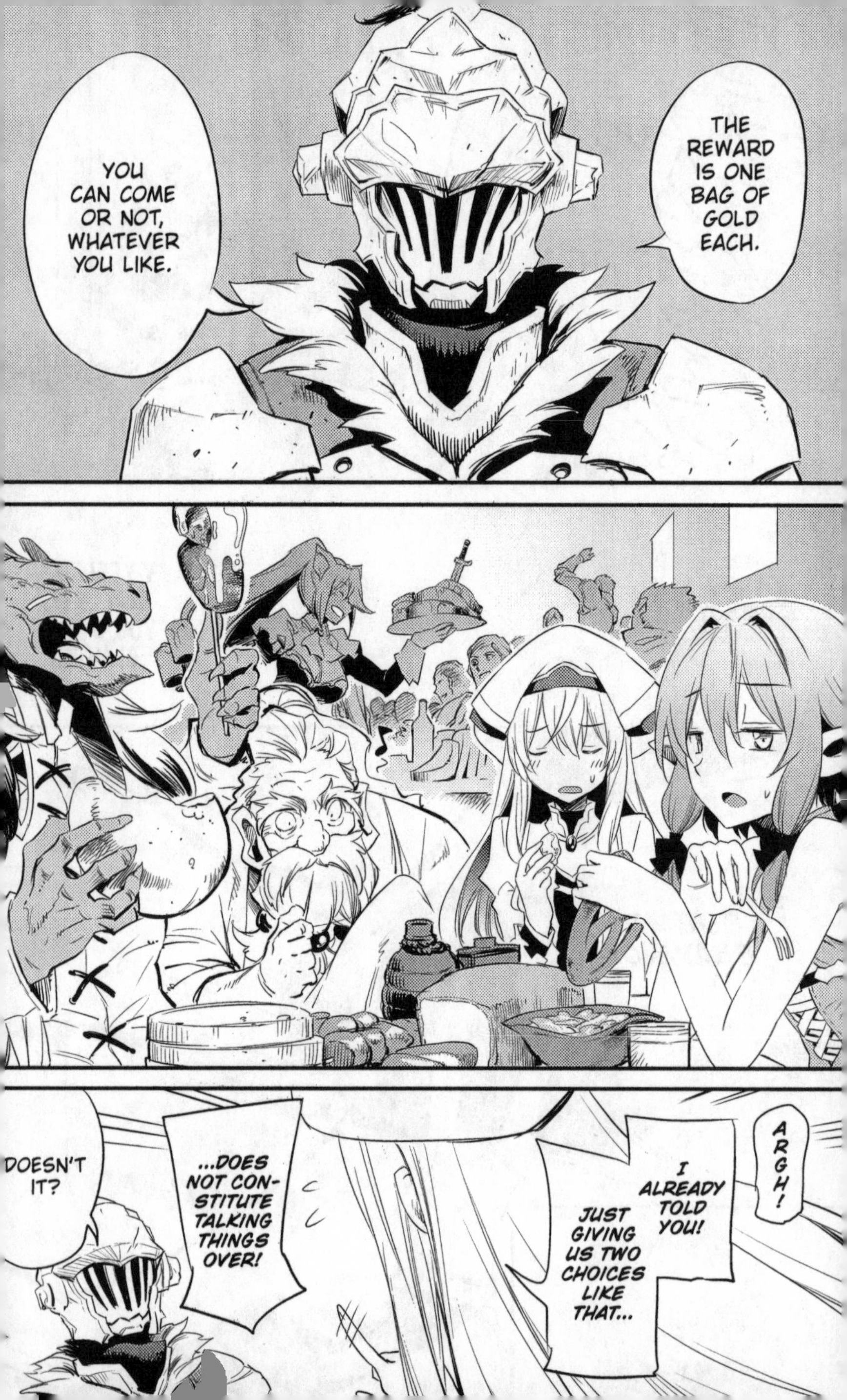
THE REWARD IS ONE BAG OF GOLD EACH.
YOU CAN COME OR NOT, WHATEVER YOU LIKE.
ARGH!
I ALREADY TOLD YOU!
JUST GIVING US TWO CHOICES LIKE THAT...
...DOES NOT CON-STITUTE TALKING THINGS OVER!
DOESN'T IT?

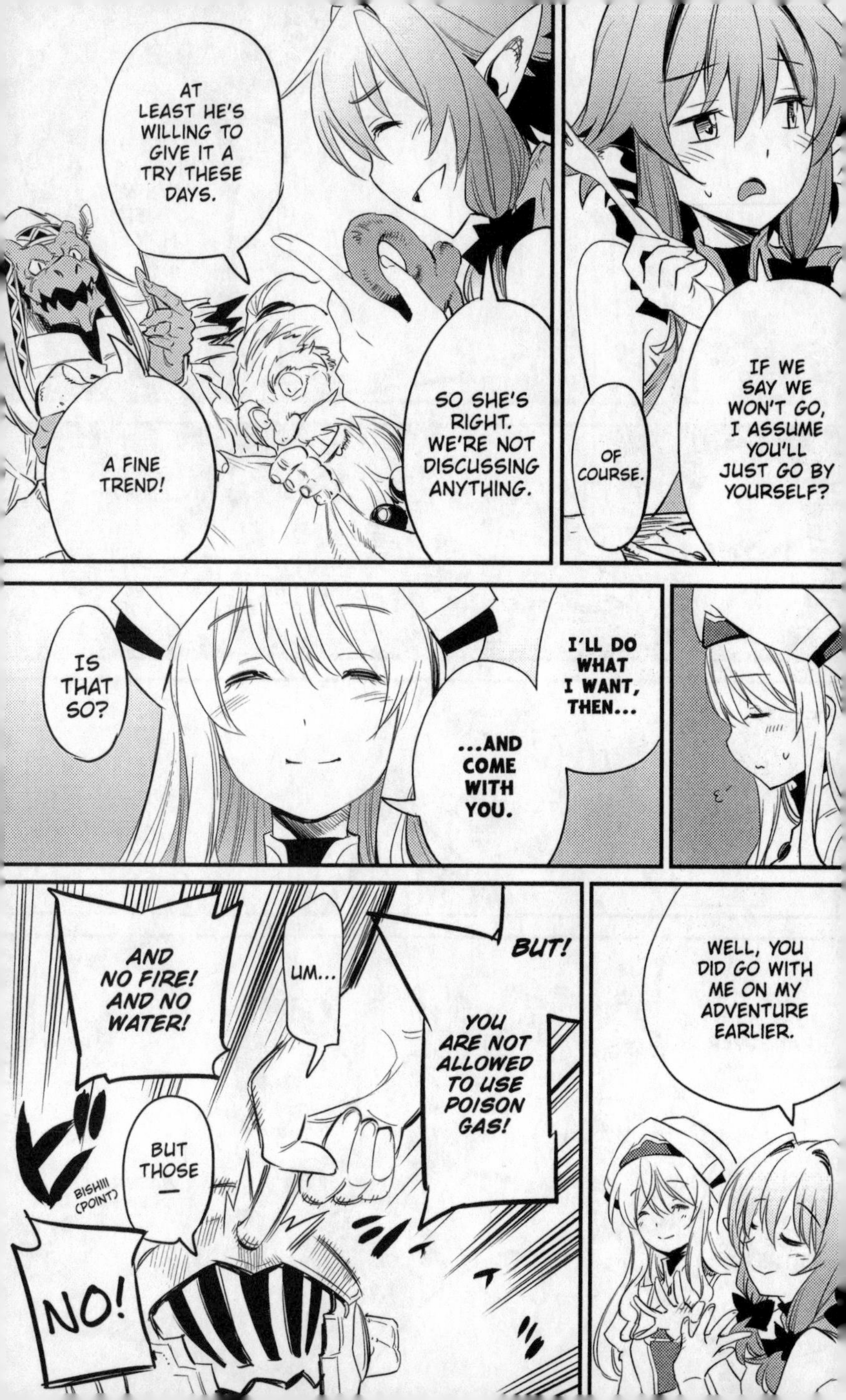
IF WE SAY WE WON'T GO, I ASSUME YOU'LL JUST GO BY YOURSELF?
OF COURSE.
SO SHE'S RIGHT. WE'RE NOT DISCUSSING ANYTHING.
AT LEAST HE'S WILLING TO GIVE IT A TRY THESE DAYS.
A FINE TREND!
I'LL DO WHAT I WANT, THEN...
...AND COME WITH YOU.
IS THAT SO?
WELL, YOU DID GO WITH ME ON MY ADVENTURE EARLIER.
BUT!
YOU ARE NOT ALLOWED TO USE POISON GAS!
UM...
AND NO FIRE! AND NO WATER!
BUT THOSE—
BISHIII (POINT)
NO!

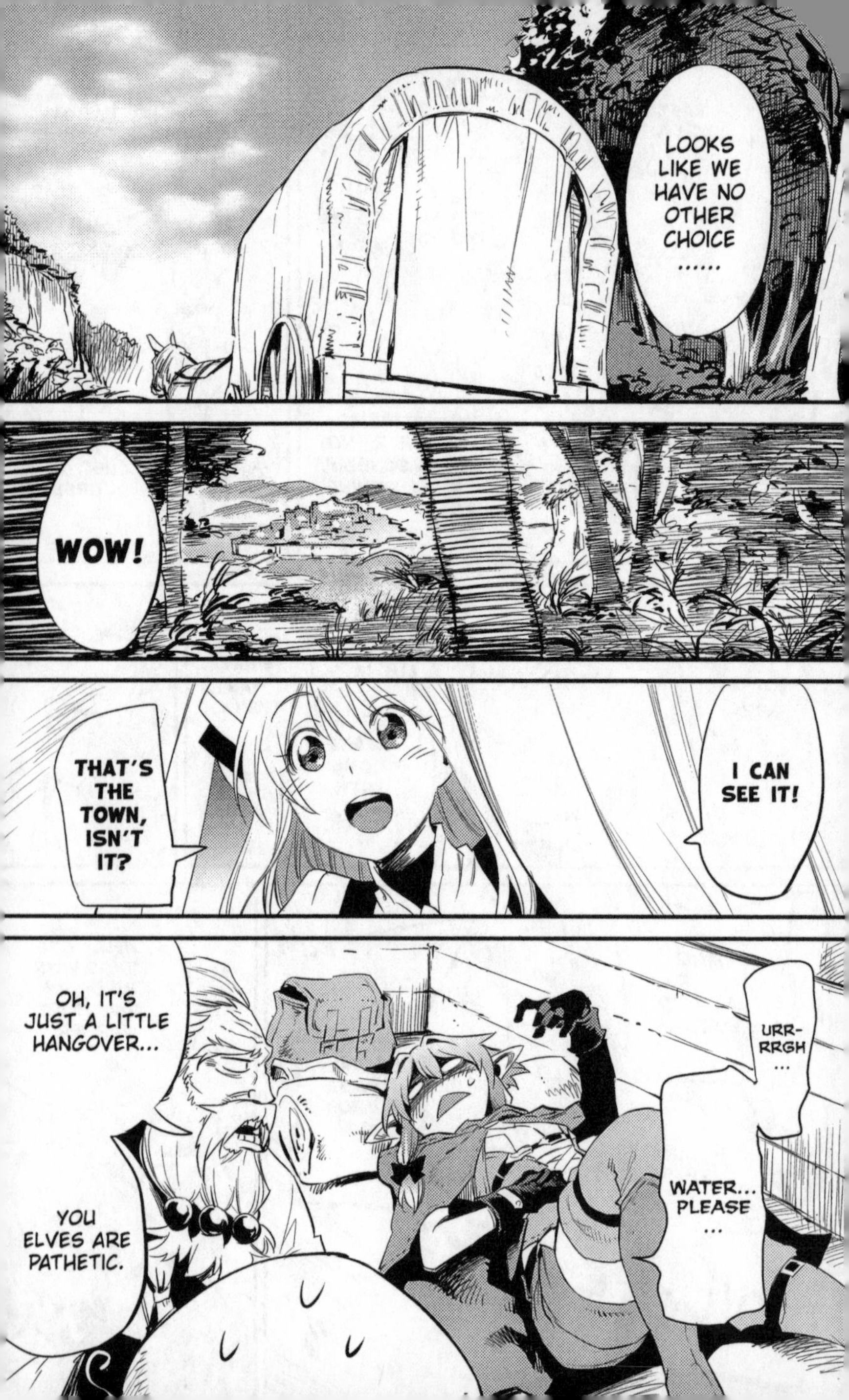
LOOKS LIKE WE HAVE NO OTHER CHOICE ......
WOW!
I CAN SEE IT!
THAT'S THE TOWN, ISN'T IT?
URR-RRGH ...
OH, IT'S JUST A LITTLE HANGOVER...
WATER... PLEASE ...
YOU ELVES ARE PATHETIC.

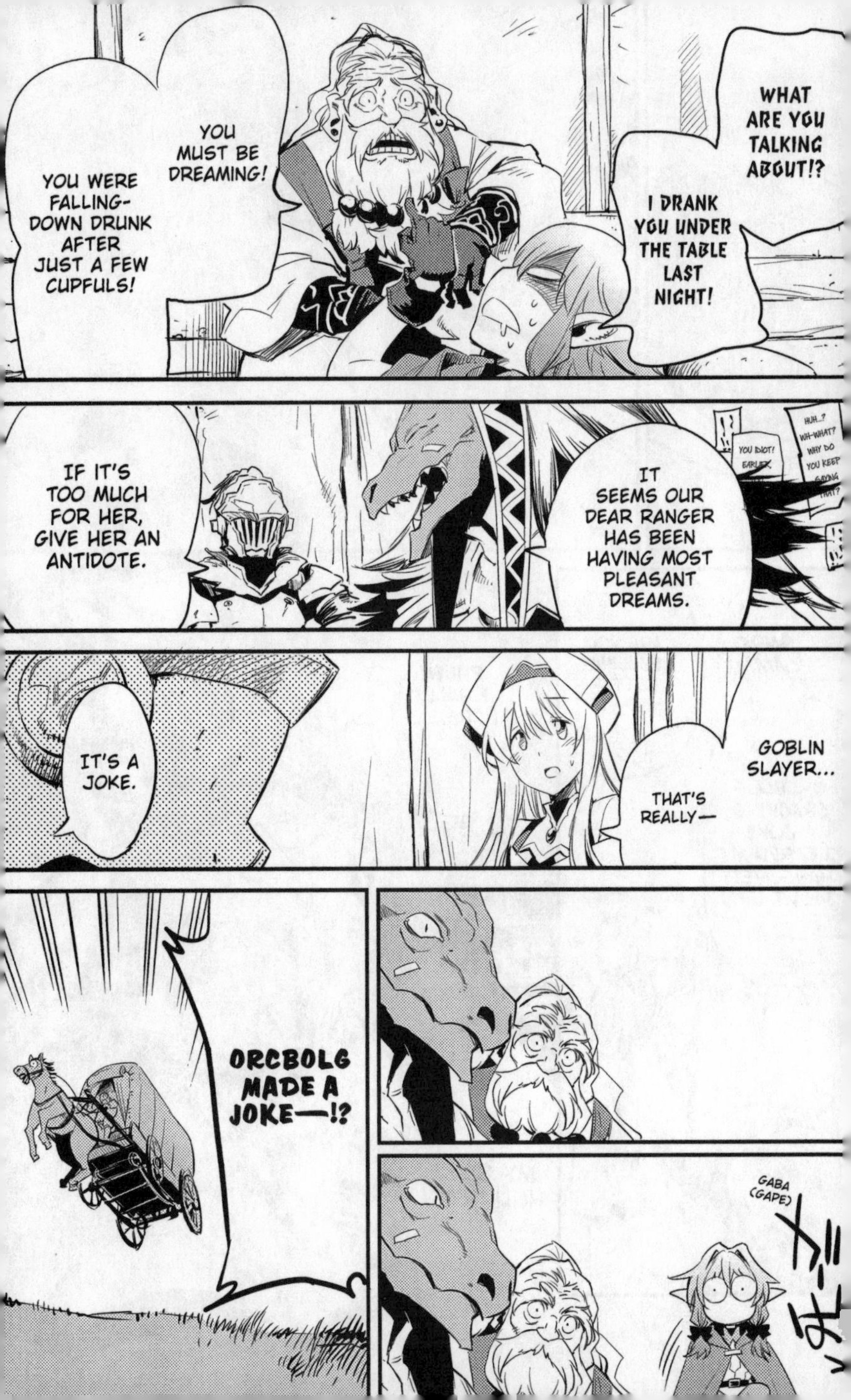
WHAT ARE YOU TALKING ABOUT!?
I DRANK YOU UNDER THE TABLE LAST NIGHT!
YOU MUST BE DREAMING!
YOU WERE FALLING-DOWN DRUNK AFTER JUST A FEW CUPFULS!
HUH...? WH-WHAT? WHY DO YOU KEEP SAYING THAT?
YOU IDIOT! EARLIER,
IT SEEMS OUR DEAR RANGER HAS BEEN HAVING MOST PLEASANT DREAMS.
IF IT'S TOO MUCH FOR HER, GIVE HER AN ANTIDOTE.
GOBLIN SLAYER...
THAT'S REALLY—
IT'S A JOKE.
GABA (GAPE)
ORCBOLG MADE A JOKE—!?

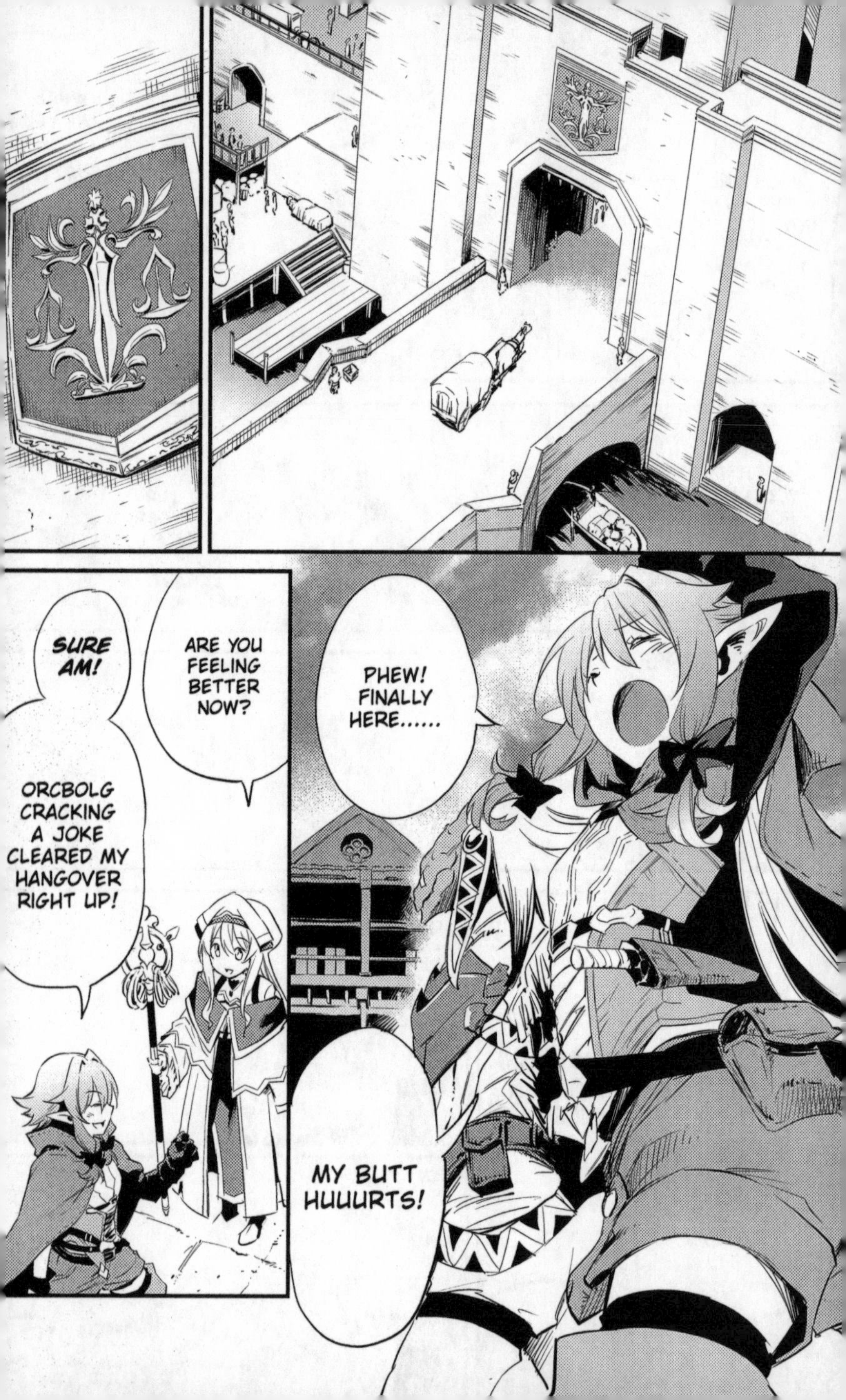
PHEW! FINALLY HERE......
MY BUTT HUUURTS!
ARE YOU FEELING BETTER NOW?
SURE AM!
ORCBOLG CRACKING A JOKE CLEARED MY HANGOVER RIGHT UP!

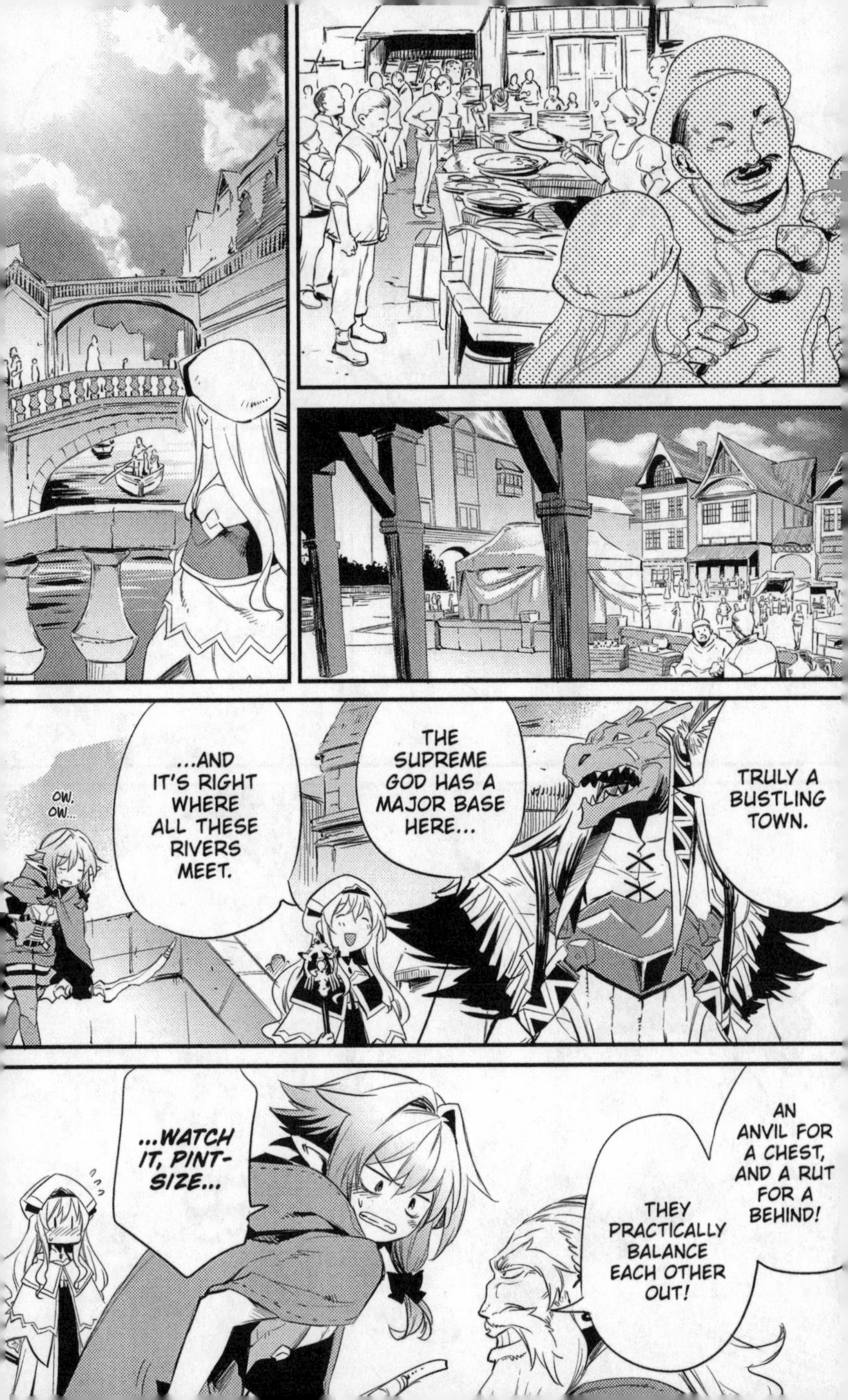
TRULY A BUSTLING TOWN.
THE SUPREME GOD HAS A MAJOR BASE HERE...
...AND IT'S RIGHT WHERE ALL THESE RIVERS MEET.
OW. OW...
AN ANVIL FOR A CHEST, AND A RUT FOR A BEHIND!
THEY PRACTICALLY BALANCE EACH OTHER OUT!
...WATCH IT, PINT-SIZE...

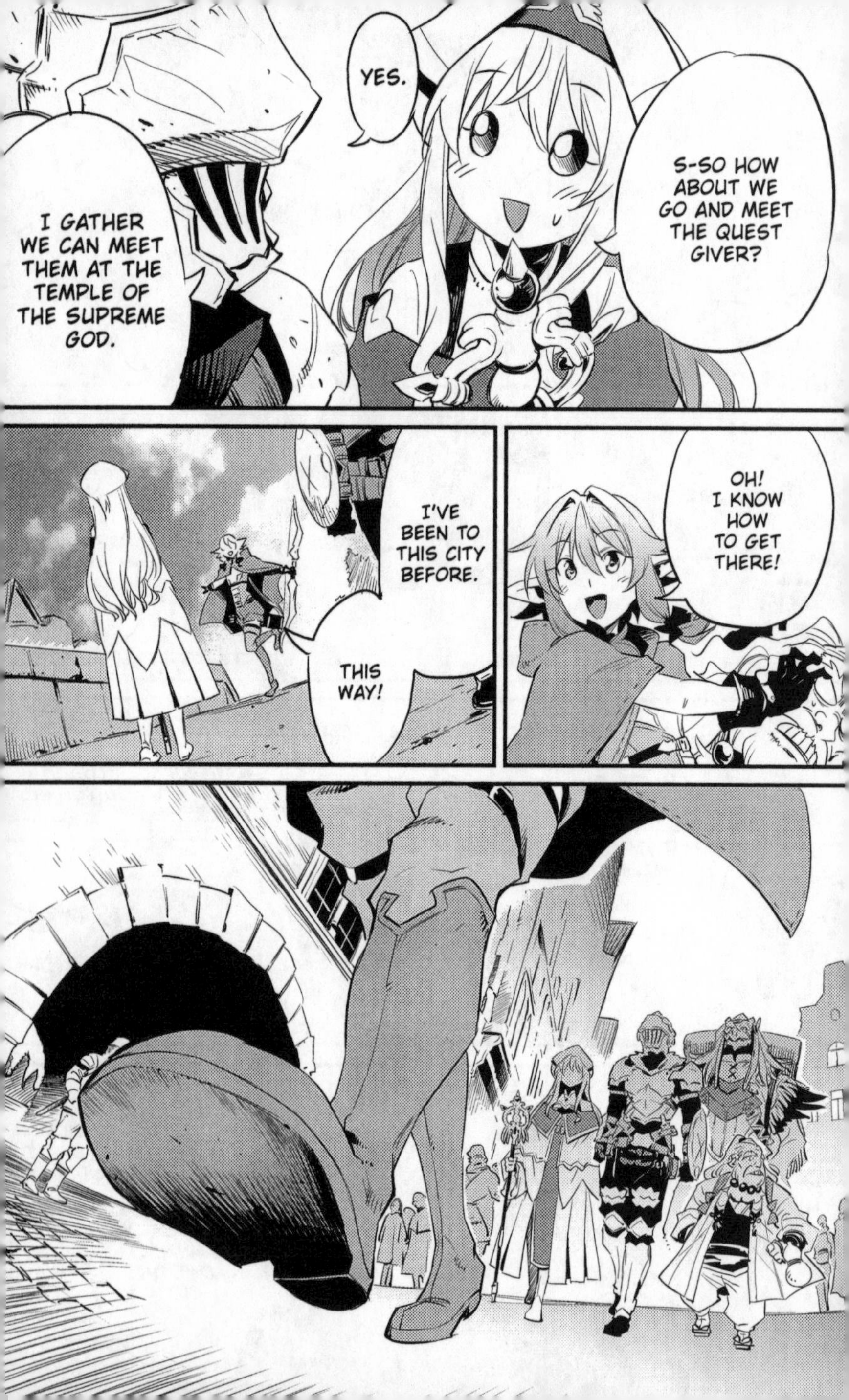
S-SO HOW ABOUT WE GO AND MEET THE QUEST GIVER?
YES.
I GATHER WE CAN MEET THEM AT THE TEMPLE OF THE SUPREME GOD.
OH! I KNOW HOW TO GET THERE!
I'VE BEEN TO THIS CITY BEFORE.
THIS WAY!

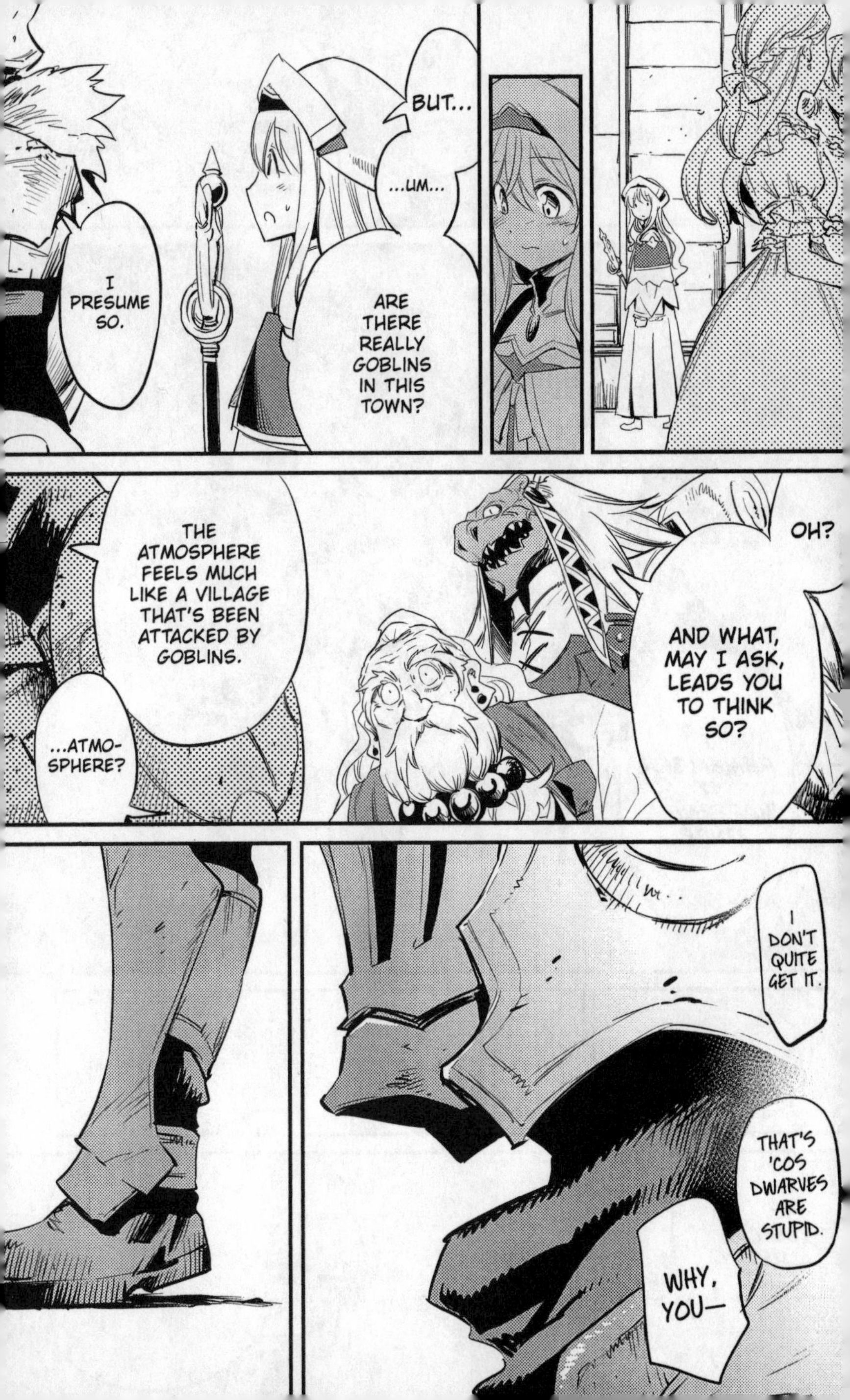
BUT...
...UM...
ARE THERE REALLY GOBLINS IN THIS TOWN?
I PRESUME SO.
THE ATMOSPHERE FEELS MUCH LIKE A VILLAGE THAT'S BEEN ATTACKED BY GOBLINS.
...ATMO-SPHERE?
OH?
AND WHAT, MAY I ASK, LEADS YOU TO THINK SO?
I DON'T QUITE GET IT.
THAT'S 'COS DWARVES ARE STUPID.
WHY, YOU—

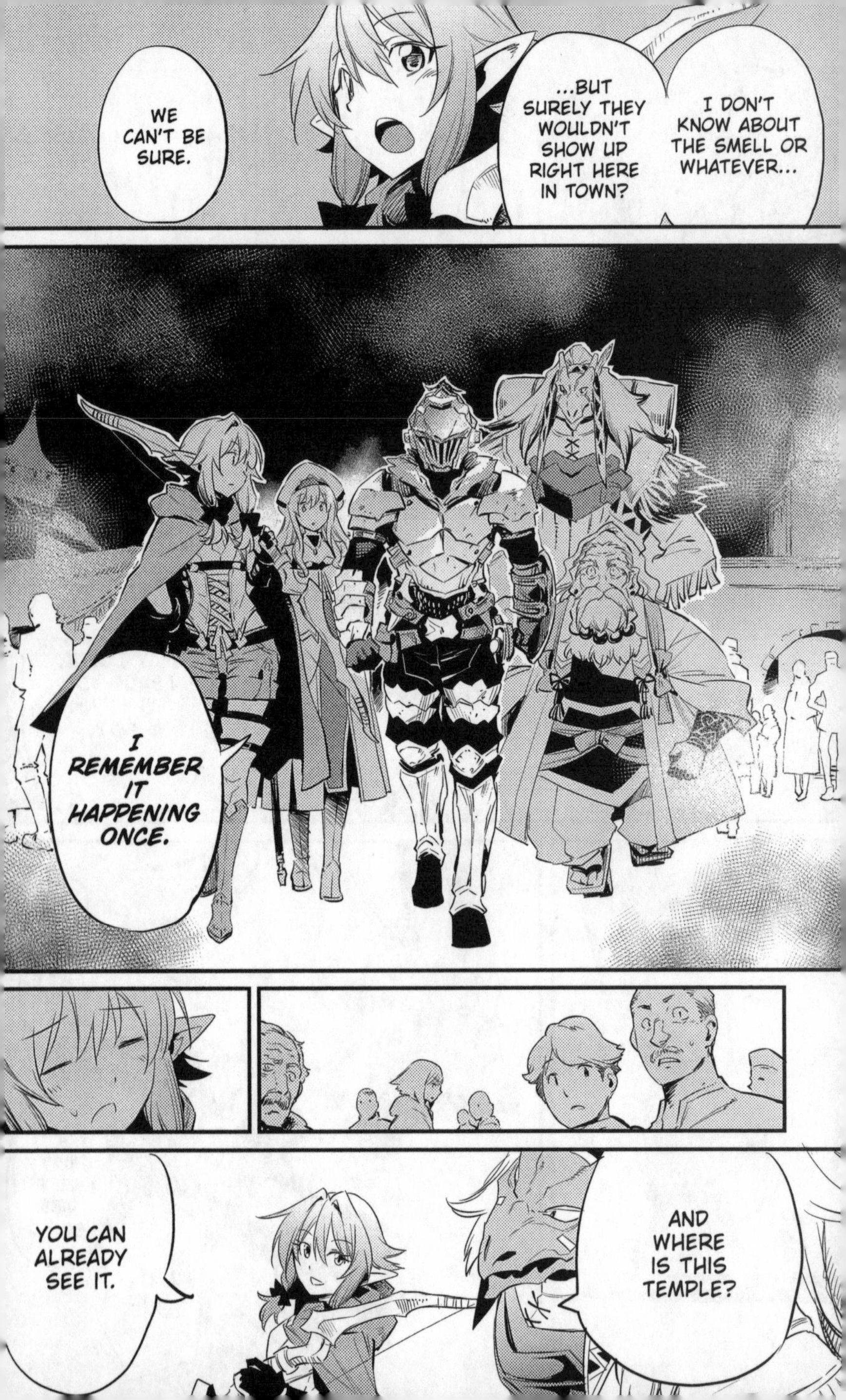
I DON'T KNOW ABOUT THE SMELL OR WHATEVER...
...BUT SURELY THEY WOULDN'T SHOW UP RIGHT HERE IN TOWN?
WE CAN'T BE SURE.
I REMEMBER IT HAPPENING ONCE.
AND WHERE IS THIS TEMPLE?
YOU CAN ALREADY SEE IT.

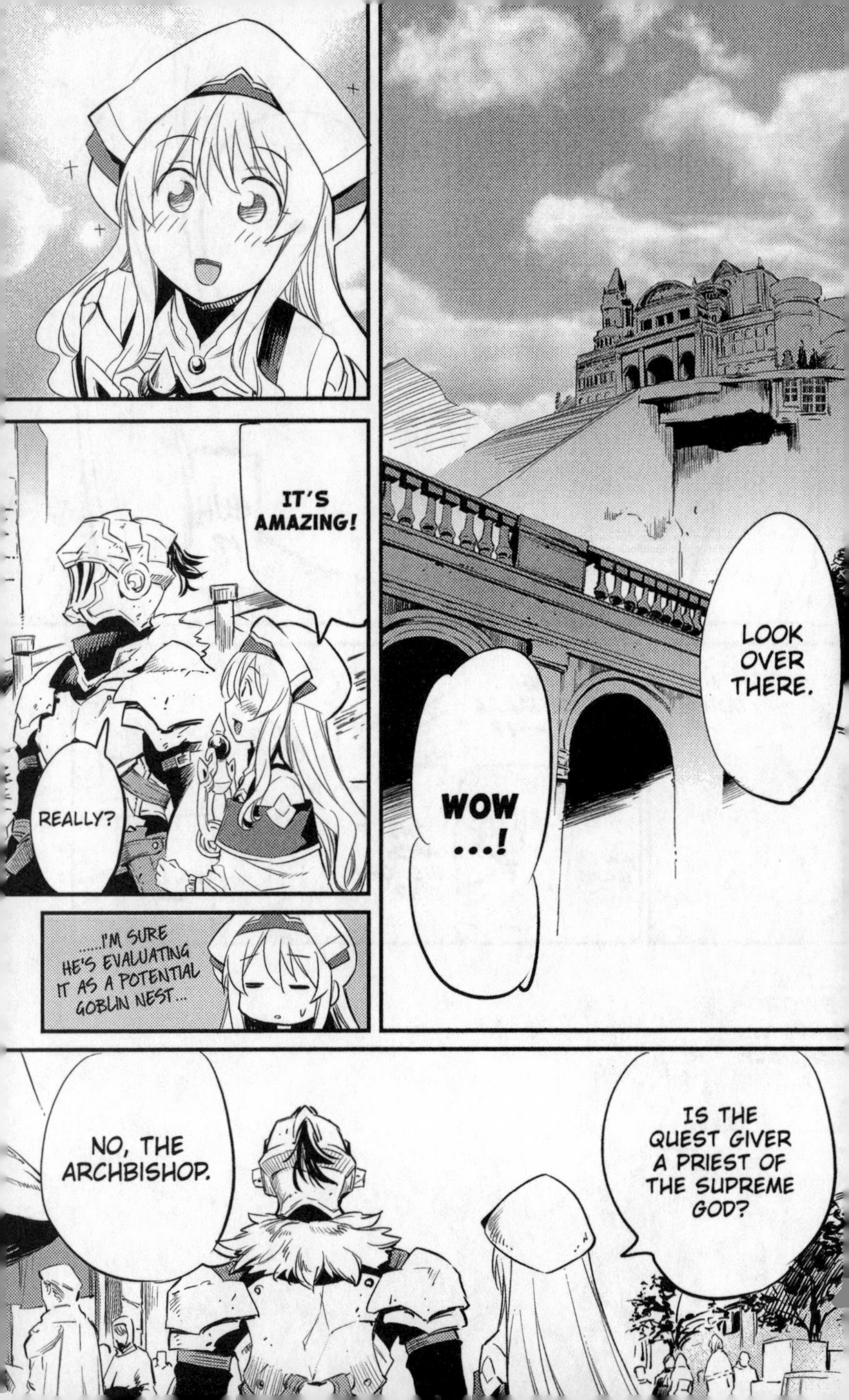
LOOK OVER THERE.
WOW ...!
IT'S AMAZING!
REALLY?
......I'M SURE HE'S EVALUATING IT AS A POTENTIAL GOBLIN NEST...
IS THE QUEST GIVER A PRIEST OF THE SUPREME GOD?
NO, THE ARCHBISHOP.

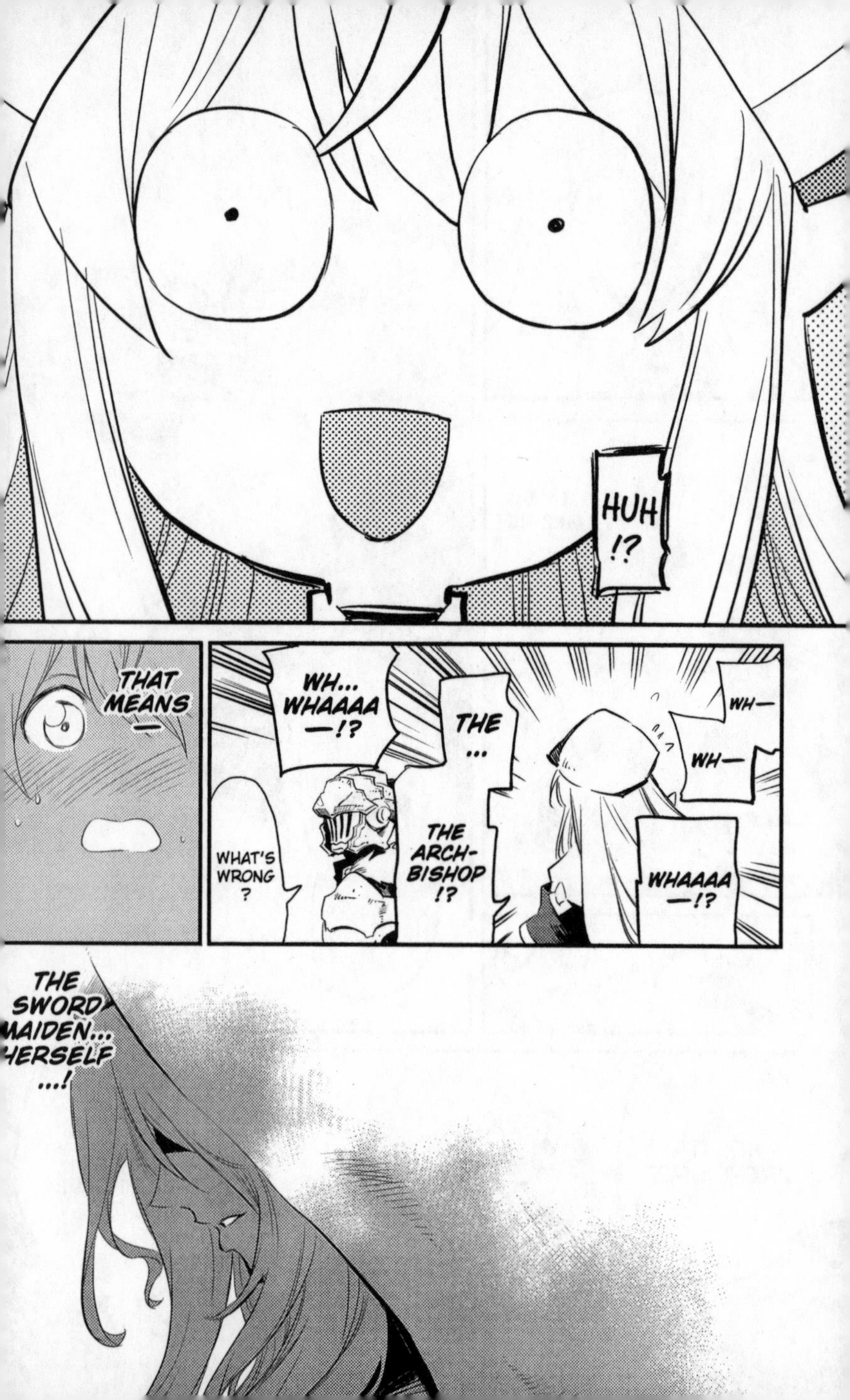
HUH!?
WH—
WH—
WHAAAA—!?
THE...
THE ARCH-BISHOP!?
WH... WHAAAA—!?
WHAT'S WRONG?
THAT MEANS—
THE SWORD MAIDEN... HERSELF...!

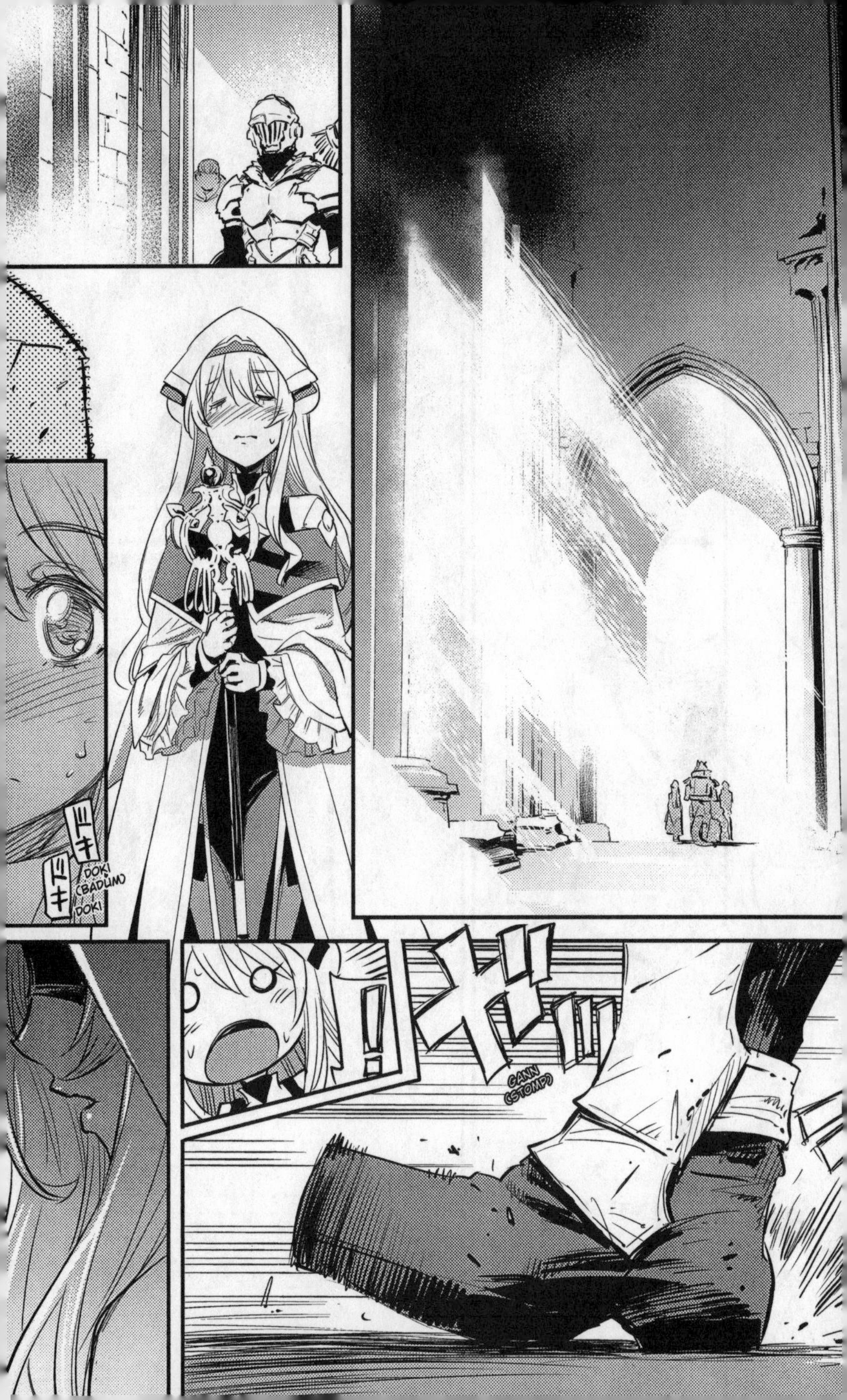
ドキ
ドキ
DOKI (BADUM) DOKI
ガン
GANN (STOMP)

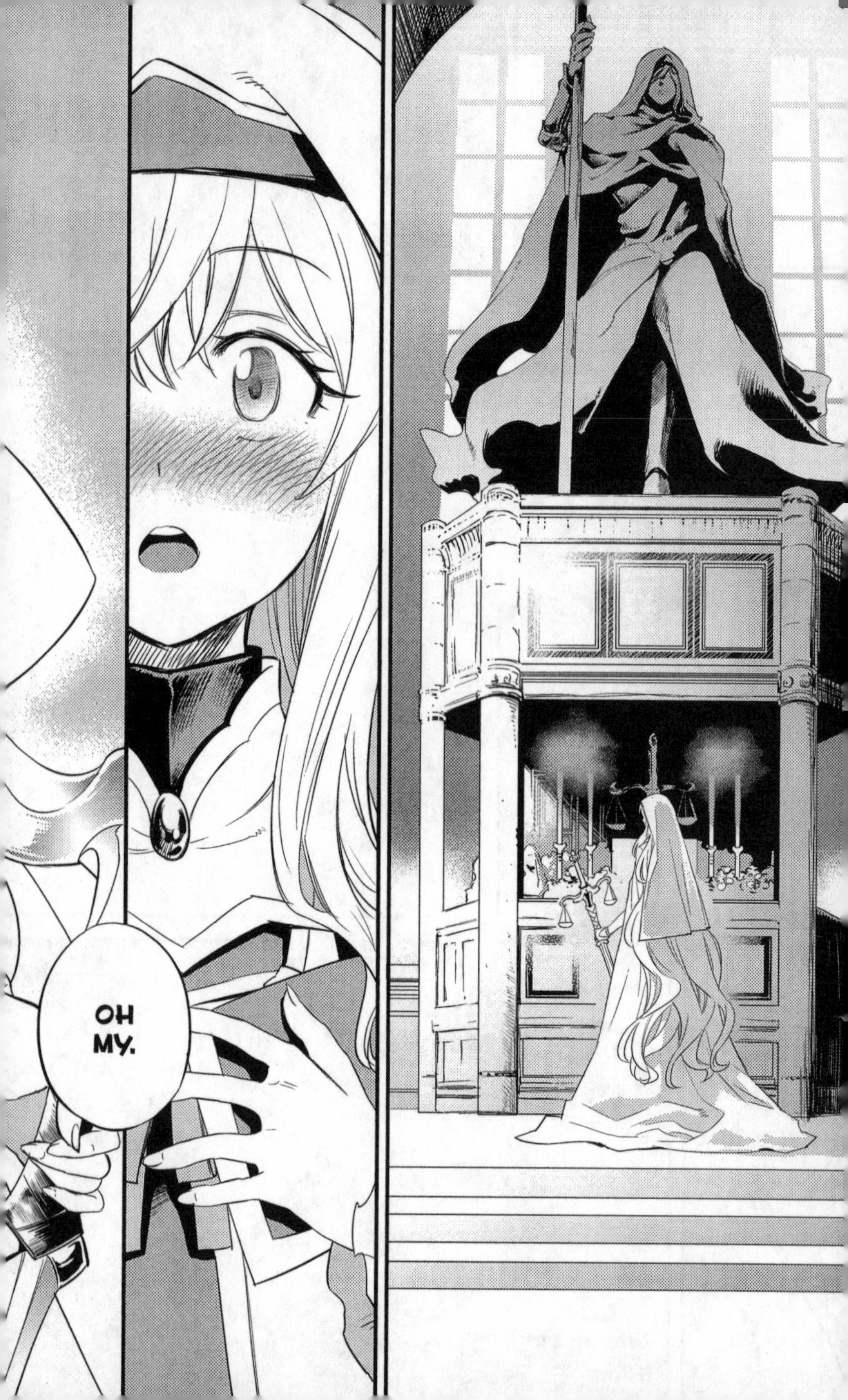
OH MY.

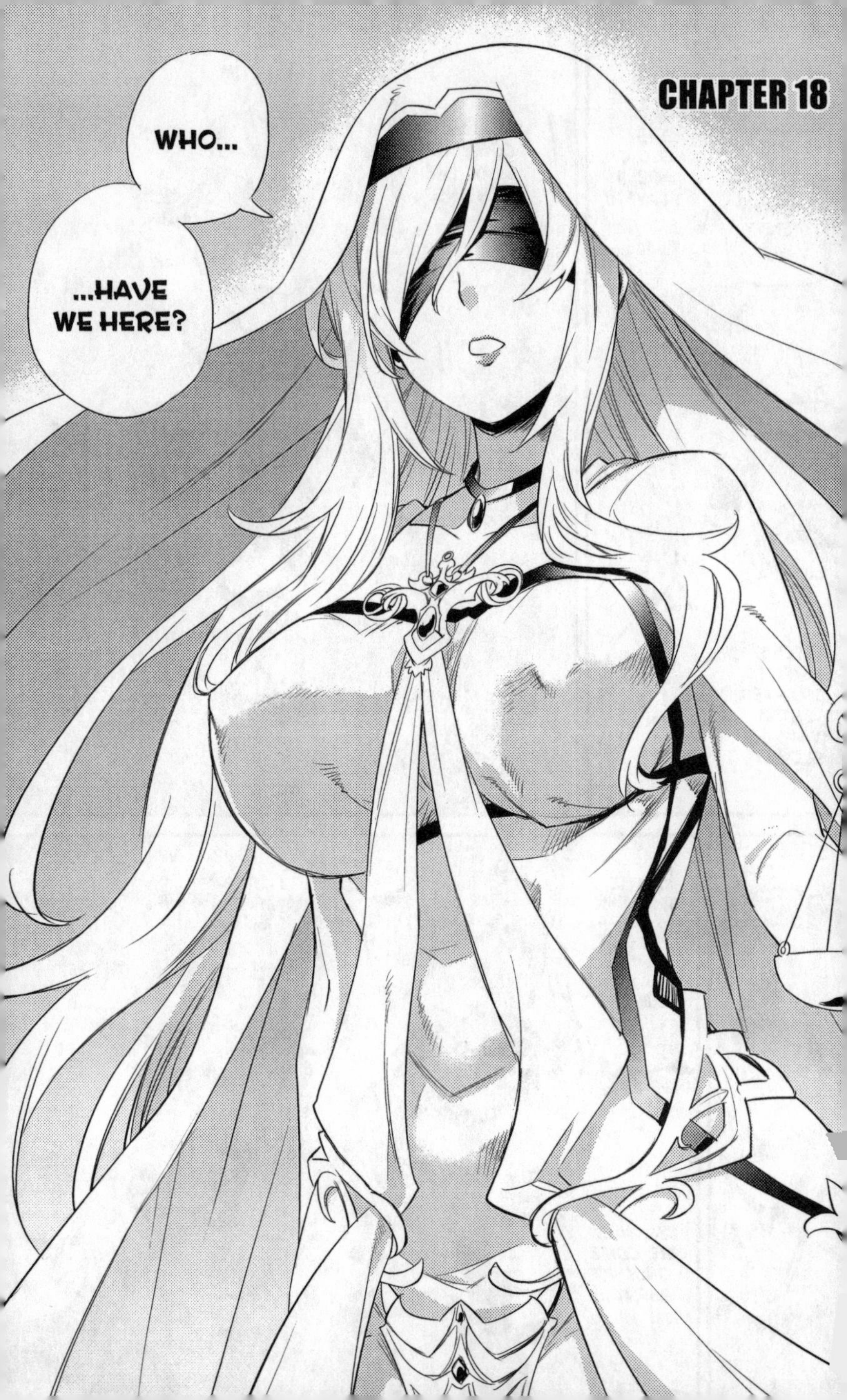
CHAPTER 18
WHO...
...HAVE WE HERE?

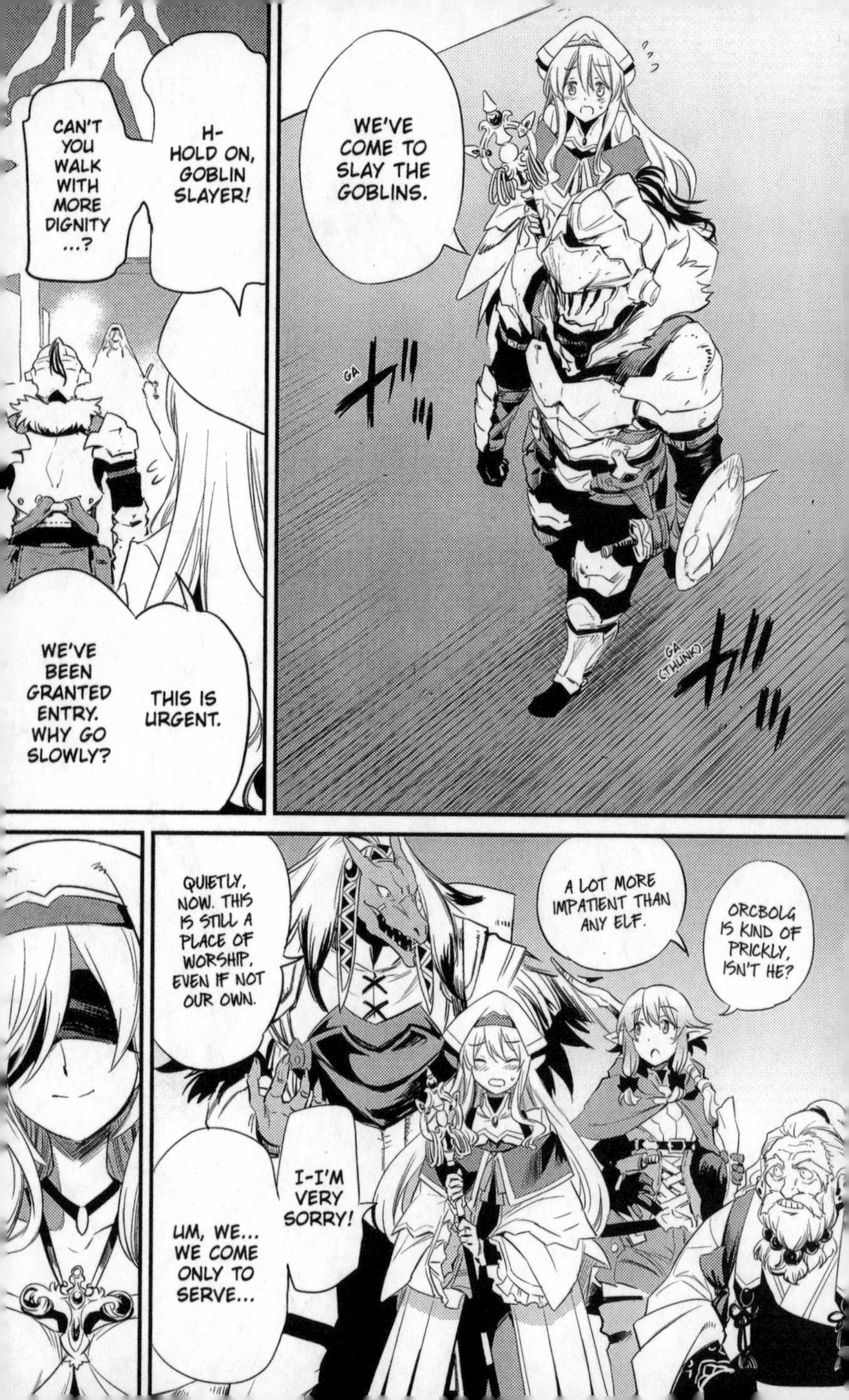
WE'VE COME TO SLAY THE GOBLINS.
GA
GA (THUNK)
H- HOLD ON, GOBLIN SLAYER!
CAN'T YOU WALK WITH MORE DIGNITY ...?
THIS IS URGENT.
WE'VE BEEN GRANTED ENTRY. WHY GO SLOWLY?
ORCBOLG IS KIND OF PRICKLY, ISN'T HE?
A LOT MORE IMPATIENT THAN ANY ELF.
QUIETLY, NOW. THIS IS STILL A PLACE OF WORSHIP, EVEN IF NOT OUR OWN.
I-I'M VERY SORRY!
UM, WE... WE COME ONLY TO SERVE...

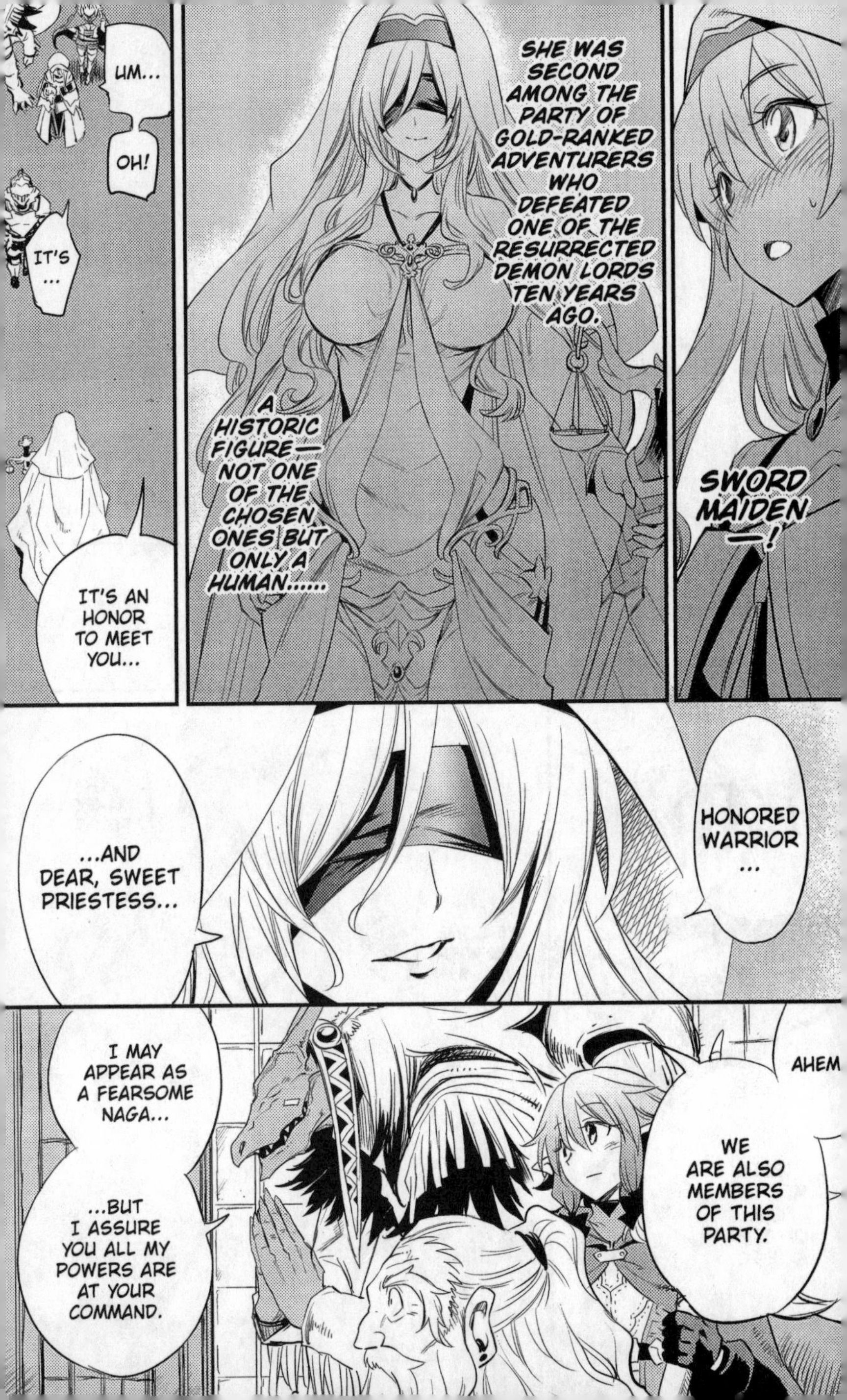
SWORD MAIDEN—!
SHE WAS SECOND AMONG THE PARTY OF GOLD-RANKED ADVENTURERS WHO DEFEATED ONE OF THE RESURRECTED DEMON LORDS TEN YEARS AGO.
A HISTORIC FIGURE—NOT ONE OF THE CHOSEN ONES BUT ONLY A HUMAN......
UM...
OH!
IT'S...
IT'S AN HONOR TO MEET YOU...
HONORED WARRIOR...
...AND DEAR, SWEET PRIESTESS...
AHEM
WE ARE ALSO MEMBERS OF THIS PARTY.
I MAY APPEAR AS A FEARSOME NAGA...
...BUT I ASSURE YOU ALL MY POWERS ARE AT YOUR COMMAND.

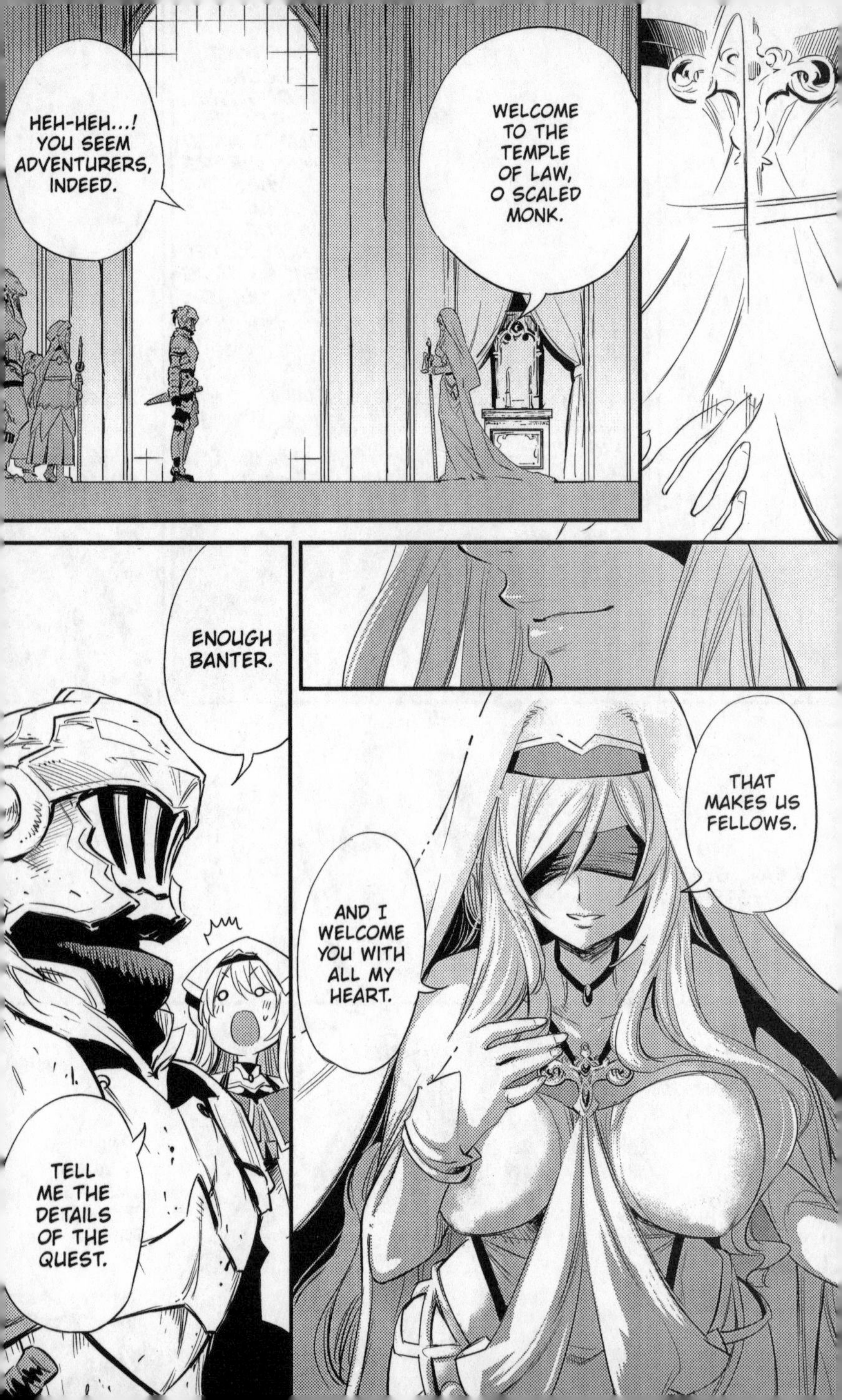

WELCOME TO THE TEMPLE OF LAW, O SCALED MONK.
HEH-HEH...! YOU SEEM ADVENTURERS, INDEED.
THAT MAKES US FELLOWS.
AND I WELCOME YOU WITH ALL MY HEART.
ENOUGH BANTER.
TELL ME THE DETAILS OF THE QUEST.

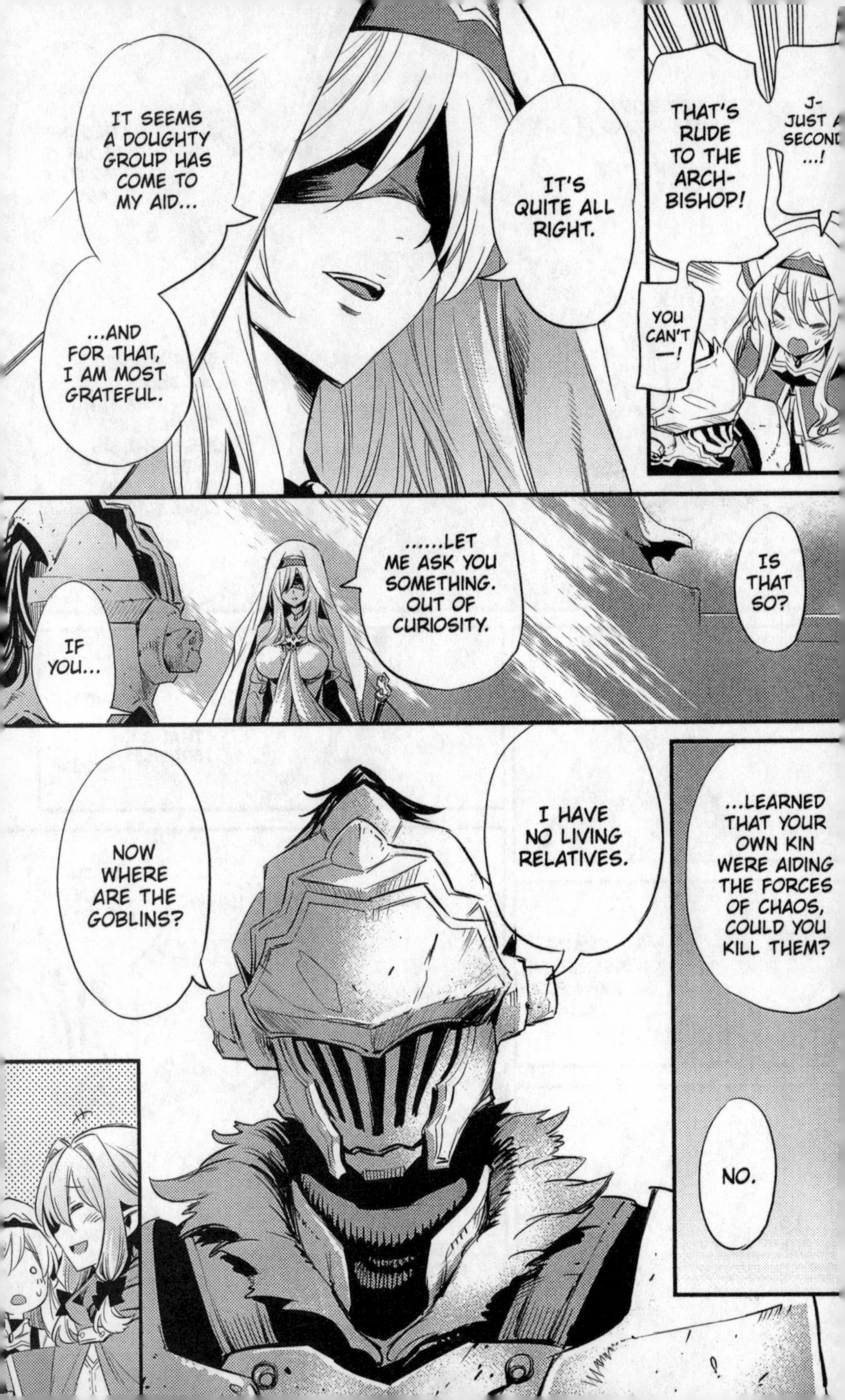

J- JUST A SECOND ...!
THAT'S RUDE TO THE ARCH-BISHOP!
YOU CAN'T —!
IT'S QUITE ALL RIGHT.
IT SEEMS A DOUGHTY GROUP HAS COME TO MY AID...
...AND FOR THAT, I AM MOST GRATEFUL.
IS THAT SO?
......LET ME ASK YOU SOMETHING. OUT OF CURIOSITY.
IF YOU...
...LEARNED THAT YOUR OWN KIN WERE AIDING THE FORCES OF CHAOS, COULD YOU KILL THEM?
NO.
I HAVE NO LIVING RELATIVES.
NOW WHERE ARE THE GOBLINS?

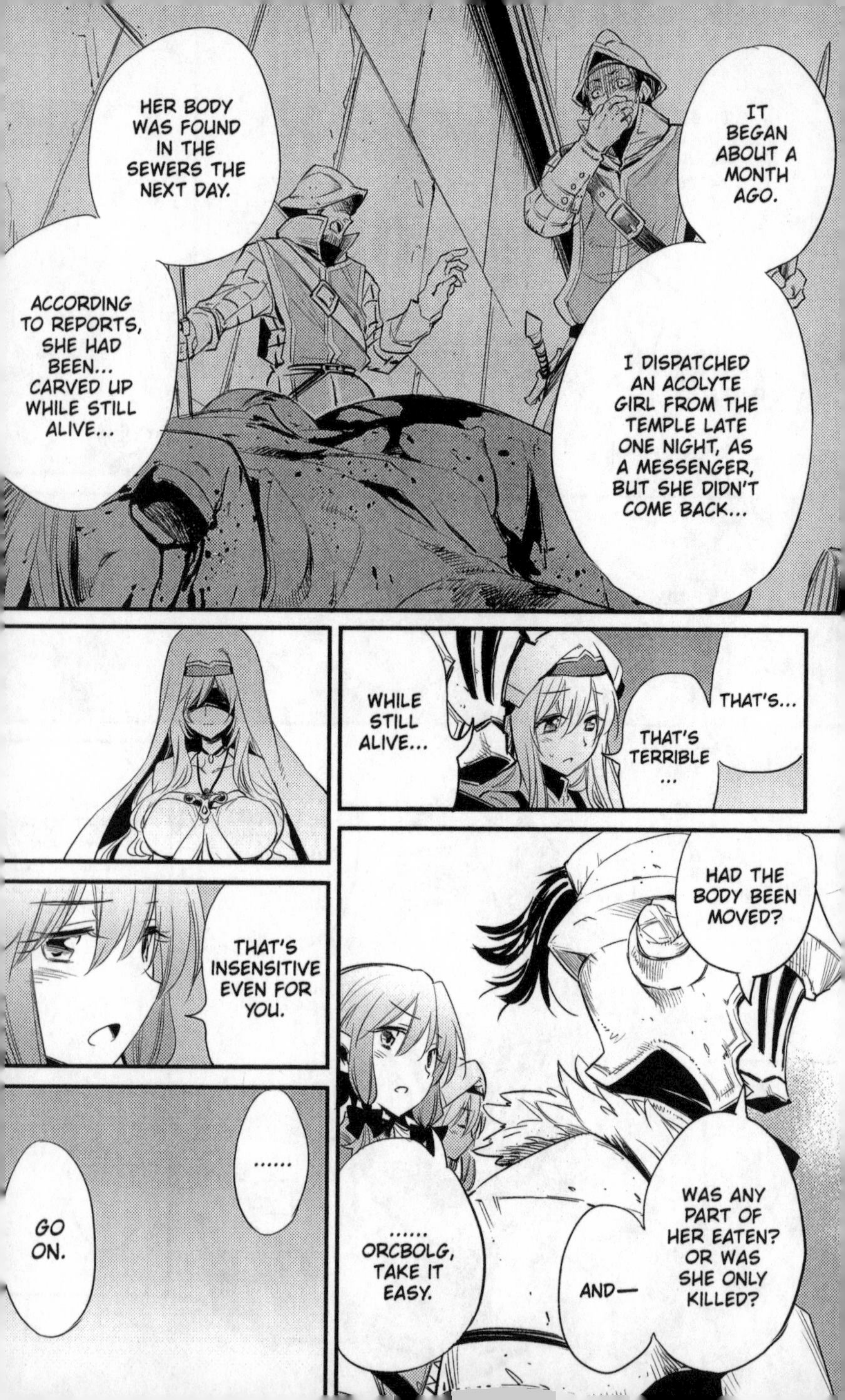
IT BEGAN ABOUT A MONTH AGO.
I DISPATCHED AN ACOLYTE GIRL FROM THE TEMPLE LATE ONE NIGHT, AS A MESSENGER, BUT SHE DIDN'T COME BACK...
HER BODY WAS FOUND IN THE SEWERS THE NEXT DAY.
ACCORDING TO REPORTS, SHE HAD BEEN... CARVED UP WHILE STILL ALIVE...
THAT'S...
THAT'S TERRIBLE ...
WHILE STILL ALIVE...
HAD THE BODY BEEN MOVED?
AND—
WAS ANY PART OF HER EATEN? OR WAS SHE ONLY KILLED?
...... ORCBOLG, TAKE IT EASY.
THAT'S INSENSITIVE EVEN FOR YOU.
......
GO ON.

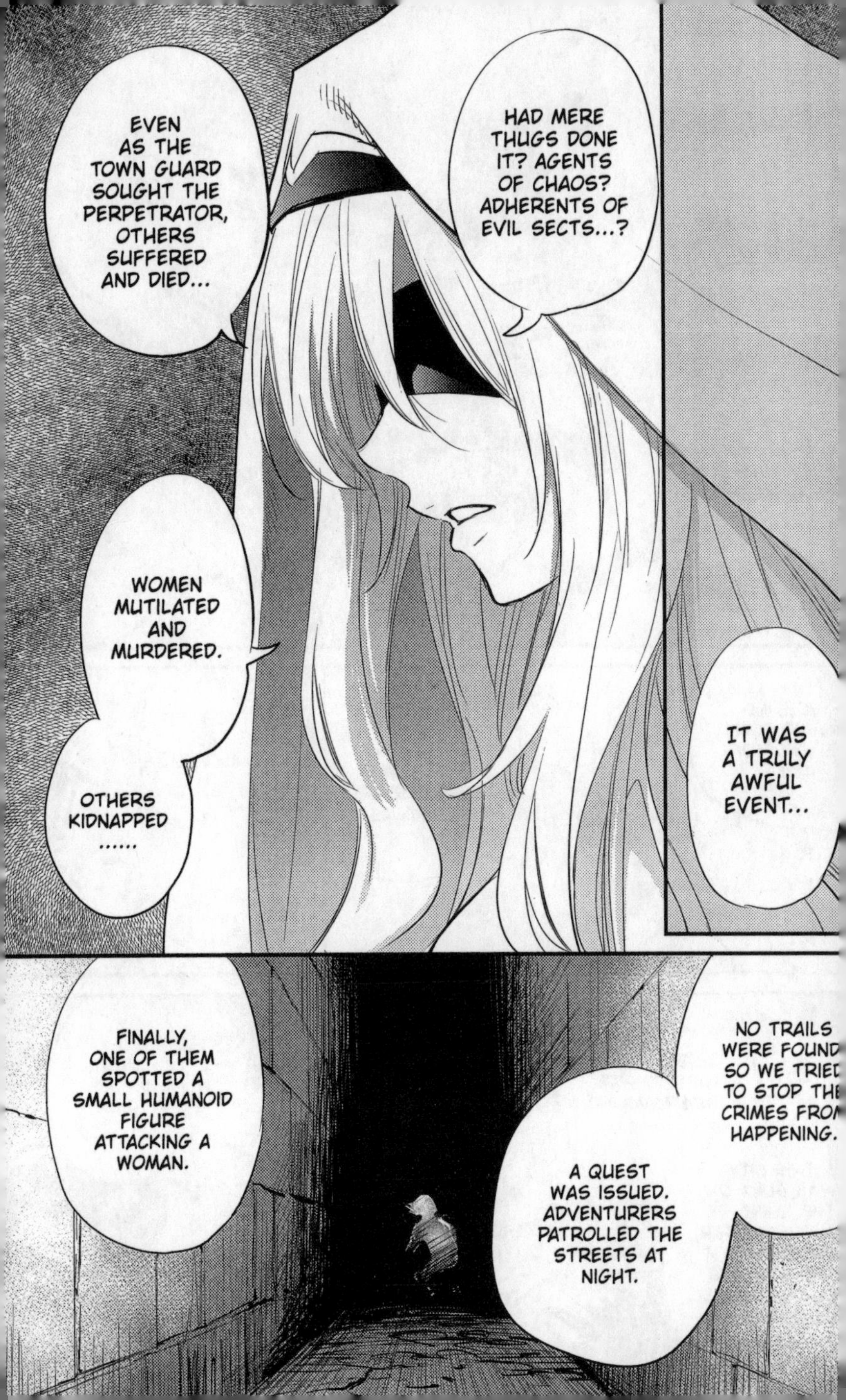

IT WAS A TRULY AWFUL EVENT...
HAD MERE THUGS DONE IT? AGENTS OF CHAOS? ADHERENTS OF EVIL SECTS...?
EVEN AS THE TOWN GUARD SOUGHT THE PERPETRATOR, OTHERS SUFFERED AND DIED...
WOMEN MUTILATED AND MURDERED.
OTHERS KIDNAPPED ......
NO TRAILS WERE FOUND SO WE TRIED TO STOP THE CRIMES FROM HAPPENING.
A QUEST WAS ISSUED. ADVENTURERS PATROLLED THE STREETS AT NIGHT.
FINALLY, ONE OF THEM SPOTTED A SMALL HUMANOID FIGURE ATTACKING A WOMAN.

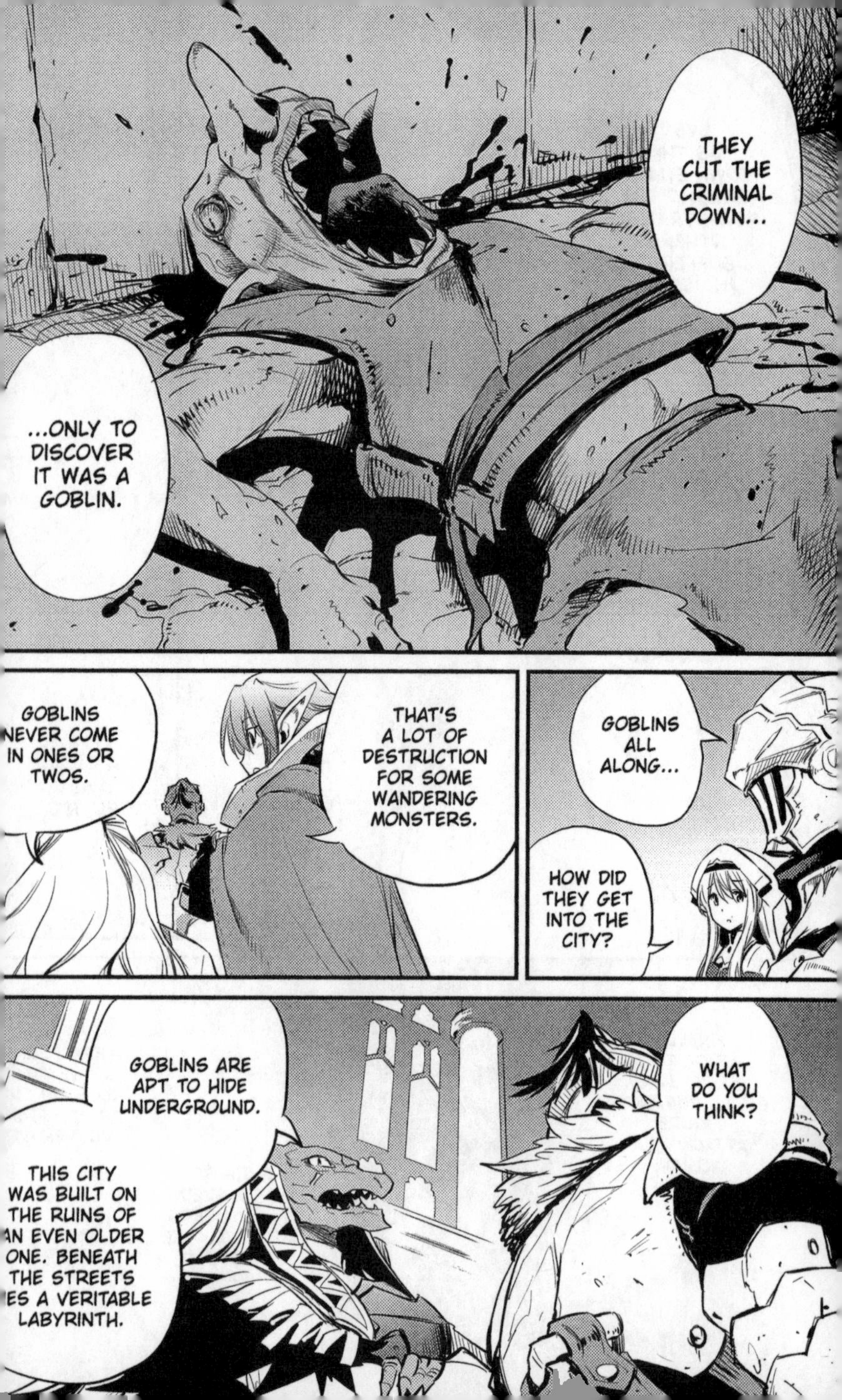
THEY CUT THE CRIMINAL DOWN...
...ONLY TO DISCOVER IT WAS A GOBLIN.
GOBLINS ALL ALONG...
HOW DID THEY GET INTO THE CITY?
THAT'S A LOT OF DESTRUCTION FOR SOME WANDERING MONSTERS.
GOBLINS NEVER COME IN ONES OR TWOS.
WHAT DO YOU THINK?
GOBLINS ARE APT TO HIDE UNDERGROUND.
THIS CITY WAS BUILT ON THE RUINS OF AN EVEN OLDER ONE. BENEATH THE STREETS ES A VERITABLE LABYRINTH.

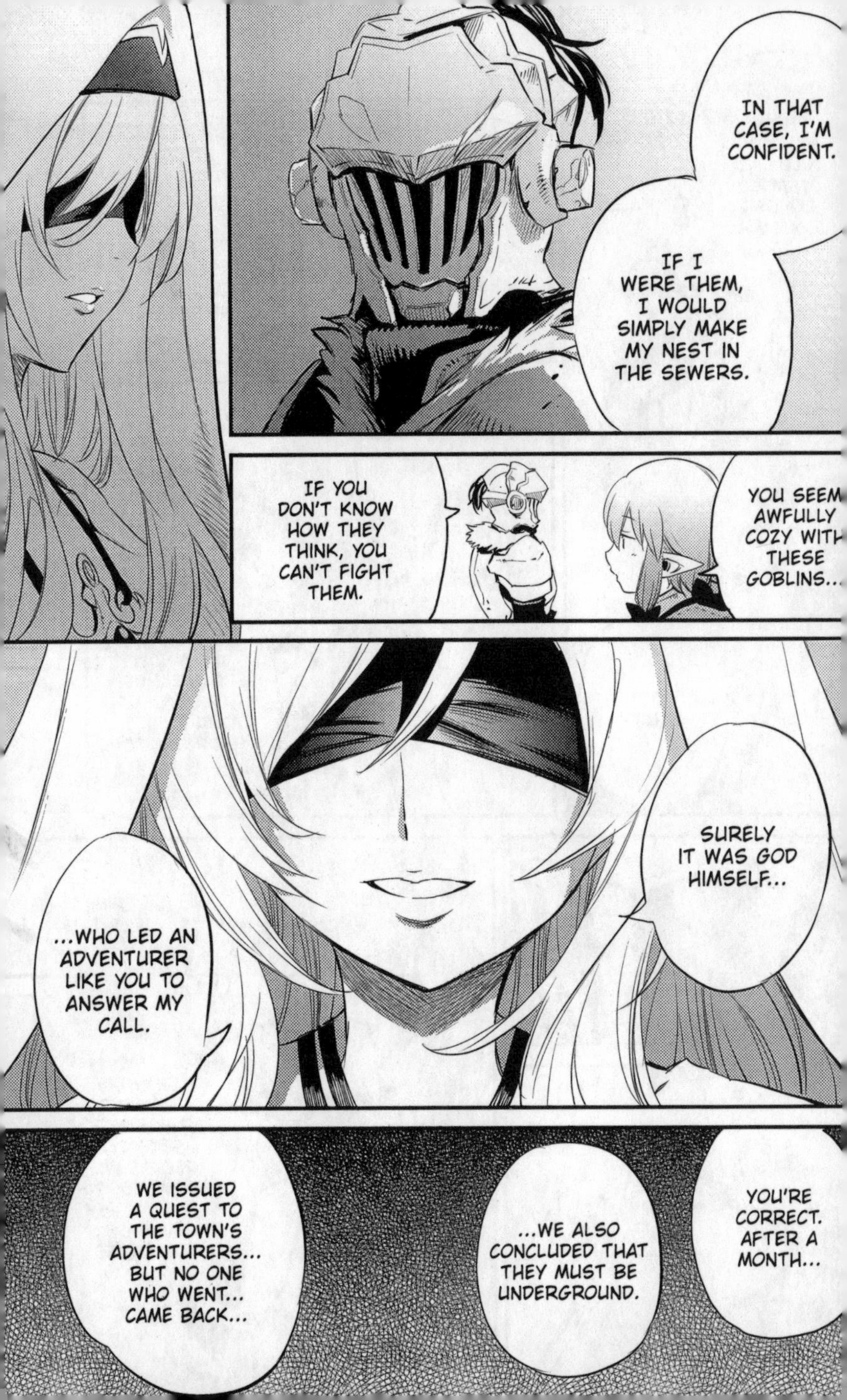
IN THAT CASE, I'M CONFIDENT.
IF I WERE THEM, I WOULD SIMPLY MAKE MY NEST IN THE SEWERS.
YOU SEEM AWFULLY COZY WITH THESE GOBLINS...
IF YOU DON'T KNOW HOW THEY THINK, YOU CAN'T FIGHT THEM.
SURELY IT WAS GOD HIMSELF...
...WHO LED AN ADVENTURER LIKE YOU TO ANSWER MY CALL.
YOU'RE CORRECT. AFTER A MONTH...
...WE ALSO CONCLUDED THAT THEY MUST BE UNDERGROUND.
WE ISSUED A QUEST TO THE TOWN'S ADVENTURERS... BUT NO ONE WHO WENT... CAME BACK...

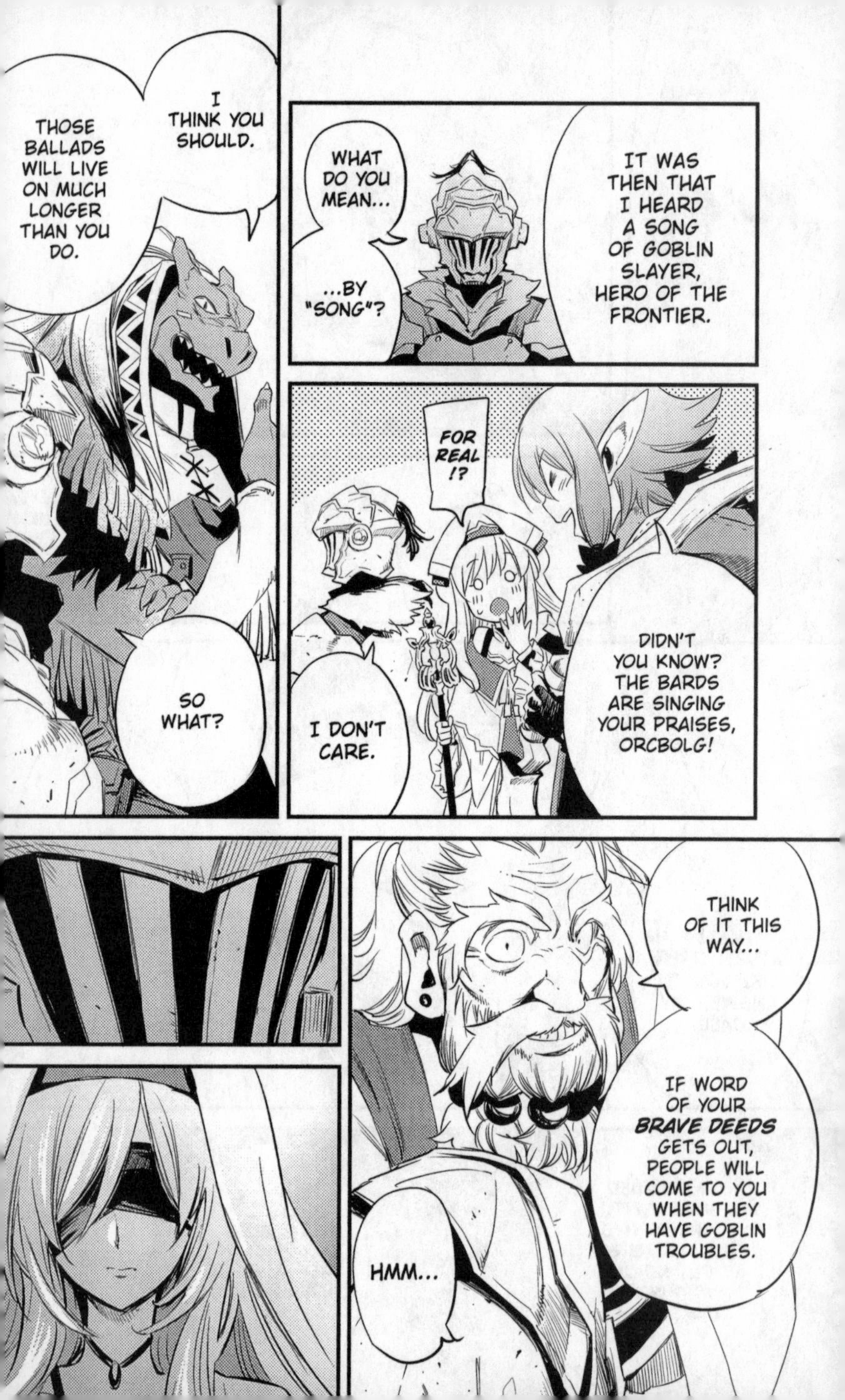
IT WAS THEN THAT I HEARD A SONG OF GOBLIN SLAYER, HERO OF THE FRONTIER.
WHAT DO YOU MEAN...
...BY "SONG"?
DIDN'T YOU KNOW? THE BARDS ARE SINGING YOUR PRAISES, ORCBOLG!
FOR REAL!?
I DON'T CARE.
I THINK YOU SHOULD.
THOSE BALLADS WILL LIVE ON MUCH LONGER THAN YOU DO.
SO WHAT?
THINK OF IT THIS WAY...
IF WORD OF YOUR BRAVE DEEDS GETS OUT, PEOPLE WILL COME TO YOU WHEN THEY HAVE GOBLIN TROUBLES.
HMM...

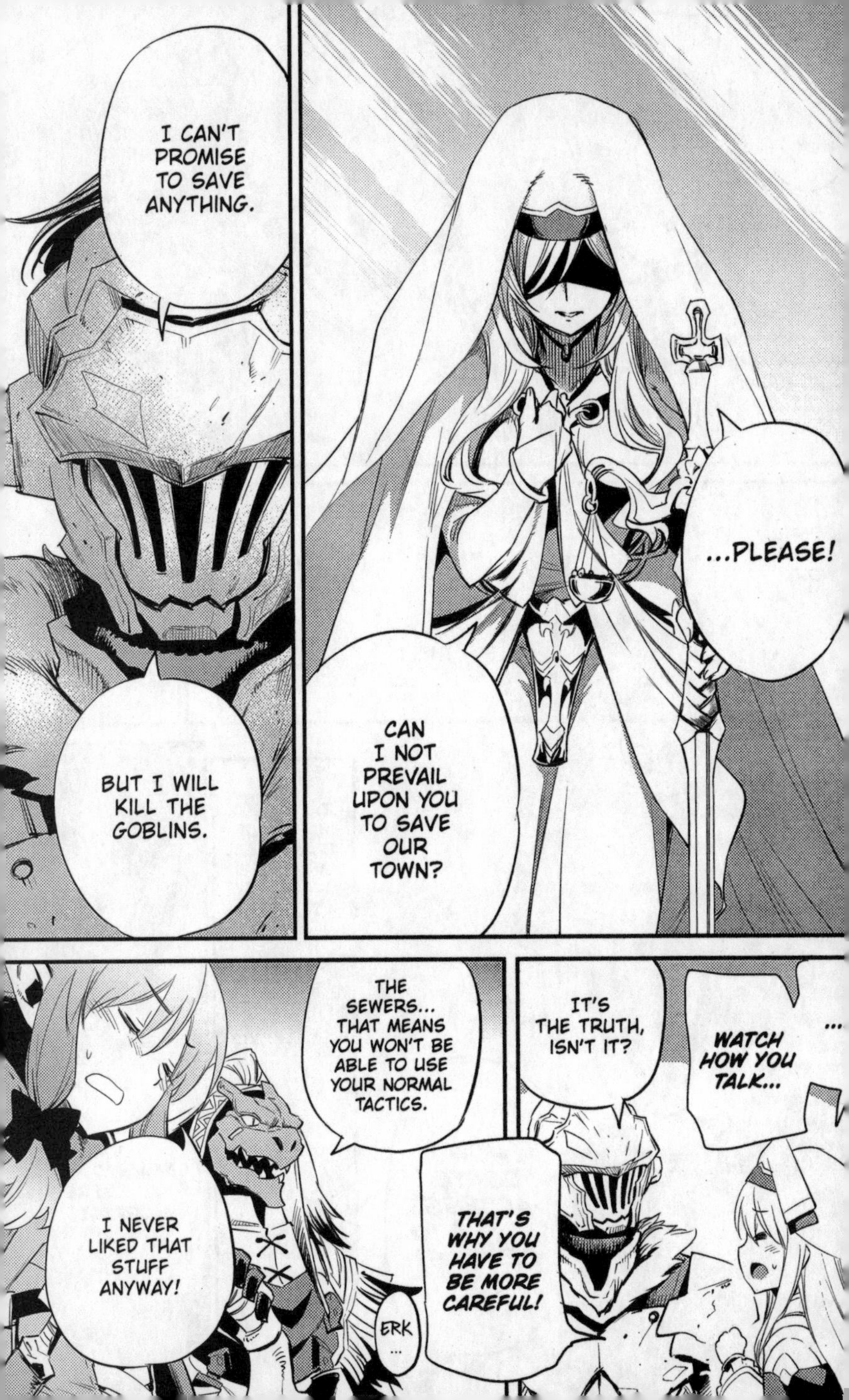
...PLEASE!
CAN I NOT PREVAIL UPON YOU TO SAVE OUR TOWN?
I CAN'T PROMISE TO SAVE ANYTHING.
BUT I WILL KILL THE GOBLINS.
...
WATCH HOW YOU TALK...
IT'S THE TRUTH, ISN'T IT?
THE SEWERS... THAT MEANS YOU WON'T BE ABLE TO USE YOUR NORMAL TACTICS.
THAT'S WHY YOU HAVE TO BE MORE CAREFUL!
I NEVER LIKED THAT STUFF ANYWAY!
ERK ...

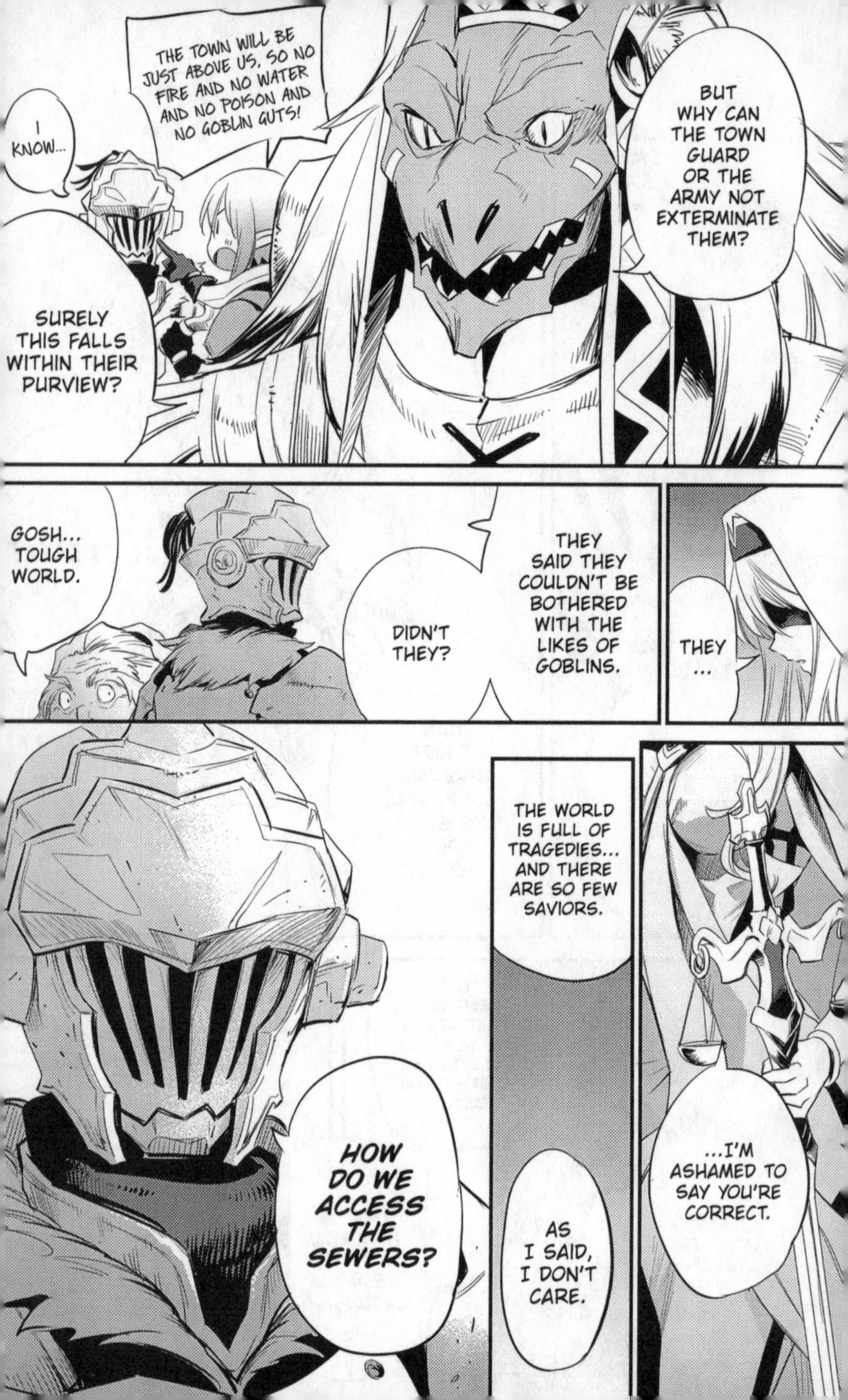
BUT WHY CAN THE TOWN GUARD OR THE ARMY NOT EXTERMINATE THEM?
THE TOWN WILL BE JUST ABOVE US, SO NO FIRE AND NO WATER AND NO POISON AND NO GOBLIN GUTS!
I KNOW...
SURELY THIS FALLS WITHIN THEIR PURVIEW?
THEY...
THEY SAID THEY COULDN'T BE BOTHERED WITH THE LIKES OF GOBLINS.
DIDN'T THEY?
GOSH... TOUGH WORLD.
...I'M ASHAMED TO SAY YOU'RE CORRECT.
THE WORLD IS FULL OF TRAGEDIES... AND THERE ARE SO FEW SAVIORS.
AS I SAID, I DON'T CARE.
HOW DO WE ACCESS THE SEWERS?

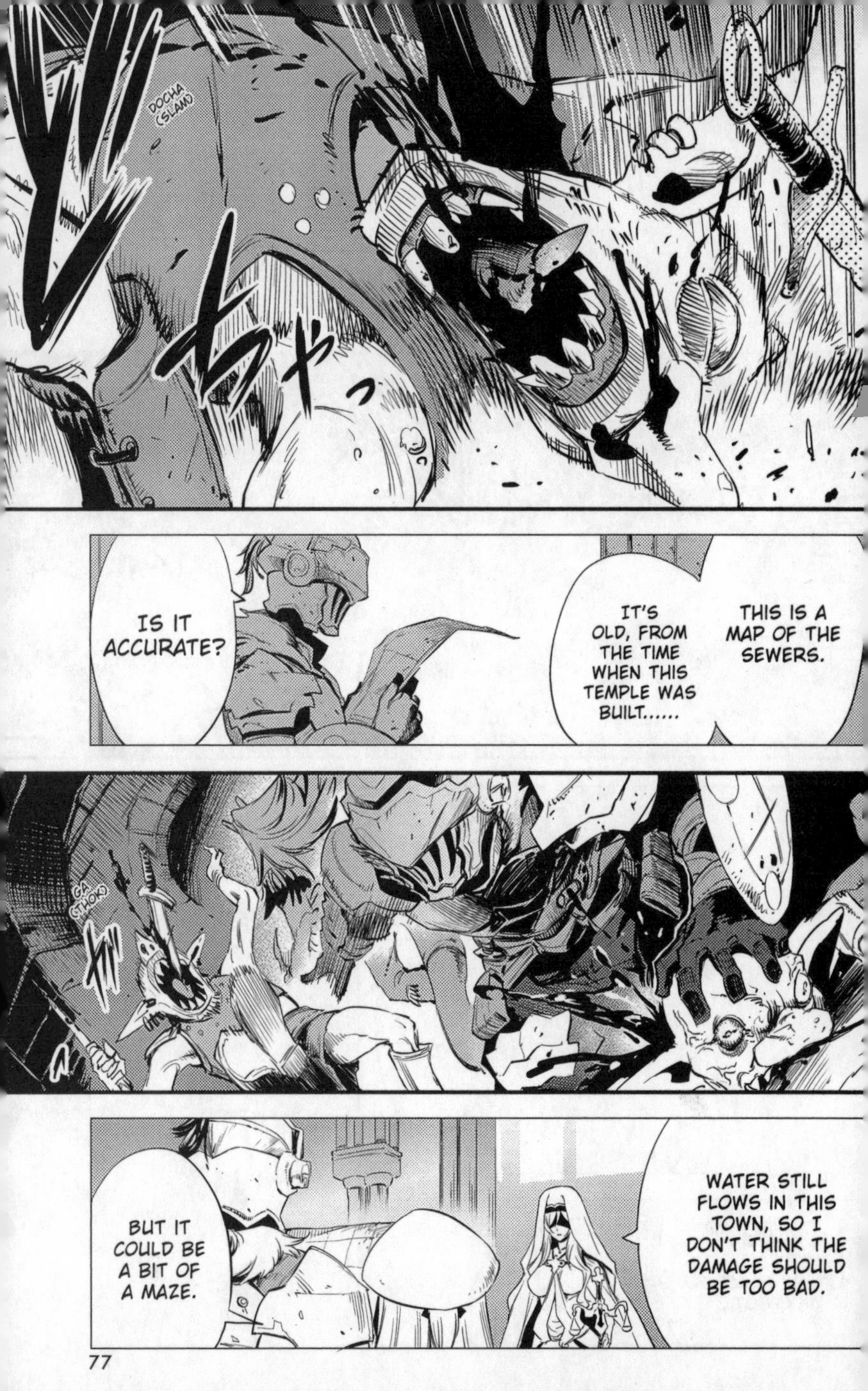
DOCHA (SLAM)
THIS IS A MAP OF THE SEWERS.
IT'S OLD, FROM THE TIME WHEN THIS TEMPLE WAS BUILT......
IS IT ACCURATE?
GA (THOK)
WATER STILL FLOWS IN THIS TOWN, SO I DON'T THINK THE DAMAGE SHOULD BE TOO BAD.
BUT IT COULD BE A BIT OF A MAZE.

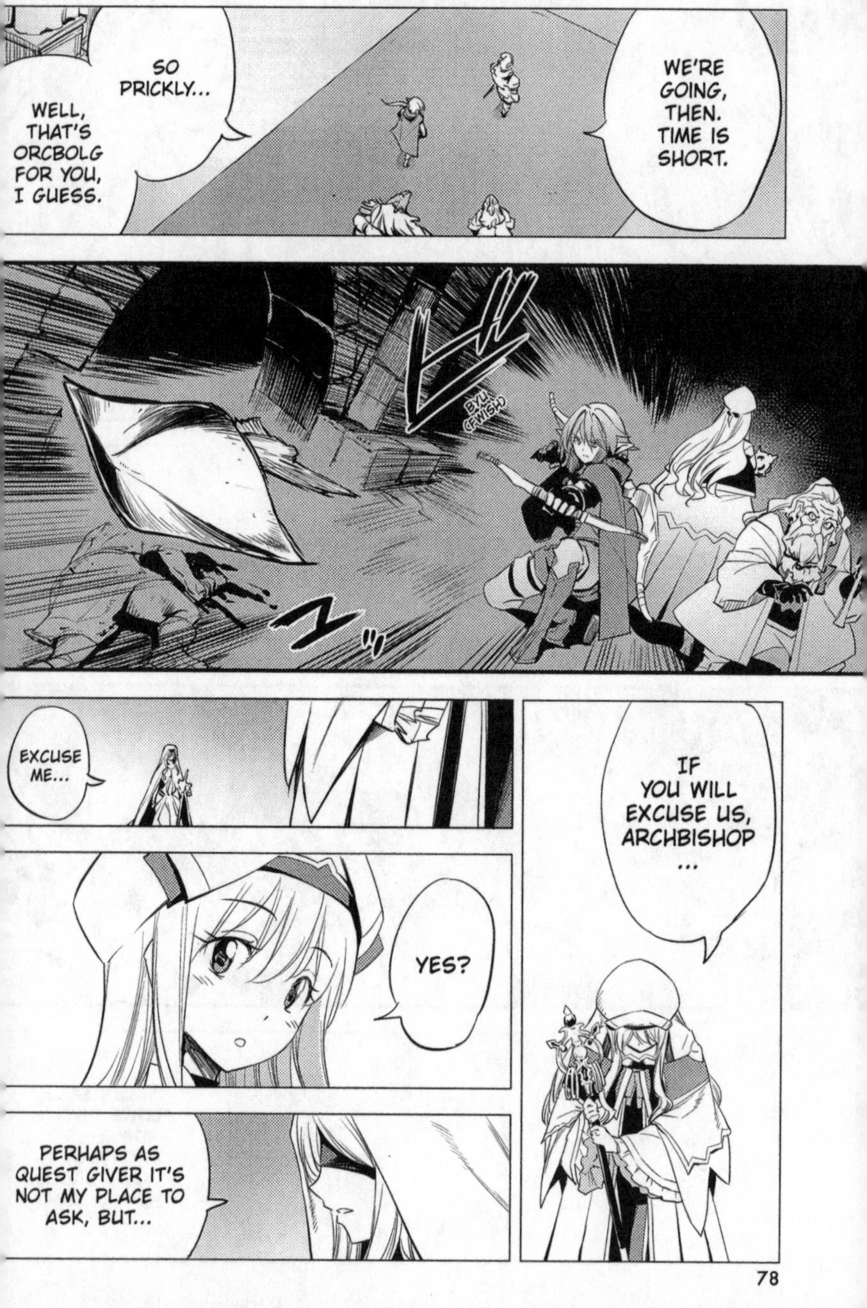
WE'RE GOING, THEN. TIME IS SHORT.
SO PRICKLY...
WELL, THAT'S ORCBOLG FOR YOU, I GUESS.
BYU (FWISH)
IF YOU WILL EXCUSE US, ARCHBISHOP...
EXCUSE ME...
YES?
PERHAPS AS QUEST GIVER IT'S NOT MY PLACE TO ASK, BUT...

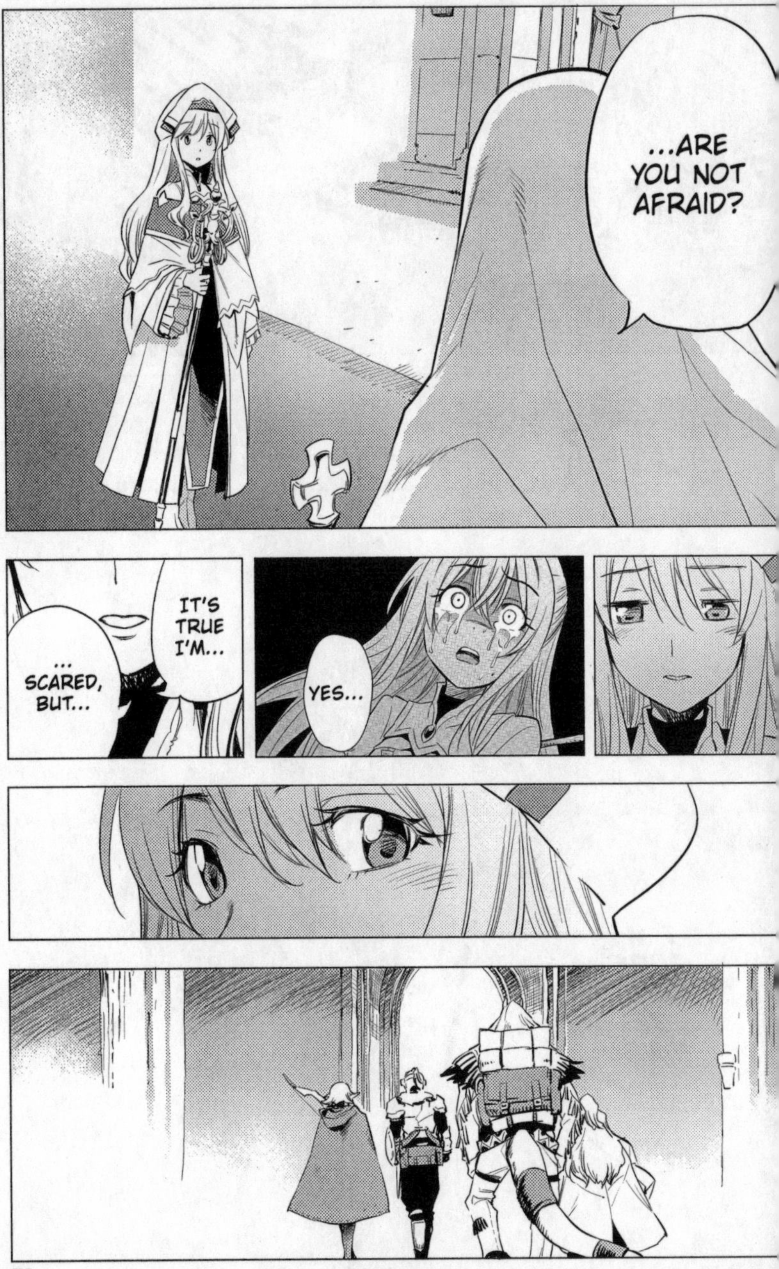
...ARE YOU NOT AFRAID?
YES...
IT'S TRUE I'M...
... SCARED, BUT...

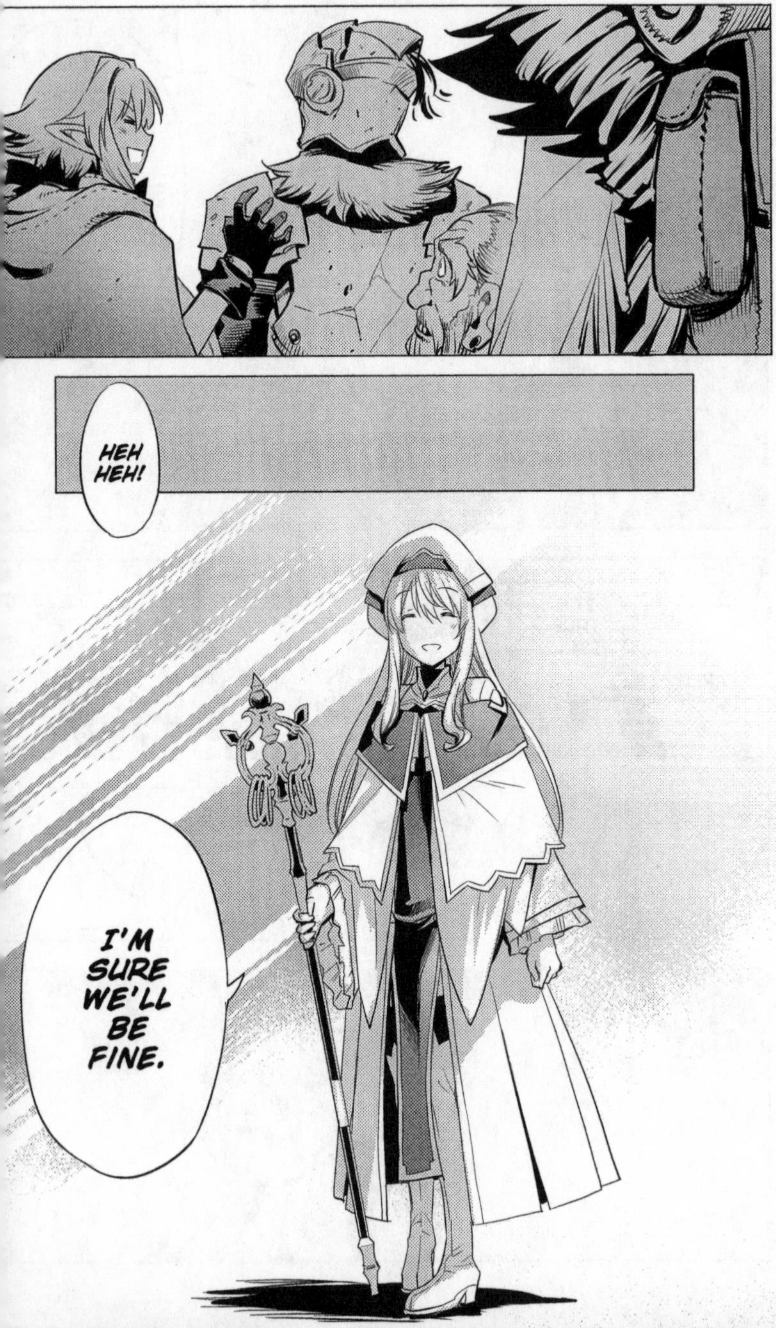
HEH HEH!
I'M SURE WE'LL BE FINE.

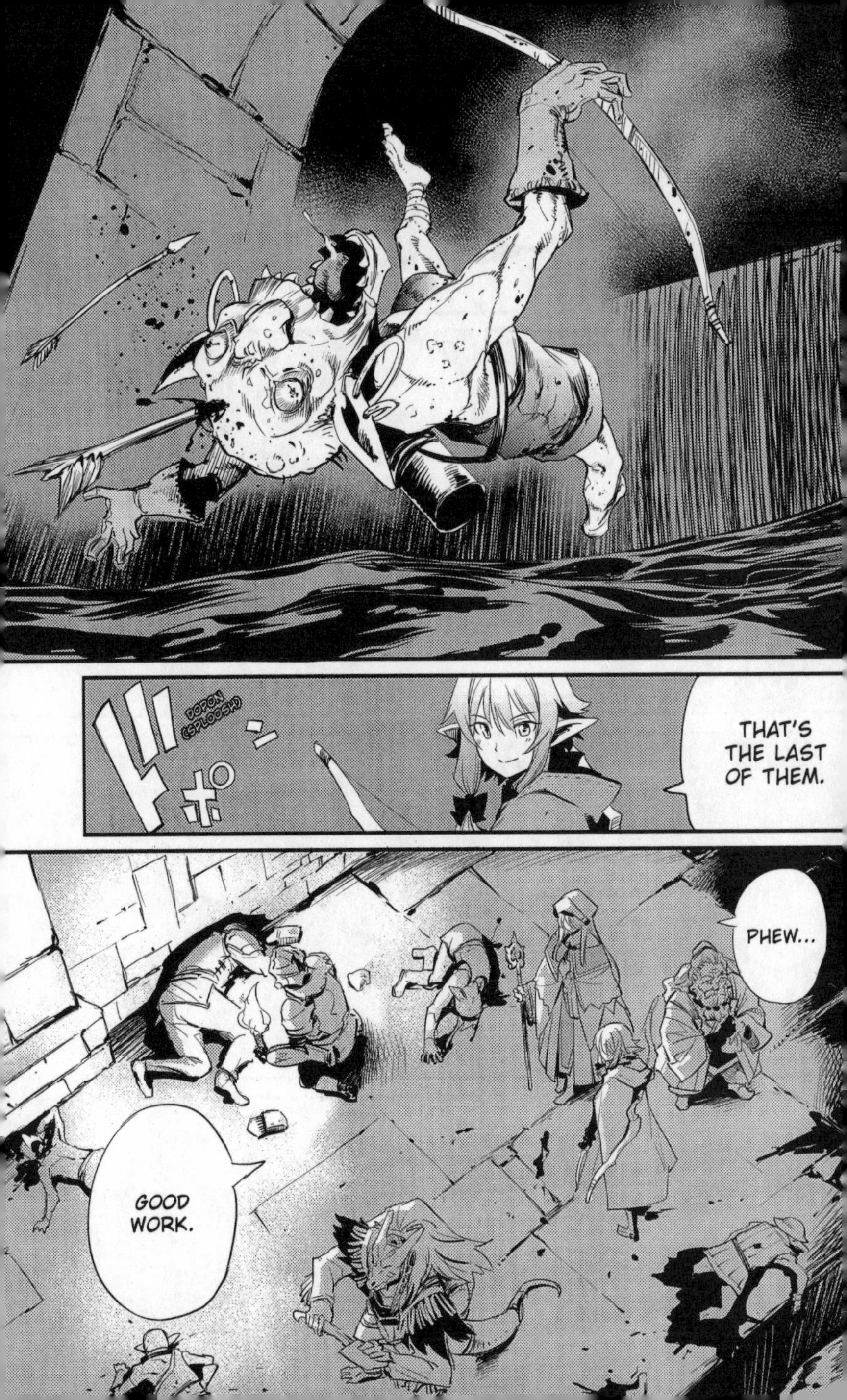
THAT'S THE LAST OF THEM.
DOPON (SPLOOSH)
PHEW...
GOOD WORK.

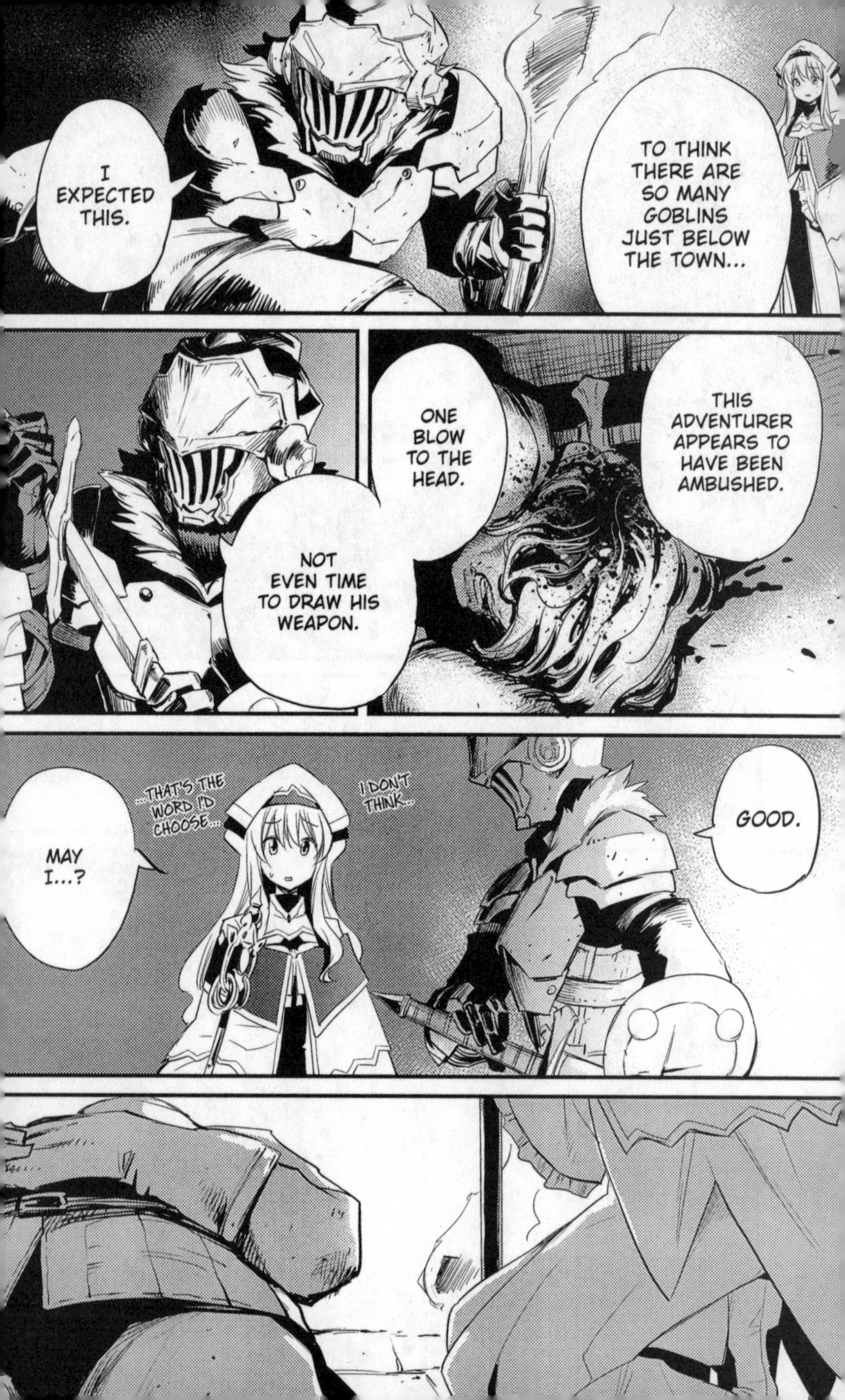
TO THINK THERE ARE SO MANY GOBLINS JUST BELOW THE TOWN...
I EXPECTED THIS.
THIS ADVENTURER APPEARS TO HAVE BEEN AMBUSHED.
ONE BLOW TO THE HEAD.
NOT EVEN TIME TO DRAW HIS WEAPON.
GOOD.
I DON'T THINK...
...THAT'S THE WORD I'D CHOOSE...
MAY I...?

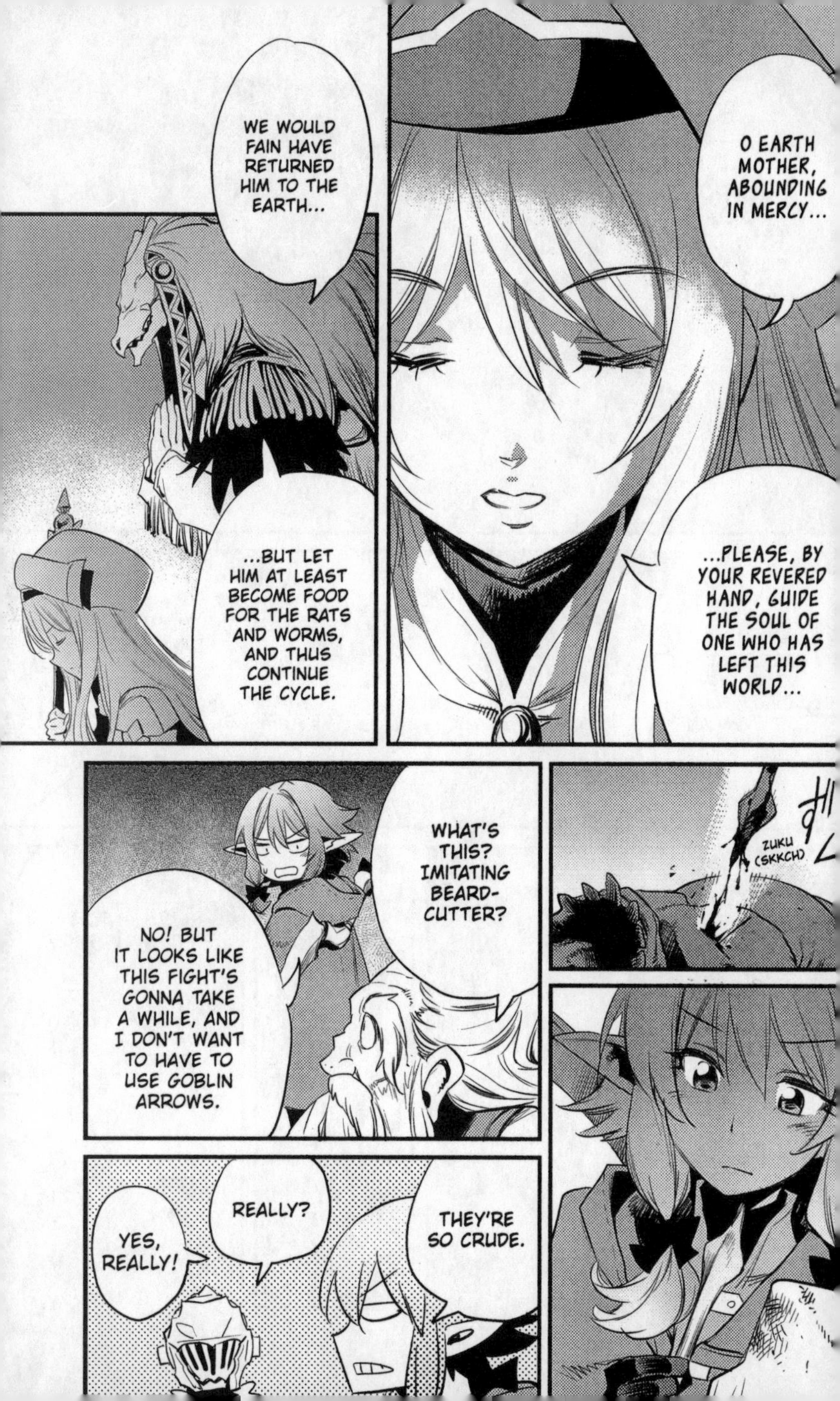
O EARTH MOTHER, ABOUNDING IN MERCY...
...PLEASE, BY YOUR REVERED HAND, GUIDE THE SOUL OF ONE WHO HAS LEFT THIS WORLD...
WE WOULD FAIN HAVE RETURNED HIM TO THE EARTH...
...BUT LET HIM AT LEAST BECOME FOOD FOR THE RATS AND WORMS, AND THUS CONTINUE THE CYCLE.
ZUKU (SKKCH)
WHAT'S THIS? IMITATING BEARD-CUTTER?
NO! BUT IT LOOKS LIKE THIS FIGHT'S GONNA TAKE A WHILE, AND I DON'T WANT TO HAVE TO USE GOBLIN ARROWS.
THEY'RE SO CRUDE.
REALLY?
YES, REALLY!

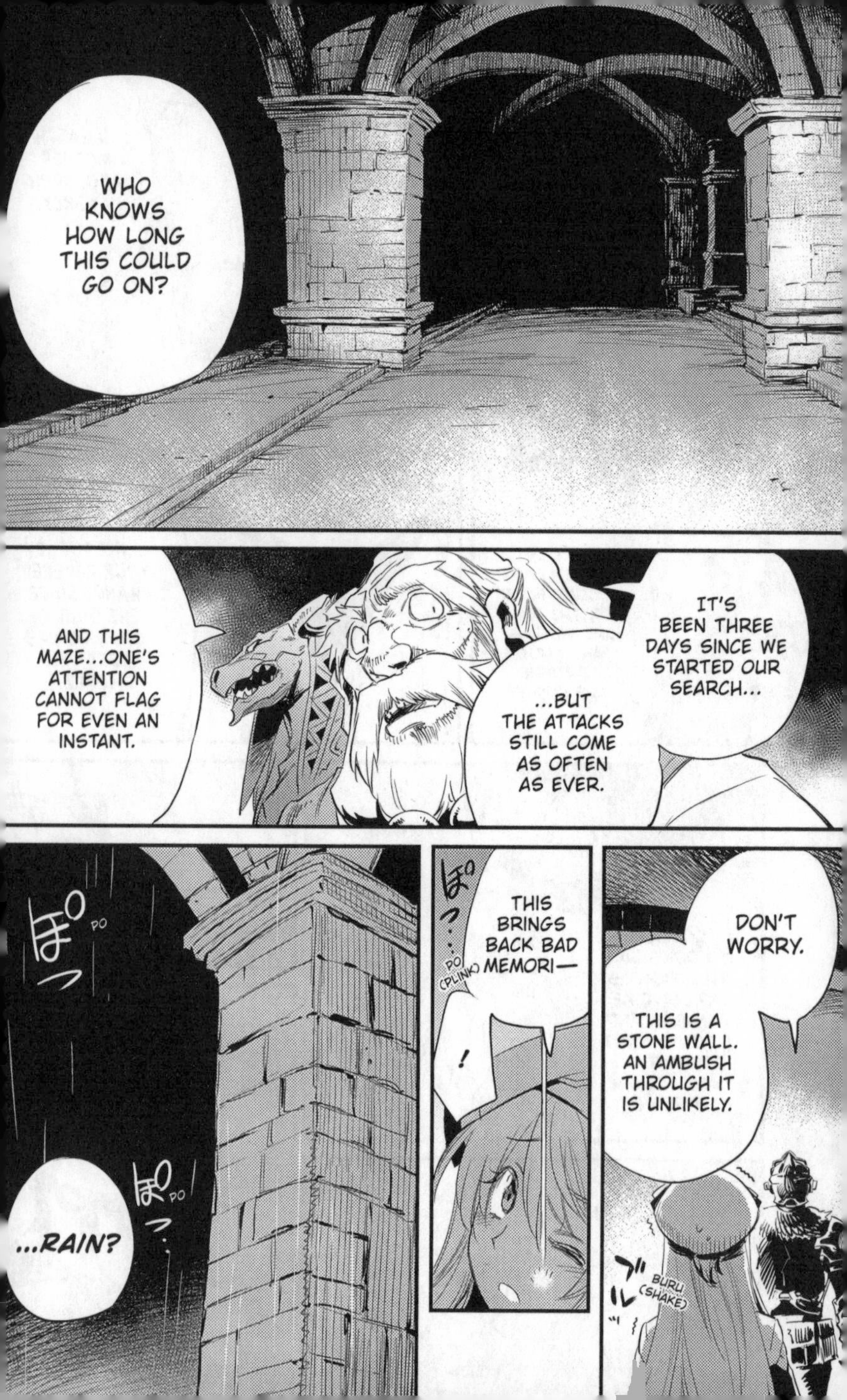
WHO KNOWS HOW LONG THIS COULD GO ON?
IT'S BEEN THREE DAYS SINCE WE STARTED OUR SEARCH...
...BUT THE ATTACKS STILL COME AS OFTEN AS EVER.
AND THIS MAZE...ONE'S ATTENTION CANNOT FLAG FOR EVEN AN INSTANT.
DON'T WORRY.
THIS IS A STONE WALL. AN AMBUSH THROUGH IT IS UNLIKELY.
ブル
BURU (SHAKE)
ぽっ
PO (PLINK)
THIS BRINGS BACK BAD MEMORI—
!
ぽっ
PO
ぽっ
PO
...RAIN?

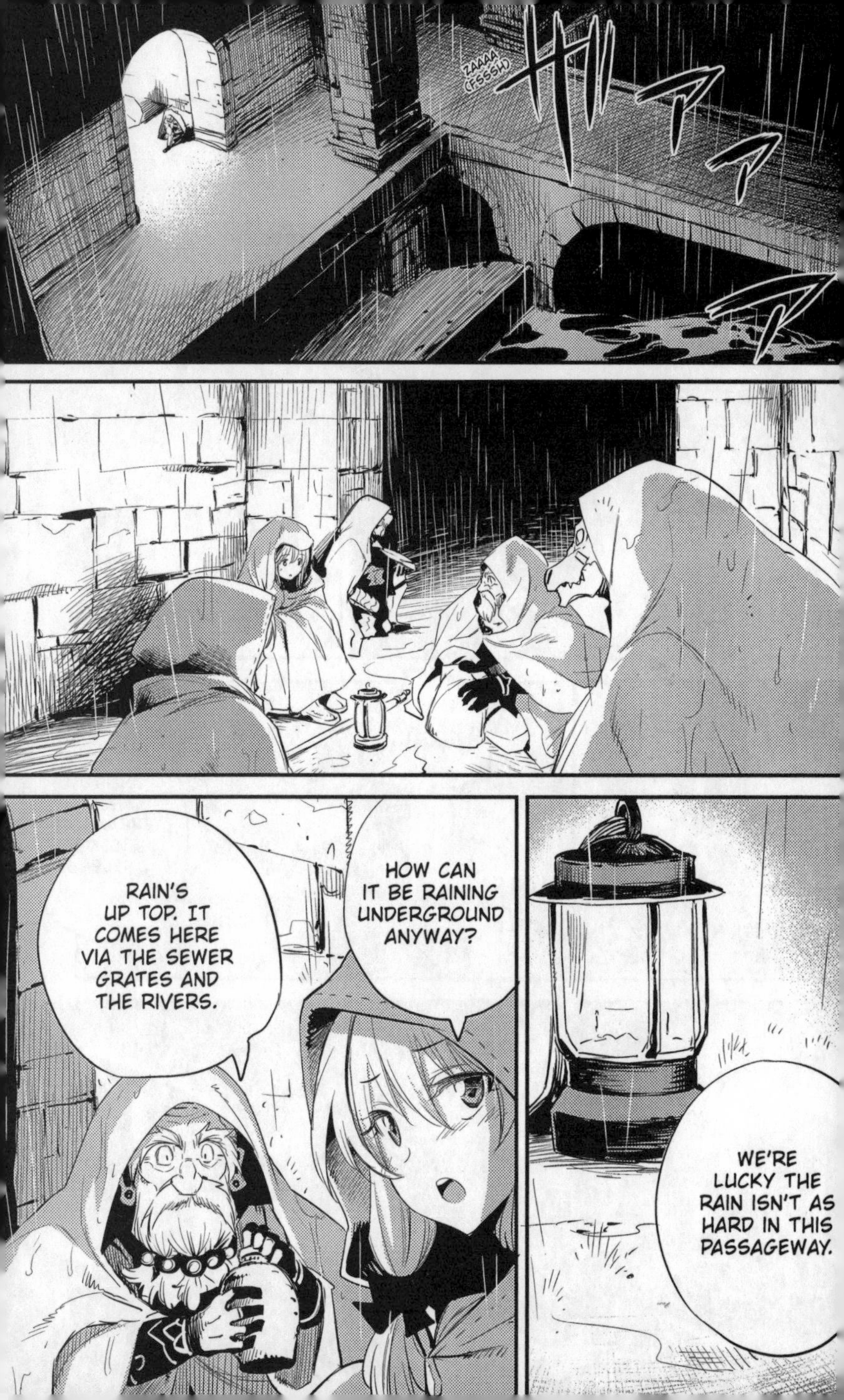
ZAAAA (FSSSH)
WE'RE LUCKY THE RAIN ISN'T AS HARD IN THIS PASSAGEWAY.
HOW CAN IT BE RAINING UNDERGROUND ANYWAY?
RAIN'S UP TOP. IT COMES HERE VIA THE SEWER GRATES AND THE RIVERS.

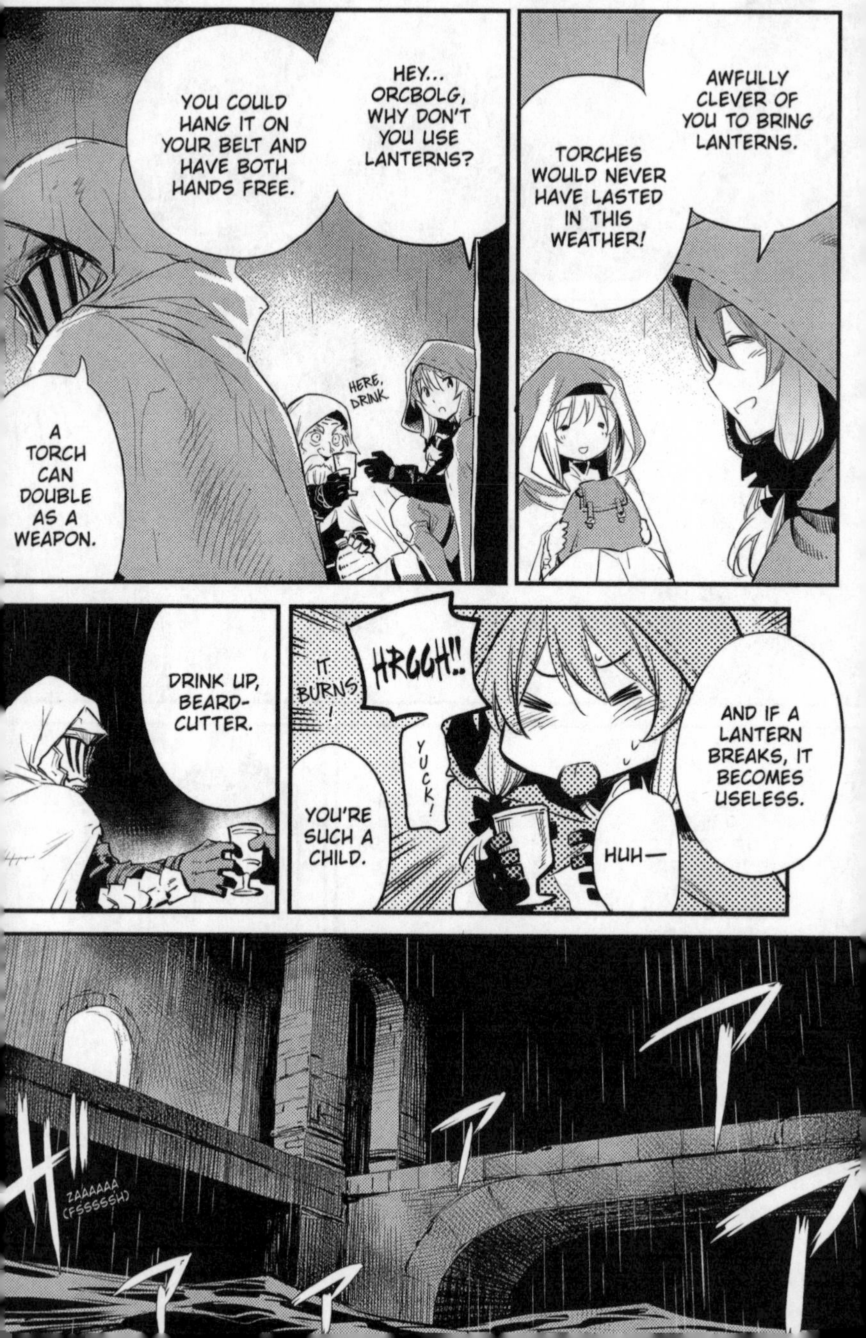
AWFULLY CLEVER OF YOU TO BRING LANTERNS.
TORCHES WOULD NEVER HAVE LASTED IN THIS WEATHER!
HEY... ORCBOLG, WHY DON'T YOU USE LANTERNS?
YOU COULD HANG IT ON YOUR BELT AND HAVE BOTH HANDS FREE.
HERE, DRINK.
A TORCH CAN DOUBLE AS A WEAPON.
AND IF A LANTERN BREAKS, IT BECOMES USELESS.
HUH—
HRGGH!!
IT BURNS!
YUCK!
YOU'RE SUCH A CHILD.
DRINK UP, BEARD-CUTTER.
ZAAAAAA (FSSSSSH)

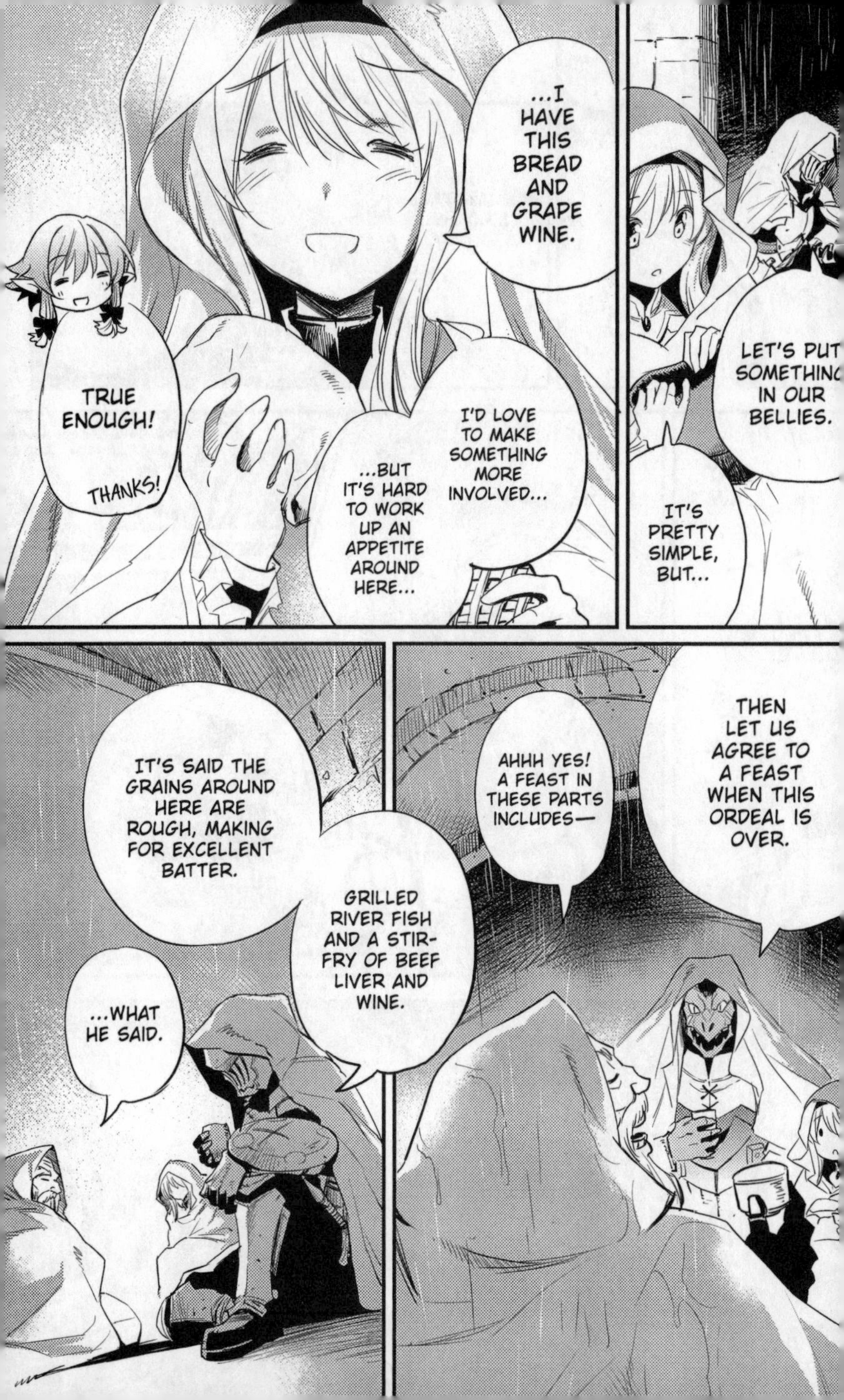
LET'S PUT SOMETHING IN OUR BELLIES.
IT'S PRETTY SIMPLE, BUT...
...I HAVE THIS BREAD AND GRAPE WINE.
I'D LOVE TO MAKE SOMETHING MORE INVOLVED...
...BUT IT'S HARD TO WORK UP AN APPETITE AROUND HERE...
TRUE ENOUGH!
THANKS!
THEN LET US AGREE TO A FEAST WHEN THIS ORDEAL IS OVER.
AHHH YES! A FEAST IN THESE PARTS INCLUDES—
GRILLED RIVER FISH AND A STIR-FRY OF BEEF LIVER AND WINE.
IT'S SAID THE GRAINS AROUND HERE ARE ROUGH, MAKING FOR EXCELLENT BATTER.
...WHAT HE SAID.

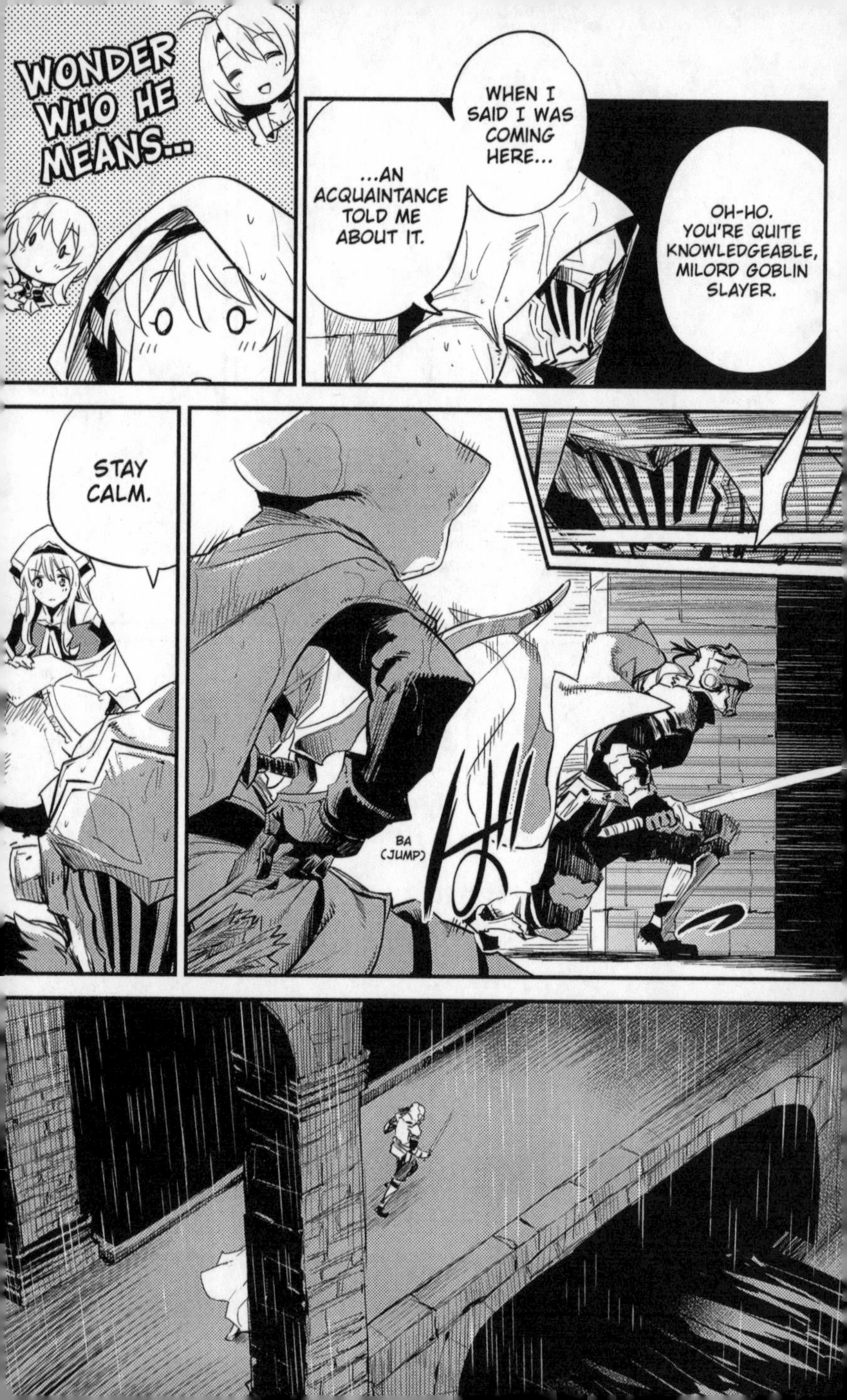
OH-HO. YOU'RE QUITE KNOWLEDGEABLE, MILORD GOBLIN SLAYER.
WHEN I SAID I WAS COMING HERE...
...AN ACQUAINTANCE TOLD ME ABOUT IT.
WONDER WHO HE MEANS...
BA (JUMP)
STAY CALM.

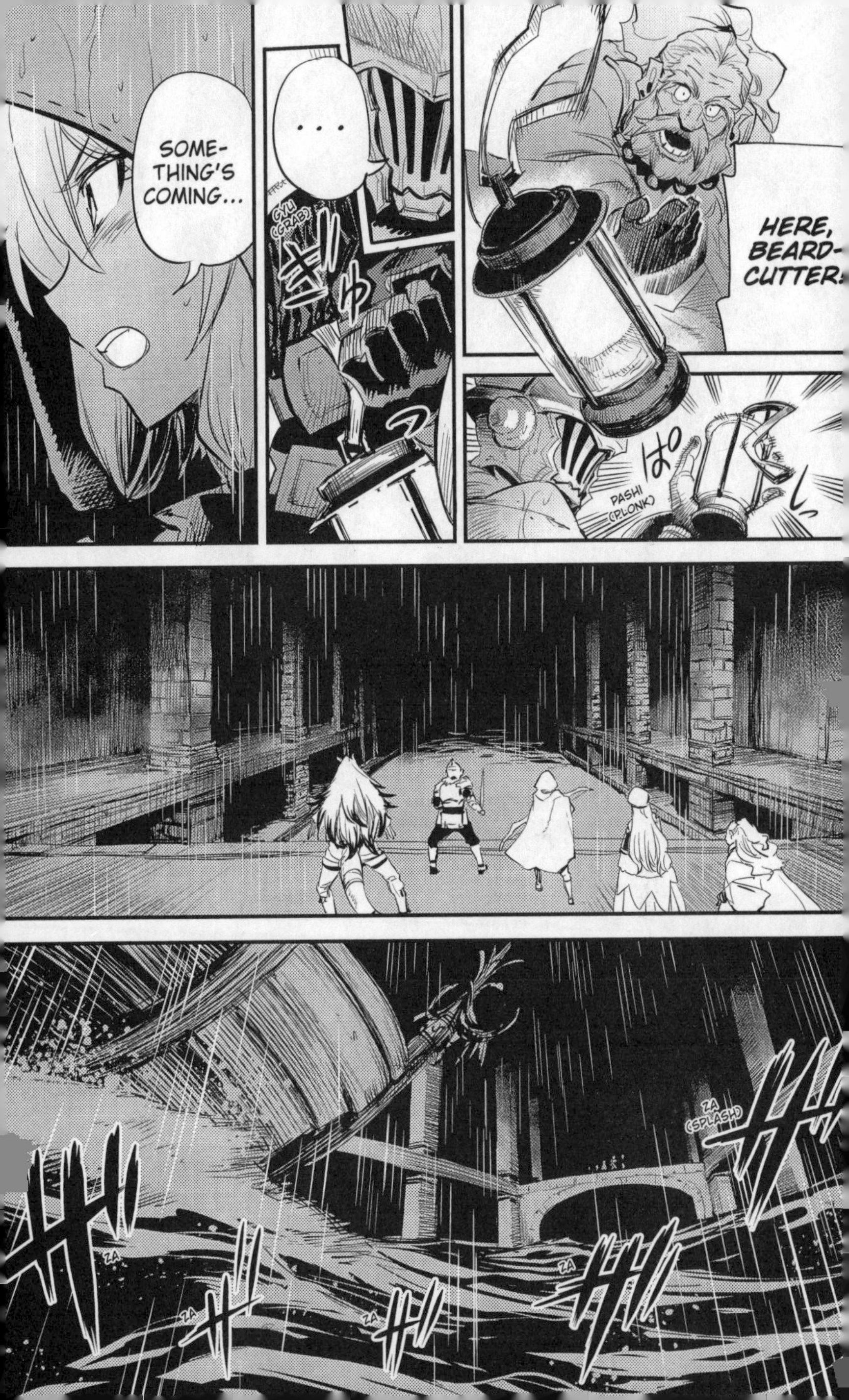
HERE, BEARD-CUTTER!
PASHI (PLONK)
...
GYU (GRAB)
SOME-THING'S COMING...
ZA (SPLASH)
ZA
ZA
ZA
ZA

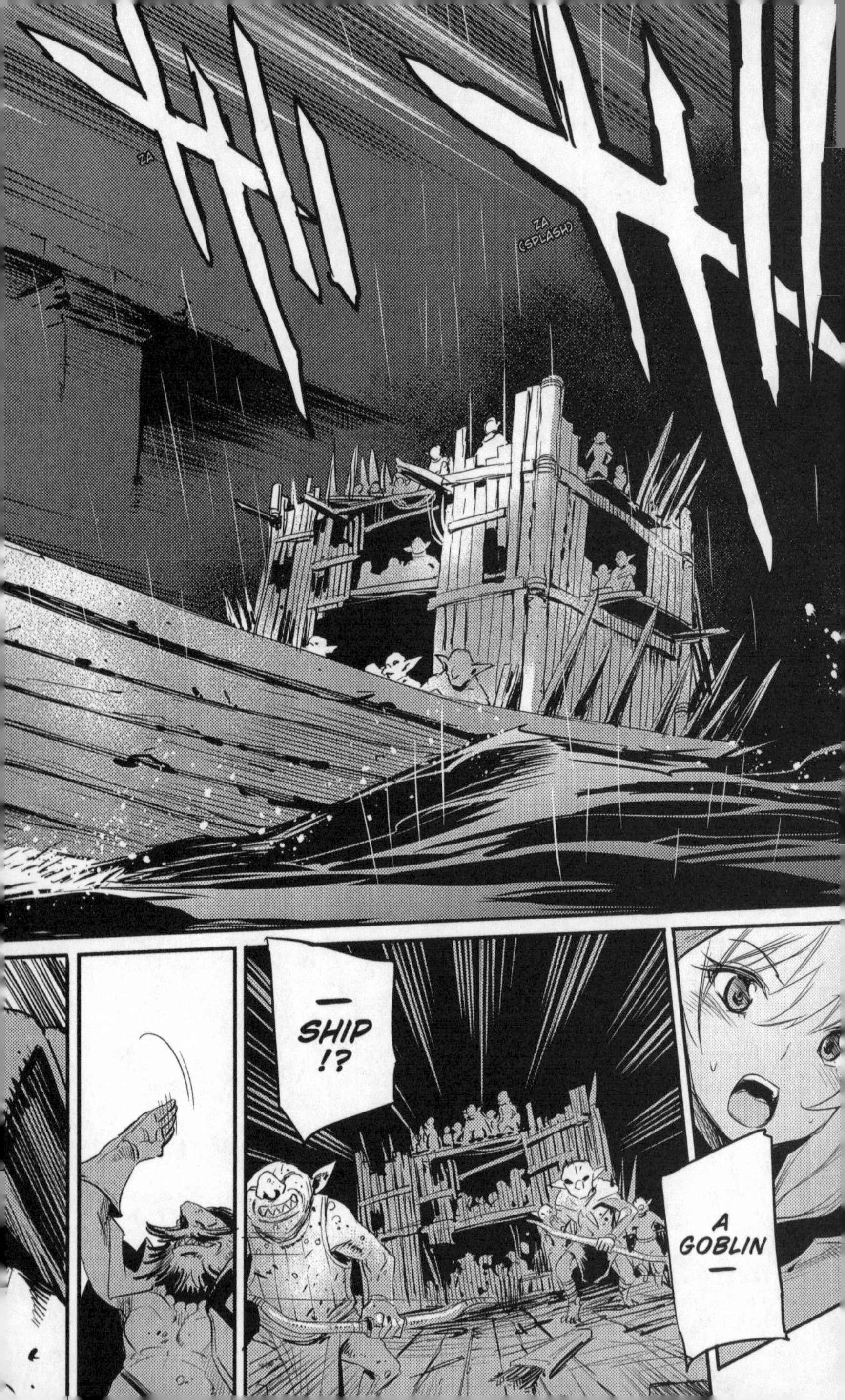
ZA
ZA (SPLASH)
A GOBLIN —
— SHIP !?

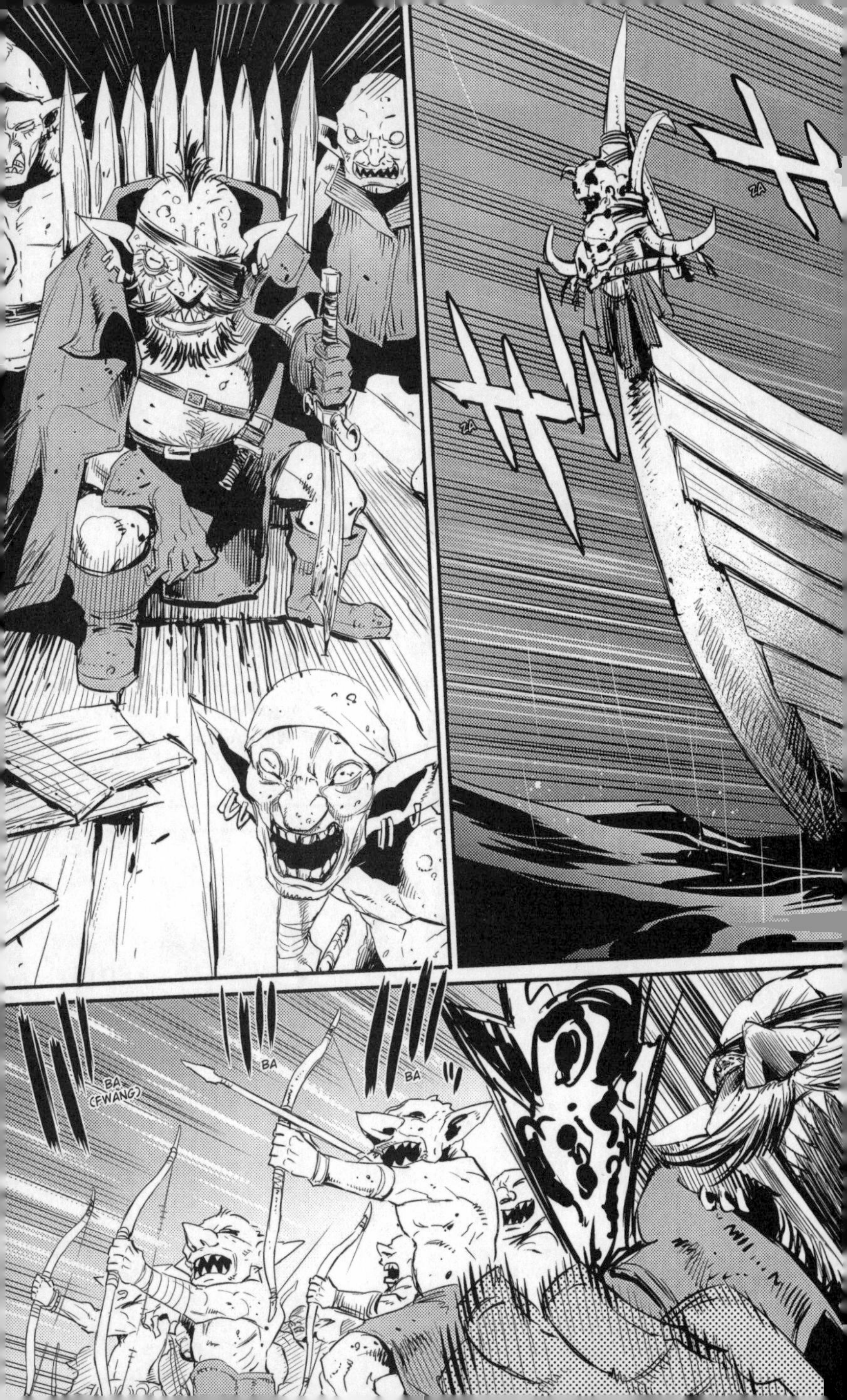
ZA
ZA
BA
BA
BA
(FWANG)

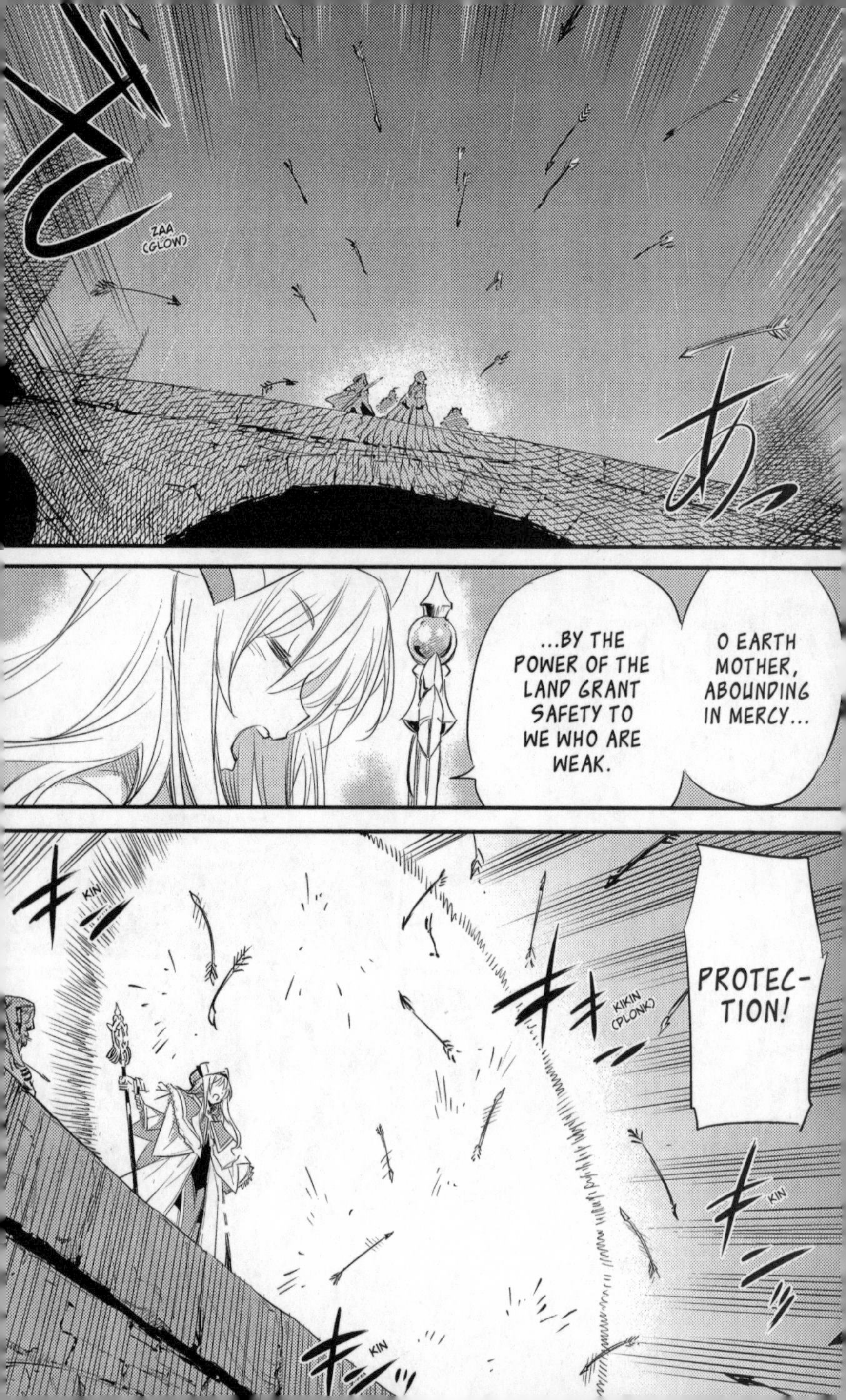
ZAA
(GLOW)
O EARTH MOTHER, ABOUNDING IN MERCY...
...BY THE POWER OF THE LAND GRANT SAFETY TO WE WHO ARE WEAK.
PROTEC-
TION!
KIKIN
(PLONK)
KIN
KIN
KIN

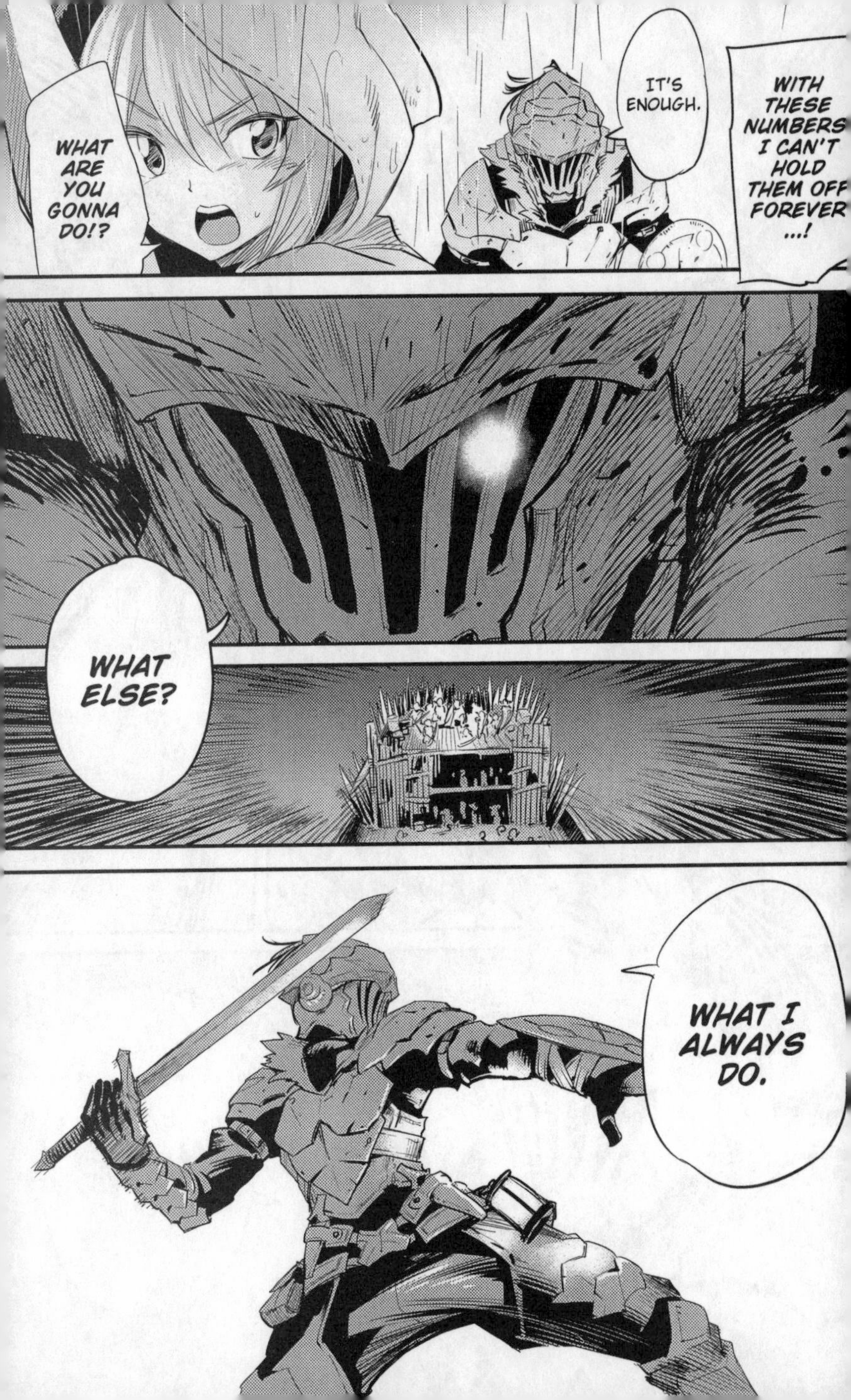
WITH THESE NUMBERS I CAN'T HOLD THEM OFF FOREVER ...!
IT'S ENOUGH.
WHAT ARE YOU GONNA DO!?
WHAT ELSE?
WHAT I ALWAYS DO.

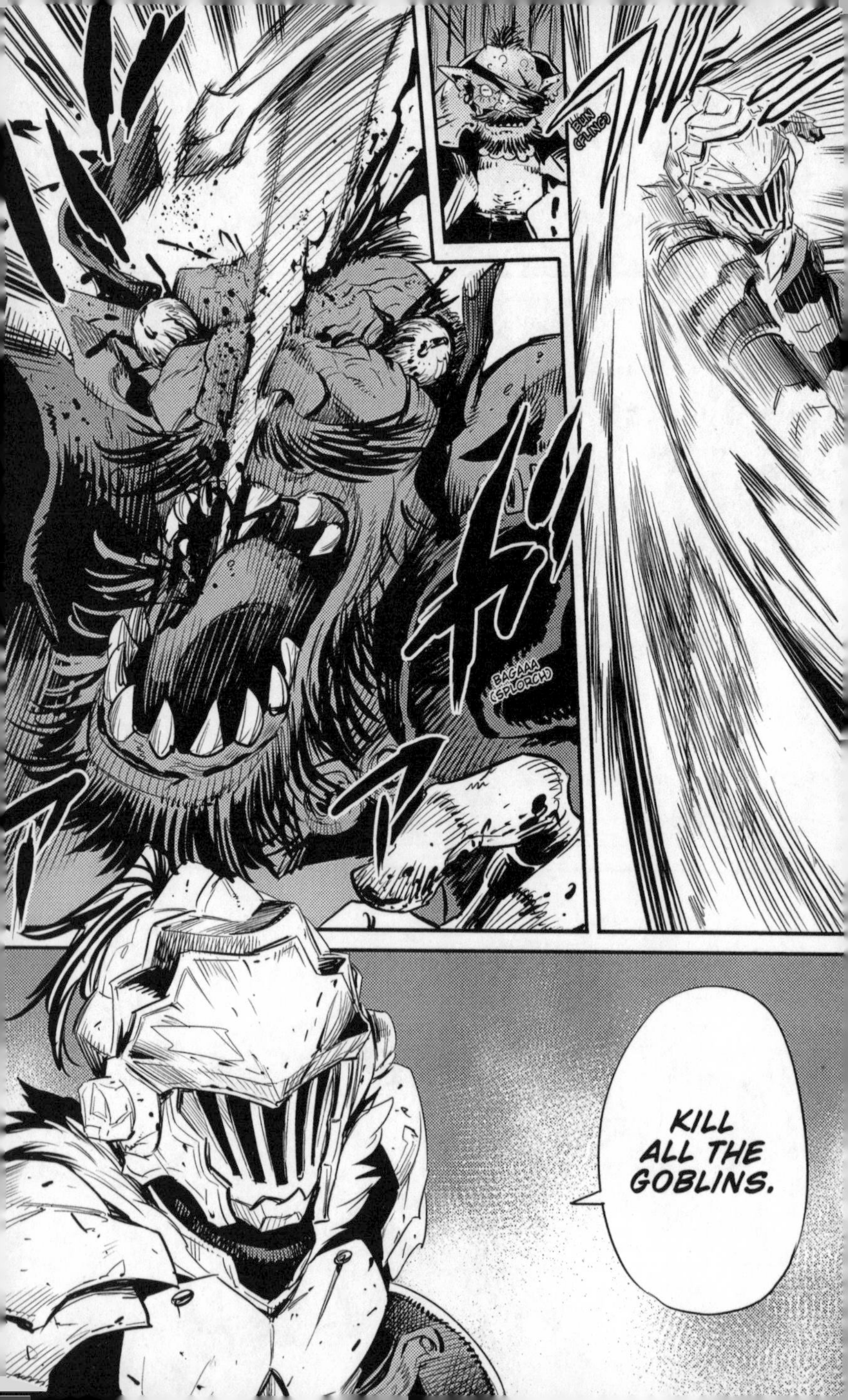
BUN (FLING)
BAGAAA (SPLORCH)
KILL ALL THE GOBLINS.

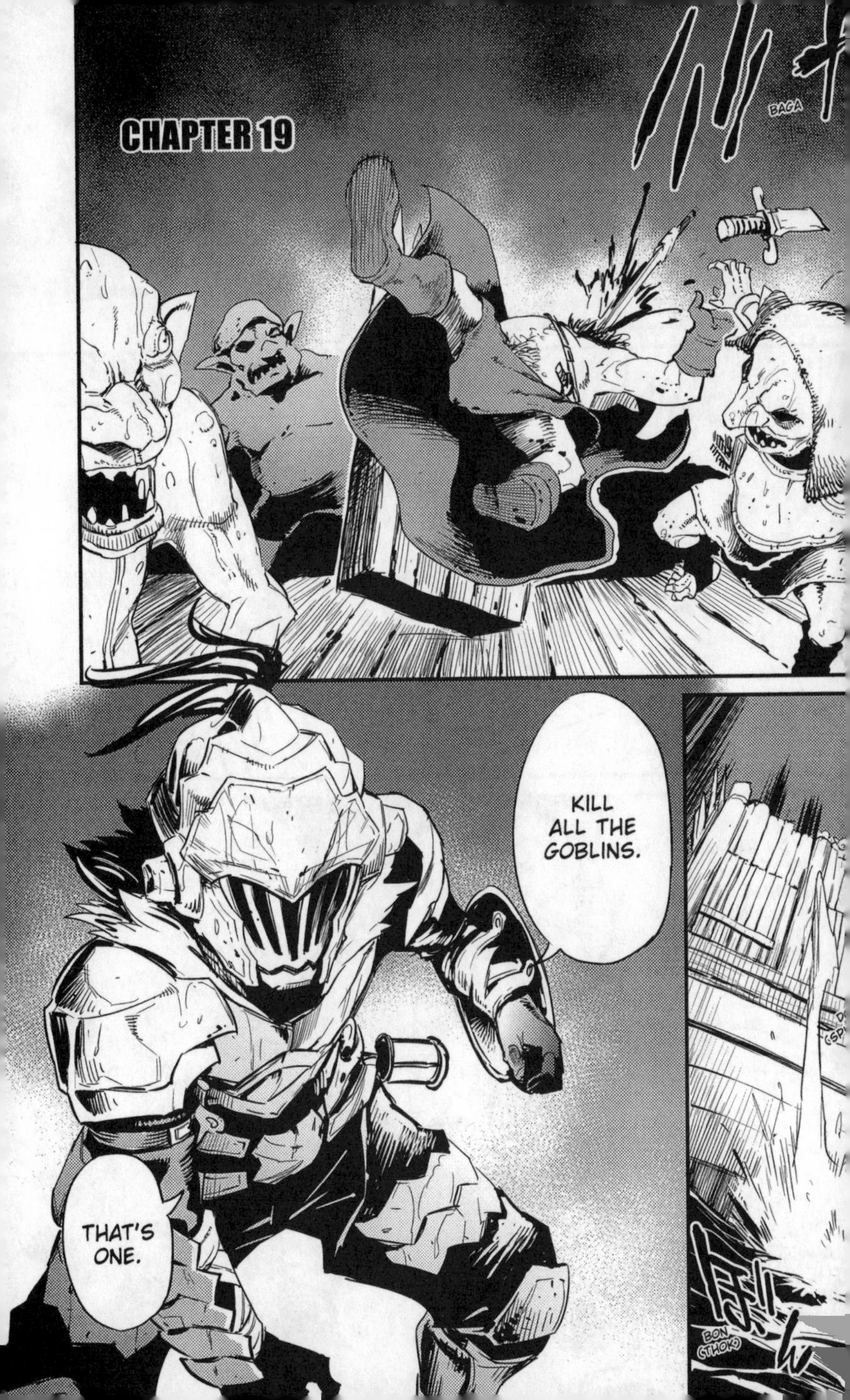
CHAPTER 19
BAGA
BON (THOK)
KILL ALL THE GOBLINS.
THAT'S ONE.

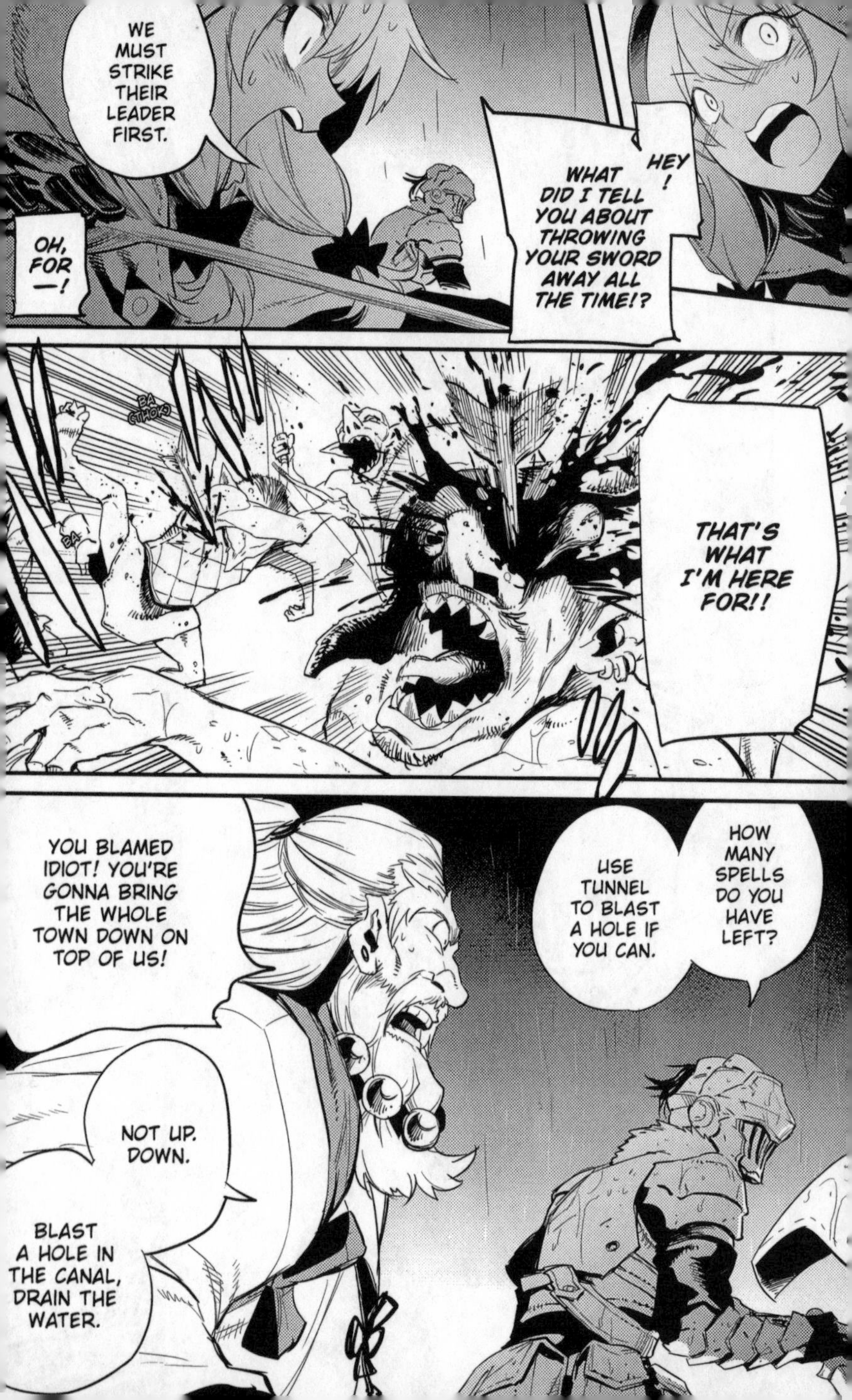
HEY! WHAT DID I TELL YOU ABOUT THROWING YOUR SWORD AWAY ALL THE TIME!?
WE MUST STRIKE THEIR LEADER FIRST.
OH, FOR—!
THAT'S WHAT I'M HERE FOR!!
BA (THOK)
BA
HOW MANY SPELLS DO YOU HAVE LEFT?
USE TUNNEL TO BLAST A HOLE IF YOU CAN.
YOU BLAMED IDIOT! YOU'RE GONNA BRING THE WHOLE TOWN DOWN ON TOP OF US!
NOT UP. DOWN.
BLAST A HOLE IN THE CANAL, DRAIN THE WATER.

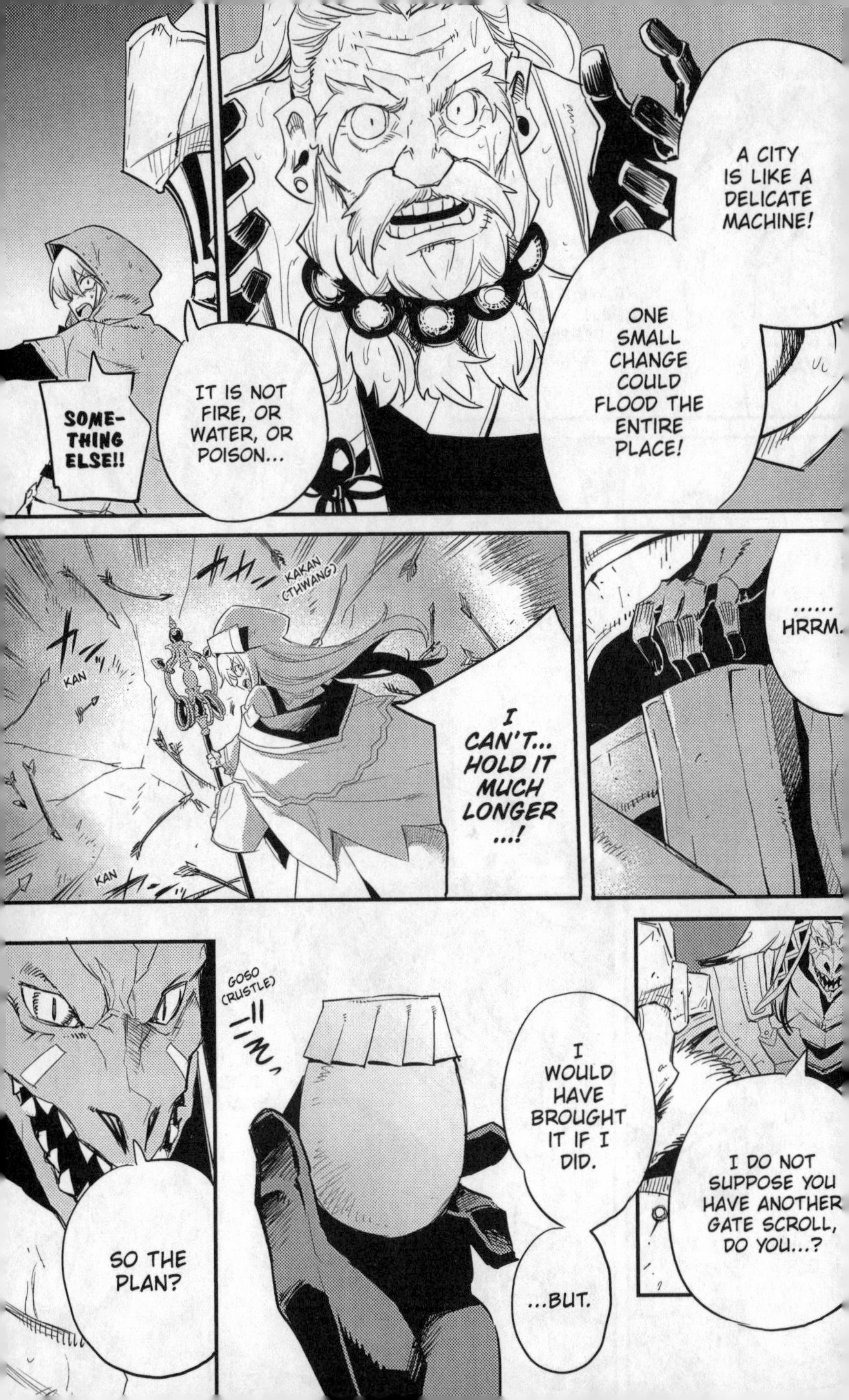
A CITY IS LIKE A DELICATE MACHINE!
ONE SMALL CHANGE COULD FLOOD THE ENTIRE PLACE!
IT IS NOT FIRE, OR WATER, OR POISON...
SOME-THING ELSE!!
......HRRM.
KAKAN (THWANG)
I CAN'T... HOLD IT MUCH LONGER ...!
KAN
KAN
I DO NOT SUPPOSE YOU HAVE ANOTHER GATE SCROLL, DO YOU...?
GOSO (RUSTLE)
I WOULD HAVE BROUGHT IT IF I DID.
...BUT.
SO THE PLAN?

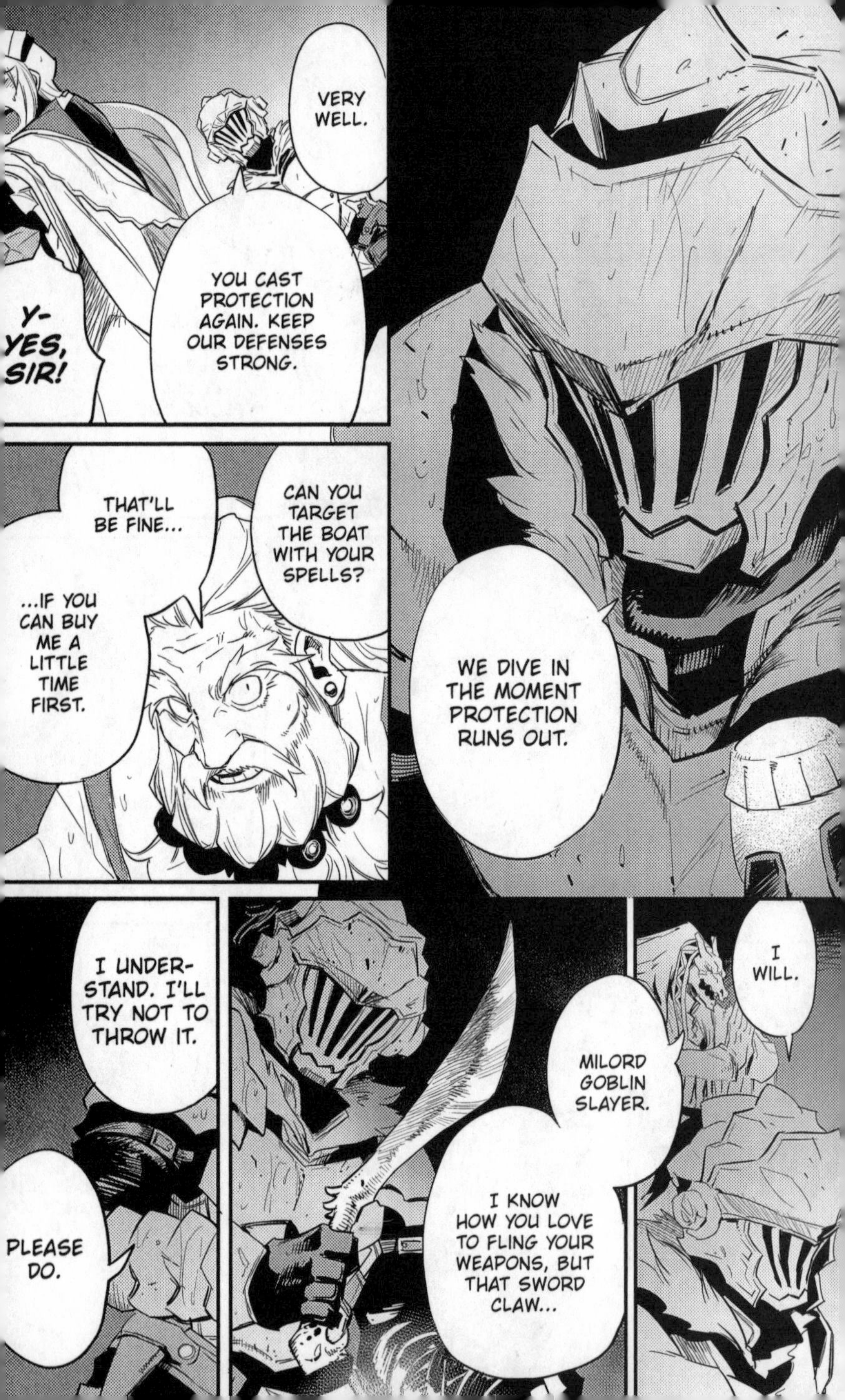
WE DIVE IN THE MOMENT PROTECTION RUNS OUT.
VERY WELL.
YOU CAST PROTECTION AGAIN. KEEP OUR DEFENSES STRONG.
Y-YES, SIR!
CAN YOU TARGET THE BOAT WITH YOUR SPELLS?
THAT'LL BE FINE...
...IF YOU CAN BUY ME A LITTLE TIME FIRST.
I WILL.
MILORD GOBLIN SLAYER.
I KNOW HOW YOU LOVE TO FLING YOUR WEAPONS, BUT THAT SWORD CLAW...
I UNDER-STAND. I'LL TRY NOT TO THROW IT.
PLEASE DO.

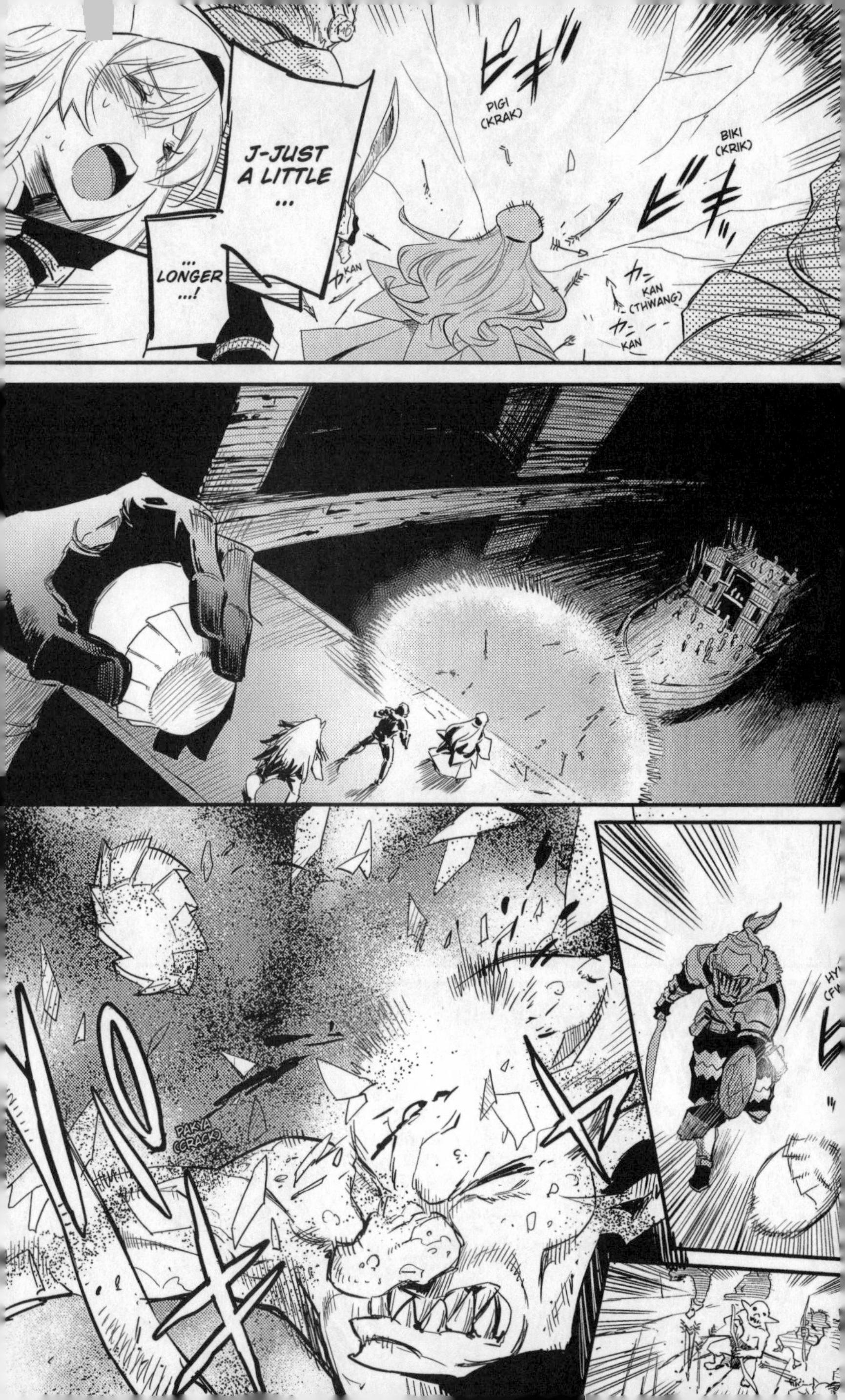
BIKI (KRIK)
PIGI (KRAK)
KAN (THWANG)
KAN
KAN
J-JUST A LITTLE ...
... LONGER ...!
HYU (FW
PAKIYA (CRACK)

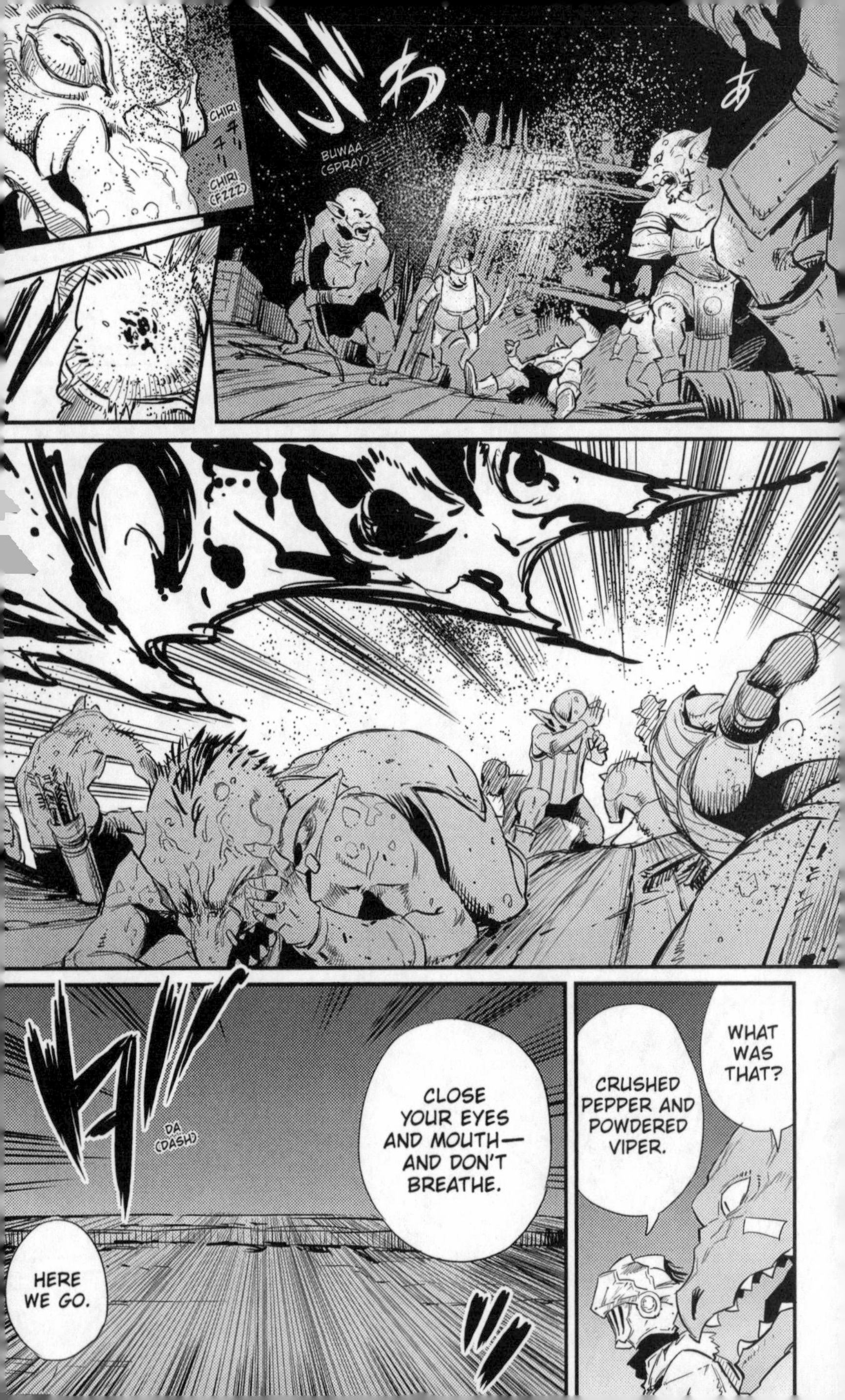
ぶわあ
BUWAA (SPRAY)
チリ チリ
CHIRI CHIRI (FZZZ)
WHAT WAS THAT?
CRUSHED PEPPER AND POWDERED VIPER.
CLOSE YOUR EYES AND MOUTH— AND DON'T BREATHE.
ダッ
DA (DASH)
HERE WE GO.

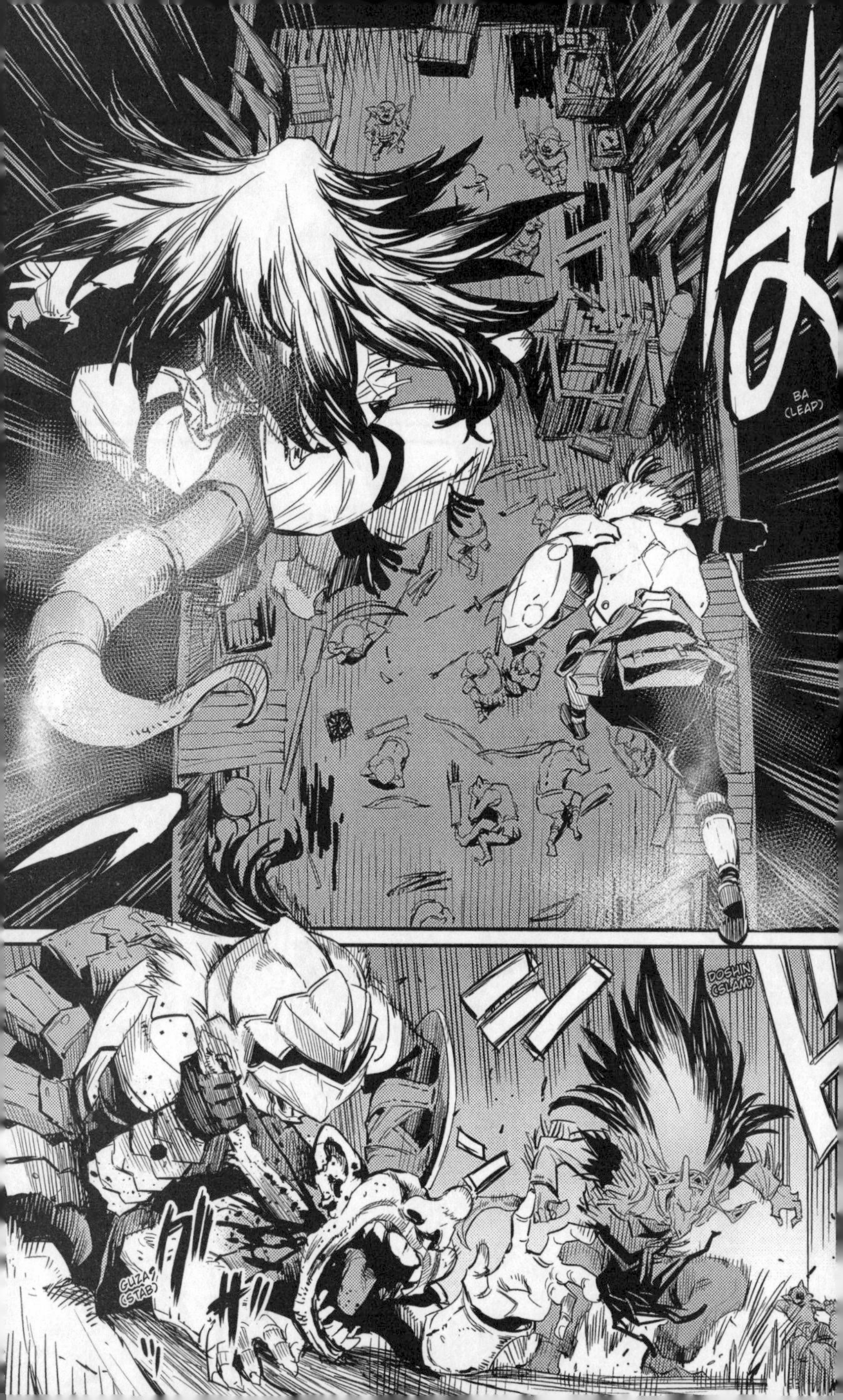
BA
(LEAP)
DOSHIN
(SLAM)
GUZA
(STAB)

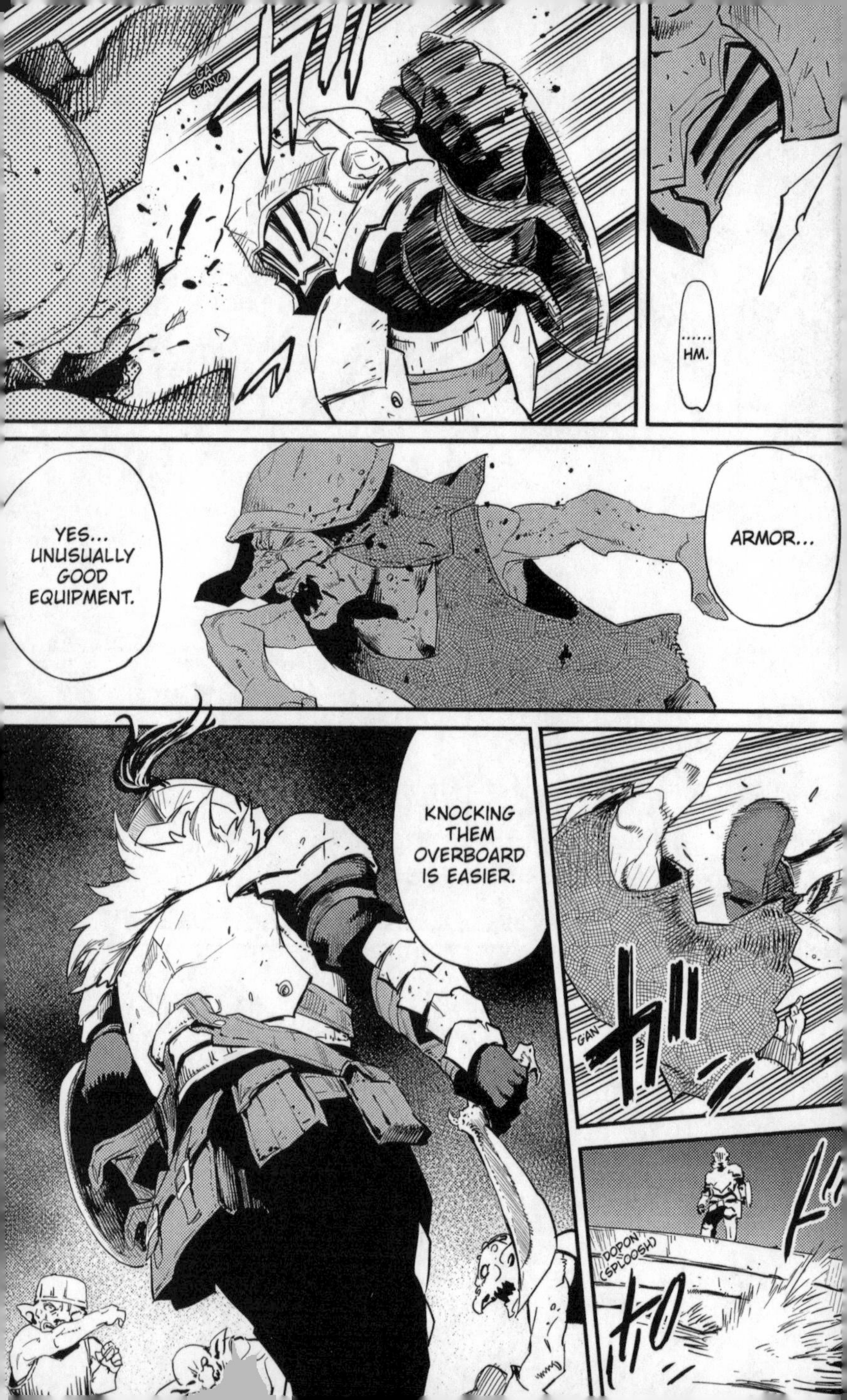
......
HM.
GA (BANG)
ARMOR...
YES... UNUSUALLY GOOD EQUIPMENT.
GAN
DOPON (SPLOOSH)
KNOCKING THEM OVERBOARD IS EASIER.

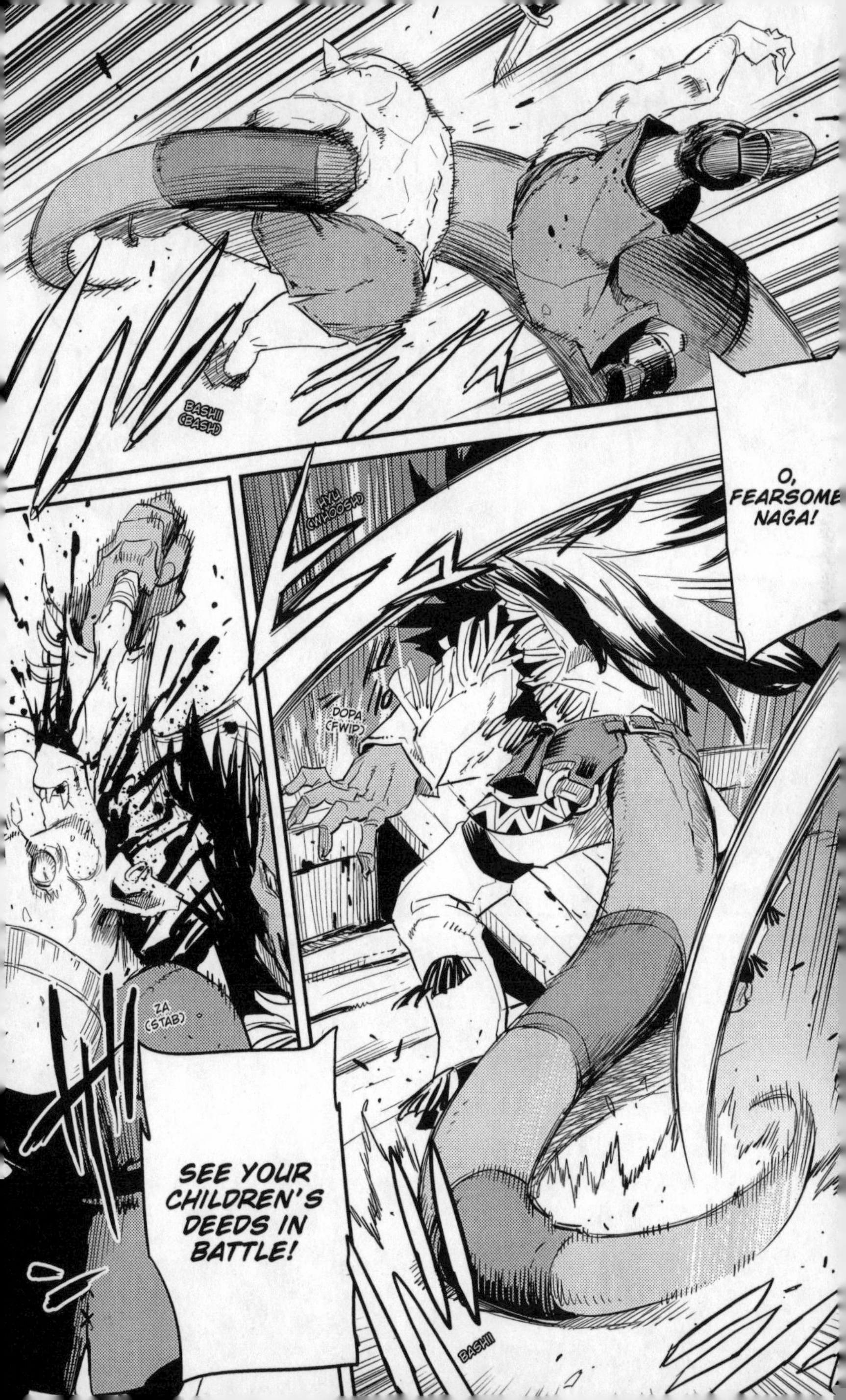
BASHI (BASH)
O, FEARSOME NAGA!
HYU (WHOOSH)
DOPA (FWIP)
ZA (STAB)
SEE YOUR CHILDREN'S DEEDS IN BATTLE!
BASHI

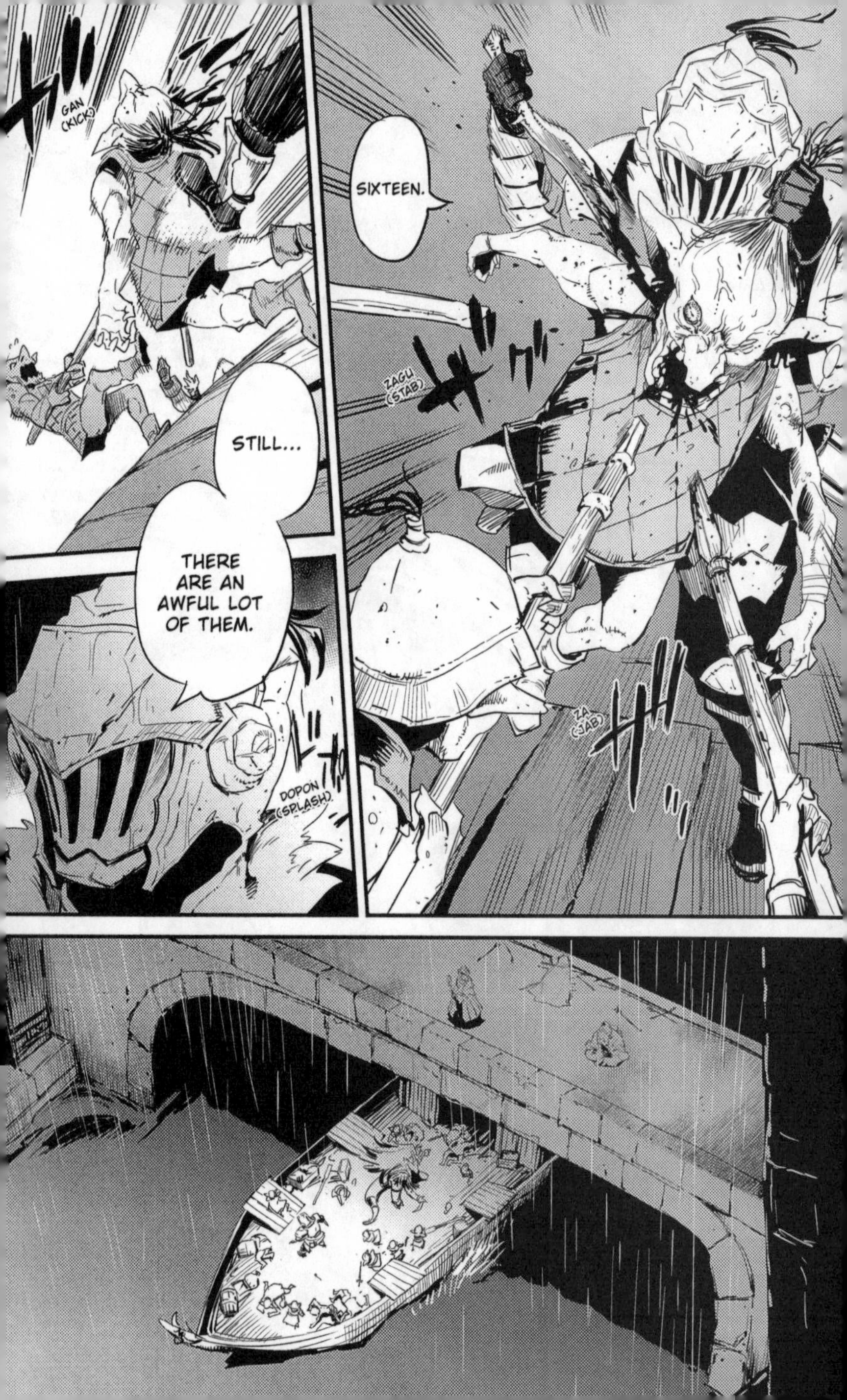
SIXTEEN.
ZAGU (STAB)
ZA (JAB)
GAN (KICK)
STILL...
THERE ARE AN AWFUL LOT OF THEM.
DOPON (SPLASH)

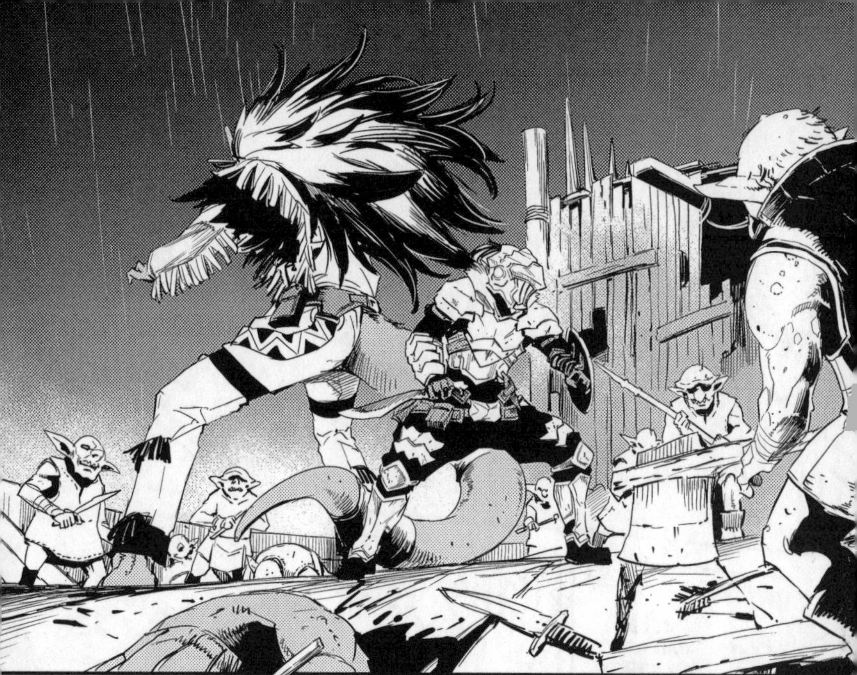
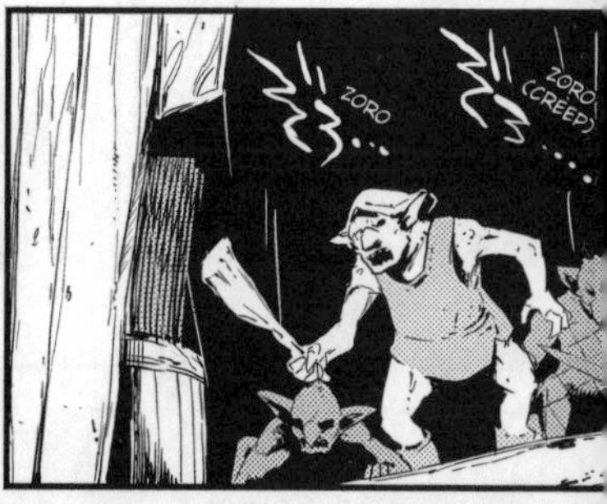
ZORO (CREEP)
ZORO
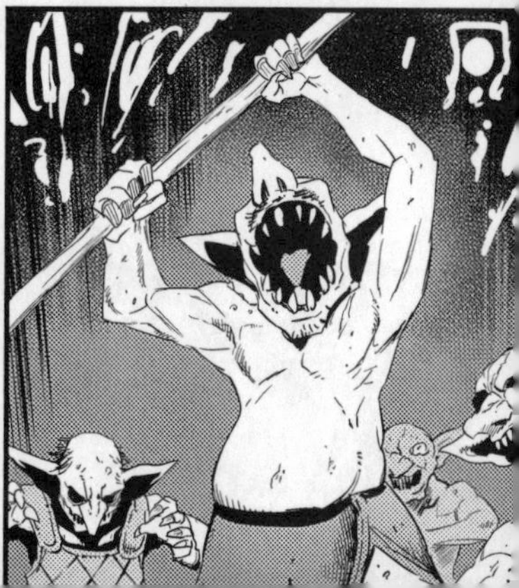
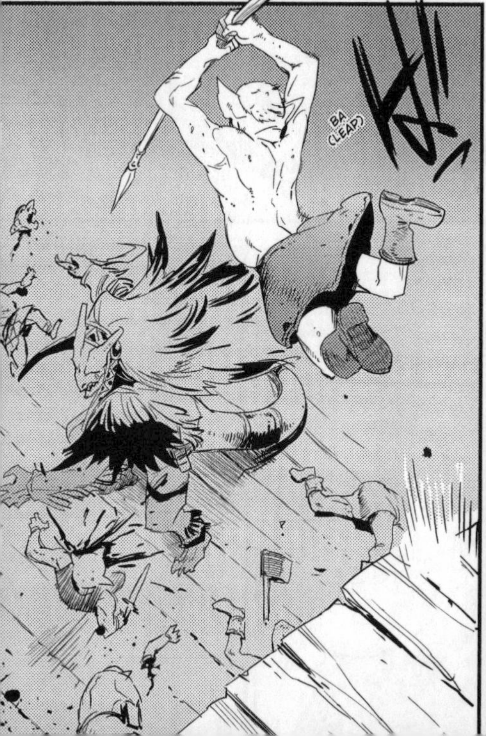
BA (LEAP)

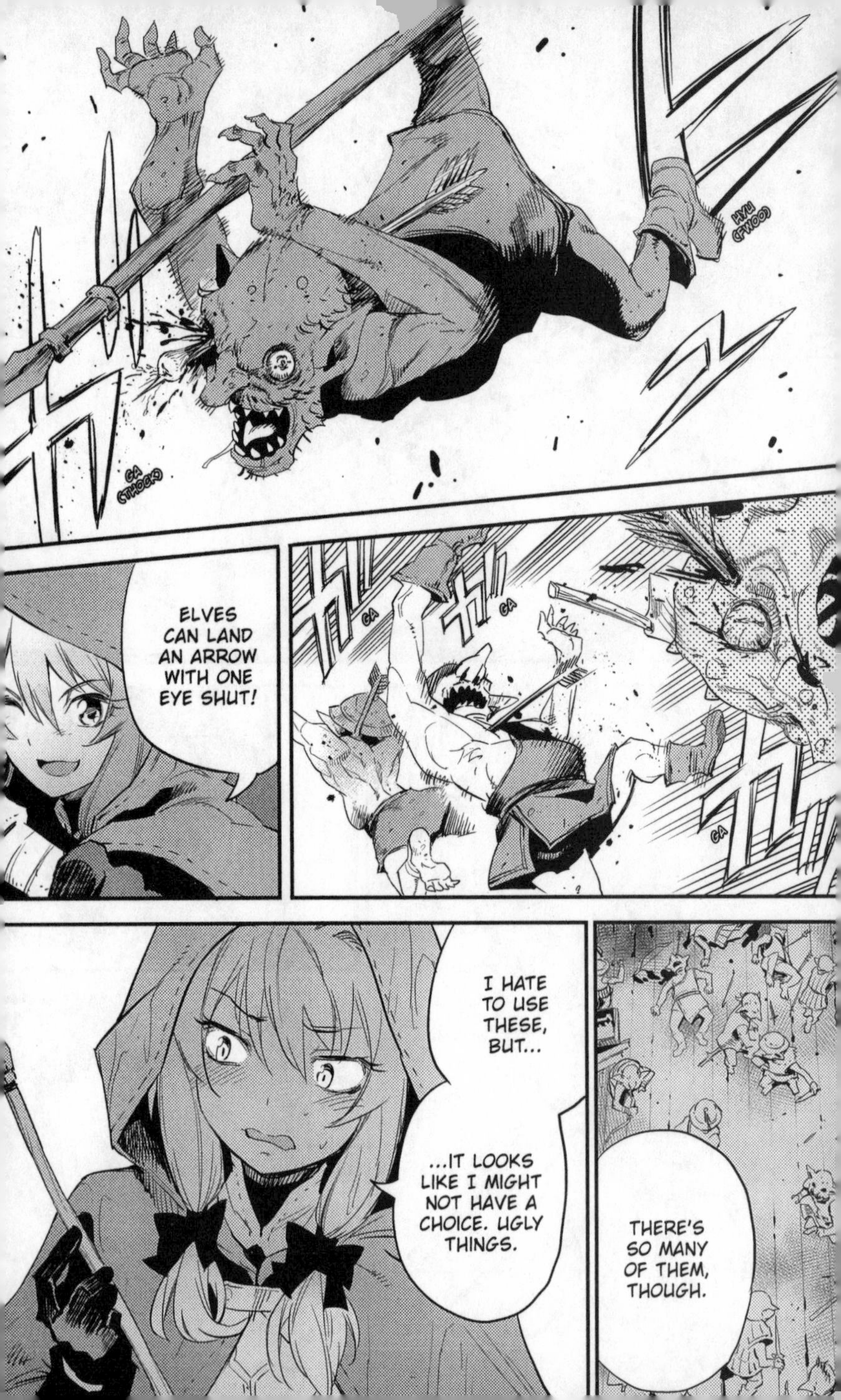
HYU (FWOO)
GA (THOCK)
GA
GA
GA
ELVES CAN LAND AN ARROW WITH ONE EYE SHUT!
THERE'S SO MANY OF THEM, THOUGH.
I HATE TO USE THESE, BUT...
...IT LOOKS LIKE I MIGHT NOT HAVE A CHOICE. UGLY THINGS.

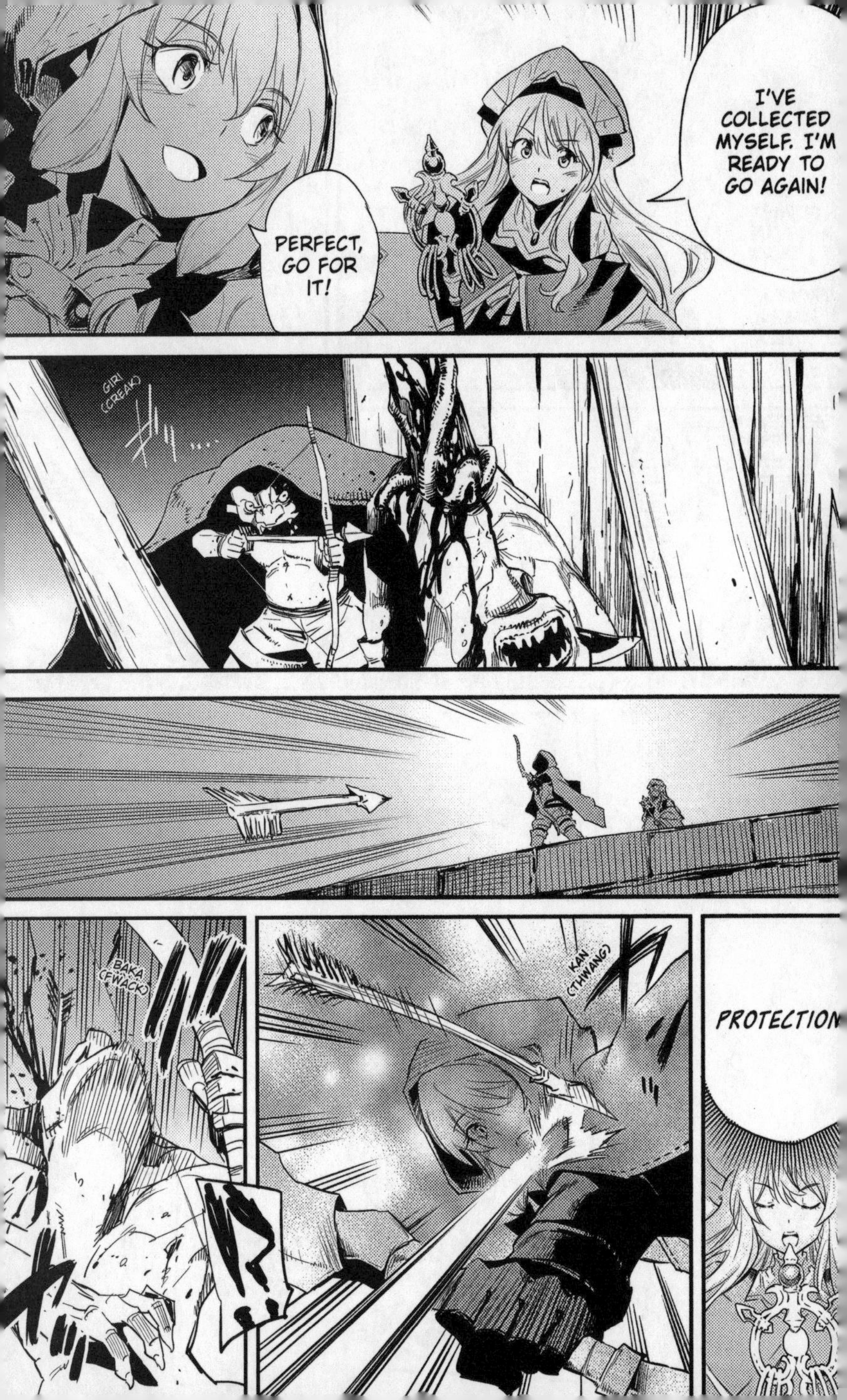
I'VE COLLECTED MYSELF. I'M READY TO GO AGAIN!
PERFECT, GO FOR IT!
GIRI (CREAK)
PROTECTION
KAN (THWANG)
BAKA (FWACK)

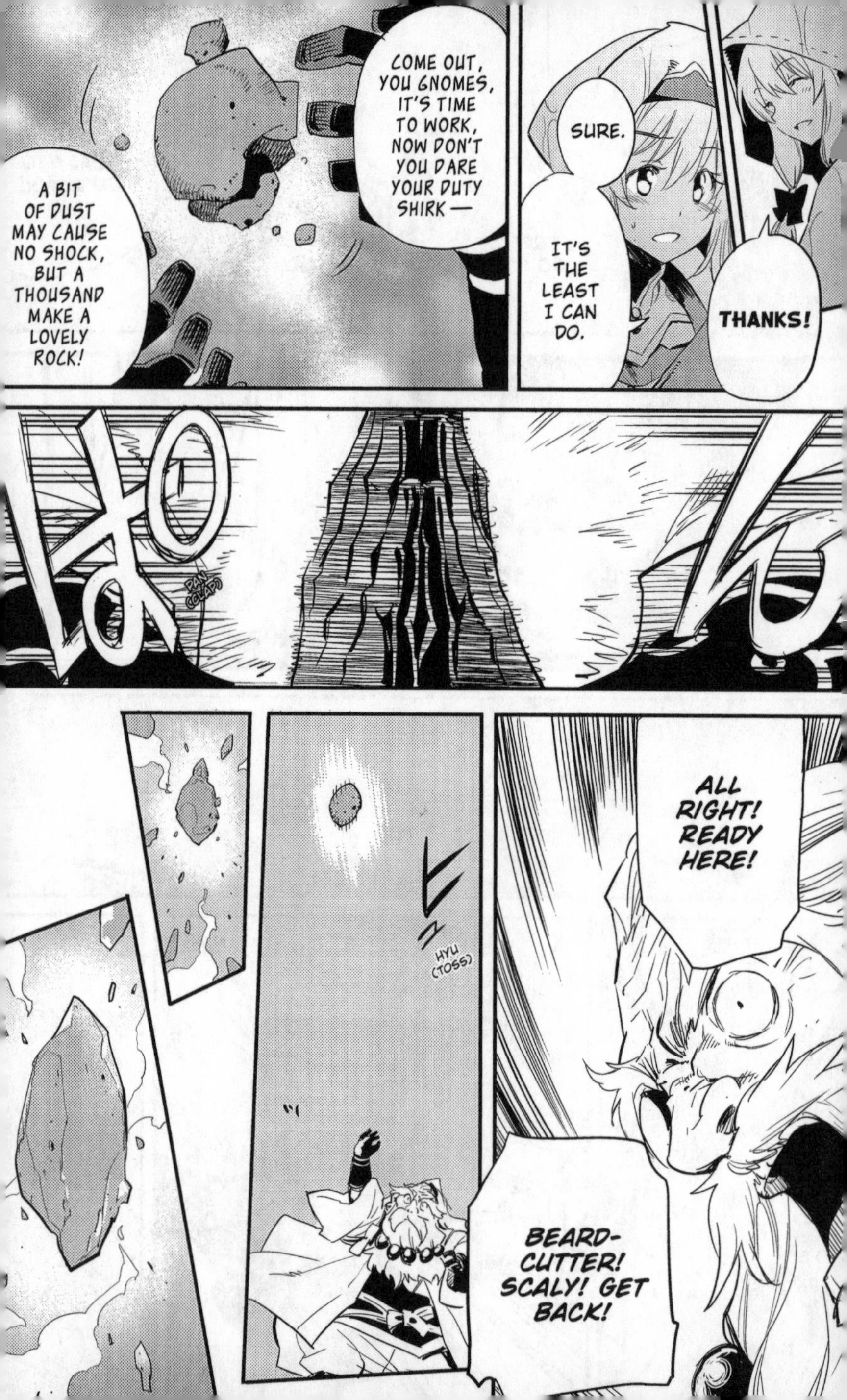
THANKS!
SURE.
IT'S THE LEAST I CAN DO.
COME OUT, YOU GNOMES, IT'S TIME TO WORK, NOW DON'T YOU DARE YOUR DUTY SHIRK—
A BIT OF DUST MAY CAUSE NO SHOCK, BUT A THOUSAND MAKE A LOVELY ROCK!
PAN (CLAP)
ALL RIGHT! READY HERE!
BEARD-CUTTER! SCALY! GET BACK!
HYU (TOSS)

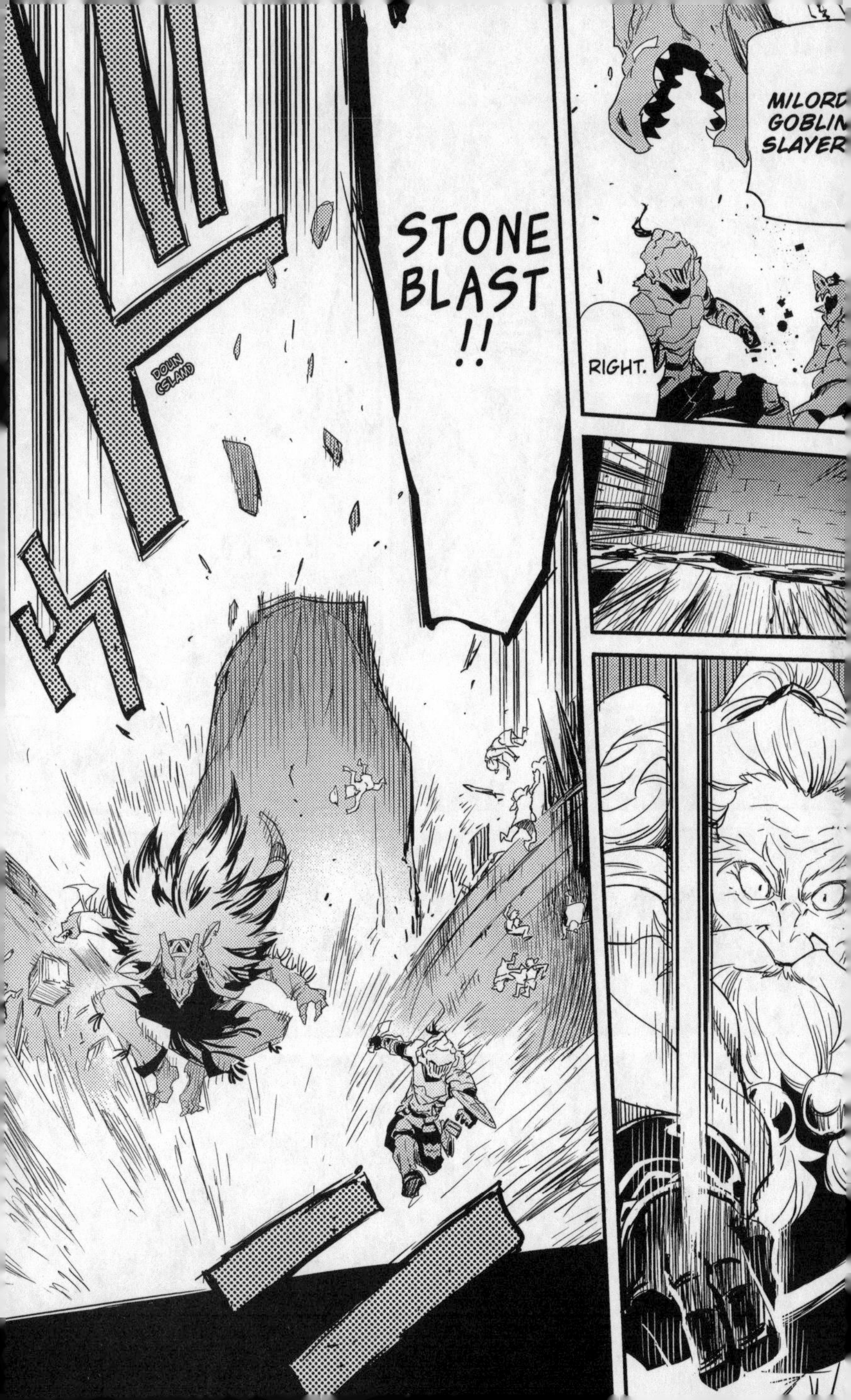
MILORD GOBLIN SLAYER
RIGHT.
STONE BLAST!!
DOWN (SLAM)

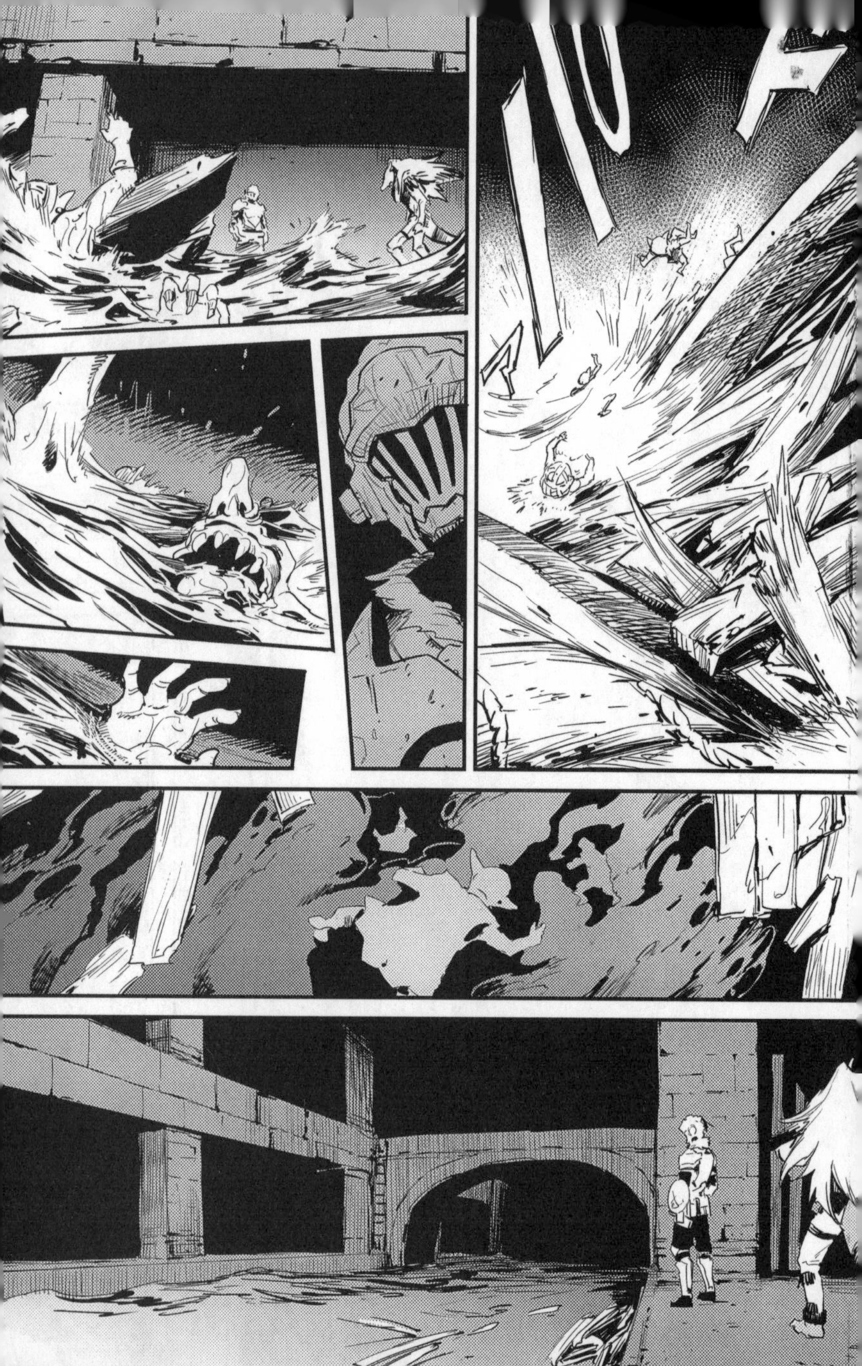

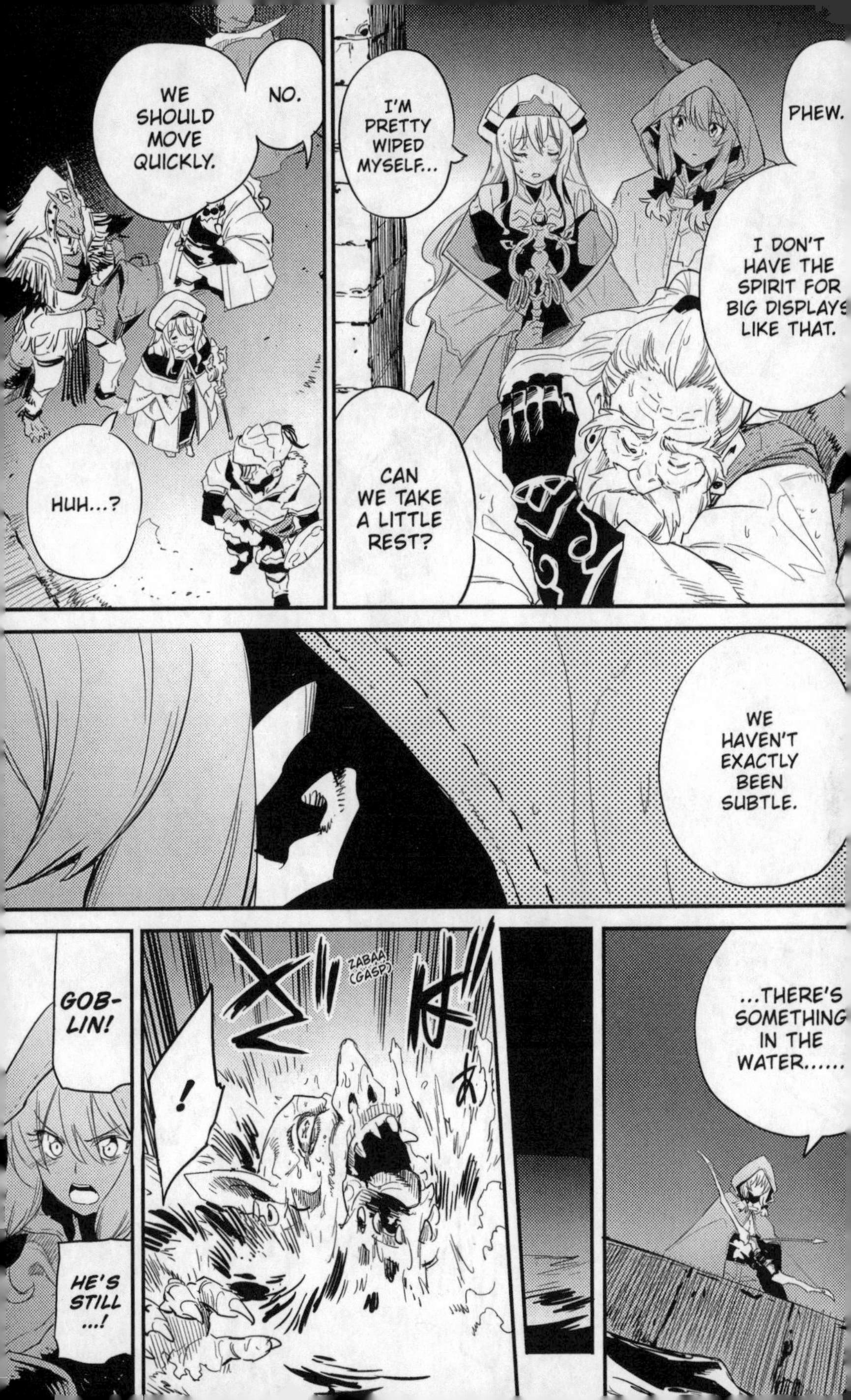
PHEW.
I DON'T HAVE THE SPIRIT FOR BIG DISPLAYS LIKE THAT.
I'M PRETTY WIPED MYSELF...
CAN WE TAKE A LITTLE REST?
NO.
WE SHOULD MOVE QUICKLY.
HUH...?
WE HAVEN'T EXACTLY BEEN SUBTLE.
...THERE'S SOMETHING IN THE WATER......
ZABAA (GASP)
!
GOB-LIN!
HE'S STILL ...!

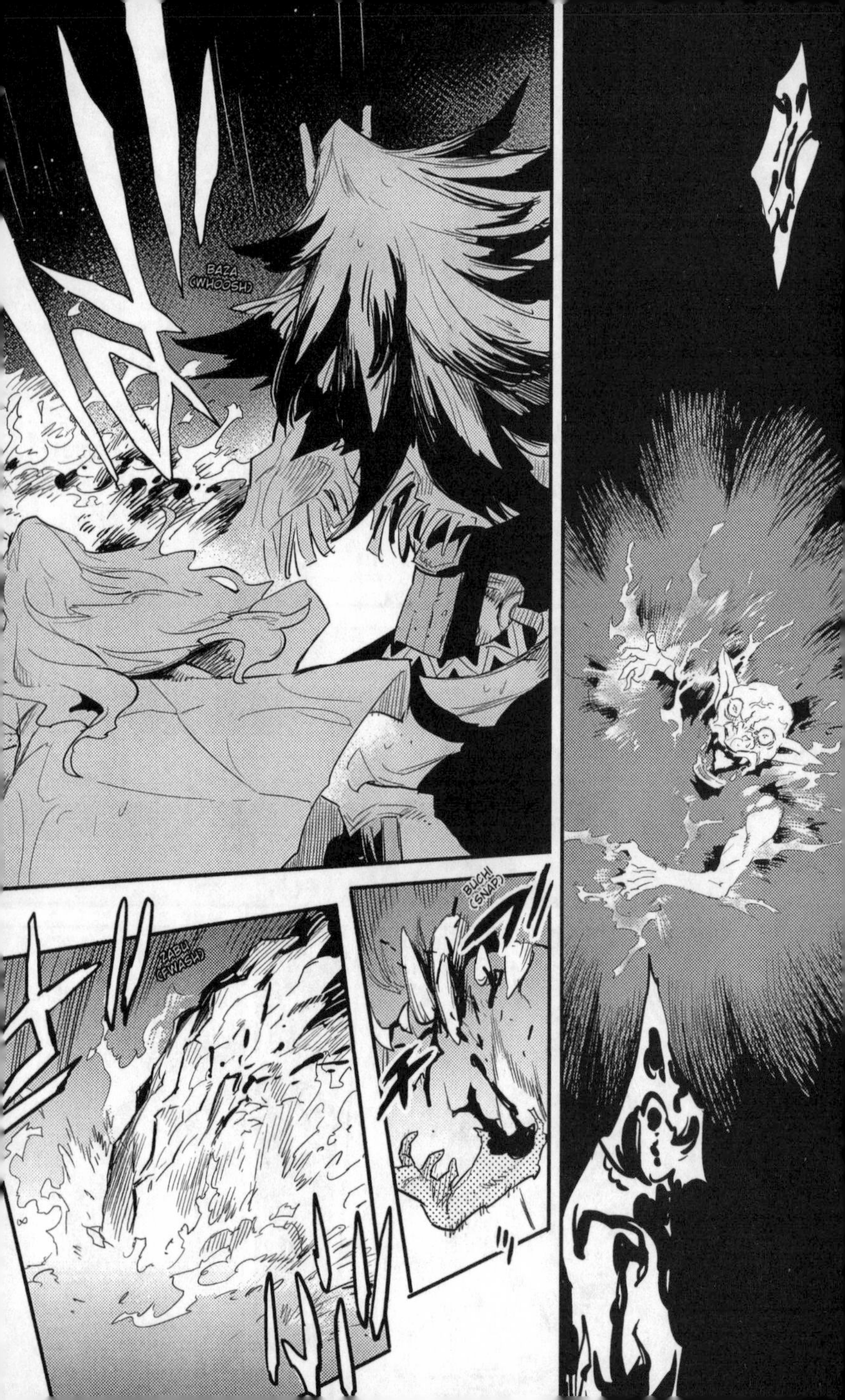
BAZA (WHOOSH)
BUCHI (SNAP)
ZABU (FWASH)

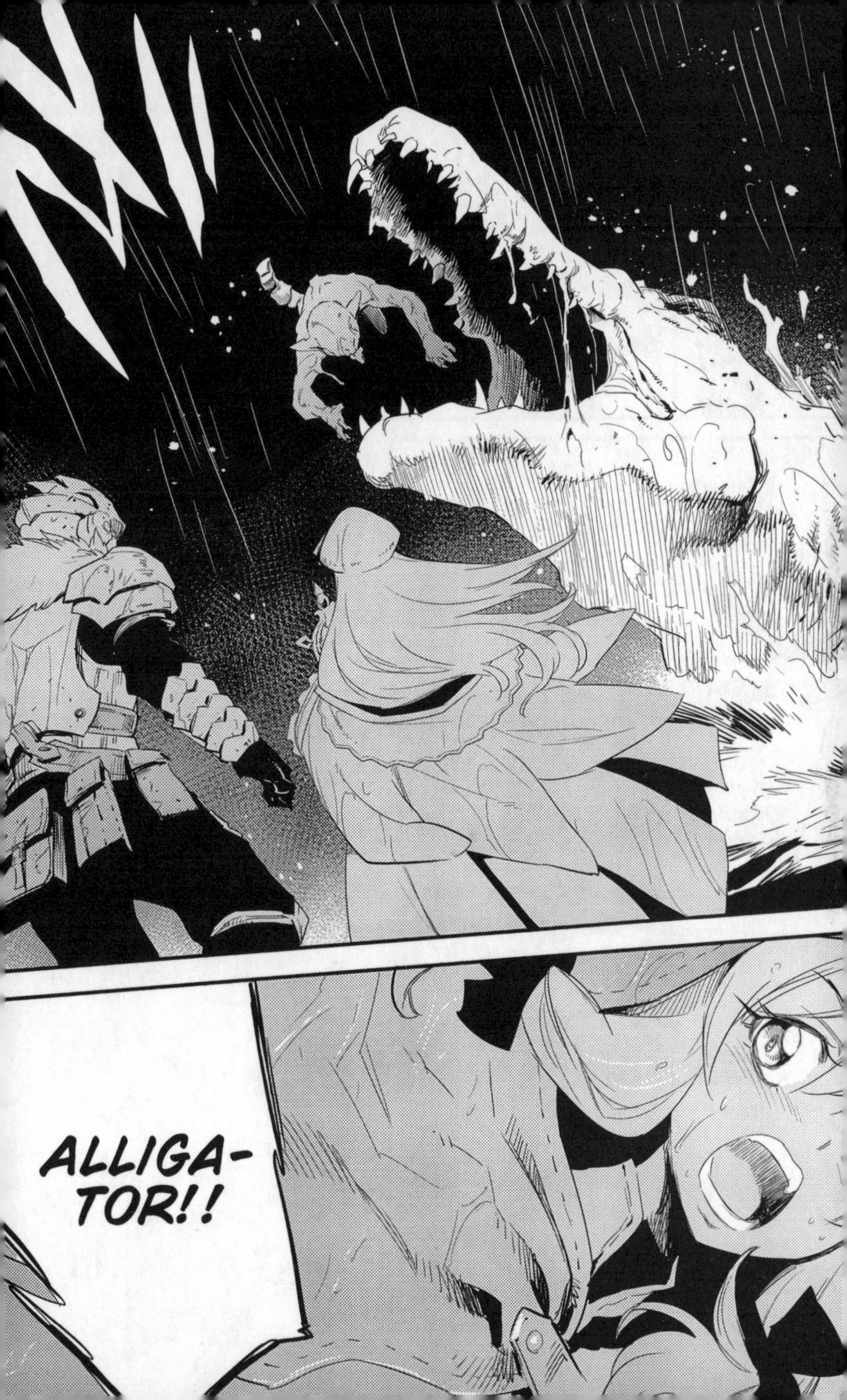
ALLIGA-
TOR!!

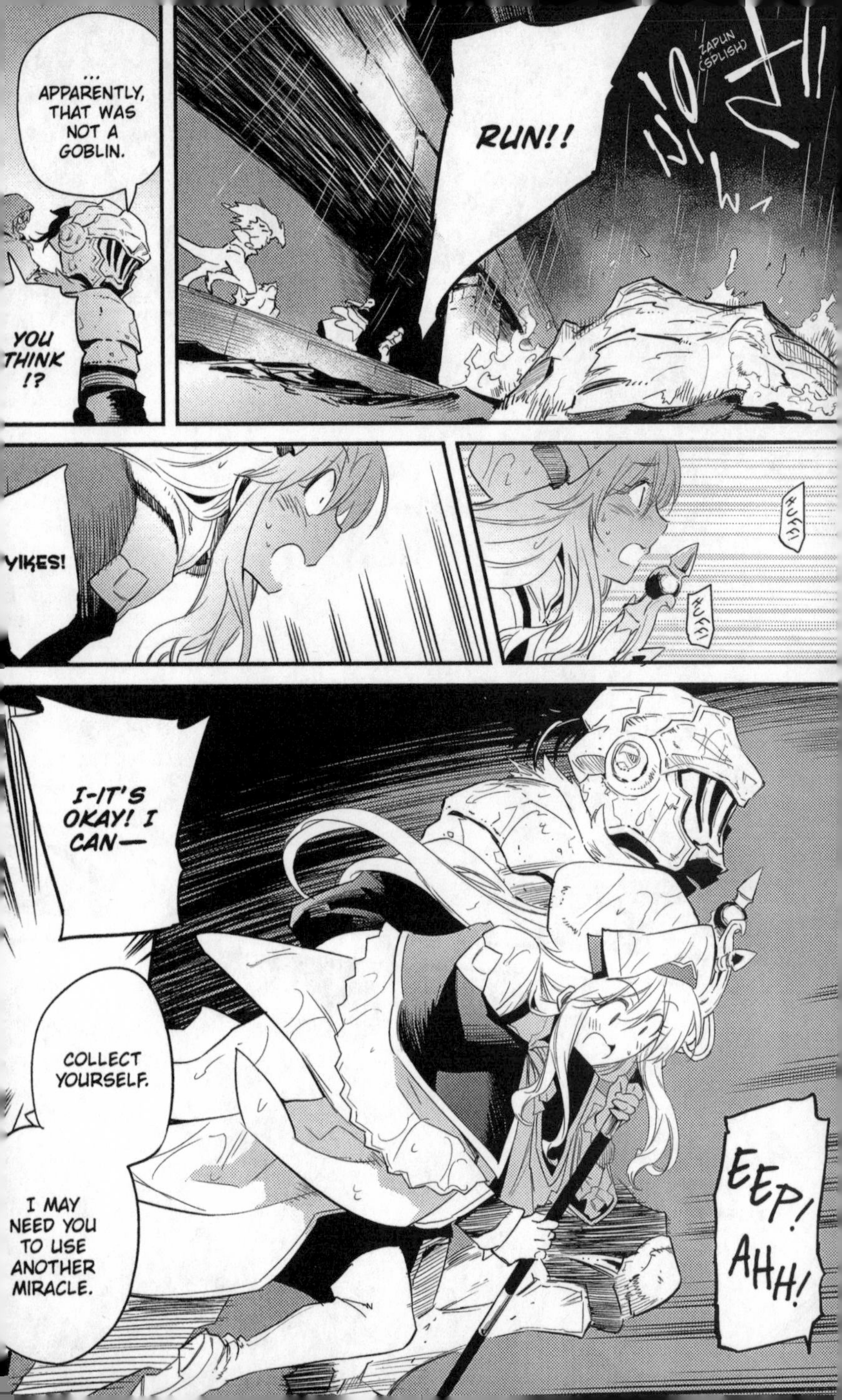
ZAPUN (SPLISH)
RUN!!
... APPARENTLY, THAT WAS NOT A GOBLIN.
YOU THINK!?
HUFF
HUFF
YIKES!
EEP! AHH!
COLLECT YOURSELF.
I MAY NEED YOU TO USE ANOTHER MIRACLE.
I-IT'S OKAY! I CAN—

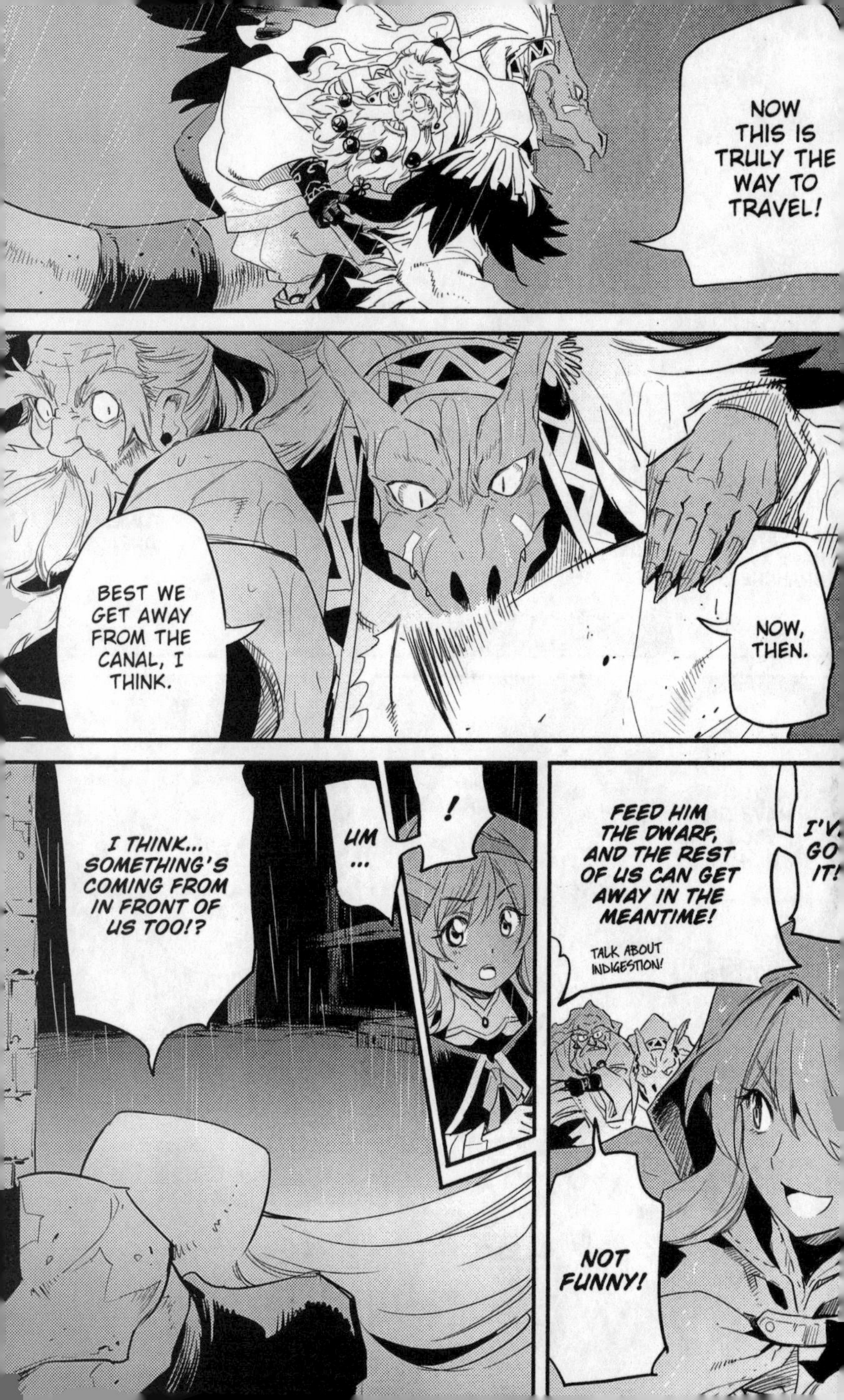
NOW THIS IS TRULY THE WAY TO TRAVEL!
!
NOW, THEN.
BEST WE GET AWAY FROM THE CANAL, I THINK.
I'V… GO IT!
FEED HIM THE DWARF, AND THE REST OF US CAN GET AWAY IN THE MEANTIME!
TALK ABOUT INDIGESTION!
NOT FUNNY!
!
UM …
I THINK… SOMETHING'S COMING FROM IN FRONT OF US TOO!?

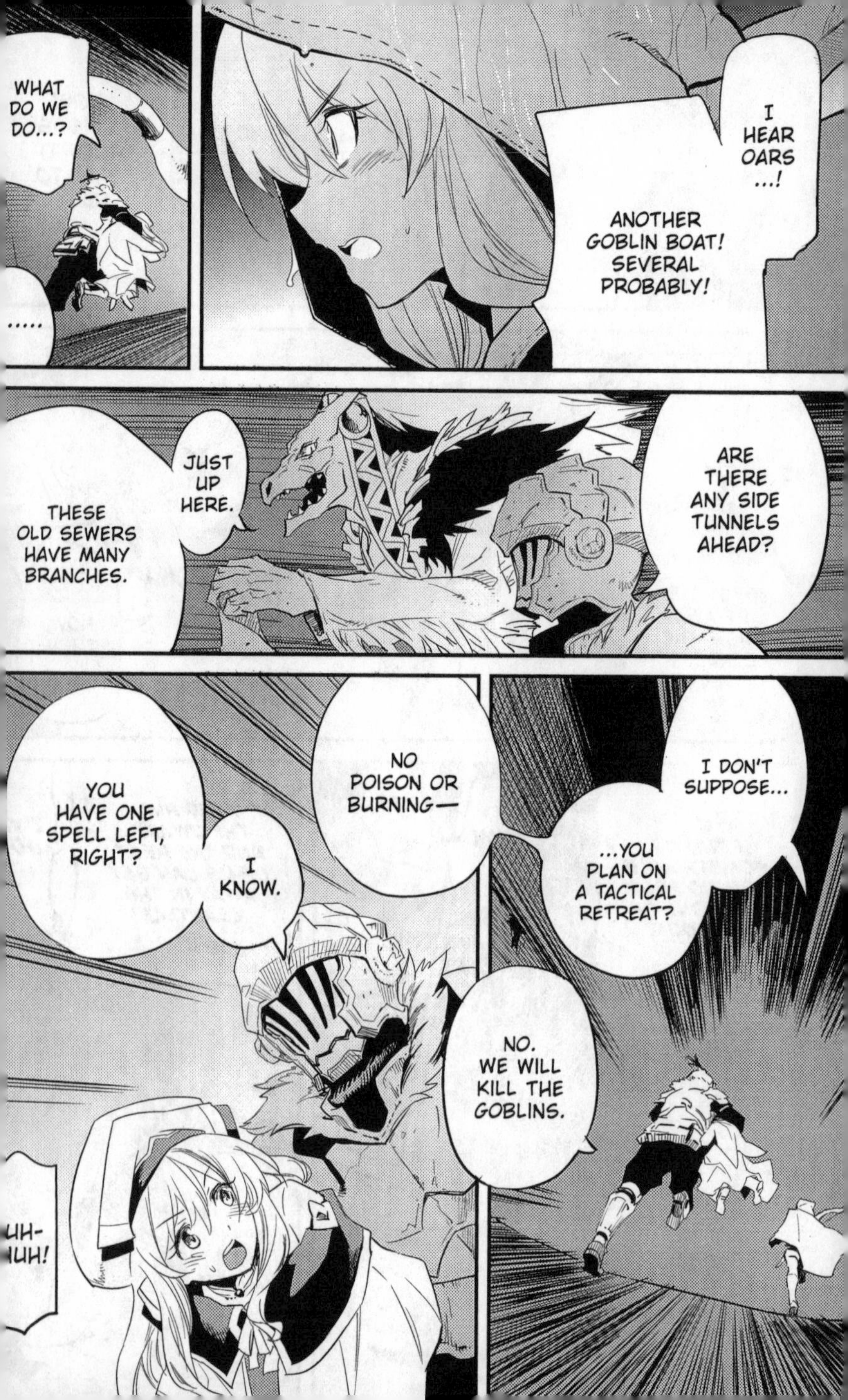

I HEAR OARS ...!
ANOTHER GOBLIN BOAT! SEVERAL PROBABLY!
WHAT DO WE DO...?
.....
ARE THERE ANY SIDE TUNNELS AHEAD?
JUST UP HERE.
THESE OLD SEWERS HAVE MANY BRANCHES.
I DON'T SUPPOSE...
...YOU PLAN ON A TACTICAL RETREAT?
NO. WE WILL KILL THE GOBLINS.
NO POISON OR BURNING—
YOU HAVE ONE SPELL LEFT, RIGHT?
I KNOW.
UH-HUH!

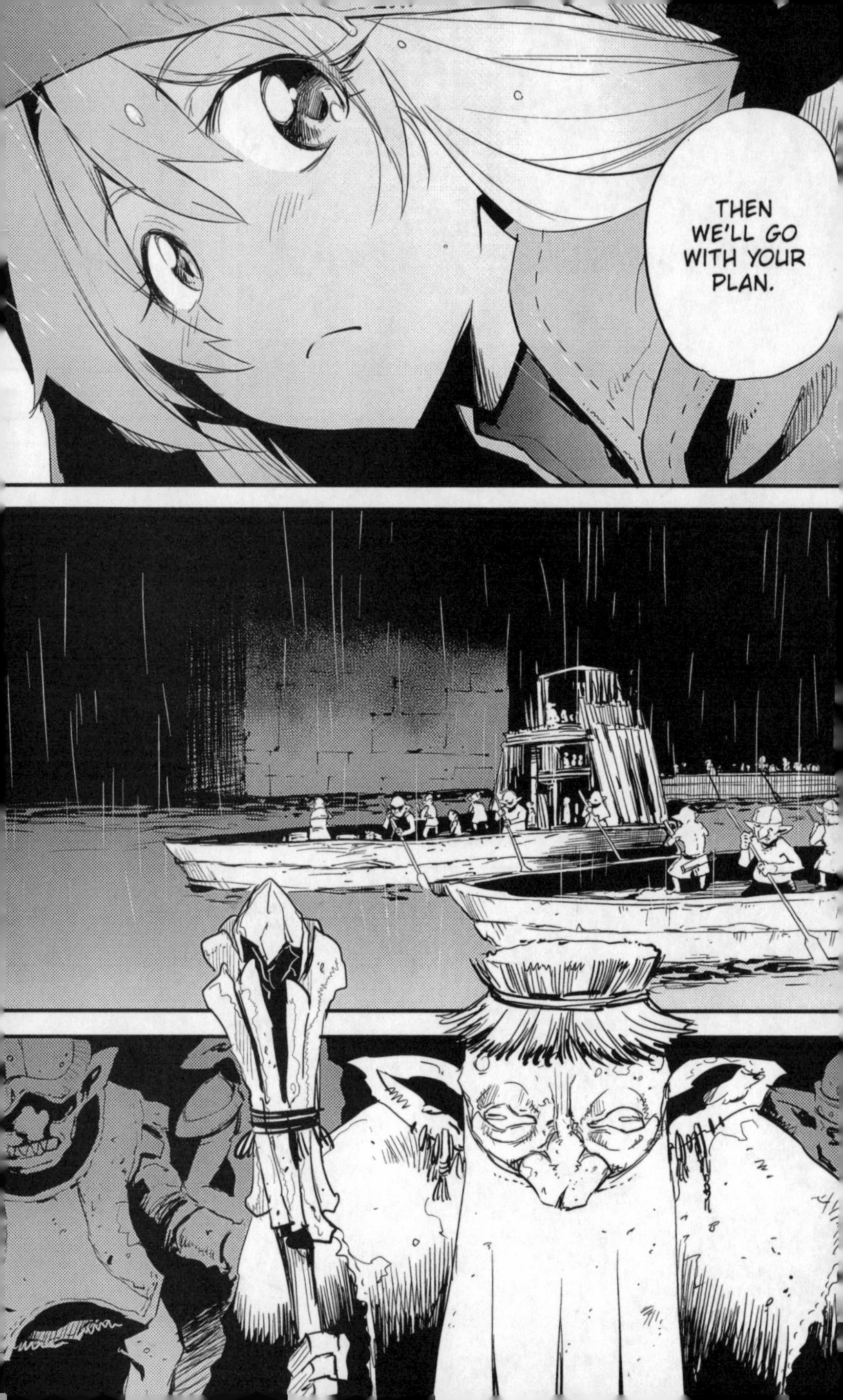
THEN WE'LL GO WITH YOUR PLAN.

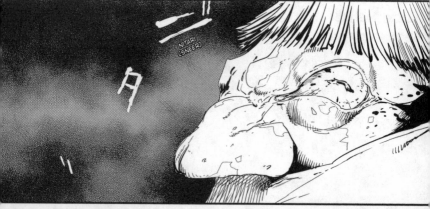

NITARI
(SNEER)

MEN! THAT IS THE LIGHT OF ADVENTURERS AHEAD!

THEY ARE WEARY FROM BATTLE!

AND SO SHALL MAKE EASY PREY FOR US!!

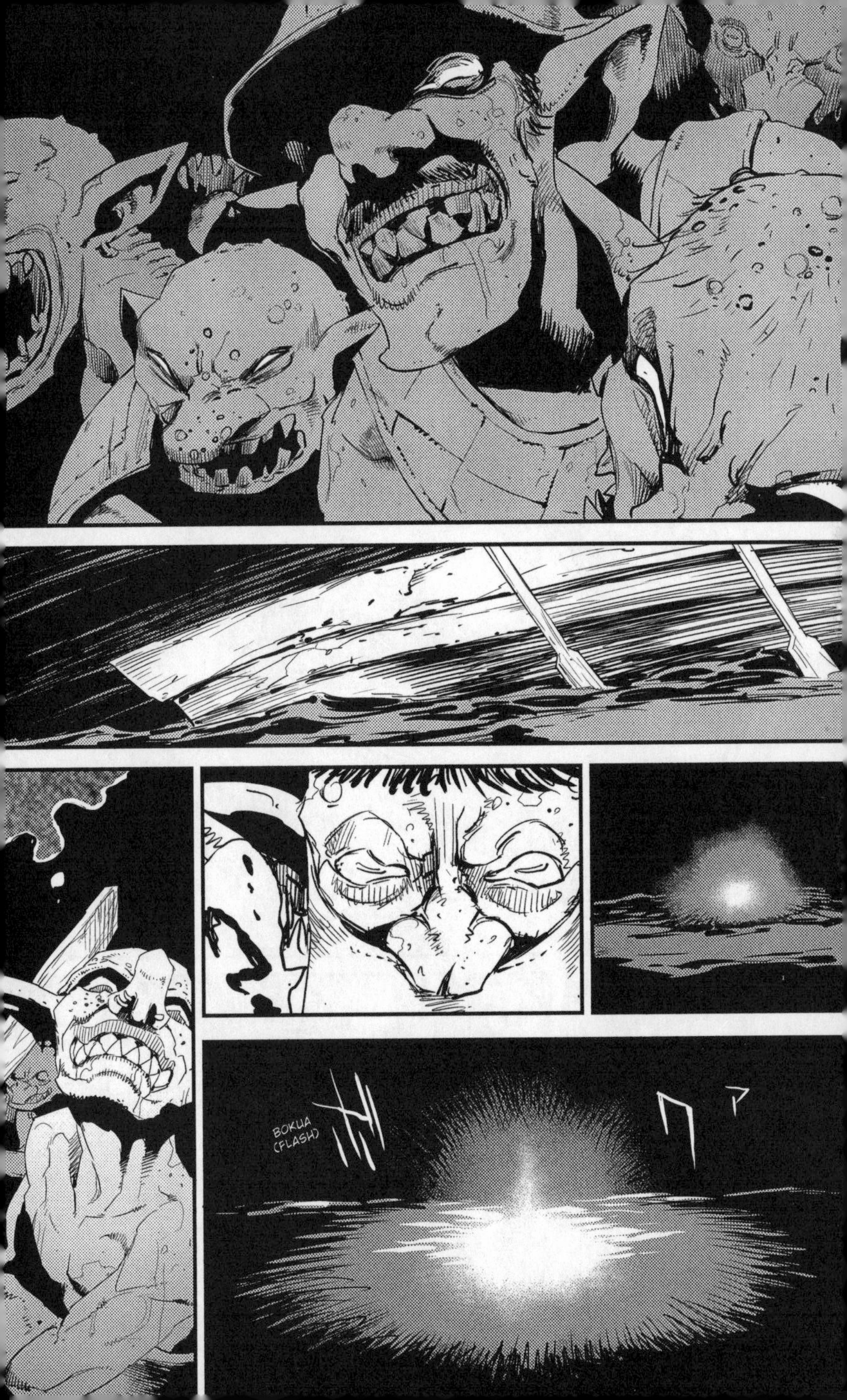
BOKUA (FLASH)

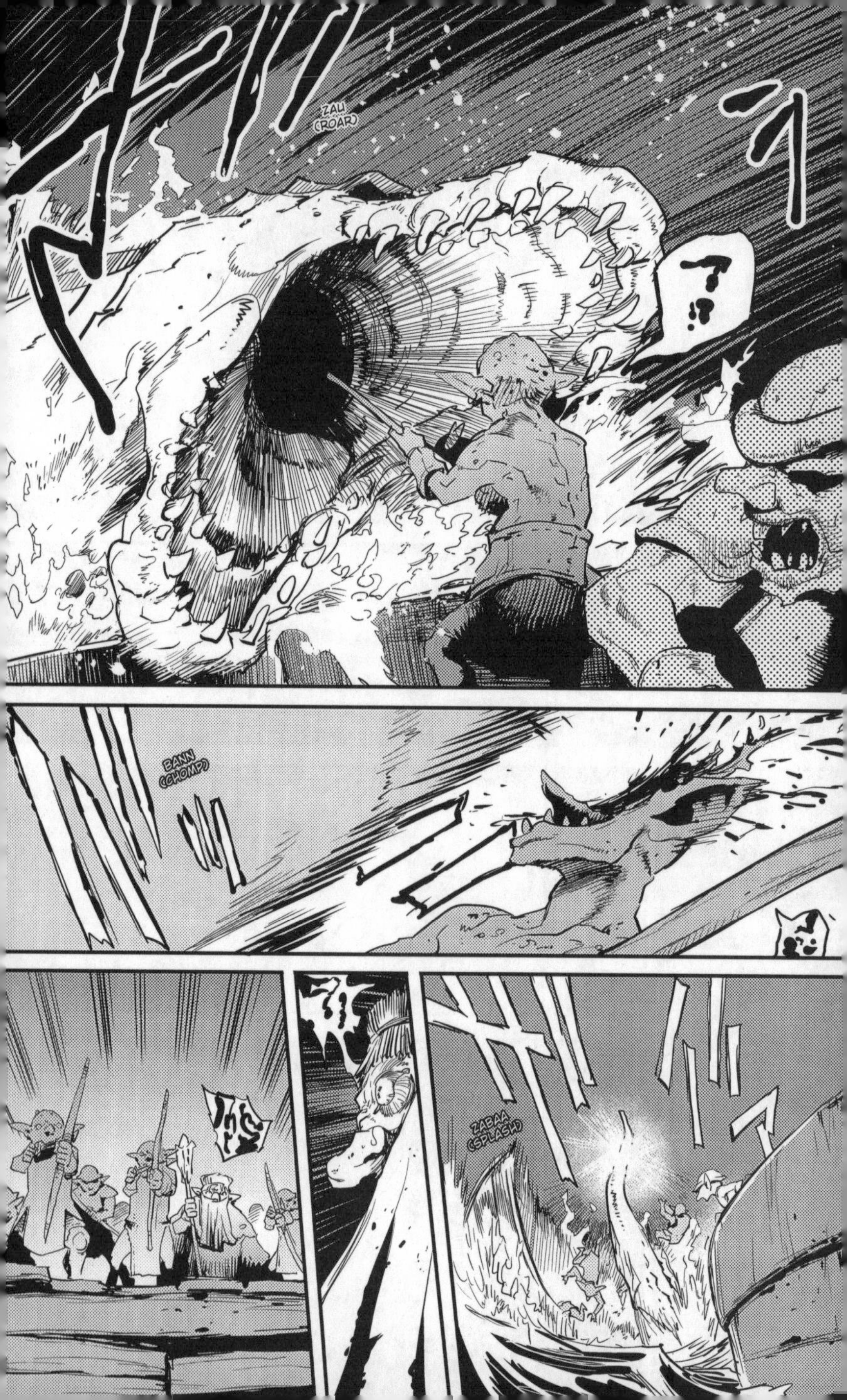
ZAU
(ROAR)
BANN
(CHOMP)
ZABAA
(SPLASH)

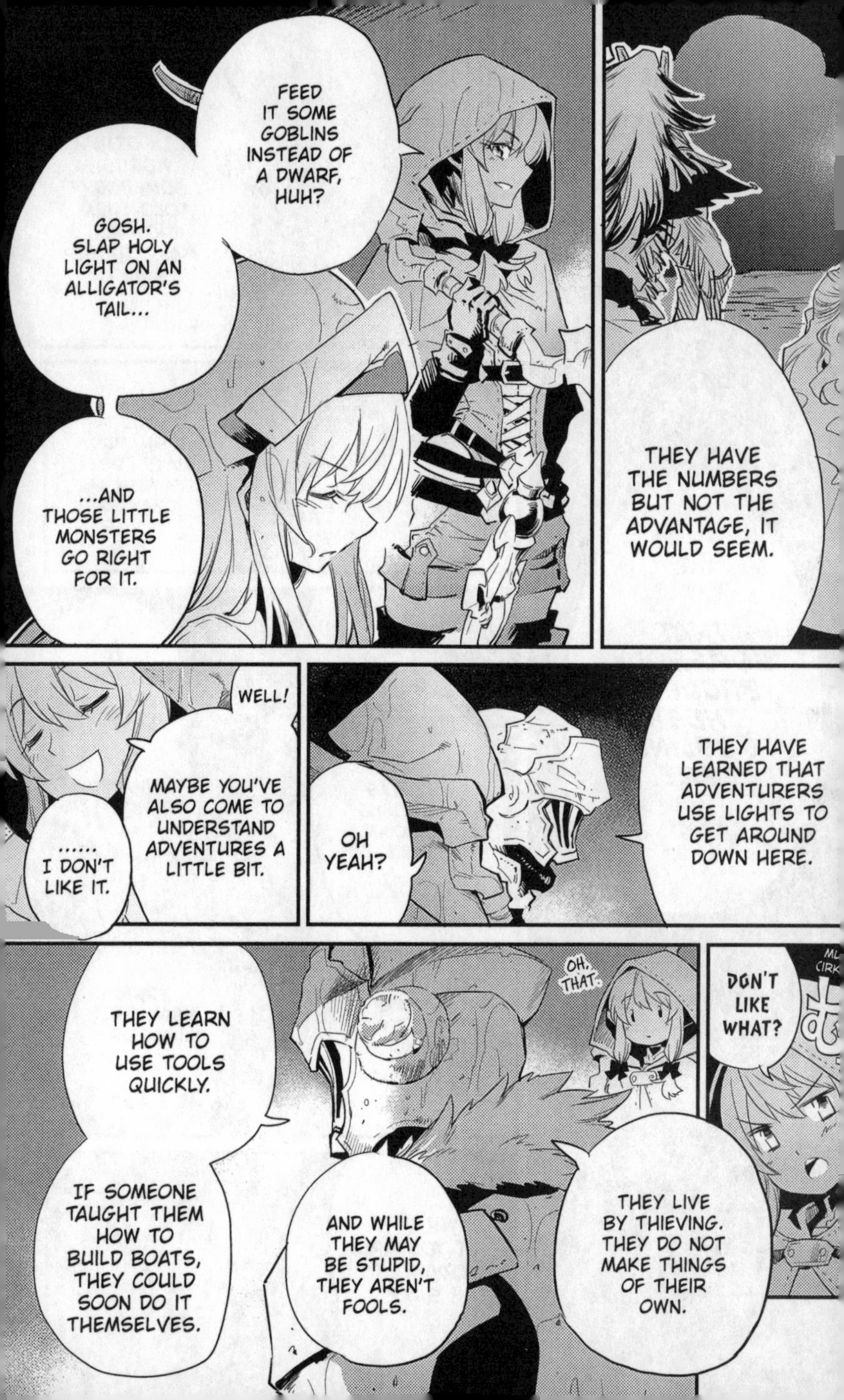
THEY HAVE THE NUMBERS BUT NOT THE ADVANTAGE, IT WOULD SEEM.
FEED IT SOME GOBLINS INSTEAD OF A DWARF, HUH?
GOSH. SLAP HOLY LIGHT ON AN ALLIGATOR'S TAIL...
...AND THOSE LITTLE MONSTERS GO RIGHT FOR IT.
THEY HAVE LEARNED THAT ADVENTURERS USE LIGHTS TO GET AROUND DOWN HERE.
OH YEAH?
WELL!
MAYBE YOU'VE ALSO COME TO UNDERSTAND ADVENTURES A LITTLE BIT.
...... I DON'T LIKE IT.
DON'T LIKE WHAT?
OH, THAT.
THEY LIVE BY THIEVING. THEY DO NOT MAKE THINGS OF THEIR OWN.
AND WHILE THEY MAY BE STUPID, THEY AREN'T FOOLS.
THEY LEARN HOW TO USE TOOLS QUICKLY.
IF SOMEONE TAUGHT THEM HOW TO BUILD BOATS, THEY COULD SOON DO IT THEMSELVES.

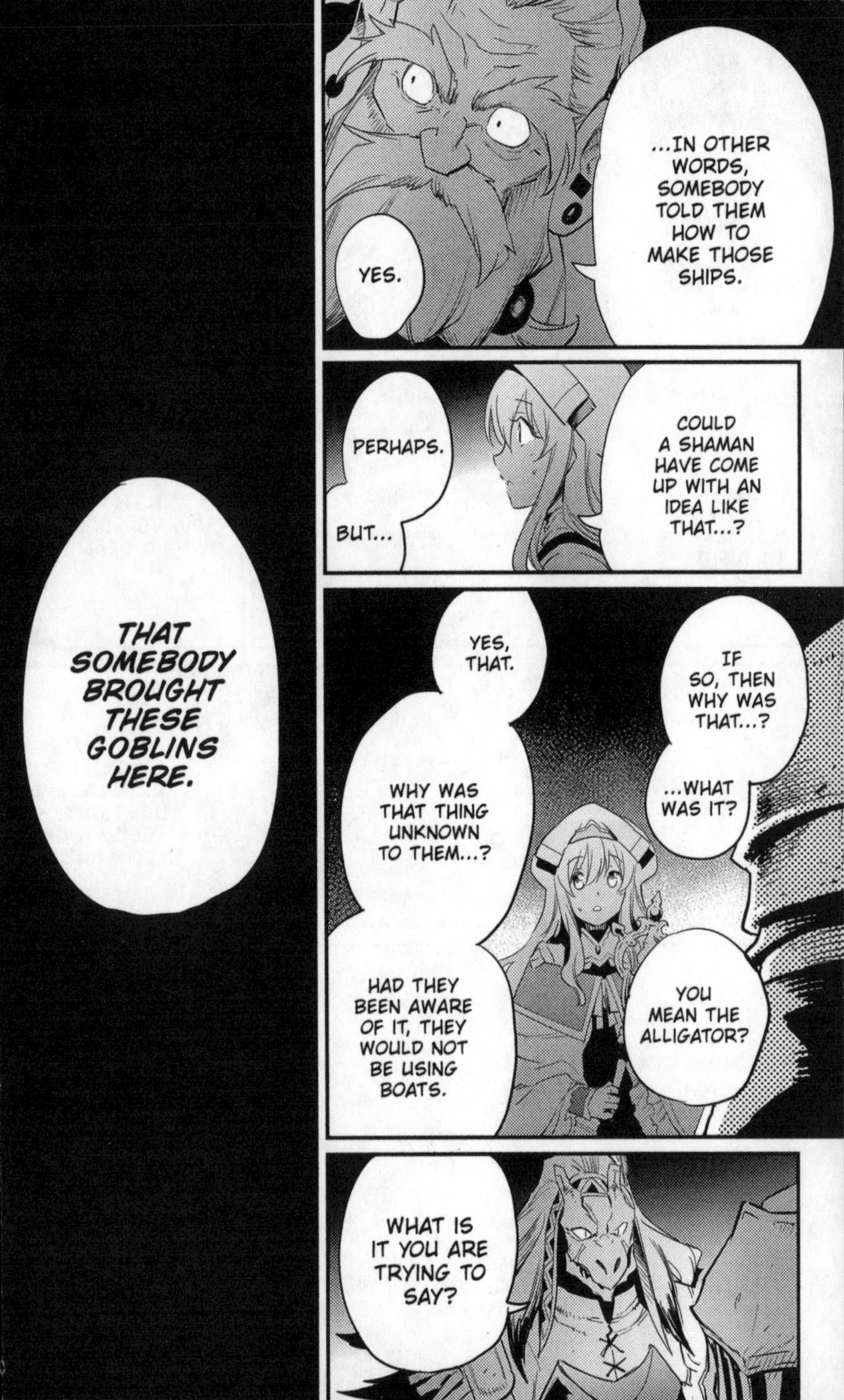
...IN OTHER WORDS, SOMEBODY TOLD THEM HOW TO MAKE THOSE SHIPS.
YES.
COULD A SHAMAN HAVE COME UP WITH AN IDEA LIKE THAT...?
PERHAPS.
BUT...
IF SO, THEN WHY WAS THAT...?
...WHAT WAS IT?
YOU MEAN THE ALLIGATOR?
YES, THAT.
WHY WAS THAT THING UNKNOWN TO THEM...?
HAD THEY BEEN AWARE OF IT, THEY WOULD NOT BE USING BOATS.
WHAT IS IT YOU ARE TRYING TO SAY?
THAT SOMEBODY BROUGHT THESE GOBLINS HERE.

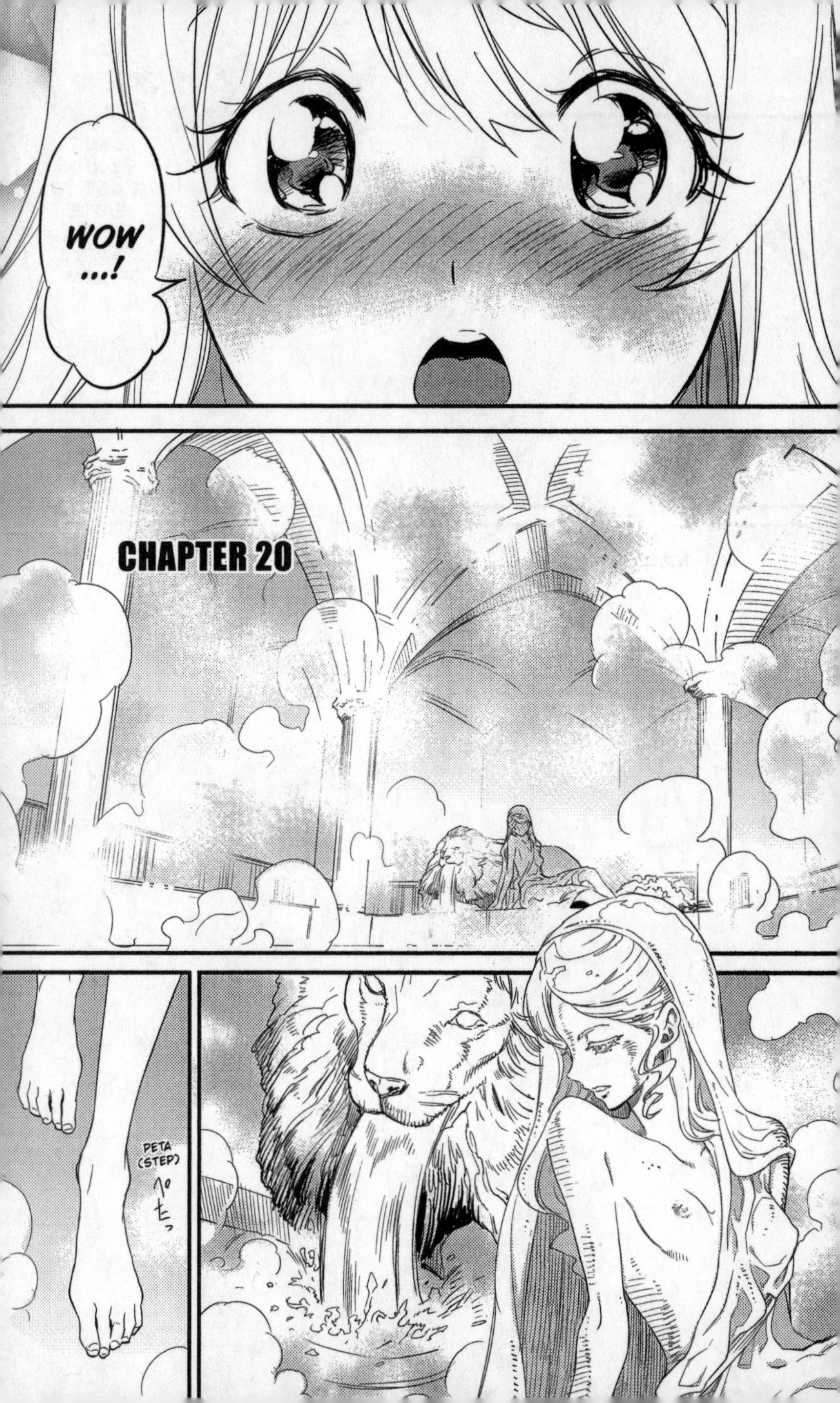
WOW ...!
CHAPTER 20
PETA (STEP)
ぺたっ

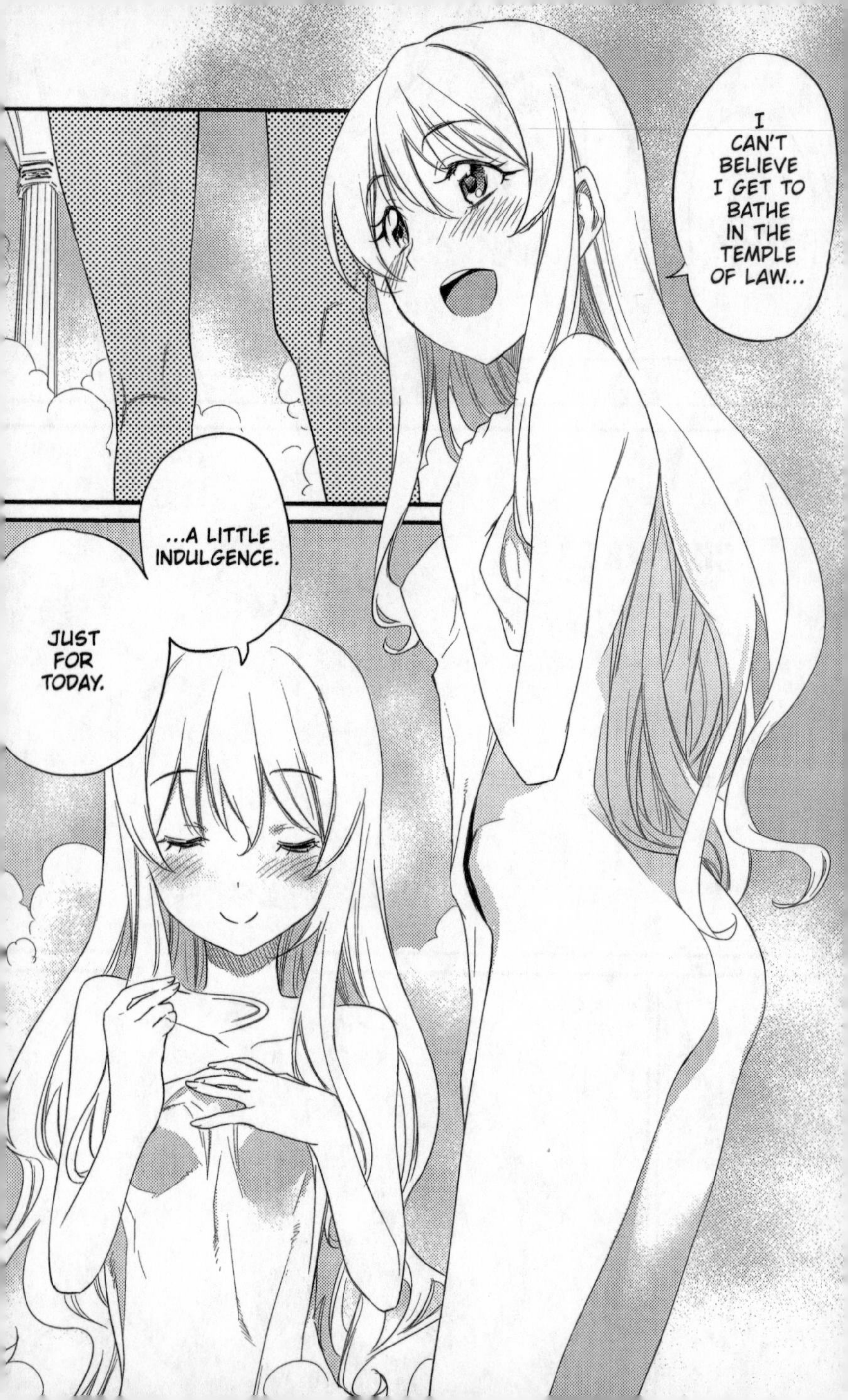
I CAN'T BELIEVE I GET TO BATHE IN THE TEMPLE OF LAW...
JUST FOR TODAY.
...A LITTLE INDULGENCE.

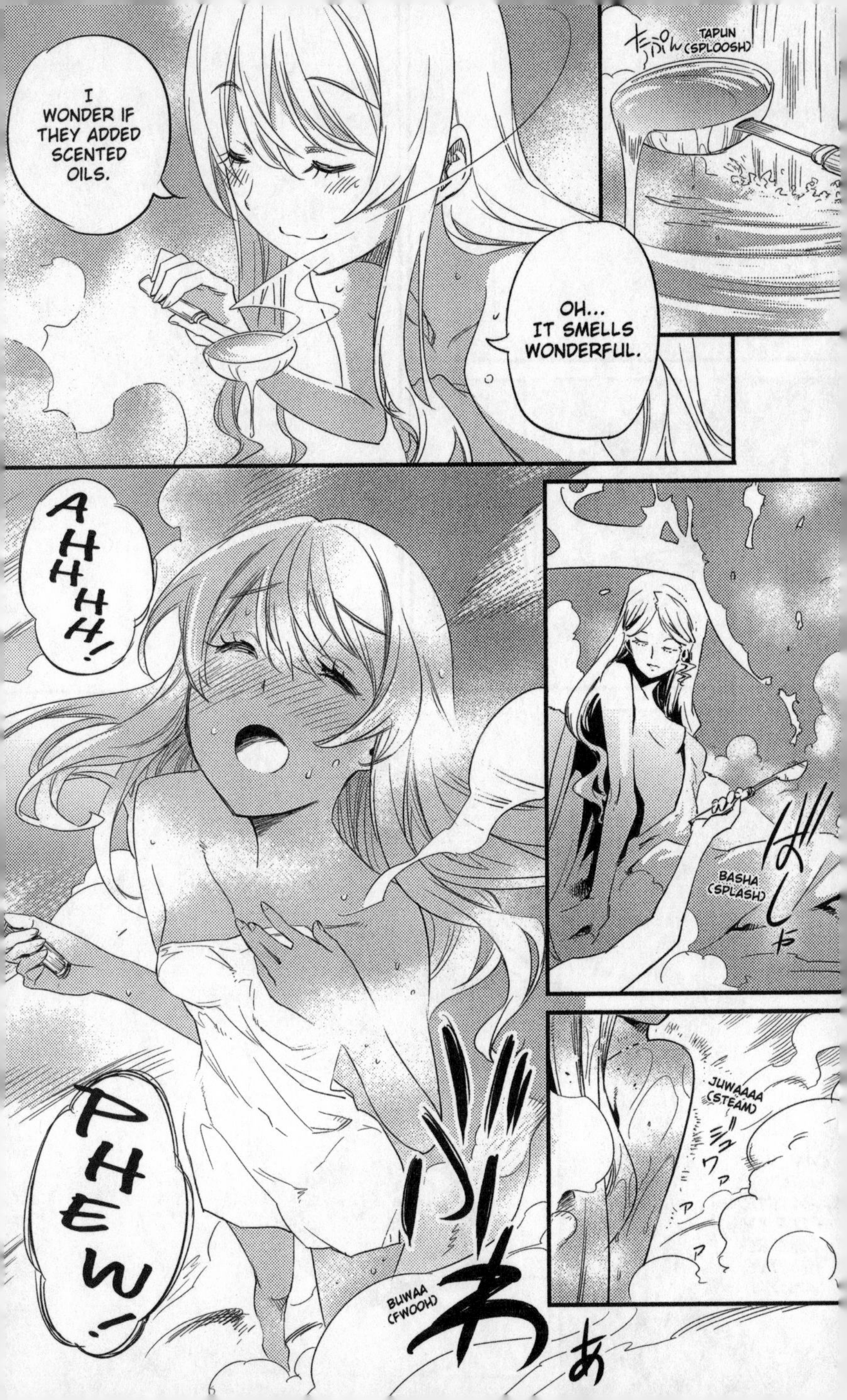
たぷん
TAPUN (SPLOOSH)
OH... IT SMELLS WONDERFUL.
I WONDER IF THEY ADDED SCENTED OILS.
ばしゃ
BASHA (SPLASH)
JUWAAAA (STEAM)
ジュワァァァ
AHHHH!
PHEW!
わぁ
BUWAA (FWOOH)

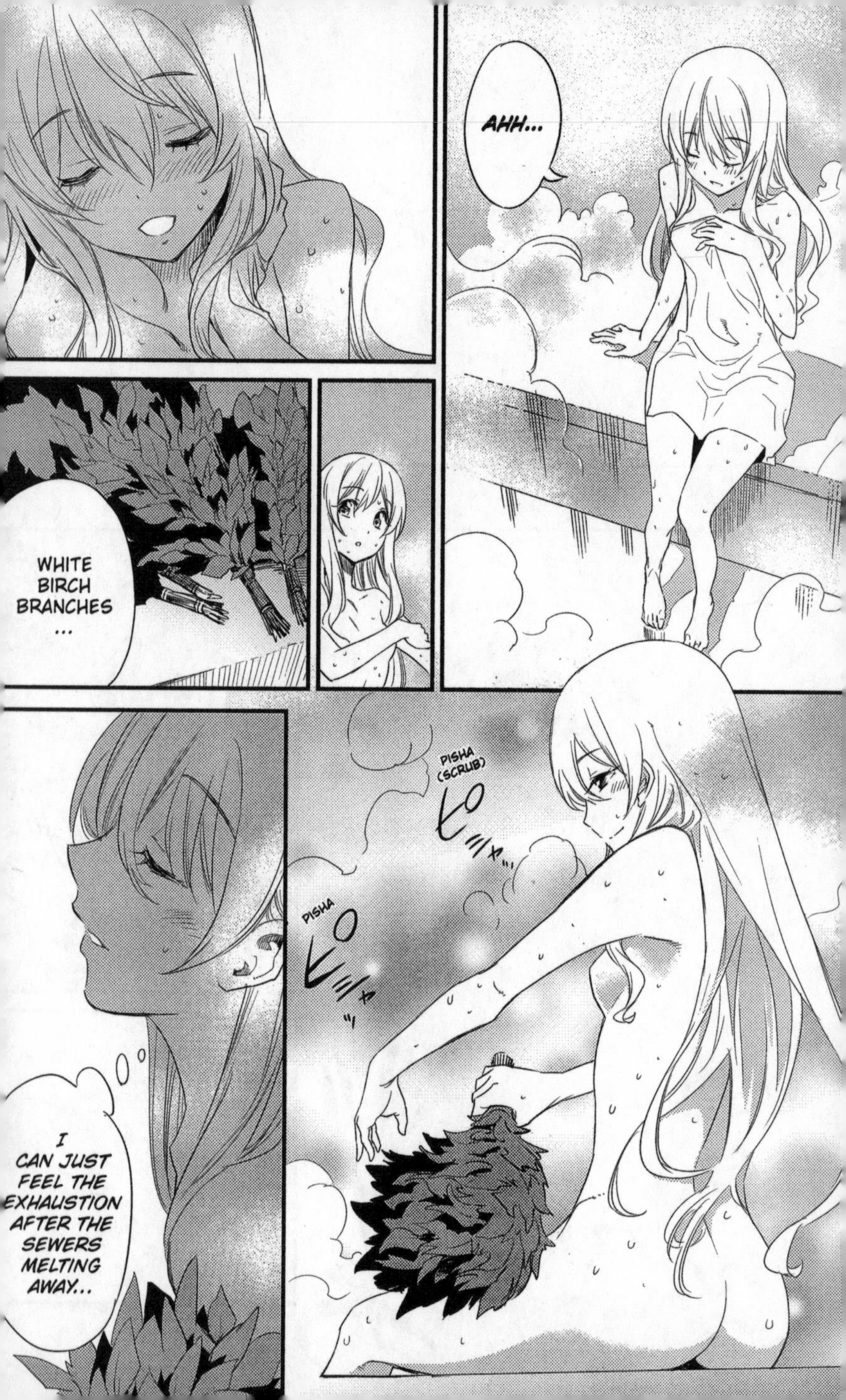
AHH...
WHITE BIRCH BRANCHES ...
PISHA (SCRUB)
PISHA
I CAN JUST FEEL THE EXHAUSTION AFTER THE SEWERS MELTING AWAY...

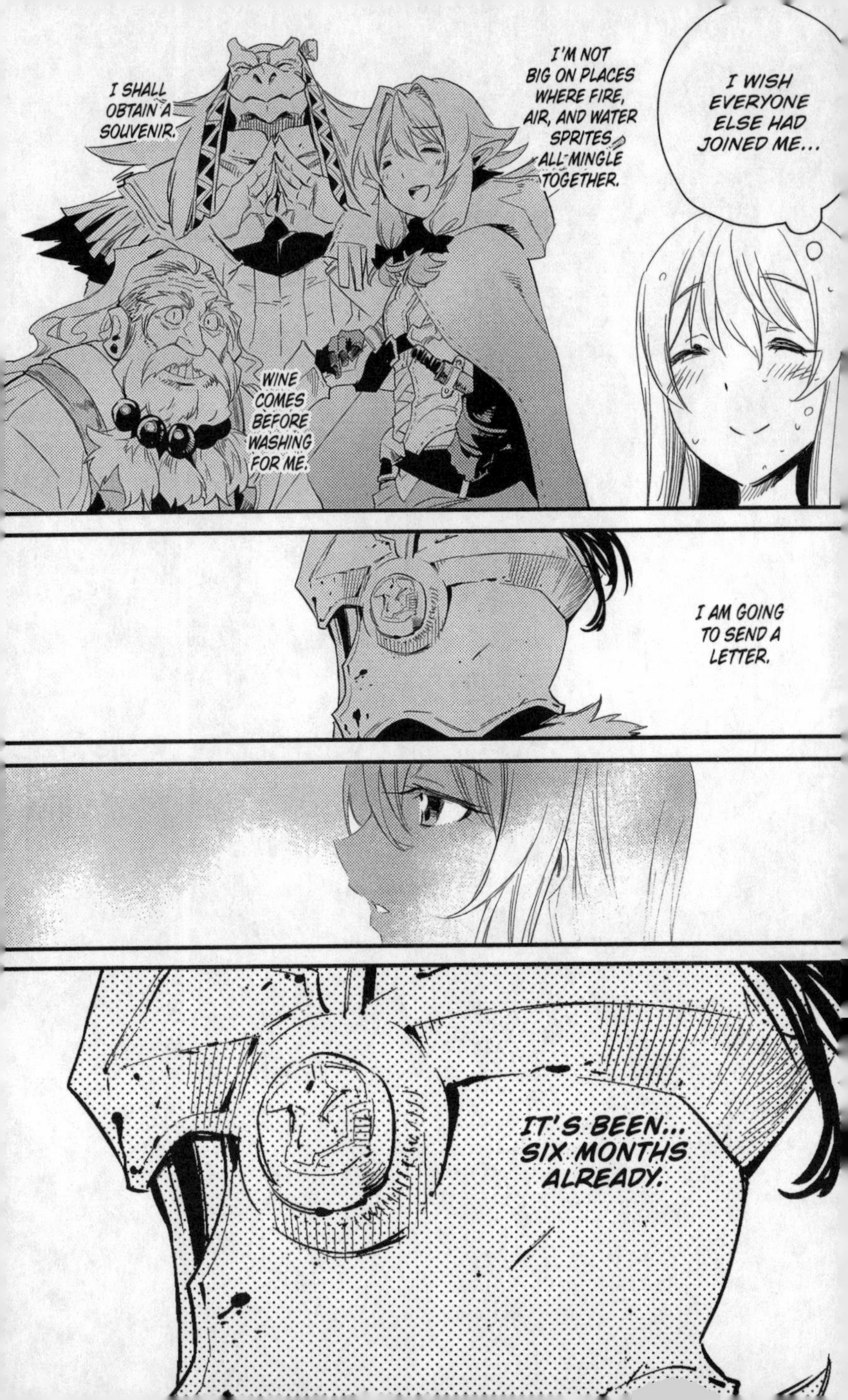
I WISH EVERYONE ELSE HAD JOINED ME...
I'M NOT BIG ON PLACES WHERE FIRE, AIR, AND WATER SPRITES ALL MINGLE TOGETHER.
I SHALL OBTAIN A SOUVENIR.
WINE COMES BEFORE WASHING FOR ME.
I AM GOING TO SEND A LETTER.
IT'S BEEN... SIX MONTHS ALREADY.

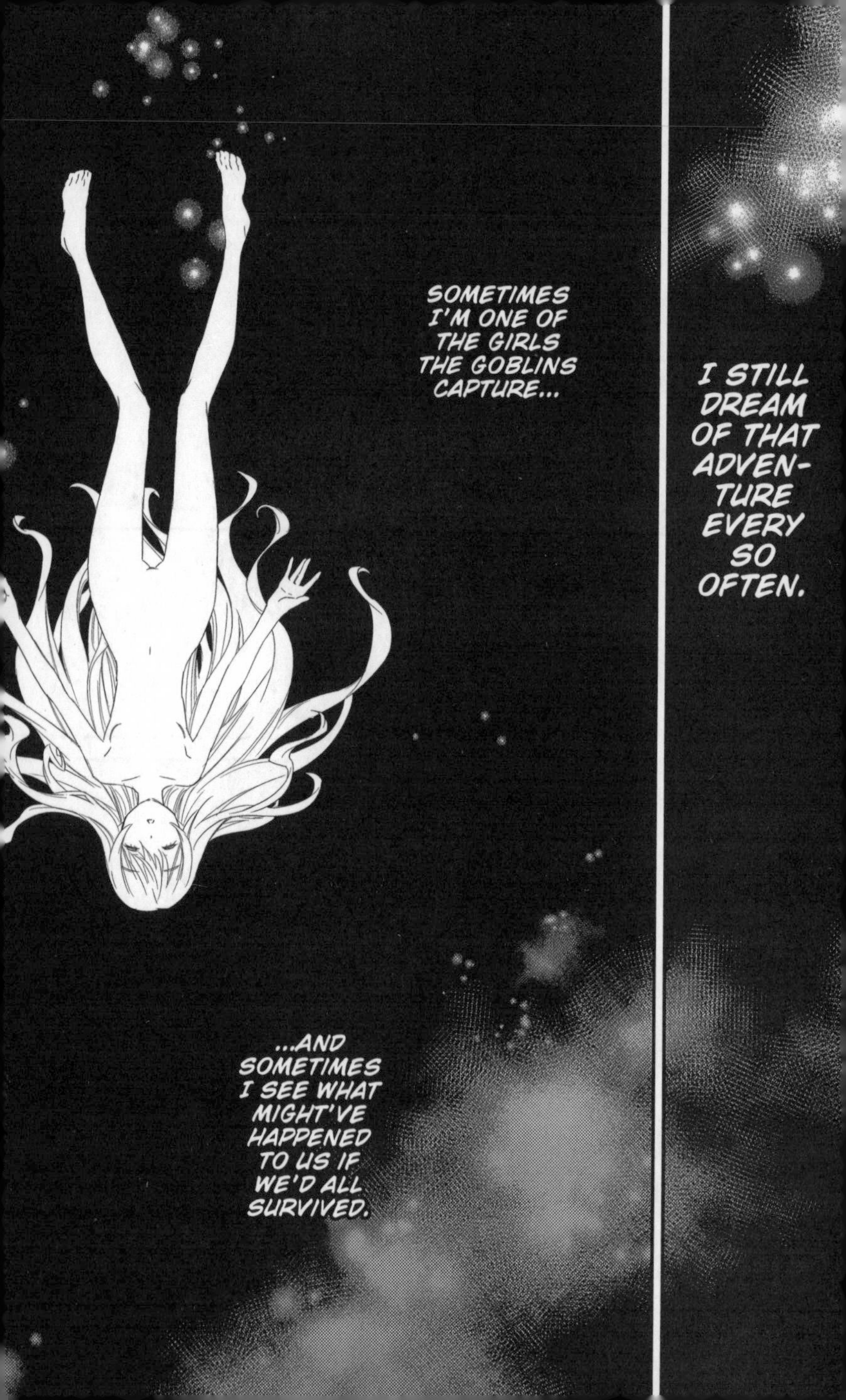
I STILL DREAM OF THAT ADVENTURE EVERY SO OFTEN.
SOMETIMES I'M ONE OF THE GIRLS THE GOBLINS CAPTURE...
...AND SOMETIMES I SEE WHAT MIGHT'VE HAPPENED TO US IF WE'D ALL SURVIVED.

IF I COULD HAVE HELPED US SUCCEED...
...I WOULDN'T HAVE MET THE FRIENDS I HAVE NOW.
I WOULDN'T HAVE VISITED THOSE RUINS OR FOUGHT THE GOBLIN LORD.
AND THE TOWN...
...MY FRIENDS ...
...HIM...
WHAT WOULD BE HAPPENING TO THEM?

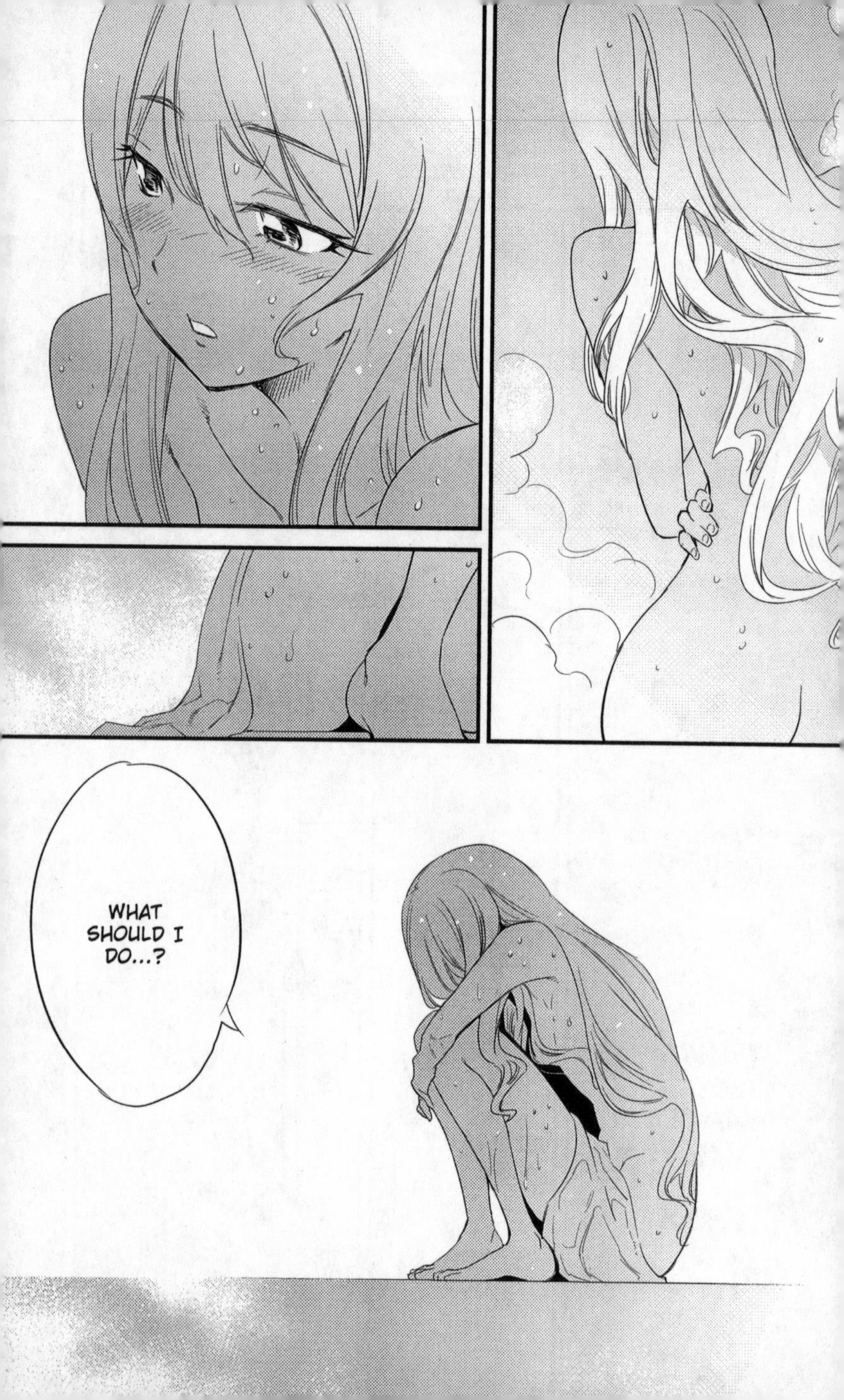
WHAT SHOULD I DO...?

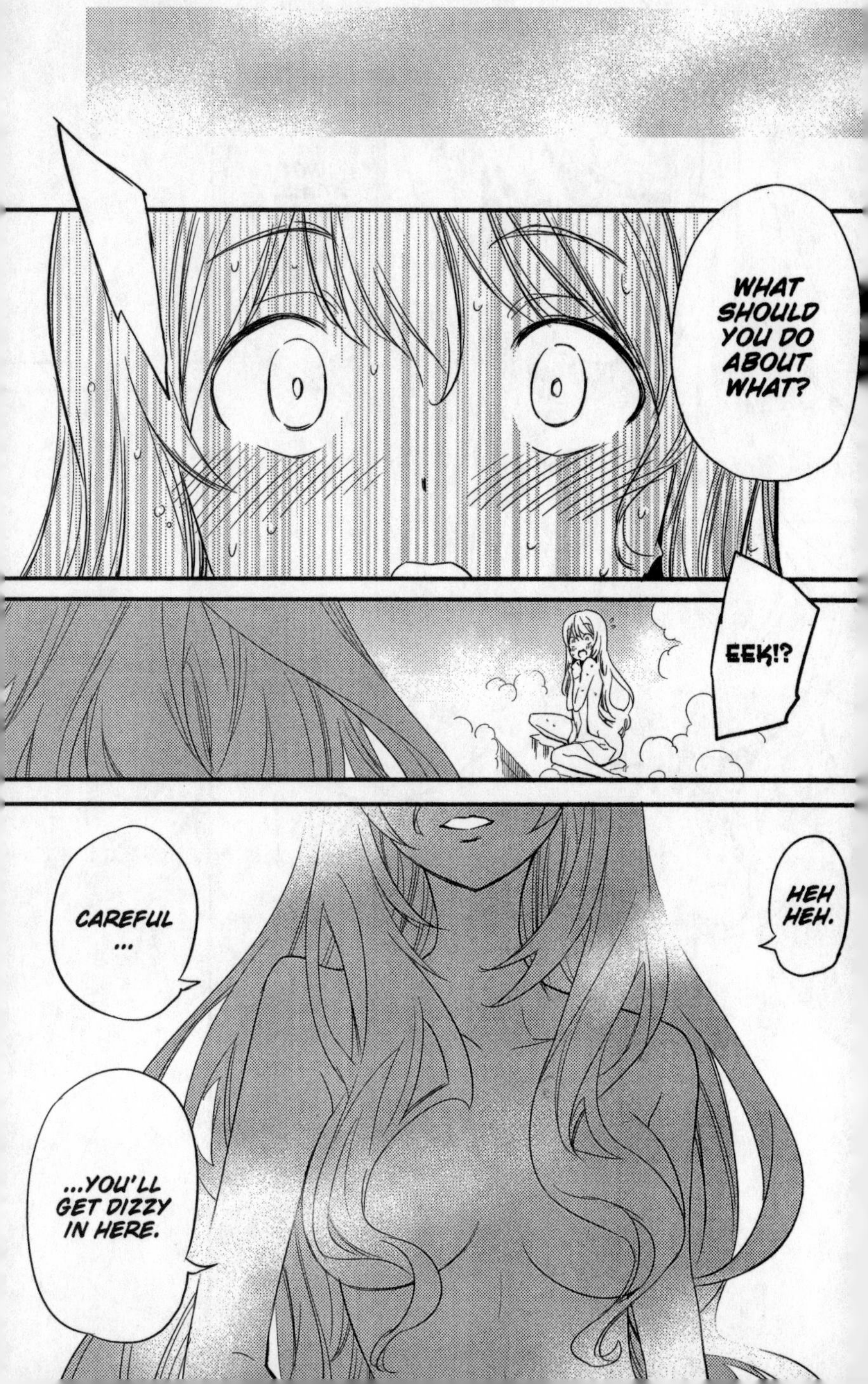
WHAT SHOULD YOU DO ABOUT WHAT?
EEK!?
HEH HEH.
CAREFUL ...
...YOU'LL GET DIZZY IN HERE.

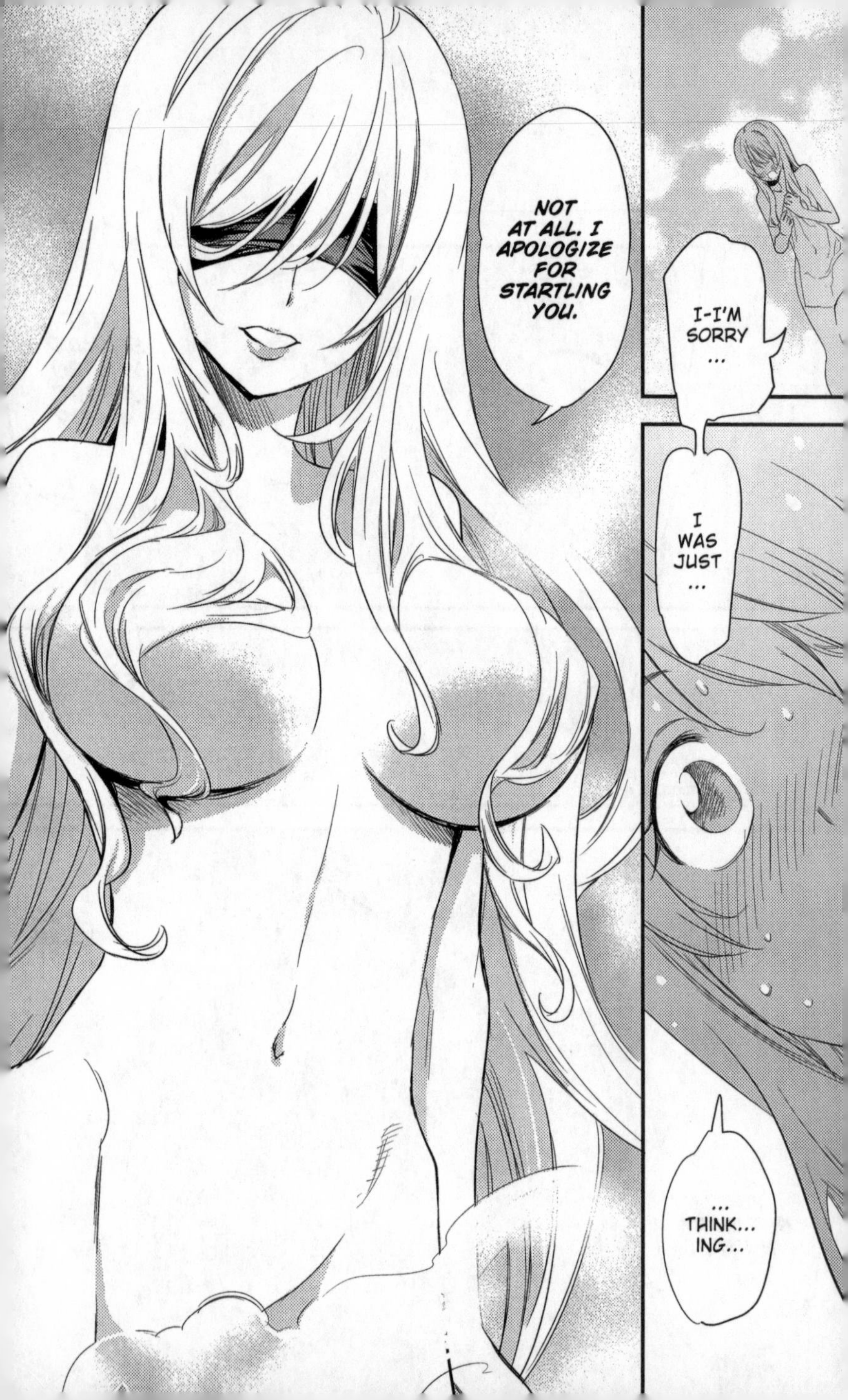
I-I'M SORRY ...
I WAS JUST ...
... THINK... ING...
NOT AT ALL. I APOLOGIZE FOR STARTLING YOU.

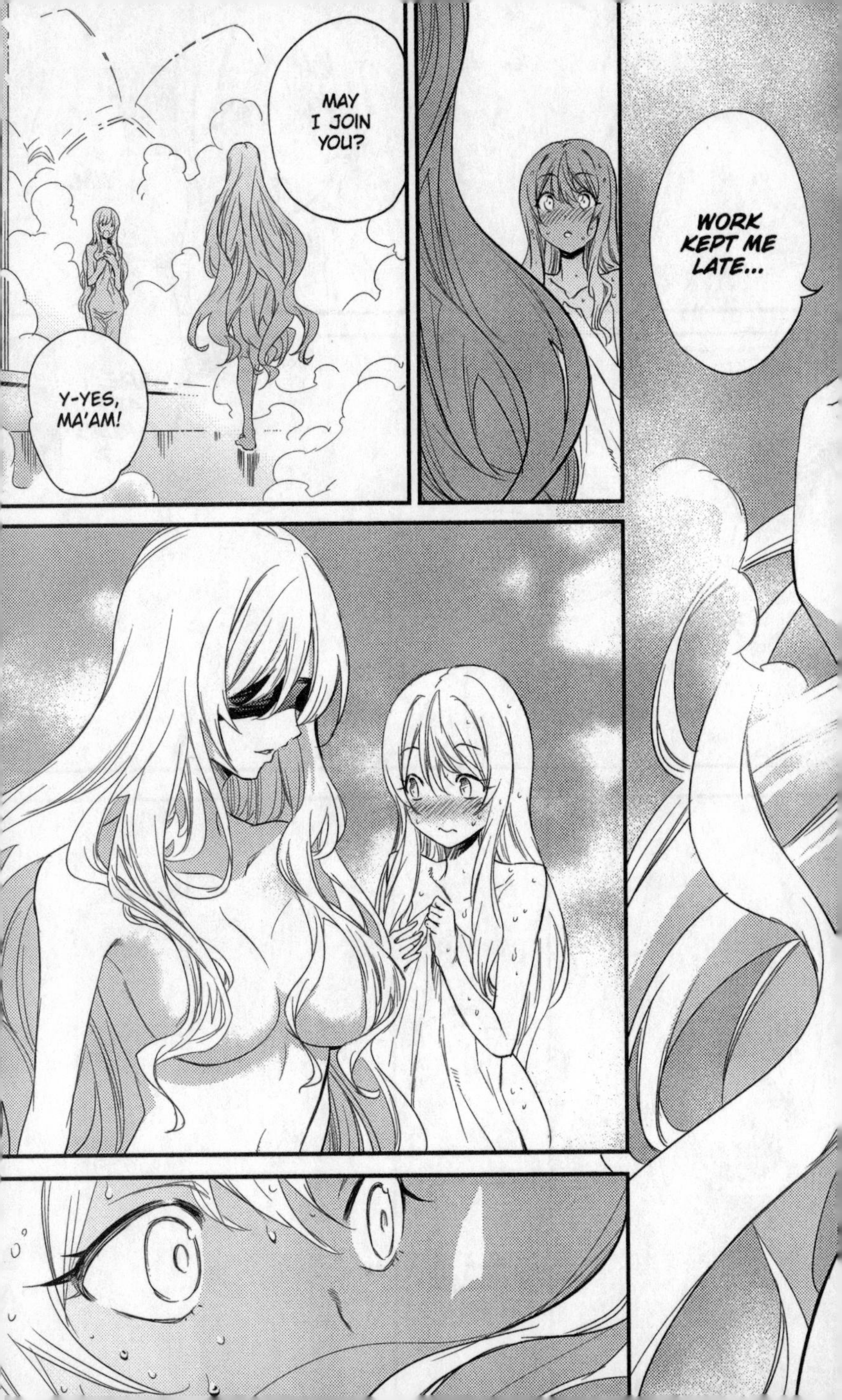
WORK KEPT ME LATE...
MAY I JOIN YOU?
Y-YES, MA'AM!

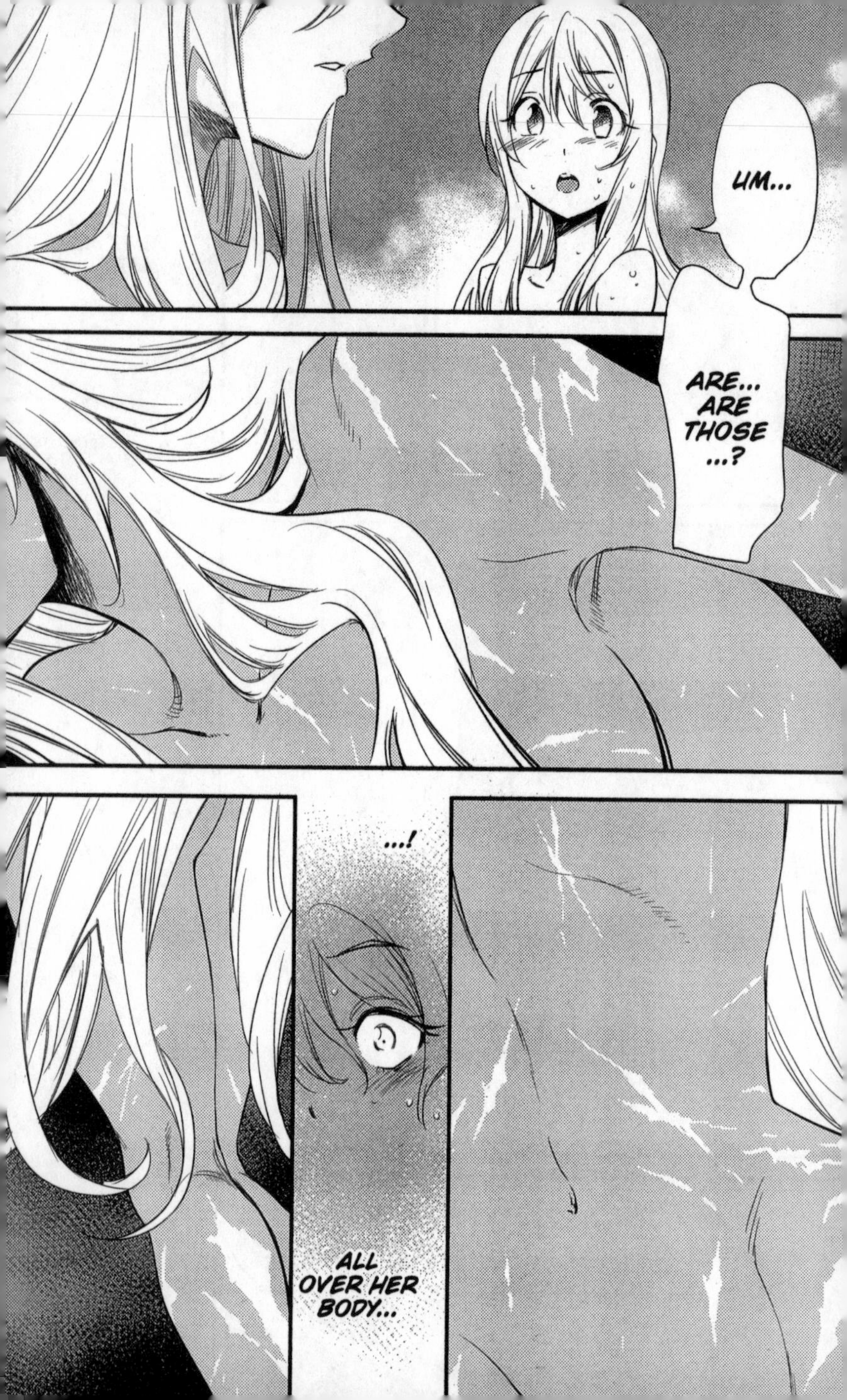
UM...
ARE... ARE THOSE ...?
...!
ALL OVER HER BODY...

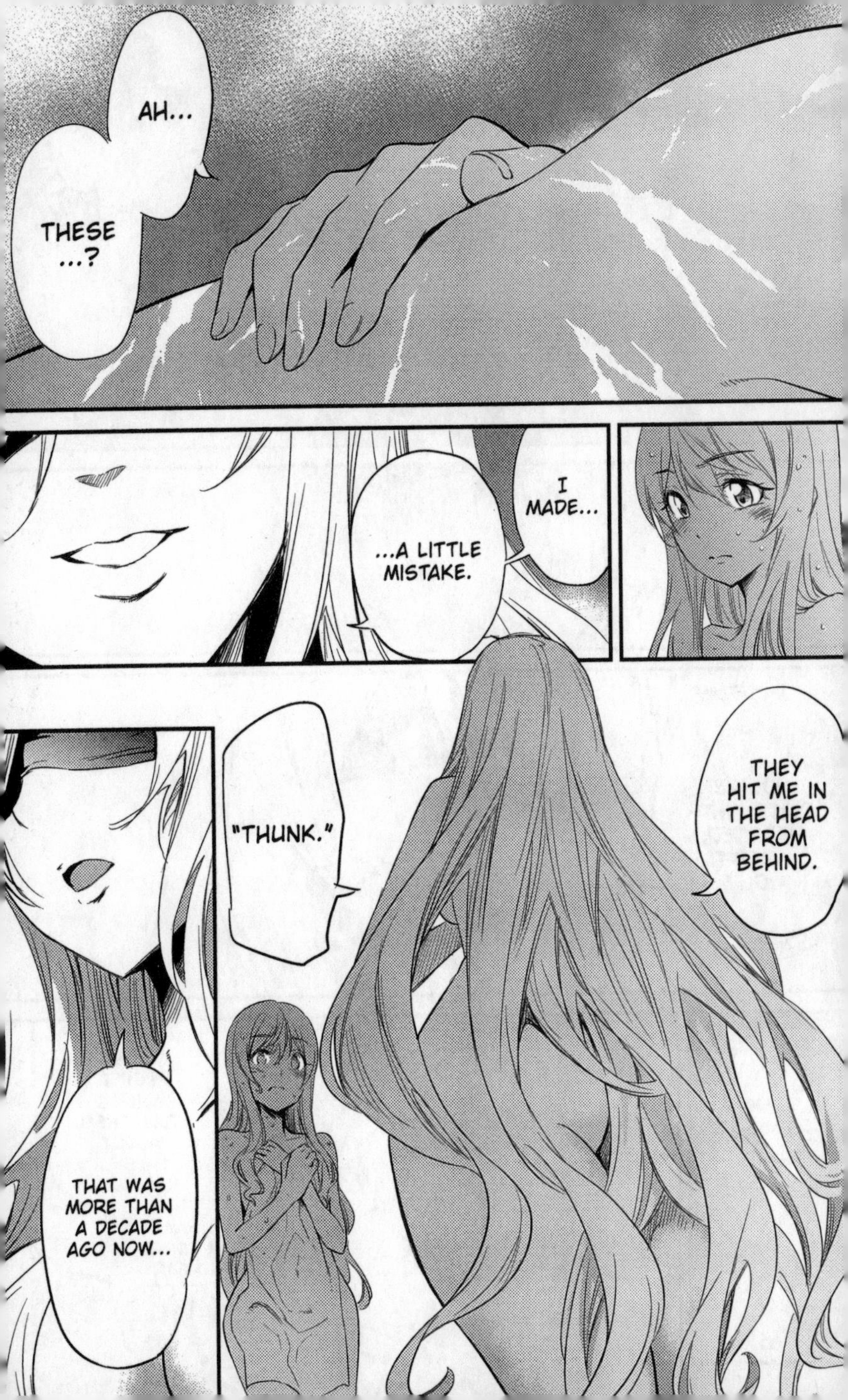
AH...
THESE ...?
I MADE...
...A LITTLE MISTAKE.
THEY HIT ME IN THE HEAD FROM BEHIND.
"THUNK."
THAT WAS MORE THAN A DECADE AGO NOW...

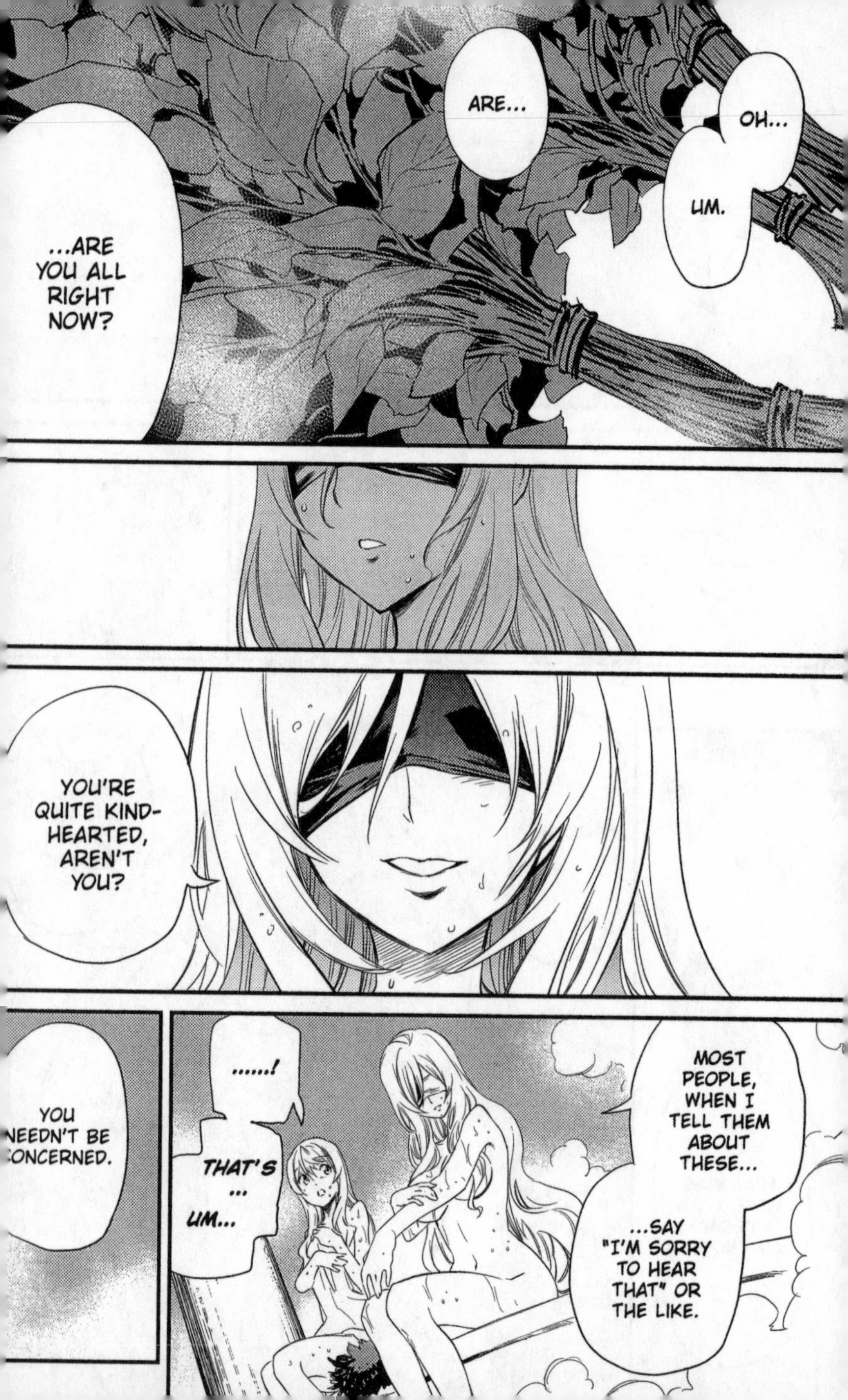
OH...
UM.
ARE...
...ARE YOU ALL RIGHT NOW?
YOU'RE QUITE KIND-HEARTED, AREN'T YOU?
MOST PEOPLE, WHEN I TELL THEM ABOUT THESE...
...SAY "I'M SORRY TO HEAR THAT" OR THE LIKE.
......!
THAT'S ... UM...
YOU NEEDN'T BE CONCERNED.

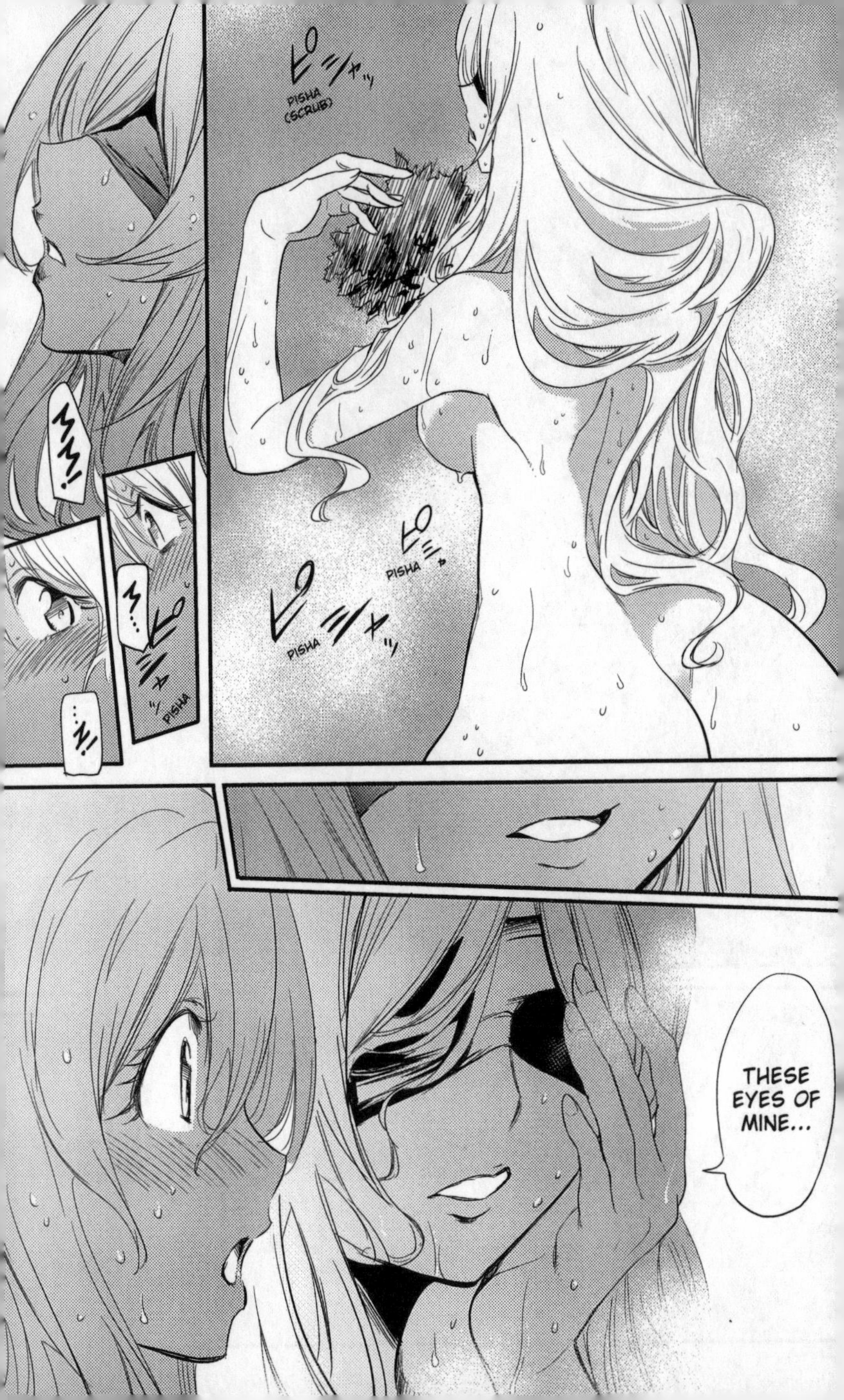

PISHA (SCRUB)
PISHA
PISHA
MM!
M...
PISHA
...N!
THESE EYES OF MINE...

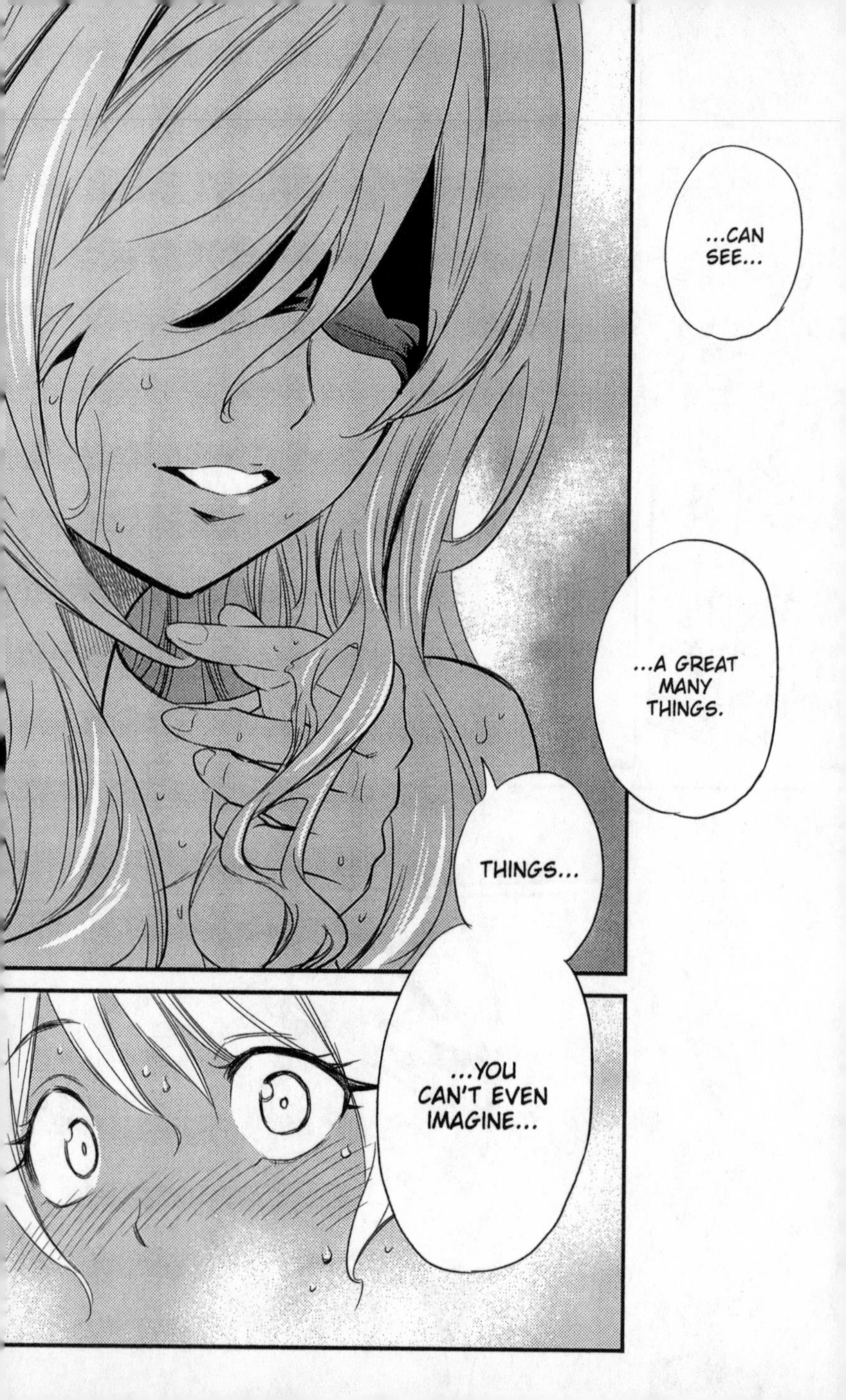

...CAN SEE...
...A GREAT MANY THINGS.
THINGS...
...YOU CAN'T EVEN IMAGINE...

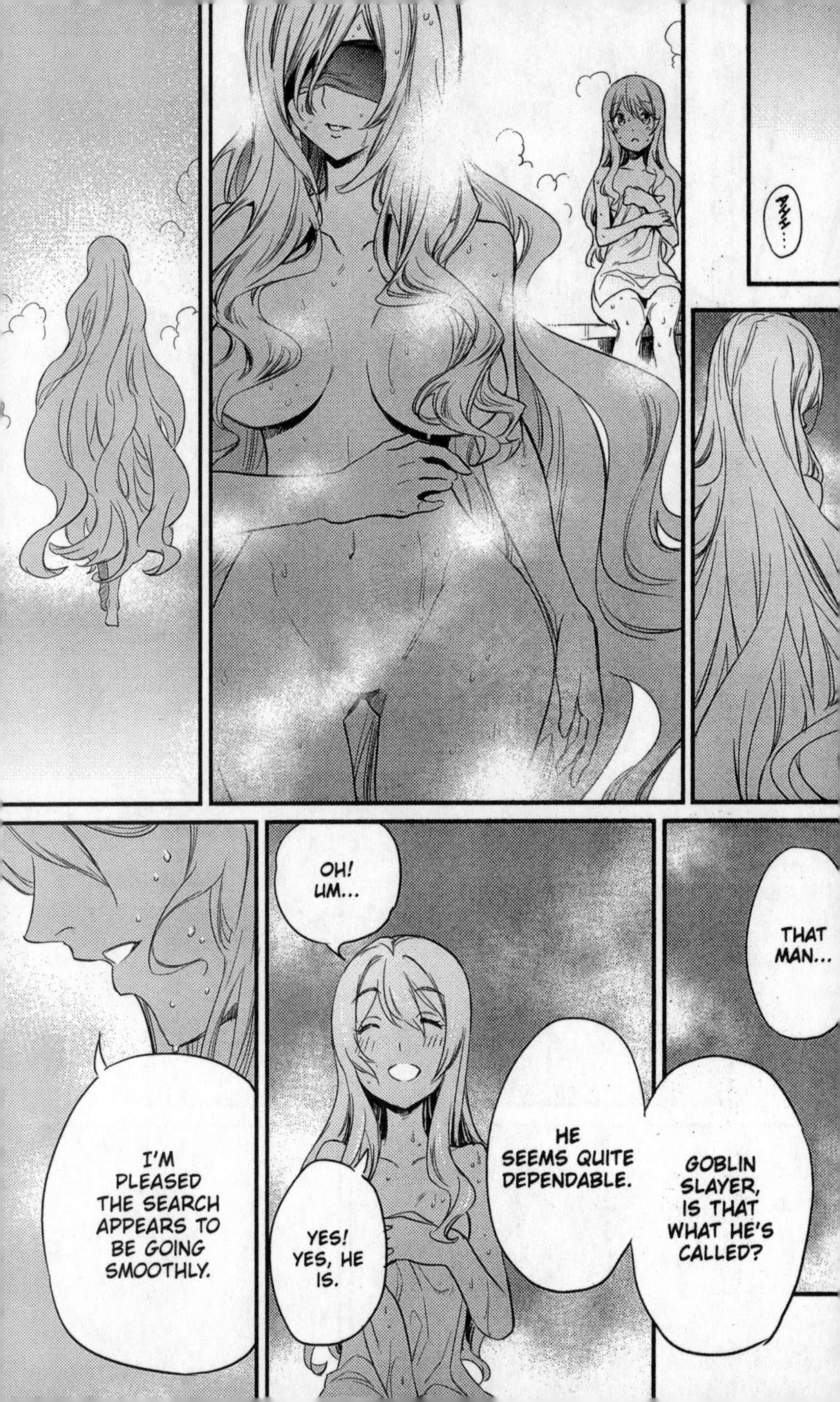
AHH...
THAT MAN...
GOBLIN SLAYER, IS THAT WHAT HE'S CALLED?
HE SEEMS QUITE DEPENDABLE.
OH! UM...
YES! YES, HE IS.
I'M PLEASED THE SEARCH APPEARS TO BE GOING SMOOTHLY.

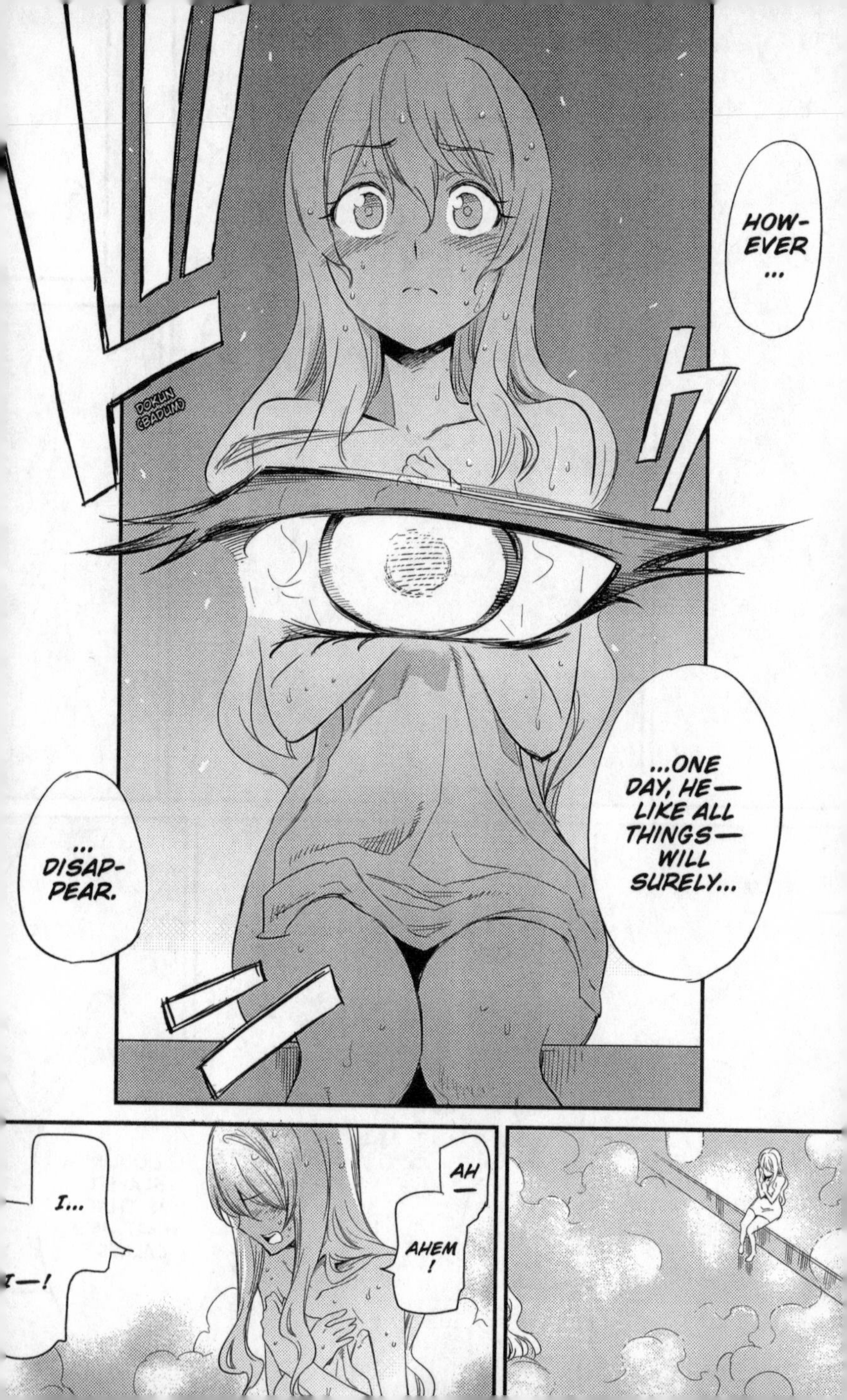
HOW-EVER...
DOKUN (BADUM)
...ONE DAY, HE—LIKE ALL THINGS—WILL SURELY...
...DISAPPEAR.
AH—
I...
AHEM!
I—!

YES.

SHE
KNOWS
...

YOU'D
BEST GET
OUT OF THE
BATH BEFORE
YOU GET
DIZZY.

SHE
KNOWS...

THAT
WOMAN...

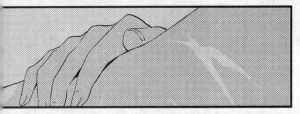

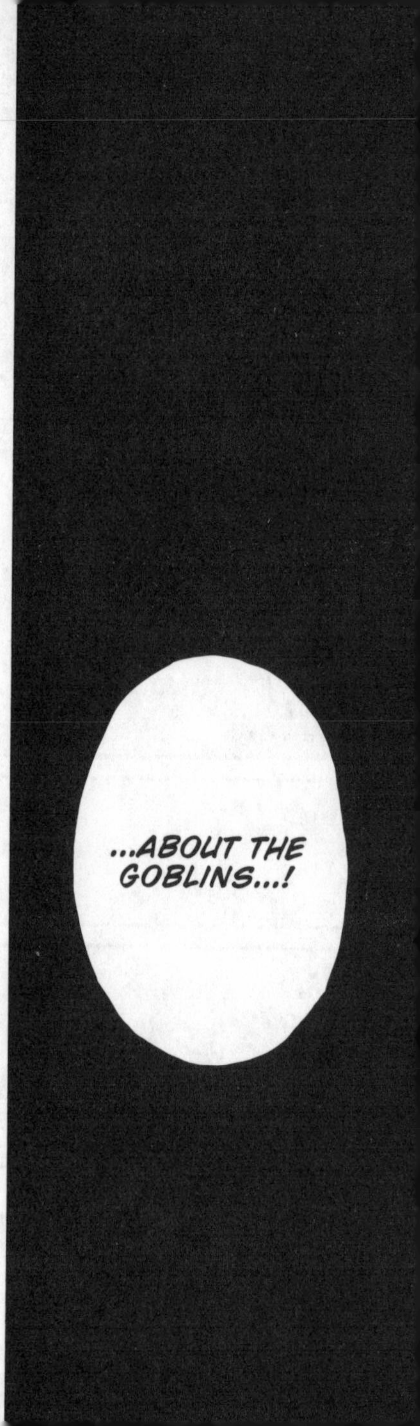
...ABOUT THE GOBLINS...!

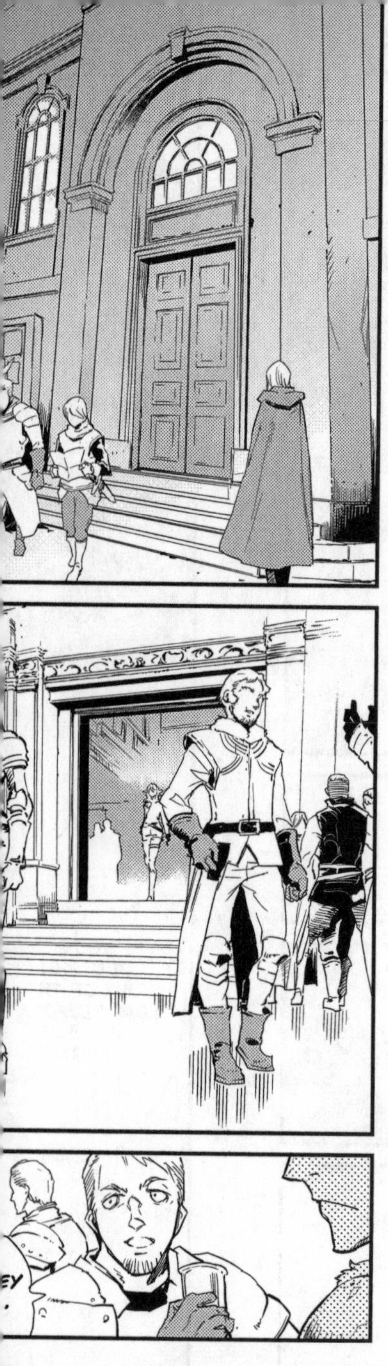

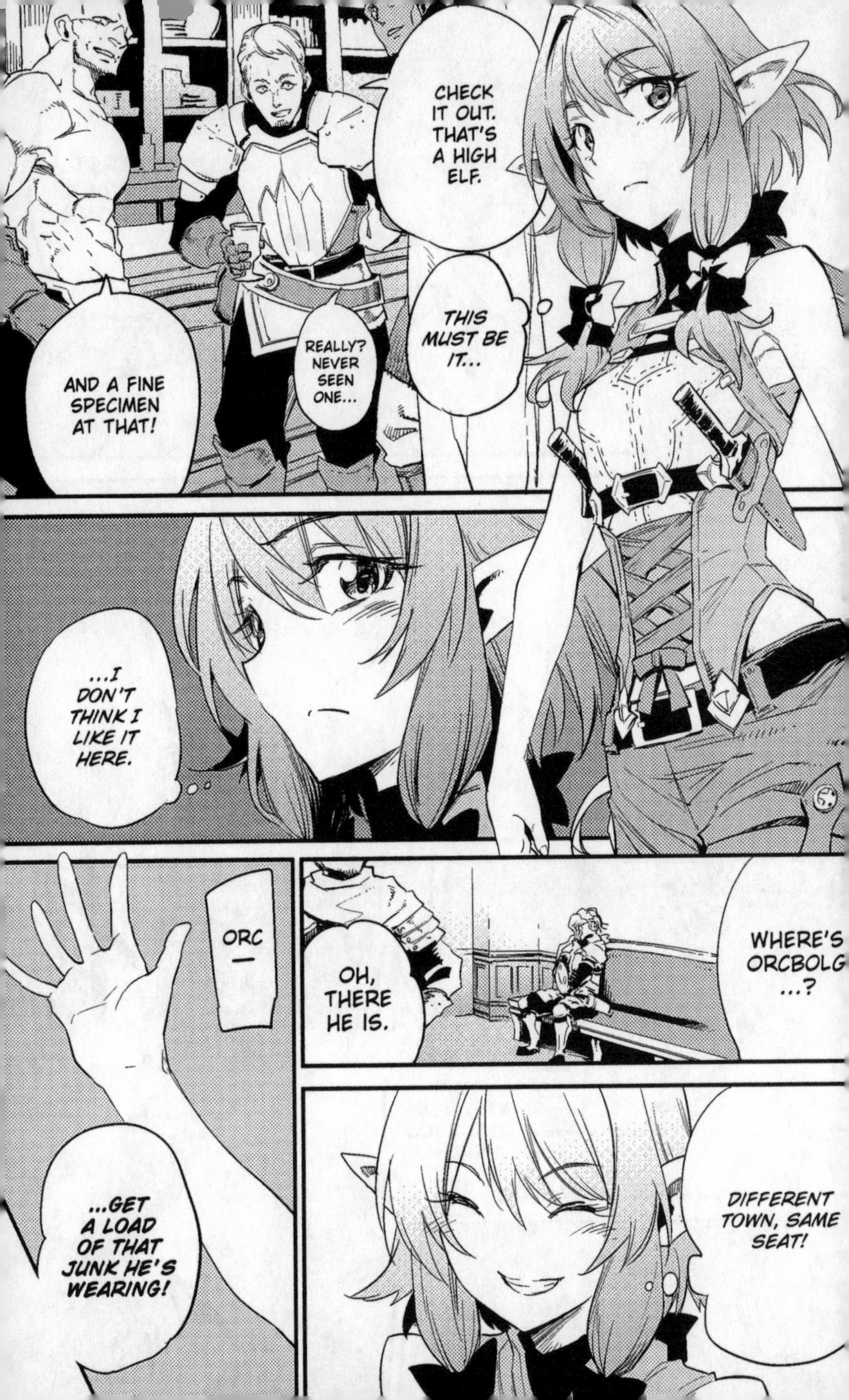
CHECK IT OUT. THAT'S A HIGH ELF.
THIS MUST BE IT...
REALLY? NEVER SEEN ONE...
AND A FINE SPECIMEN AT THAT!
...I DON'T THINK I LIKE IT HERE.
WHERE'S ORCBOLG ...?
OH, THERE HE IS.
DIFFERENT TOWN, SAME SEAT!
ORC—
...GET A LOAD OF THAT JUNK HE'S WEARING!

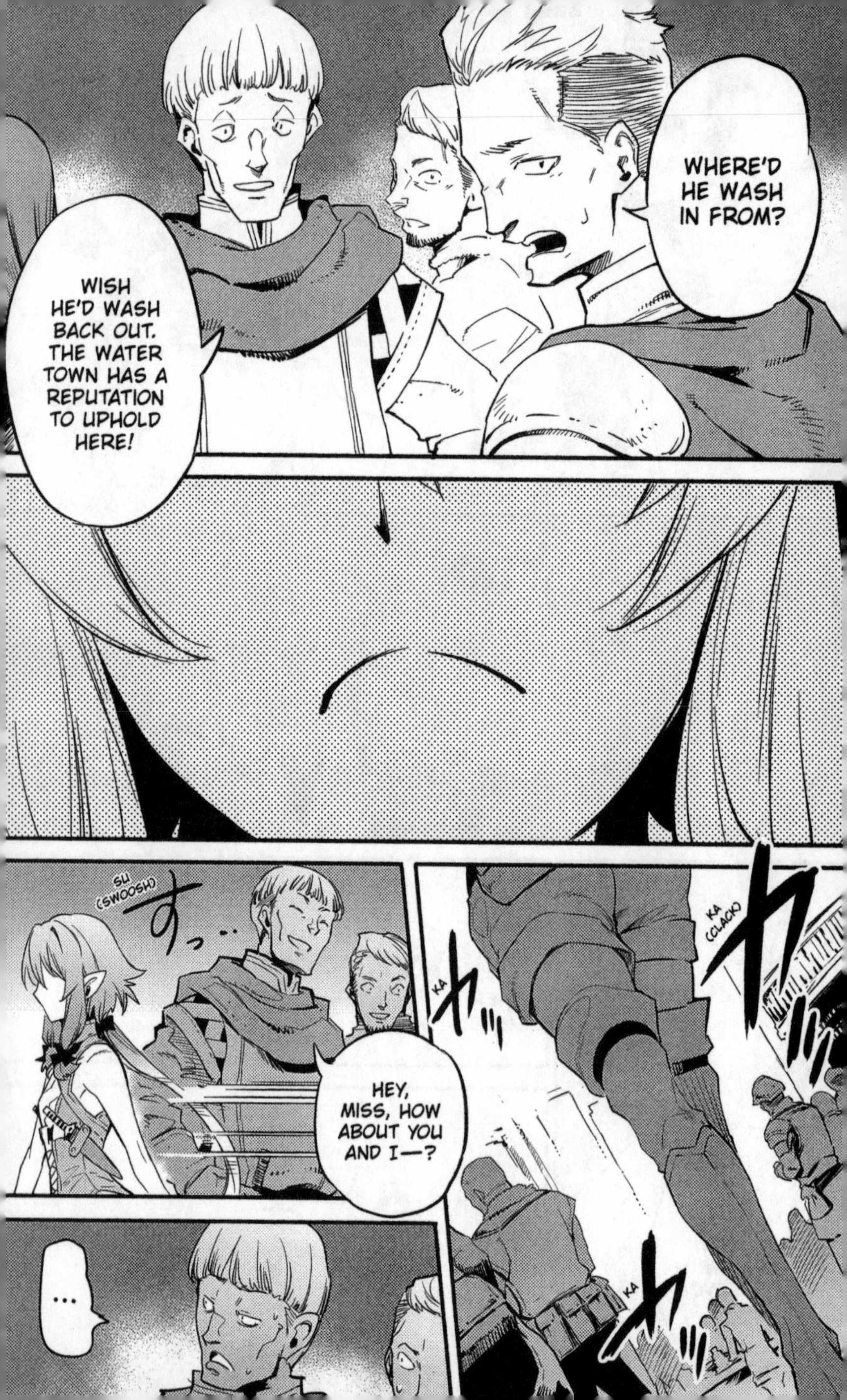
WHERE'D HE WASH IN FROM?
WISH HE'D WASH BACK OUT. THE WATER TOWN HAS A REPUTATION TO UPHOLD HERE!
KA (CLACK)
KA
KA
SU (SWOOSH)
HEY, MISS, HOW ABOUT YOU AND I—?
...

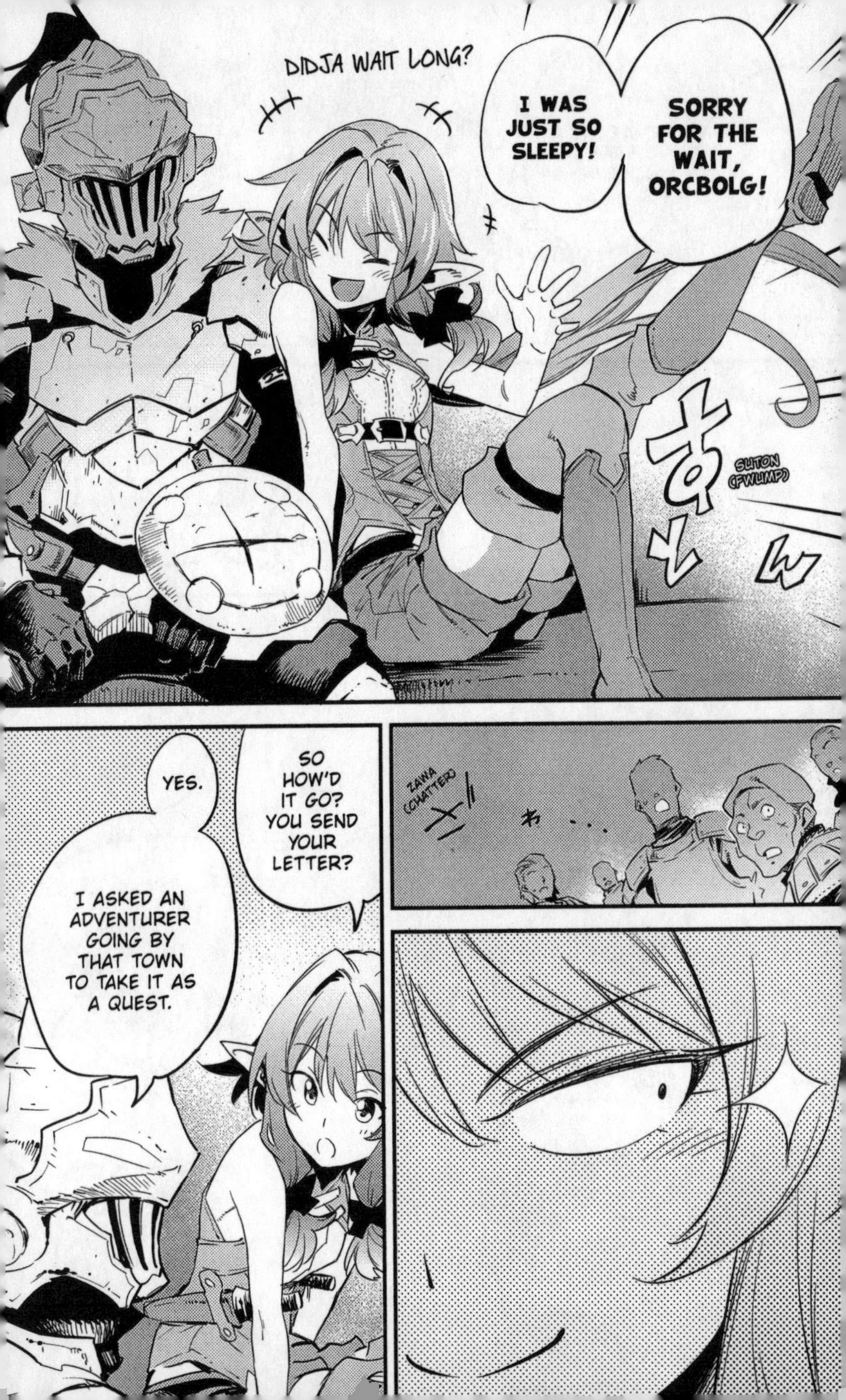
SORRY FOR THE WAIT, ORCBOLG!
I WAS JUST SO SLEEPY!
DIDJA WAIT LONG?
すとん
SUTON (FWUMP)
ZAWA (CHATTER)
SO HOW'D IT GO? YOU SEND YOUR LETTER?
YES.
I ASKED AN ADVENTURER GOING BY THAT TOWN TO TAKE IT AS A QUEST.

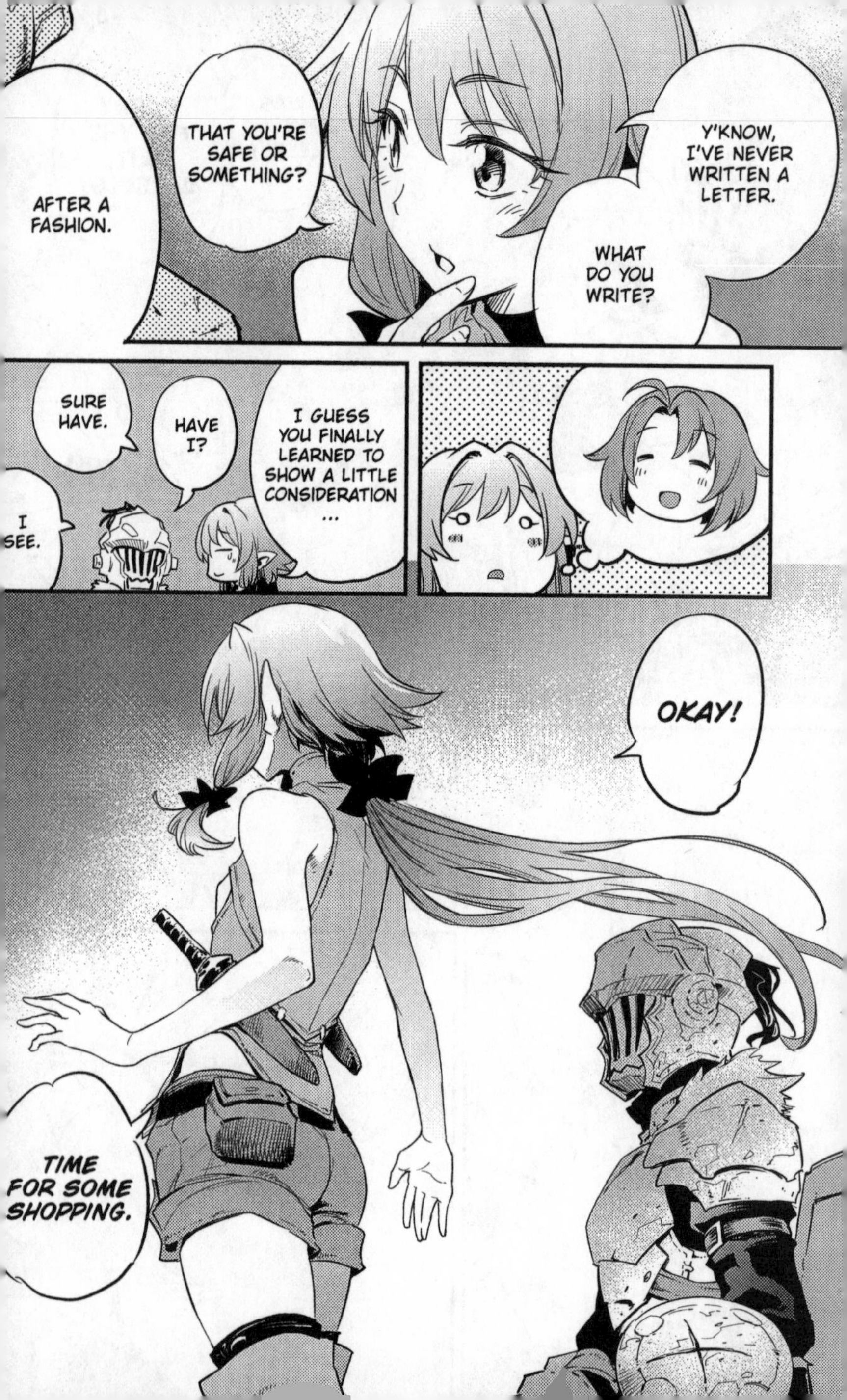
Y'KNOW, I'VE NEVER WRITTEN A LETTER.
WHAT DO YOU WRITE?
THAT YOU'RE SAFE OR SOMETHING?
AFTER A FASHION.
I GUESS YOU FINALLY LEARNED TO SHOW A LITTLE CONSIDERATION ...
HAVE I?
SURE HAVE.
I SEE.
OKAY!
TIME FOR SOME SHOPPING.

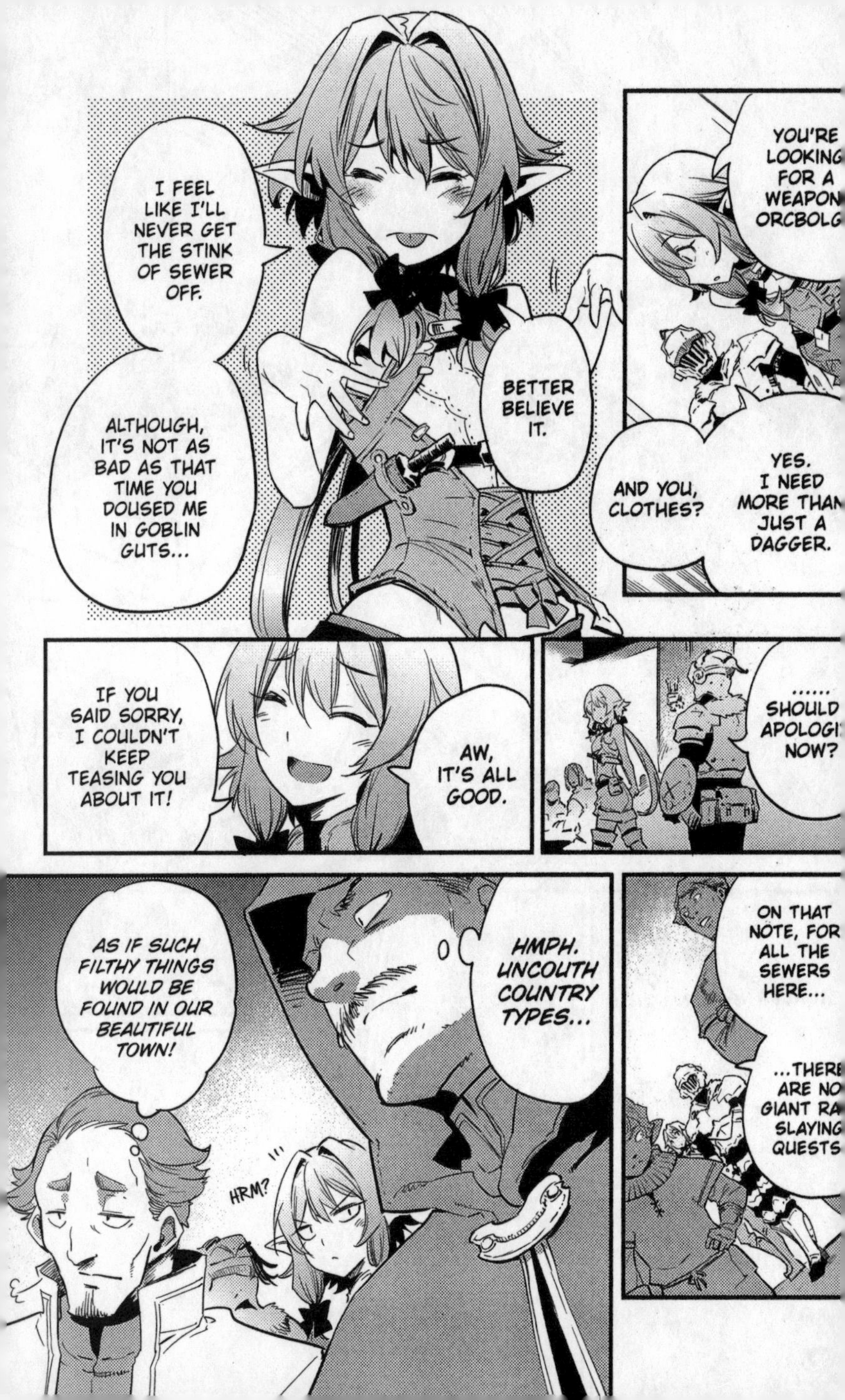

YOU'RE LOOKING FOR A WEAPON ORCBOLG
YES. I NEED MORE THAN JUST A DAGGER.
AND YOU, CLOTHES?
BETTER BELIEVE IT.
I FEEL LIKE I'LL NEVER GET THE STINK OF SEWER OFF.
ALTHOUGH, IT'S NOT AS BAD AS THAT TIME YOU DOUSED ME IN GOBLIN GUTS...
......SHOULD APOLOGI NOW?
AW, IT'S ALL GOOD.
IF YOU SAID SORRY, I COULDN'T KEEP TEASING YOU ABOUT IT!
ON THAT NOTE, FOR ALL THE SEWERS HERE...
...THERE ARE NO GIANT RA SLAYING QUESTS
HMPH. UNCOUTH COUNTRY TYPES...
AS IF SUCH FILTHY THINGS WOULD BE FOUND IN OUR BEAUTIFUL TOWN!
HRM?

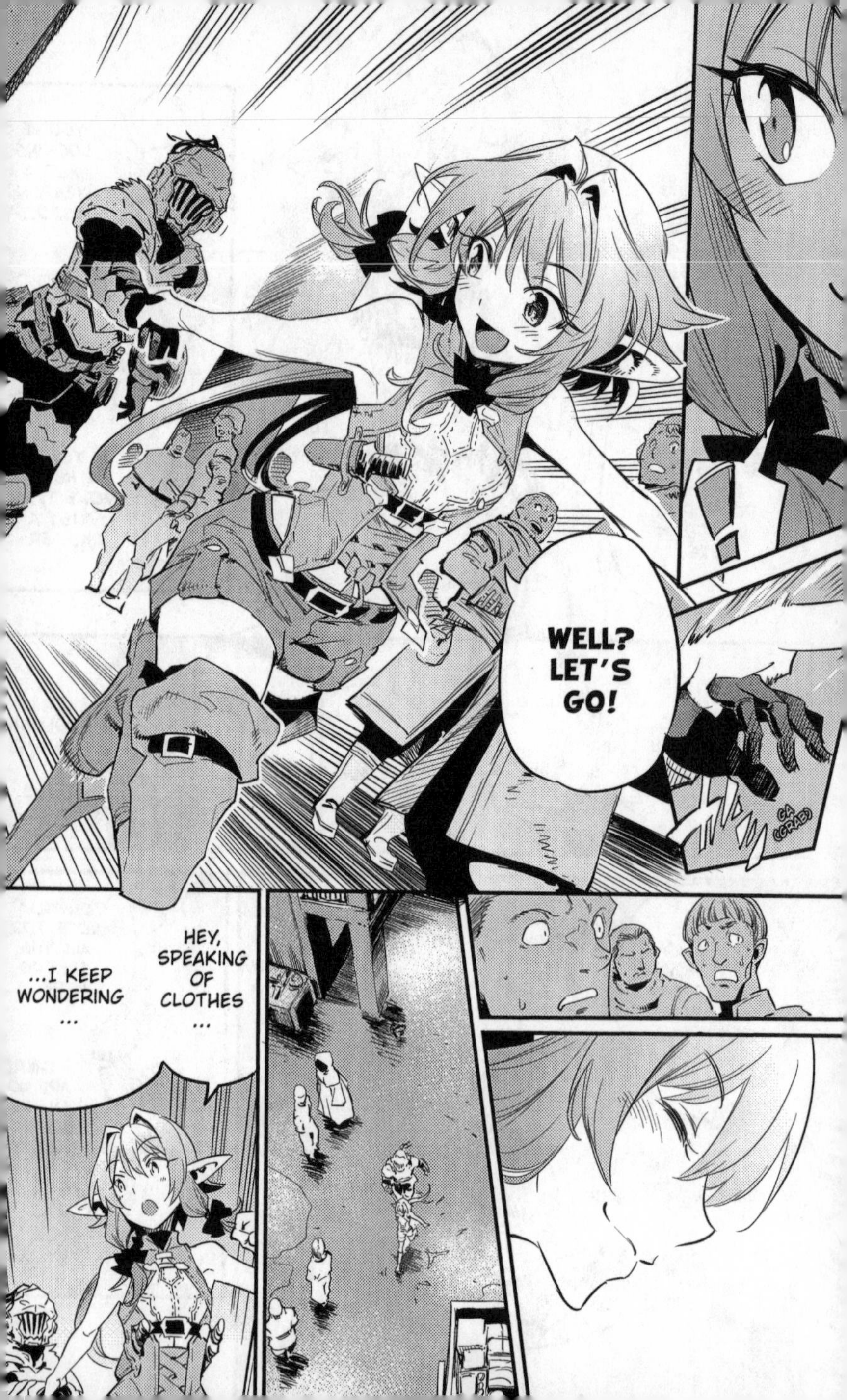
GA (GRAB)
WELL? LET'S GO!
HEY, SPEAKING OF CLOTHES ...
...I KEEP WONDERING ...

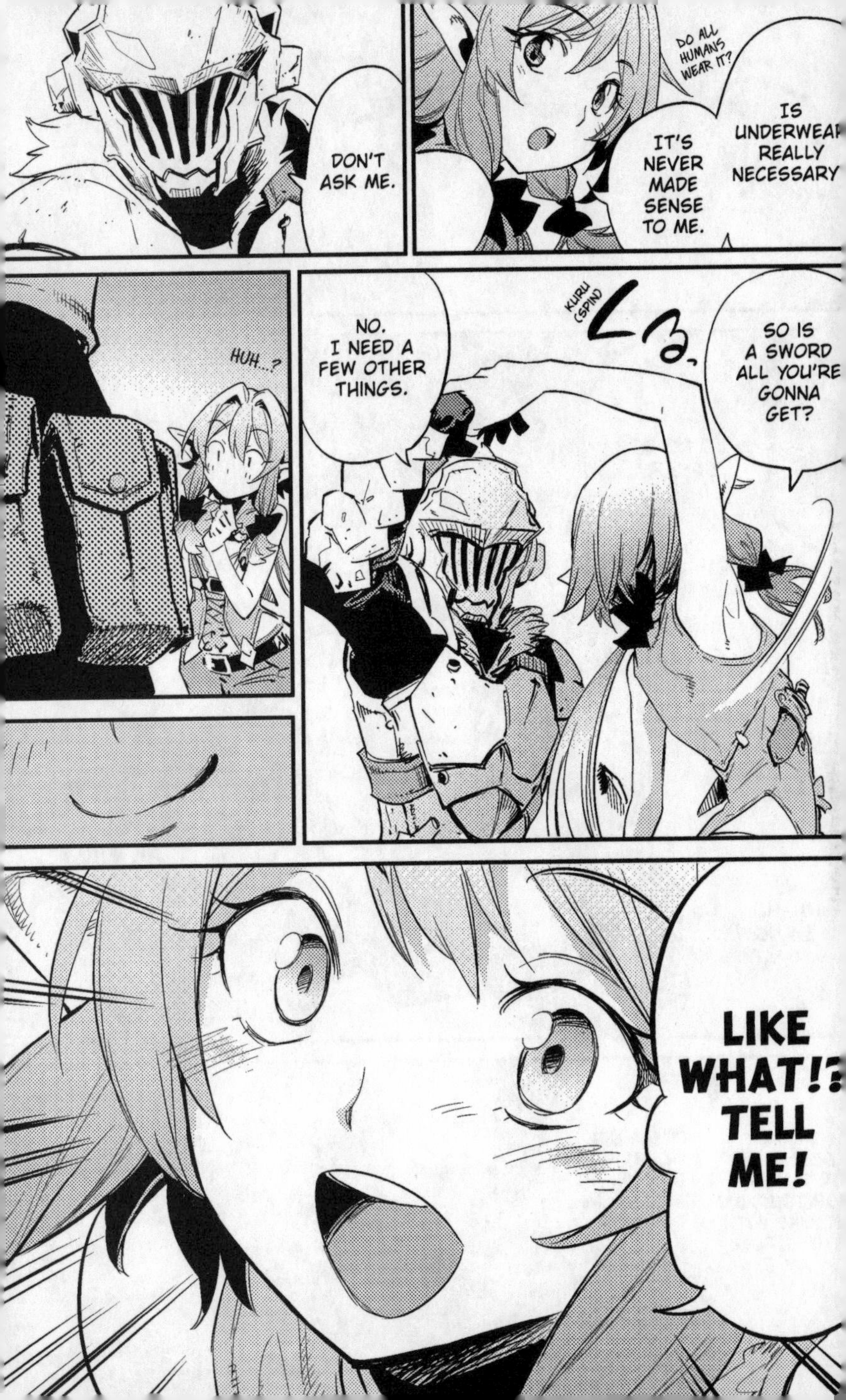
IS UNDERWEAR REALLY NECESSARY
DO ALL HUMANS WEAR IT?
IT'S NEVER MADE SENSE TO ME.
DON'T ASK ME.
SO IS A SWORD ALL YOU'RE GONNA GET?
くる
KURU (SPIN)
NO. I NEED A FEW OTHER THINGS.
HUH...?
LIKE WHAT!? TELL ME!

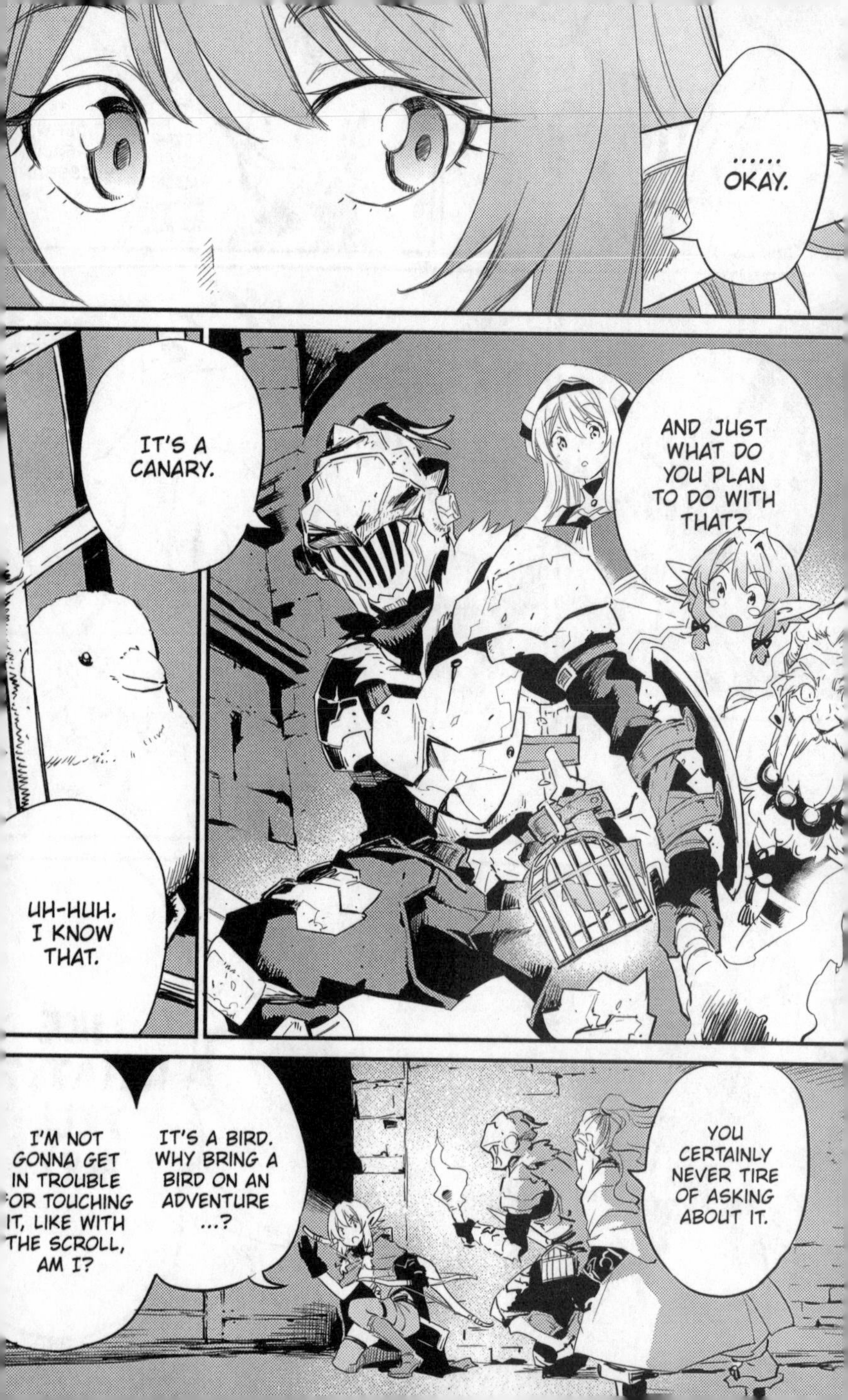
......OKAY.
AND JUST WHAT DO YOU PLAN TO DO WITH THAT?
IT'S A CANARY.
UH-HUH. I KNOW THAT.
YOU CERTAINLY NEVER TIRE OF ASKING ABOUT IT.
IT'S A BIRD. WHY BRING A BIRD ON AN ADVENTURE ...?
I'M NOT GONNA GET IN TROUBLE FOR TOUCHING IT, LIKE WITH THE SCROLL, AM I?

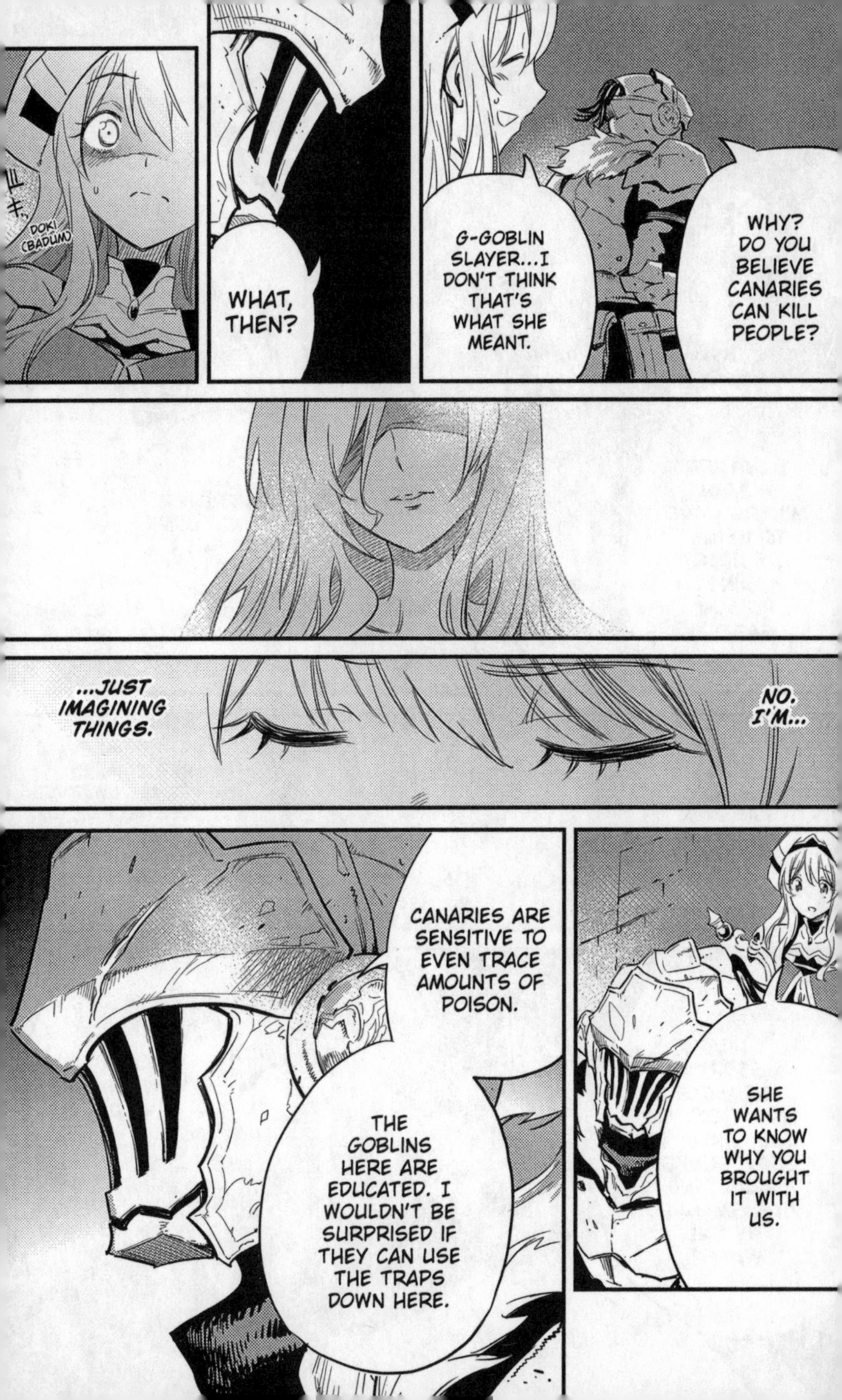
WHY? DO YOU BELIEVE CANARIES CAN KILL PEOPLE?
G-GOBLIN SLAYER...I DON'T THINK THAT'S WHAT SHE MEANT.
WHAT, THEN?
DOKI (BADUM)
NO. I'M...
...JUST IMAGINING THINGS.
SHE WANTS TO KNOW WHY YOU BROUGHT IT WITH US.
CANARIES ARE SENSITIVE TO EVEN TRACE AMOUNTS OF POISON.
THE GOBLINS HERE ARE EDUCATED. I WOULDN'T BE SURPRISED IF THEY CAN USE THE TRAPS DOWN HERE.

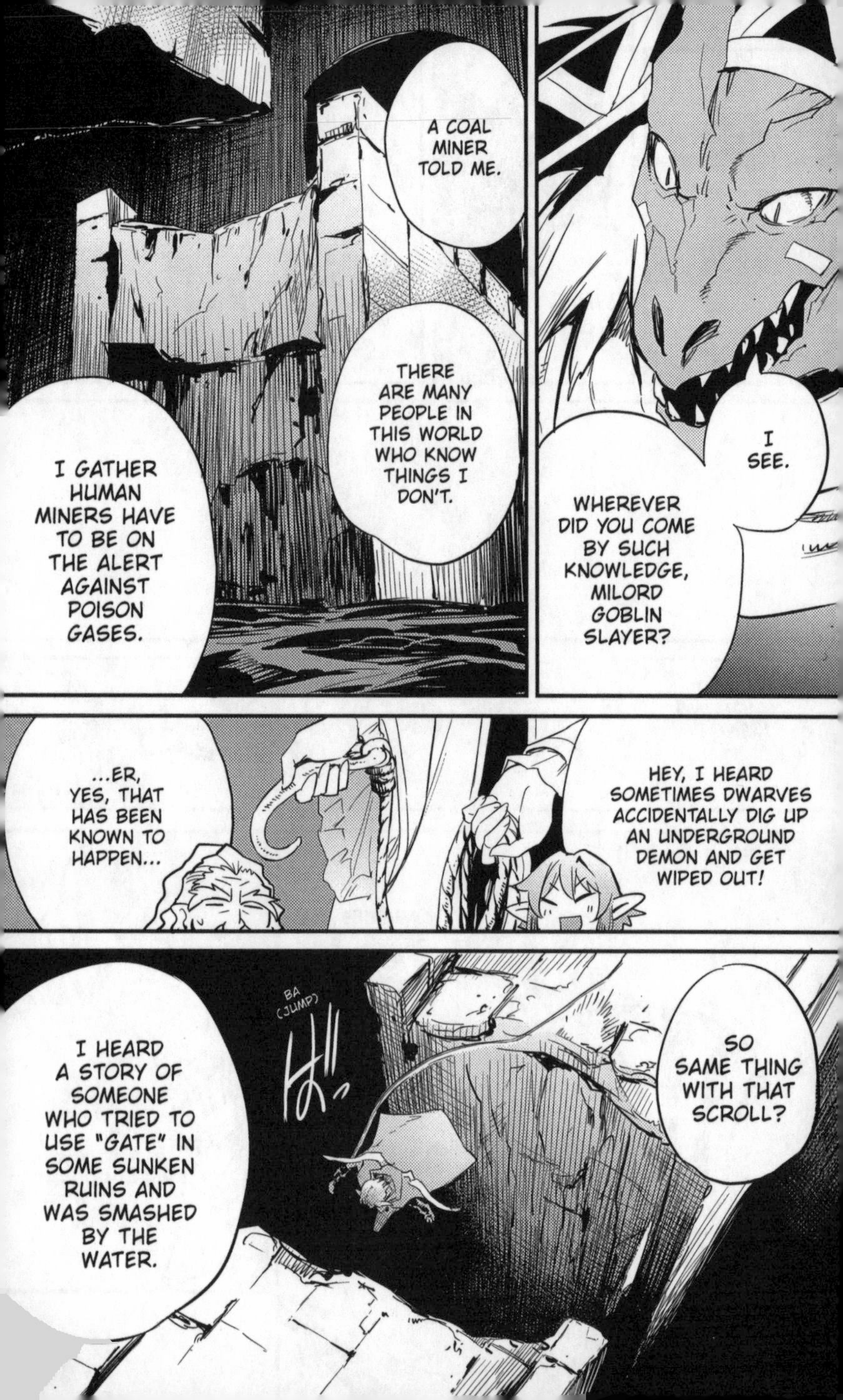
I SEE.
WHEREVER DID YOU COME BY SUCH KNOWLEDGE, MILORD GOBLIN SLAYER?
A COAL MINER TOLD ME.
THERE ARE MANY PEOPLE IN THIS WORLD WHO KNOW THINGS I DON'T.
I GATHER HUMAN MINERS HAVE TO BE ON THE ALERT AGAINST POISON GASES.
HEY, I HEARD SOMETIMES DWARVES ACCIDENTALLY DIG UP AN UNDERGROUND DEMON AND GET WIPED OUT!
...ER, YES, THAT HAS BEEN KNOWN TO HAPPEN...
SO SAME THING WITH THAT SCROLL?
BA (JUMP)
I HEARD A STORY OF SOMEONE WHO TRIED TO USE "GATE" IN SOME SUNKEN RUINS AND WAS SMASHED BY THE WATER.

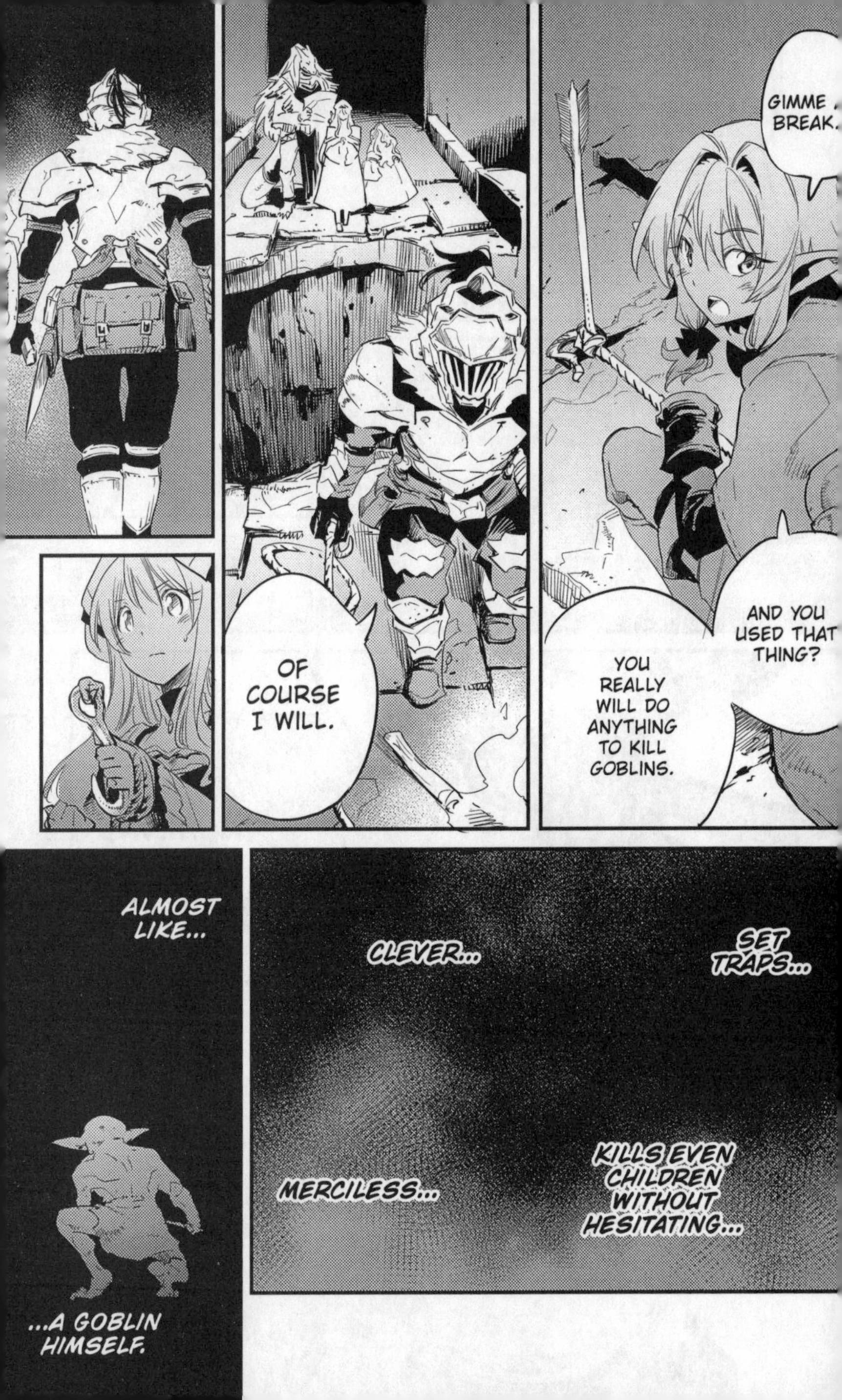
GIMME
BREAK.
AND YOU USED THAT THING?
YOU REALLY WILL DO ANYTHING TO KILL GOBLINS.
OF COURSE I WILL.
SET TRAPS...
CLEVER...
KILLS EVEN CHILDREN WITHOUT HESITATING...
MERCILESS...
ALMOST LIKE...
...A GOBLIN HIMSELF.

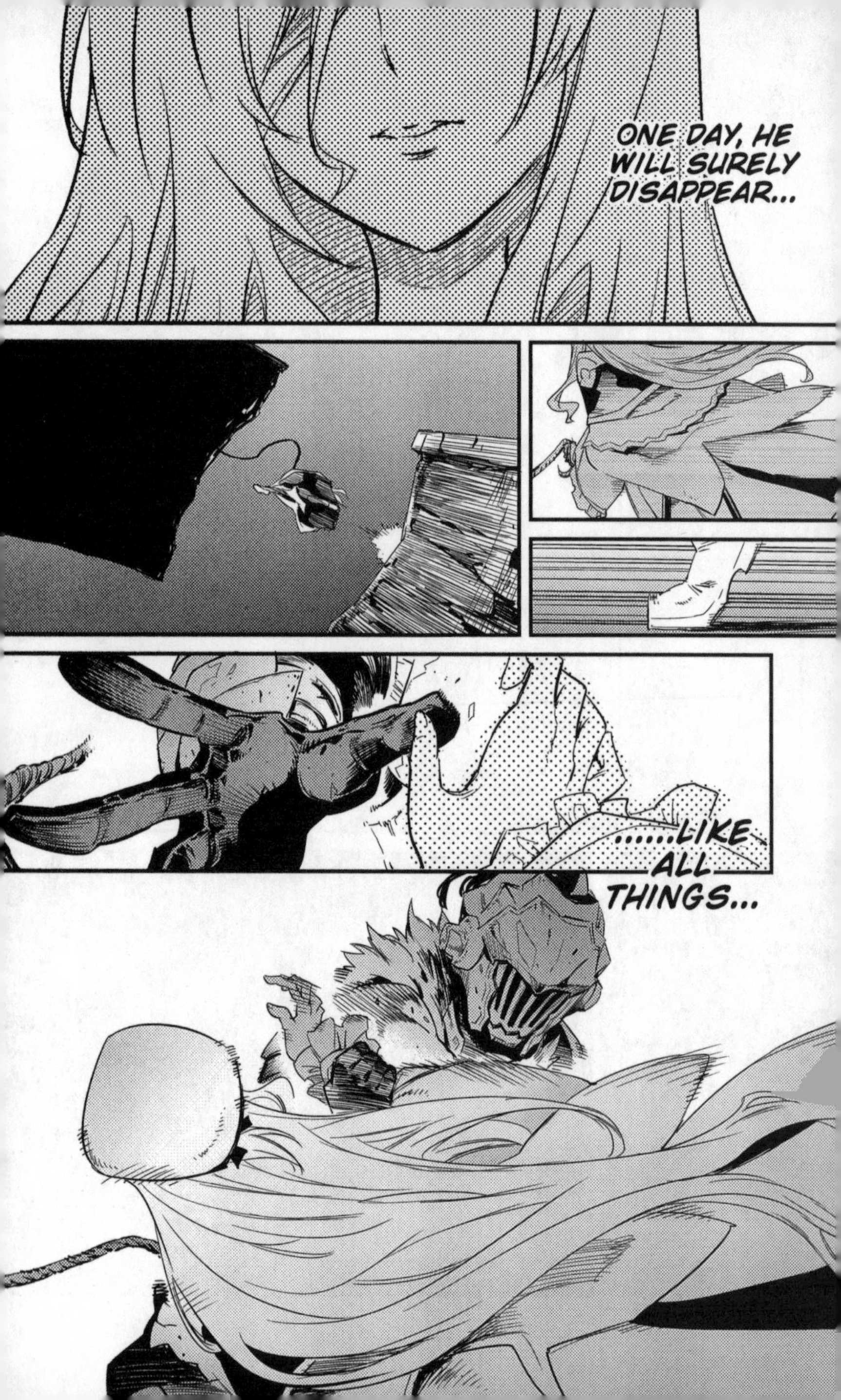
ONE DAY, HE WILL SURELY DISAPPEAR...
......LIKE ALL THINGS...

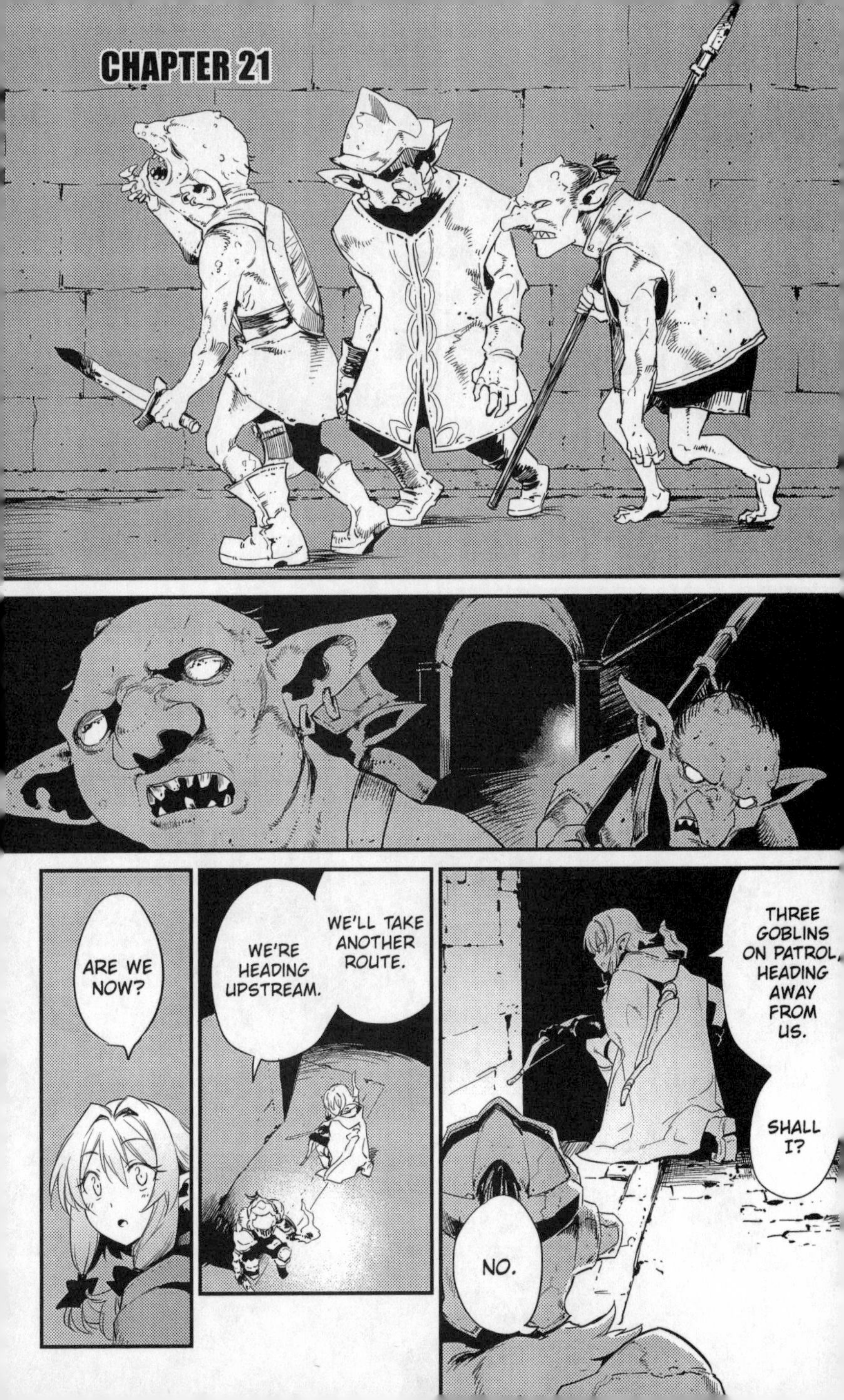
CHAPTER 21
THREE GOBLINS ON PATROL, HEADING AWAY FROM US.
SHALL I?
NO.
WE'LL TAKE ANOTHER ROUTE.
WE'RE HEADING UPSTREAM.
ARE WE NOW?

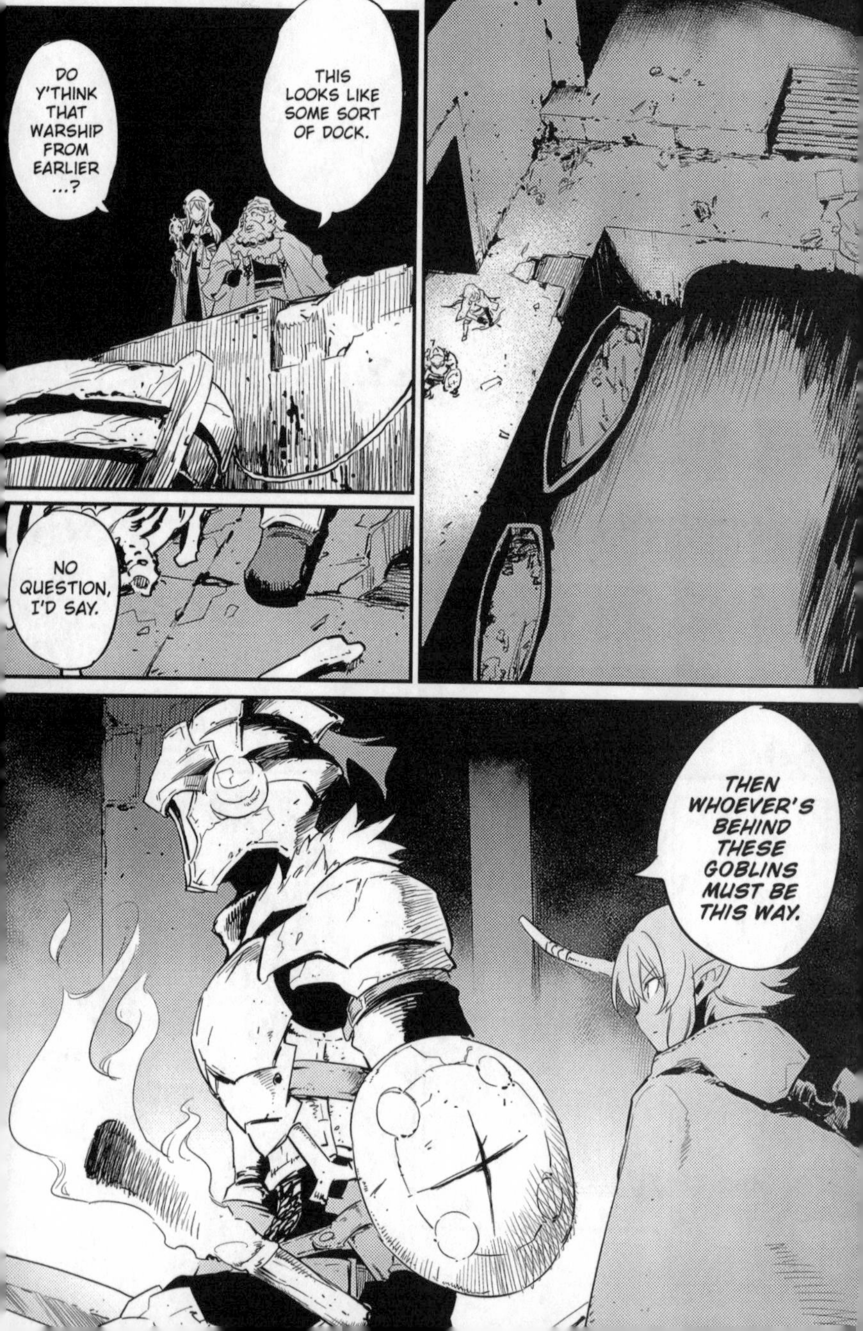
THIS LOOKS LIKE SOME SORT OF DOCK.
DO Y'THINK THAT WARSHIP FROM EARLIER ...?
NO QUESTION, I'D SAY.
THEN WHOEVER'S BEHIND THESE GOBLINS MUST BE THIS WAY.

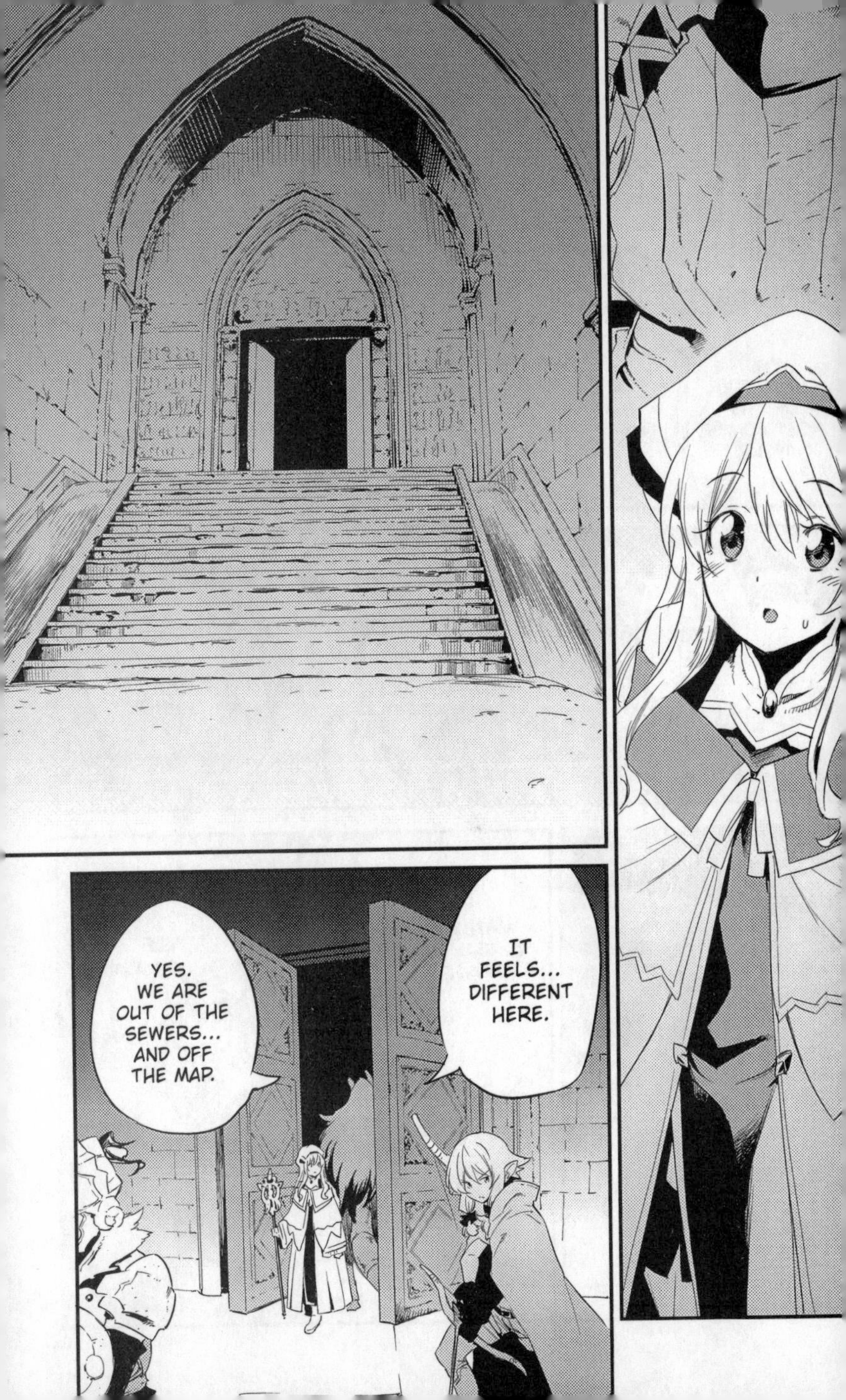
IT FEELS... DIFFERENT HERE.
YES. WE ARE OUT OF THE SEWERS... AND OFF THE MAP.

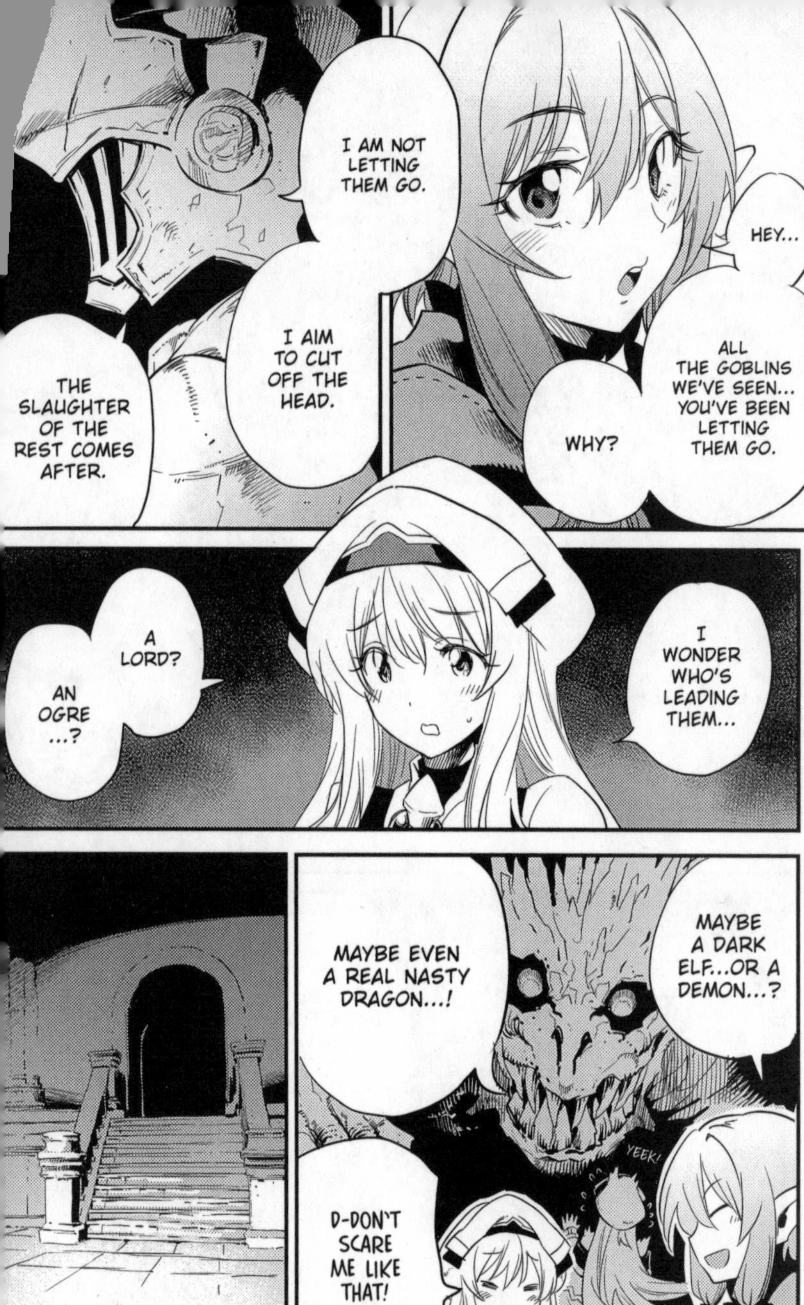
HEY...
ALL THE GOBLINS WE'VE SEEN... YOU'VE BEEN LETTING THEM GO.
WHY?
I AM NOT LETTING THEM GO.
I AIM TO CUT OFF THE HEAD.
THE SLAUGHTER OF THE REST COMES AFTER.
I WONDER WHO'S LEADING THEM...
A LORD?
AN OGRE ...?
MAYBE A DARK ELF...OR A DEMON...?
MAYBE EVEN A REAL NASTY DRAGON...!
YEEK!
D-DON'T SCARE ME LIKE THAT!

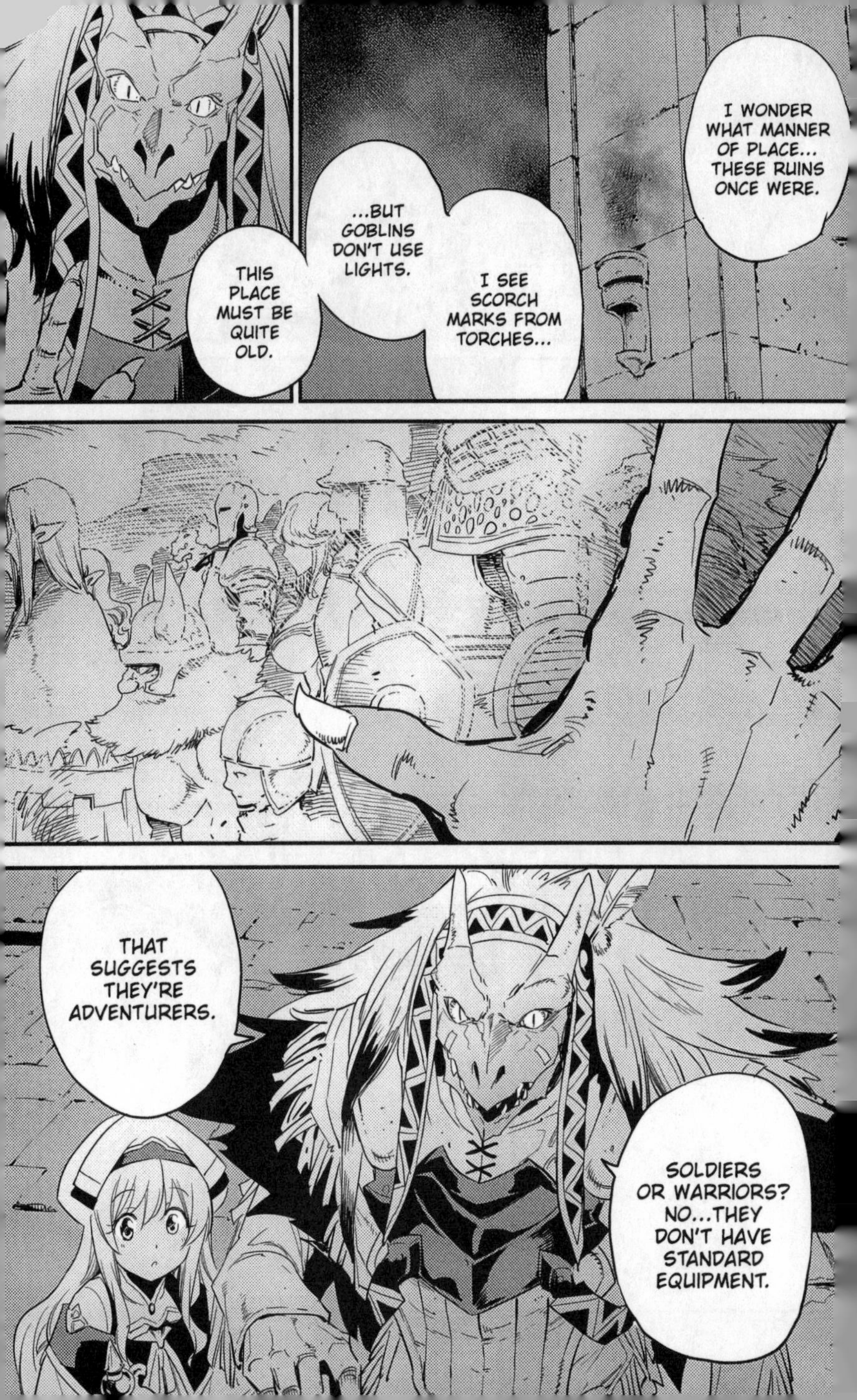
I WONDER WHAT MANNER OF PLACE... THESE RUINS ONCE WERE.
I SEE SCORCH MARKS FROM TORCHES...
...BUT GOBLINS DON'T USE LIGHTS.
THIS PLACE MUST BE QUITE OLD.
SOLDIERS OR WARRIORS? NO...THEY DON'T HAVE STANDARD EQUIPMENT.
THAT SUGGESTS THEY'RE ADVENTURERS.

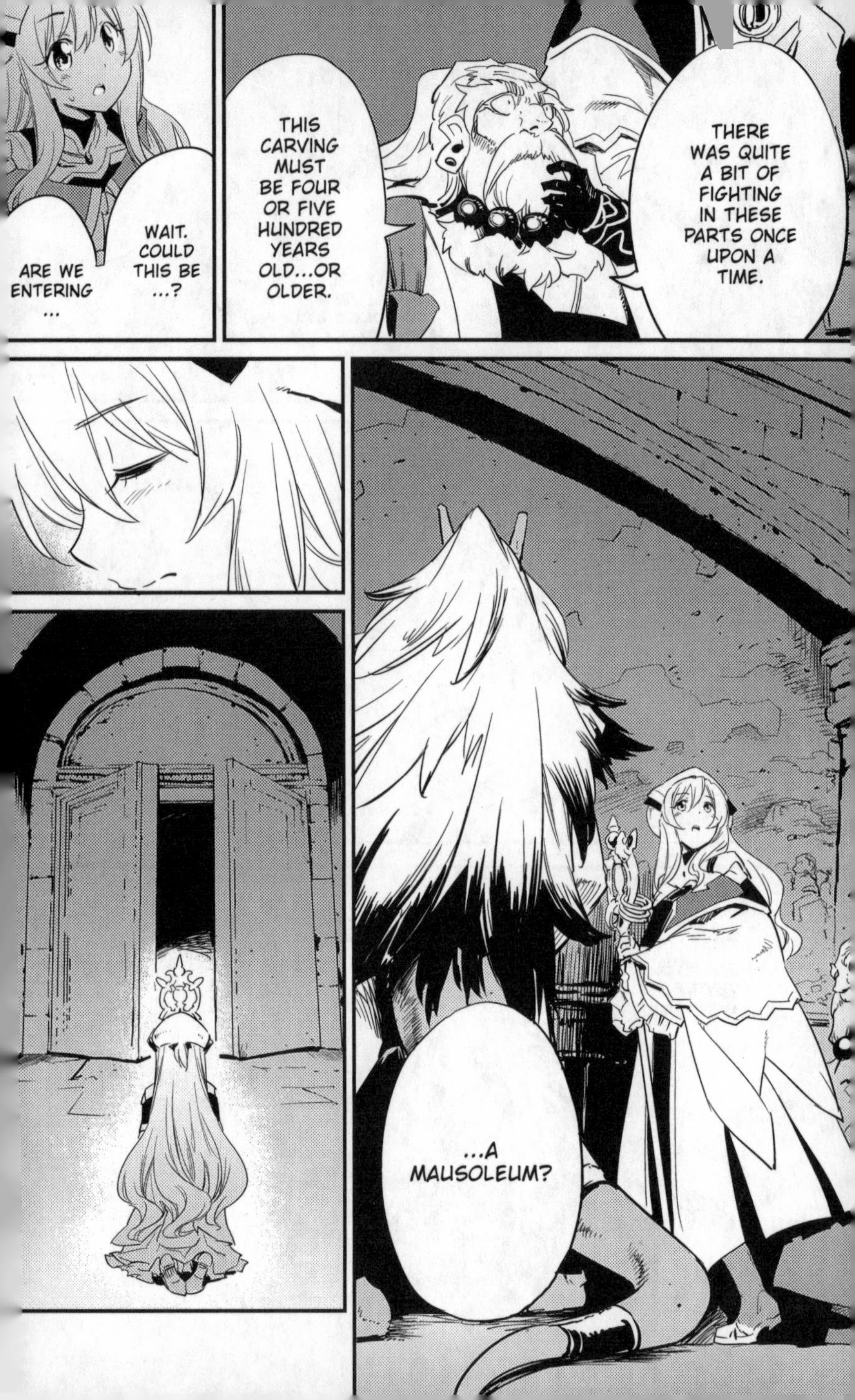
THERE WAS QUITE A BIT OF FIGHTING IN THESE PARTS ONCE UPON A TIME.
THIS CARVING MUST BE FOUR OR FIVE HUNDRED YEARS OLD...OR OLDER.
WAIT. COULD THIS BE ...?
ARE WE ENTERING ...
...A MAUSOLEUM?

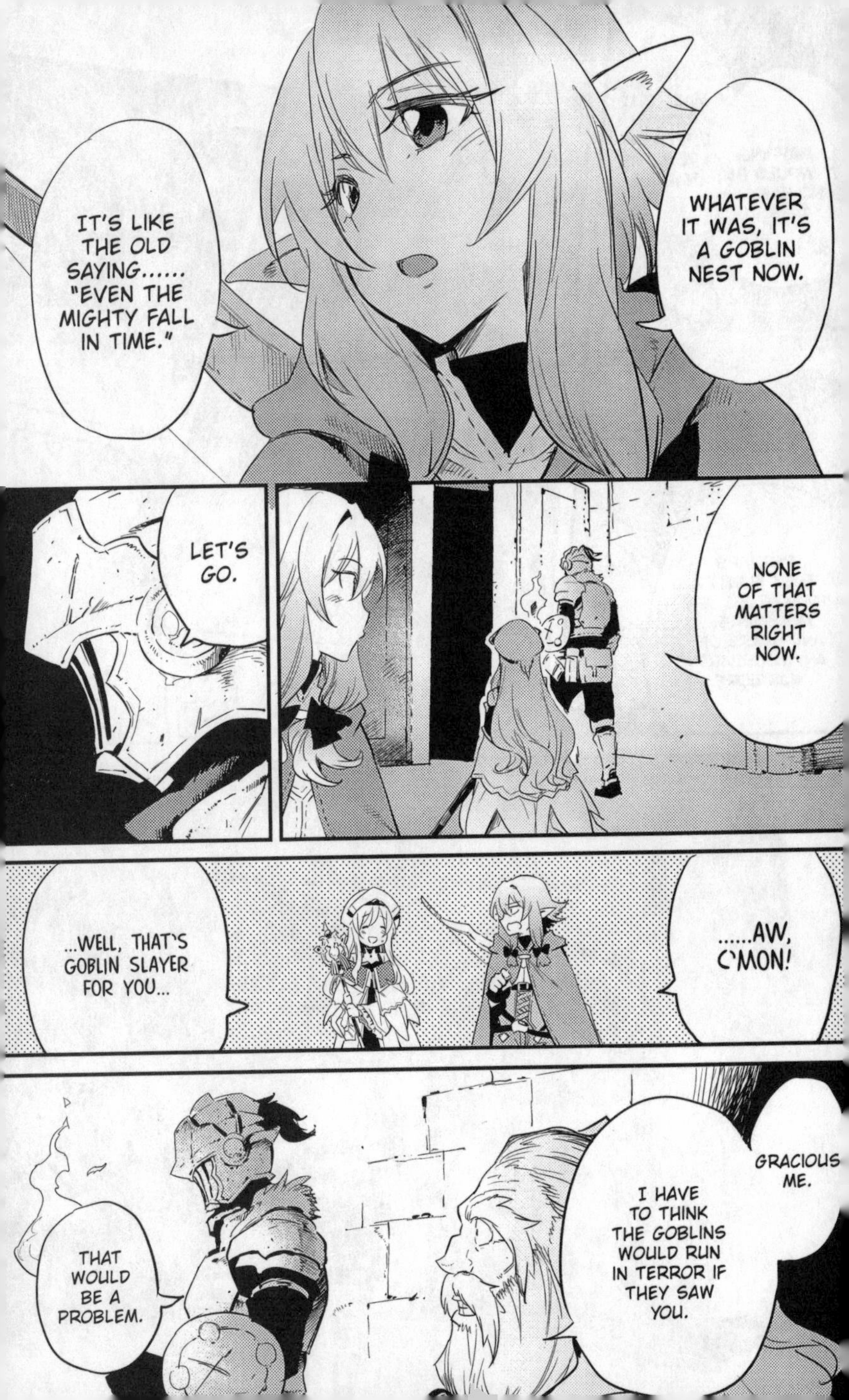
WHATEVER IT WAS, IT'S A GOBLIN NEST NOW.
IT'S LIKE THE OLD SAYING...... "EVEN THE MIGHTY FALL IN TIME."
NONE OF THAT MATTERS RIGHT NOW.
LET'S GO.
......AW, C'MON!
...WELL, THAT'S GOBLIN SLAYER FOR YOU...
GRACIOUS ME.
I HAVE TO THINK THE GOBLINS WOULD RUN IN TERROR IF THEY SAW YOU.
THAT WOULD BE A PROBLEM.

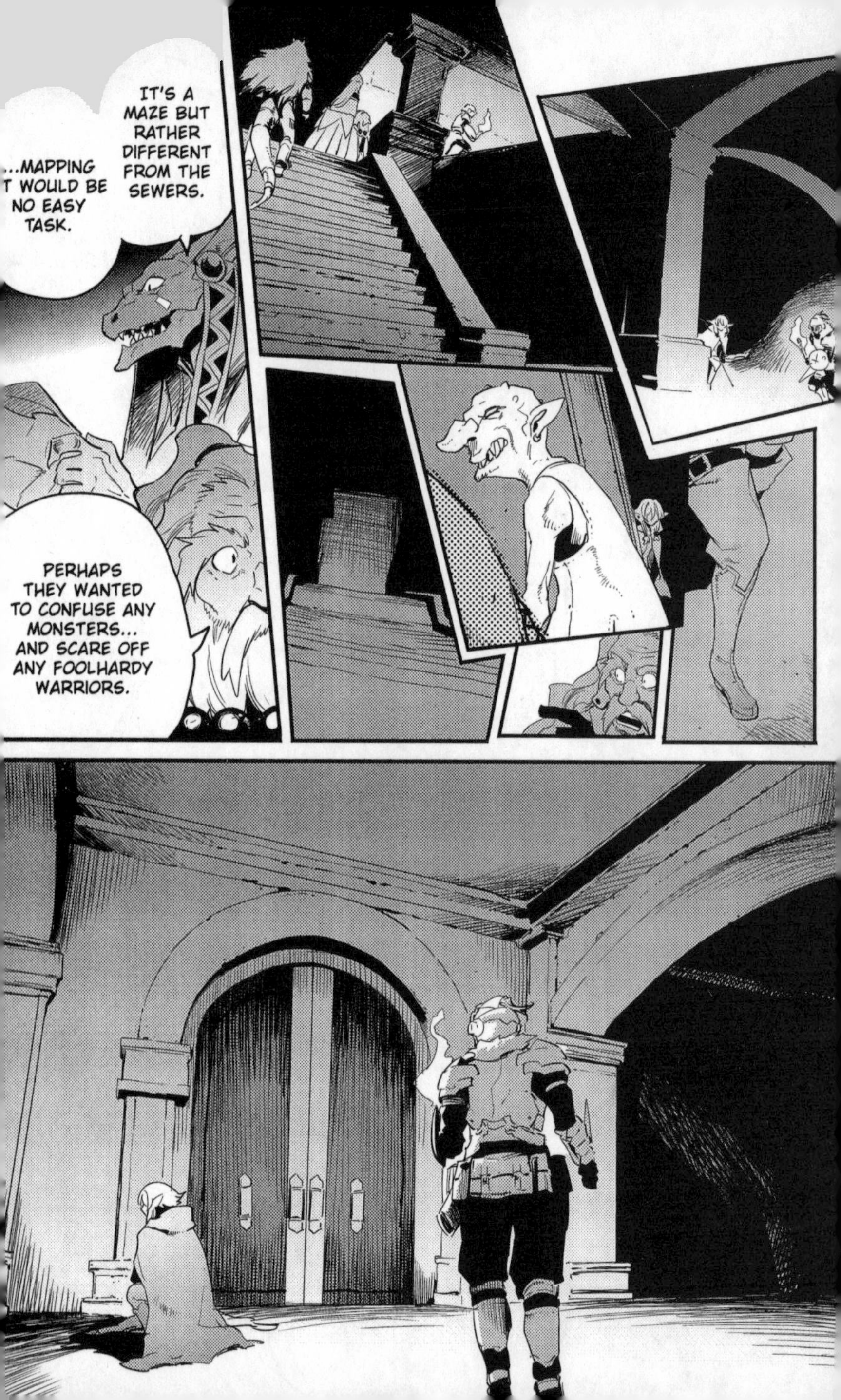
IT'S A MAZE BUT RATHER DIFFERENT FROM THE SEWERS.
...MAPPING T WOULD BE NO EASY TASK.
PERHAPS THEY WANTED TO CONFUSE ANY MONSTERS... AND SCARE OFF ANY FOOLHARDY WARRIORS.

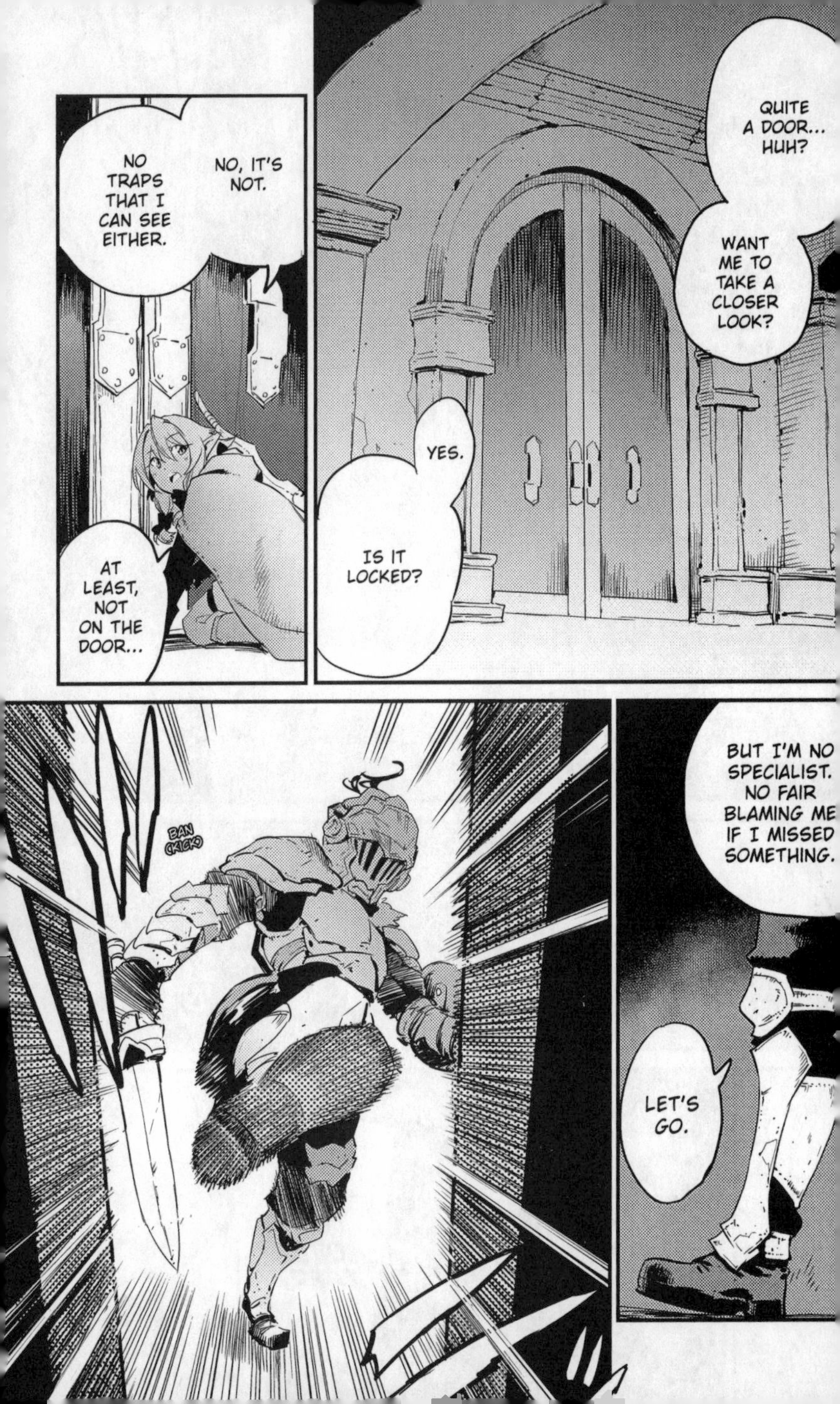
QUITE A DOOR... HUH?
WANT ME TO TAKE A CLOSER LOOK?
YES.
IS IT LOCKED?
NO, IT'S NOT.
NO TRAPS THAT I CAN SEE EITHER.
AT LEAST, NOT ON THE DOOR...
BUT I'M NO SPECIALIST. NO FAIR BLAMING ME IF I MISSED SOMETHING.
LET'S GO.
BAN (KICK)

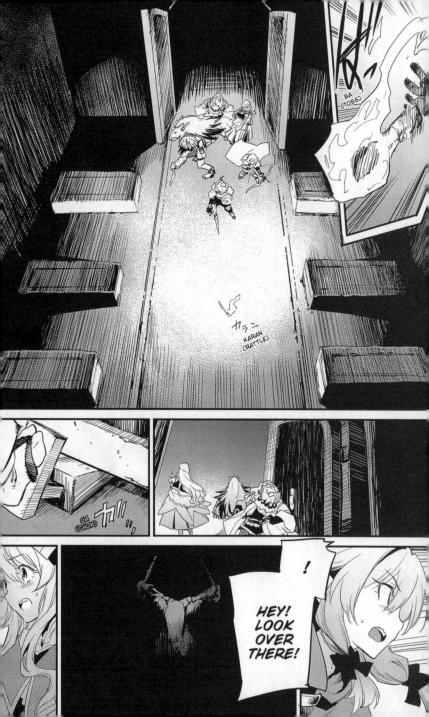

BA
(TOSS)

カラン
KARAN
(RATTLE)

GA
(CHOK)

!

HEY!
LOOK
OVER
THERE!

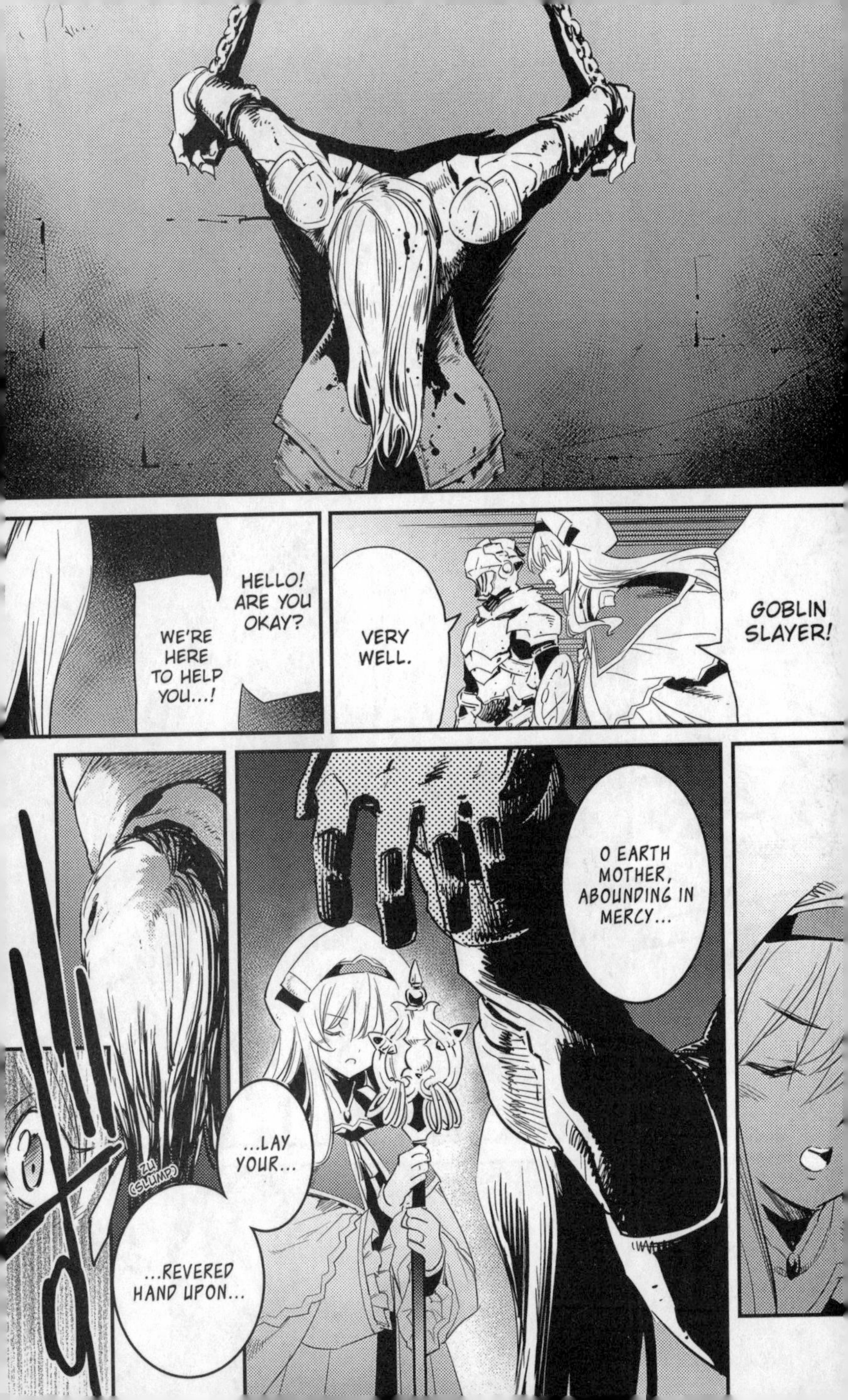
GOBLIN SLAYER!
VERY WELL.
HELLO! ARE YOU OKAY?
WE'RE HERE TO HELP YOU...!
O EARTH MOTHER, ABOUNDING IN MERCY...
...LAY YOUR...
...REVERED HAND UPON...
ZU (SLUMP)

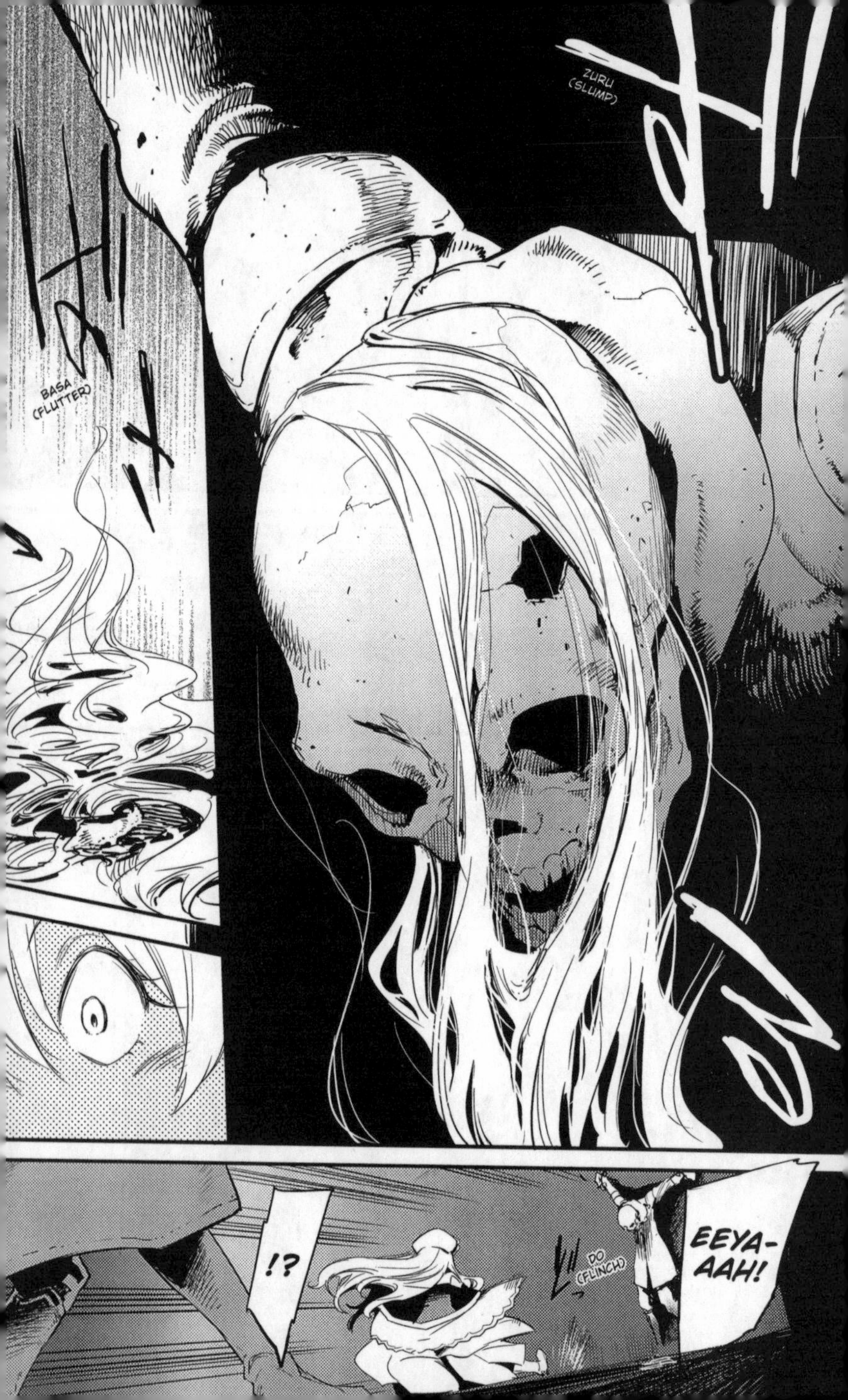
ZURU
(SLUMP)
BASA
(FLUTTER)
EEYA-
AAH!
DO
(FLINCH)
!?

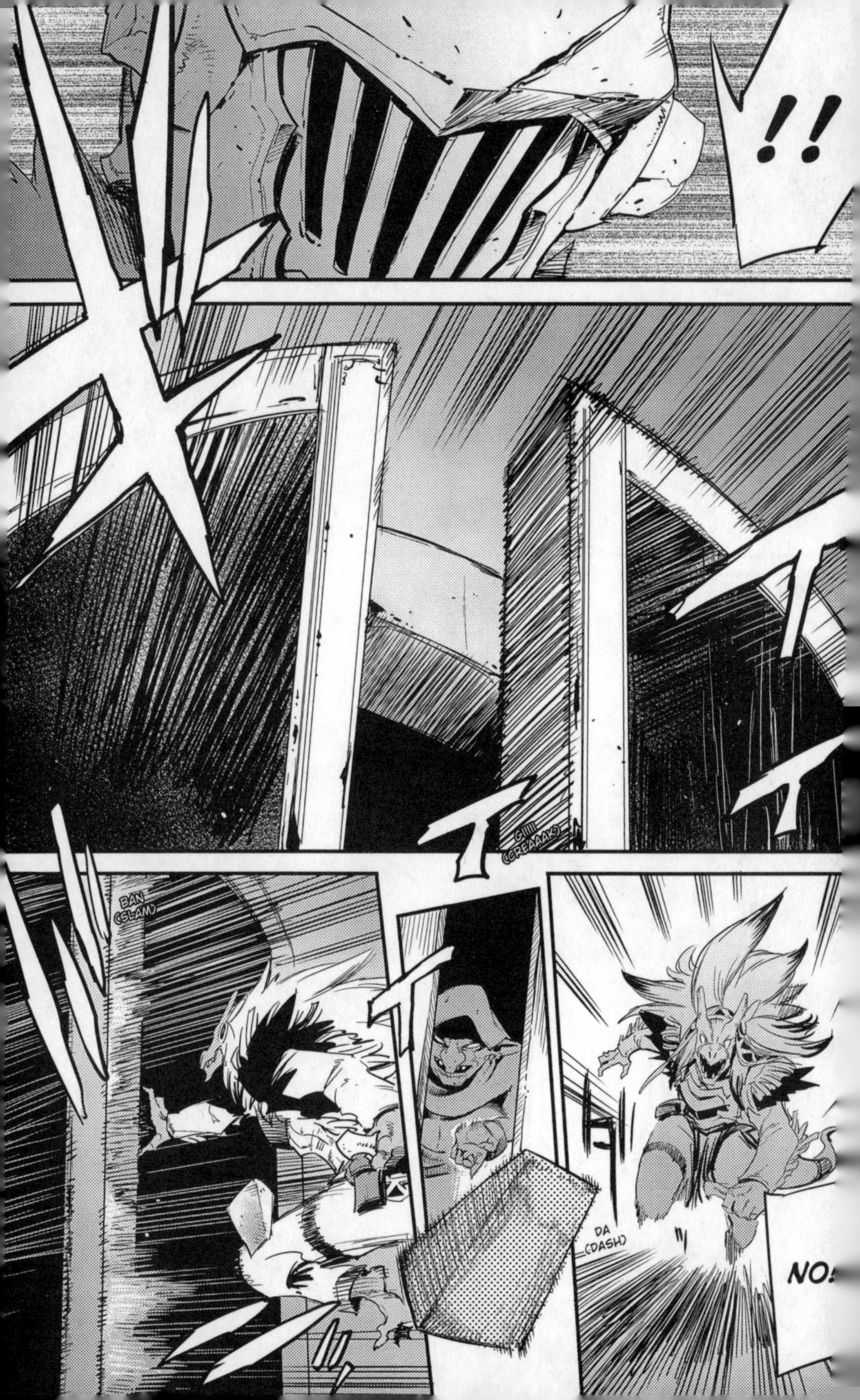
!!
GIIII
(CREAAAK)
DA
(DASH)
NO!
BAN
(SLAM)

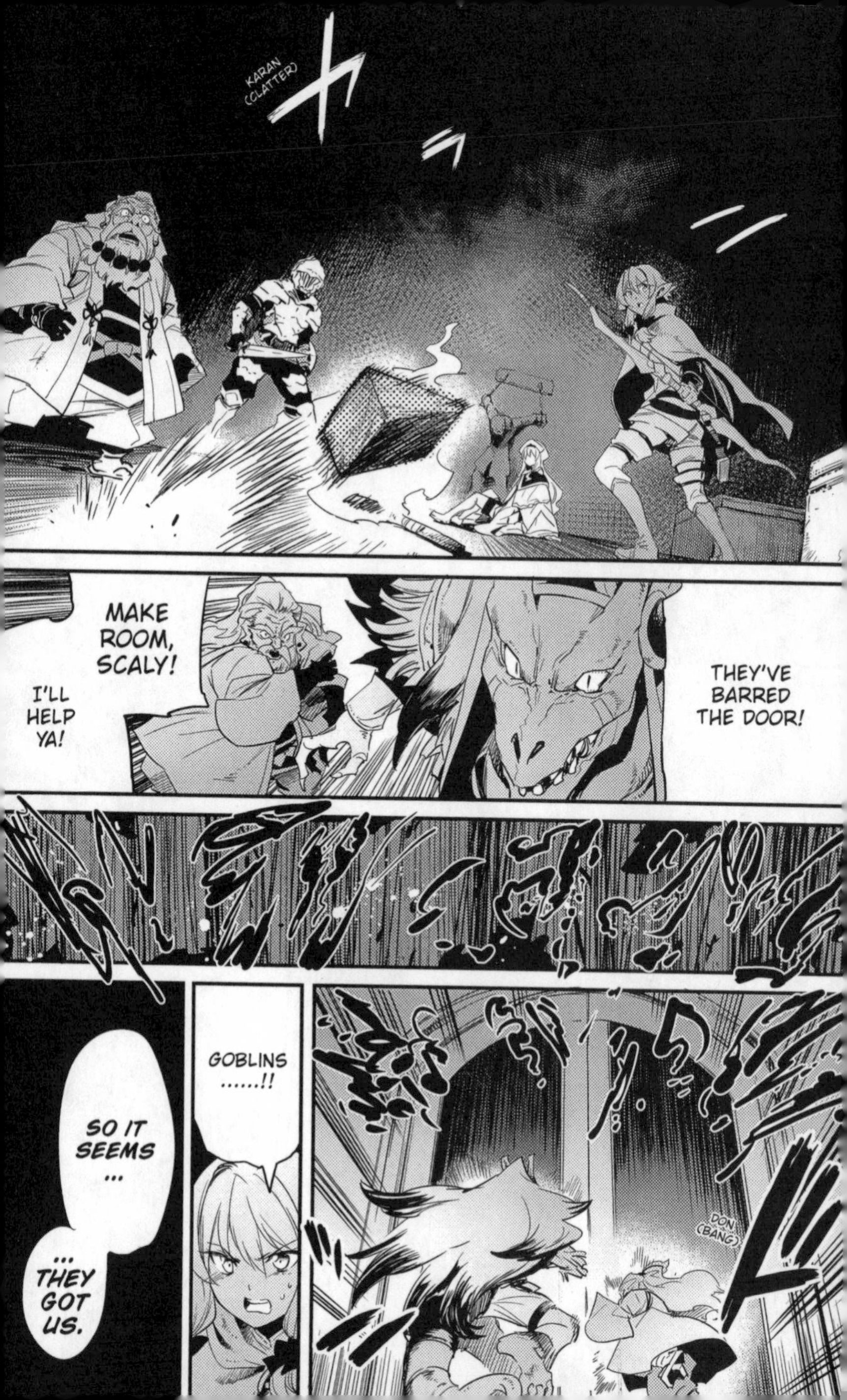
KARAN (CLATTER)
THEY'VE BARRED THE DOOR!
MAKE ROOM, SCALY!
I'LL HELP YA!
DON (BANG)
GOBLINS ......!!
SO IT SEEMS ...
... THEY GOT US.

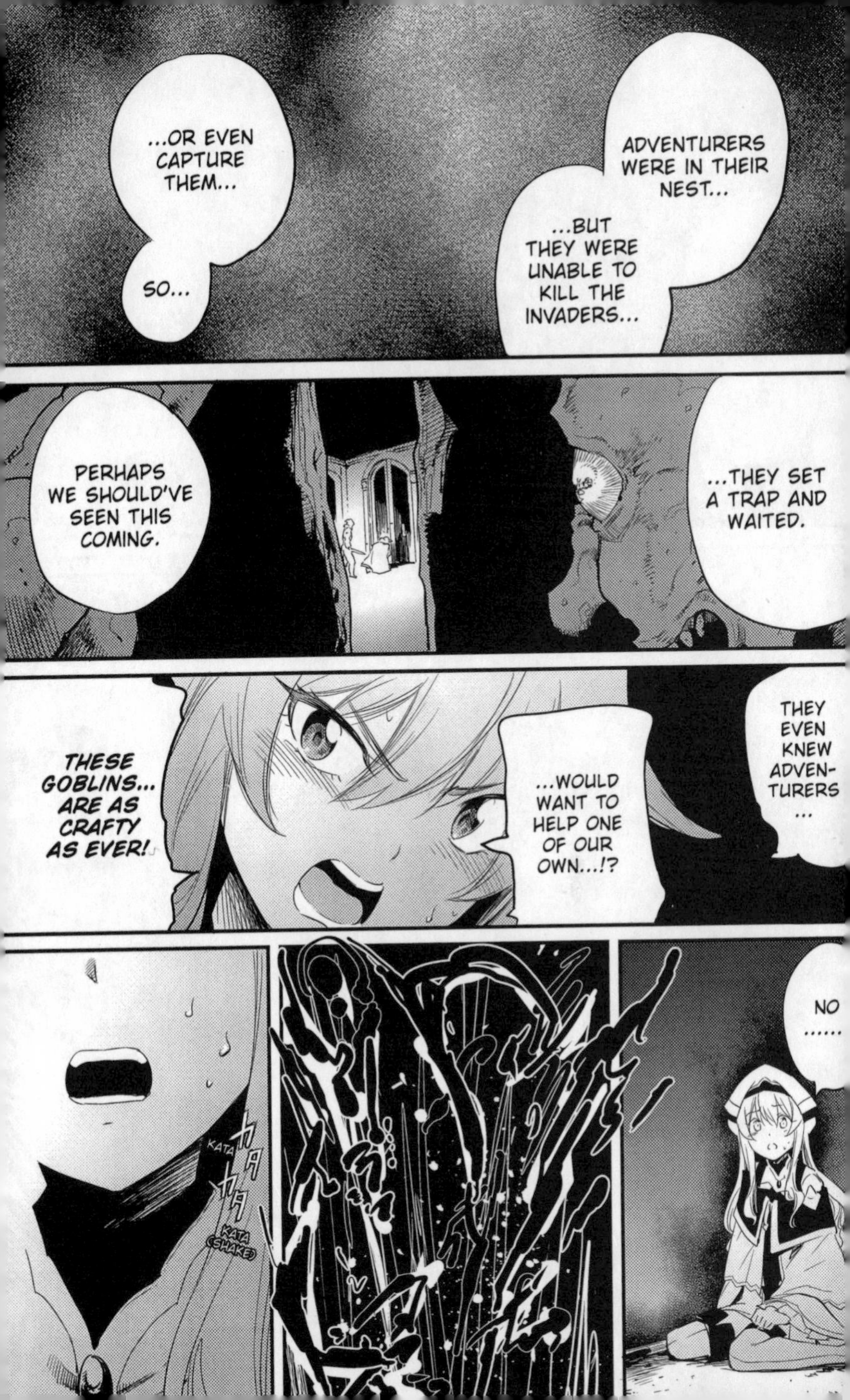
ADVENTURERS WERE IN THEIR NEST...
...BUT THEY WERE UNABLE TO KILL THE INVADERS...
...OR EVEN CAPTURE THEM...
SO...
...THEY SET A TRAP AND WAITED.
PERHAPS WE SHOULD'VE SEEN THIS COMING.
THEY EVEN KNEW ADVEN-TURERS...
...WOULD WANT TO HELP ONE OF OUR OWN...!?
THESE GOBLINS... ARE AS CRAFTY AS EVER!
NO ......
KATA KATA (SHAKE)

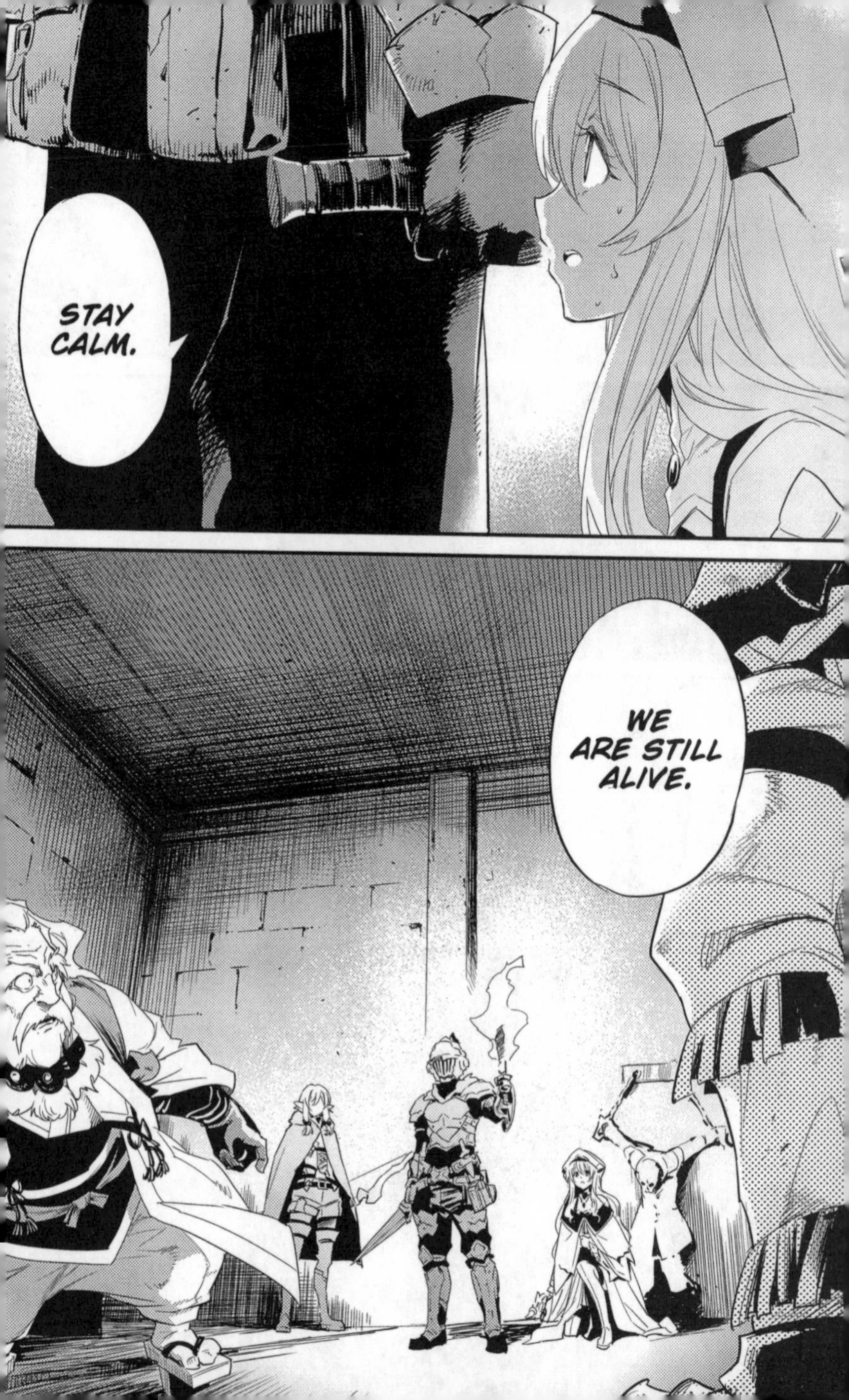
STAY CALM.
WE ARE STILL ALIVE.

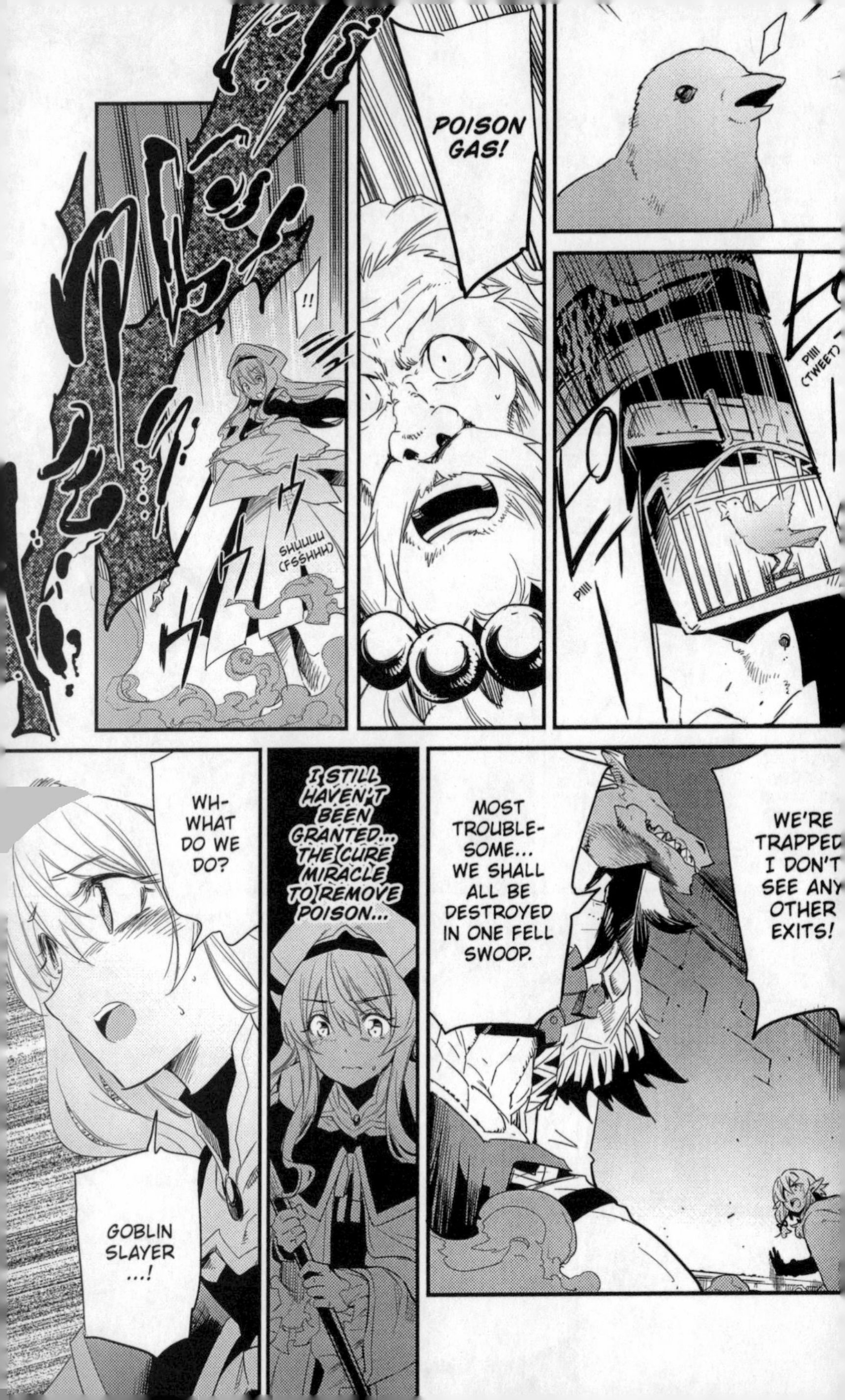
PIIII (TWEET)
PIIII
POISON GAS!
!!
SHUUUU (FSSHHH)
WE'RE TRAPPED I DON'T SEE ANY OTHER EXITS!
MOST TROUBLE-SOME... WE SHALL ALL BE DESTROYED IN ONE FELL SWOOP.
I STILL HAVEN'T BEEN GRANTED... THE CURE MIRACLE TO REMOVE POISON...
WH-WHAT DO WE DO?
GOBLIN SLAYER ...!

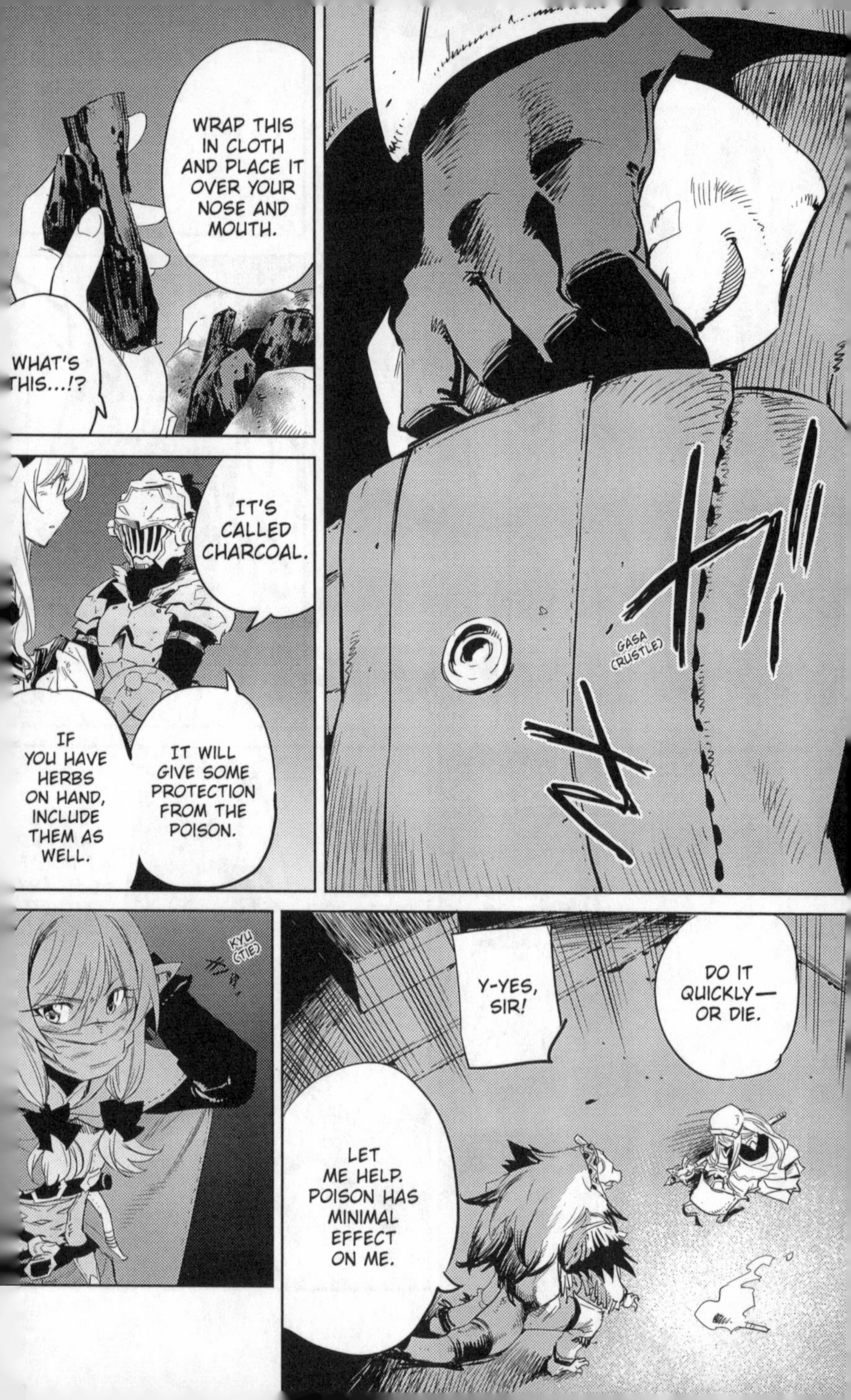
GASA (RUSTLE)
WRAP THIS IN CLOTH AND PLACE IT OVER YOUR NOSE AND MOUTH.
WHAT'S THIS...!?
IT'S CALLED CHARCOAL.
IT WILL GIVE SOME PROTECTION FROM THE POISON.
IF YOU HAVE HERBS ON HAND, INCLUDE THEM AS WELL.
DO IT QUICKLY— OR DIE.
Y-YES, SIR!
LET ME HELP. POISON HAS MINIMAL EFFECT ON ME.
KYU (TIE)

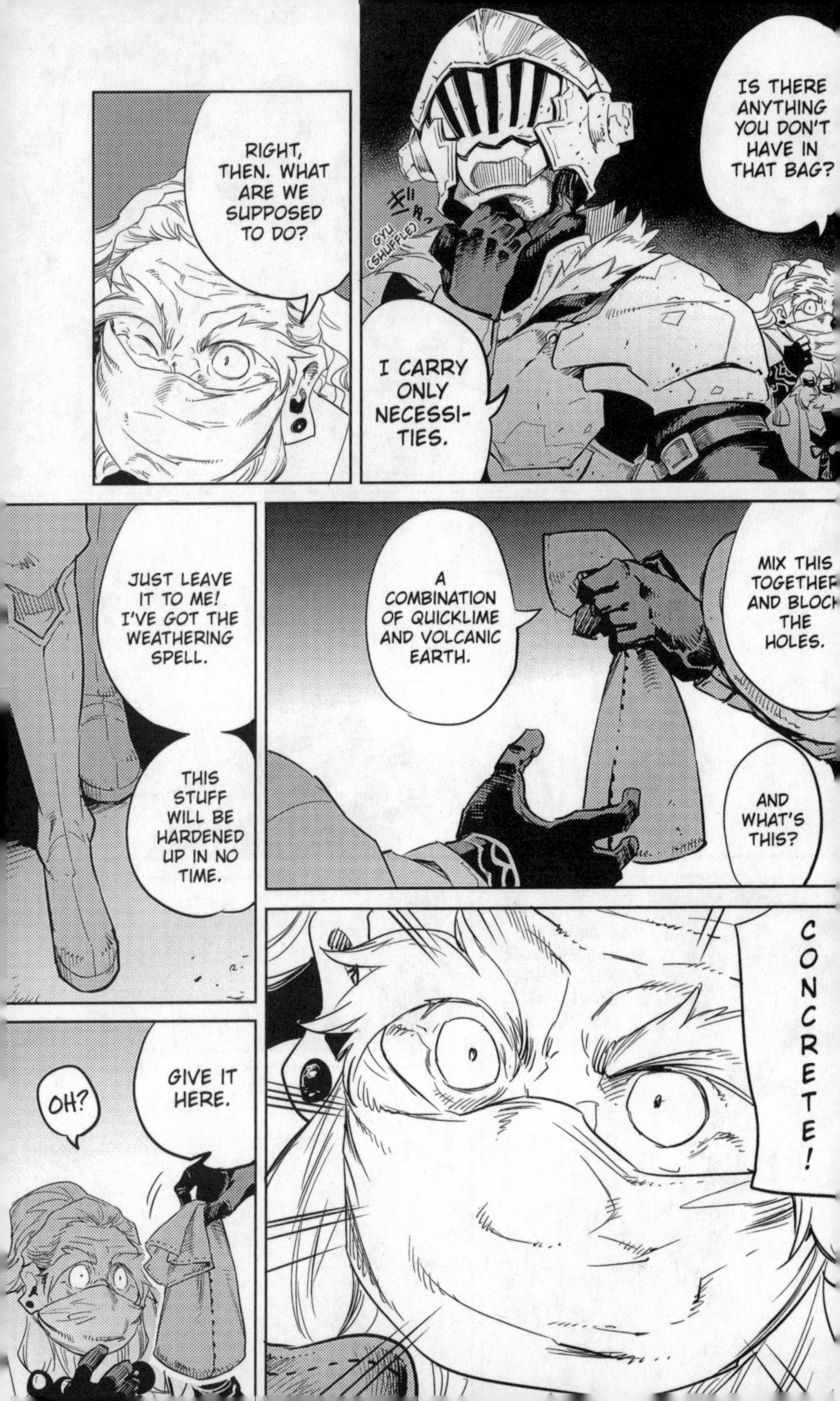
IS THERE ANYTHING YOU DON'T HAVE IN THAT BAG?
GYU (SHUFFLE)
I CARRY ONLY NECESSITIES.
RIGHT, THEN. WHAT ARE WE SUPPOSED TO DO?
MIX THIS TOGETHER AND BLOCK THE HOLES.
A COMBINATION OF QUICKLIME AND VOLCANIC EARTH.
AND WHAT'S THIS?
JUST LEAVE IT TO ME! I'VE GOT THE WEATHERING SPELL.
THIS STUFF WILL BE HARDENED UP IN NO TIME.
CONCRETE!
GIVE IT HERE.
OH?

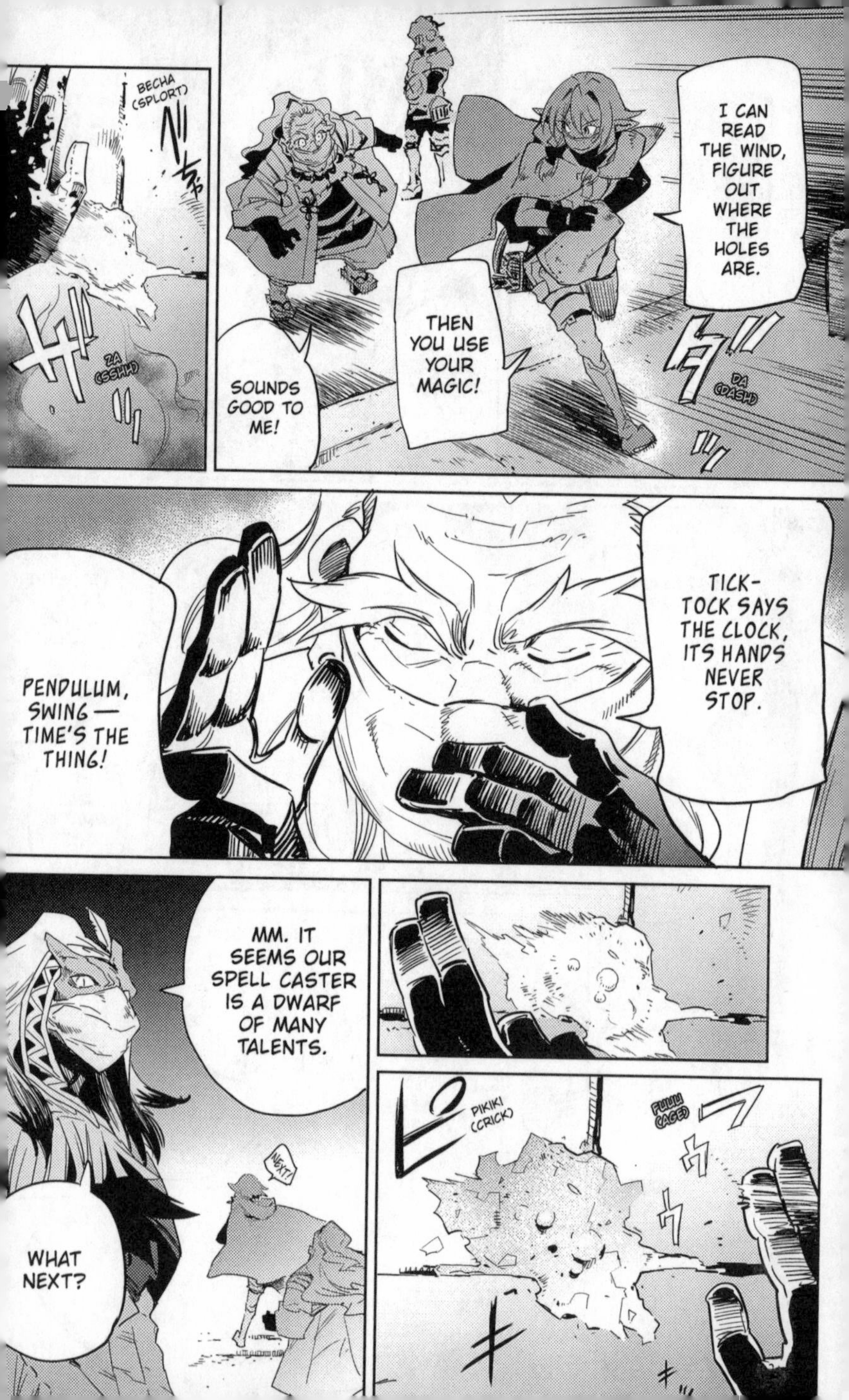
I CAN READ THE WIND, FIGURE OUT WHERE THE HOLES ARE.
DA (DASH)
THEN YOU USE YOUR MAGIC!
SOUNDS GOOD TO ME!
BECHA (SPLORT)
ZA (SSHH)
TICK-TOCK SAYS THE CLOCK, ITS HANDS NEVER STOP.
PENDULUM, SWING— TIME'S THE THING!
FUUU (CAGED)
PIKIKI (CRICK)
MM. IT SEEMS OUR SPELL CASTER IS A DWARF OF MANY TALENTS.
NEXT!
WHAT NEXT?

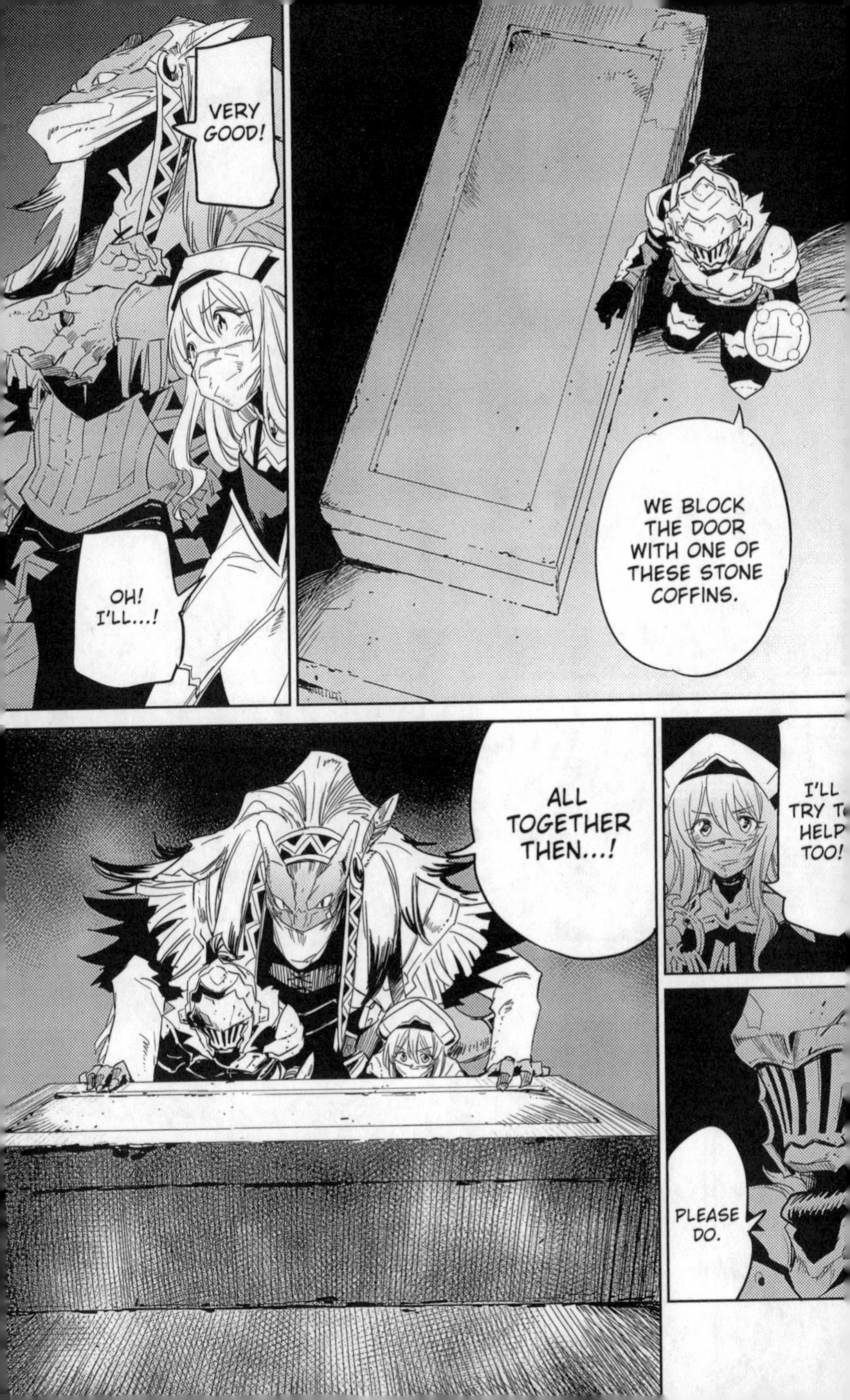
WE BLOCK THE DOOR WITH ONE OF THESE STONE COFFINS.
VERY GOOD!
OH! I'LL...!
I'LL TRY T HELP TOO!
PLEASE DO.
ALL TOGETHER THEN...!

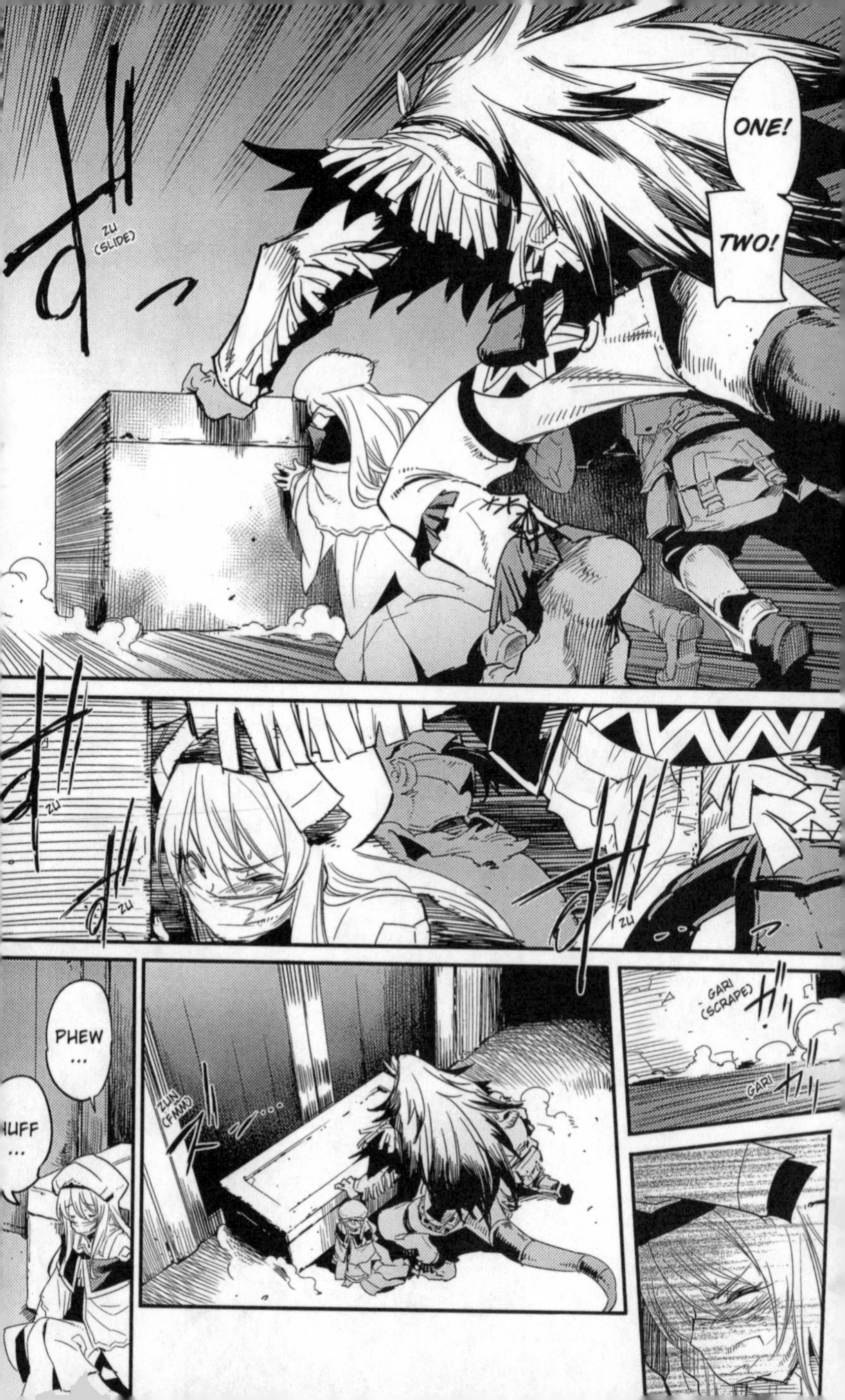
ONE!
TWO!
ZU (SLIDE)
ZU
ZU
ZU
GARI (SCRAPE)
GARI
ZUN (FMM)
PHEW...
HUFF...

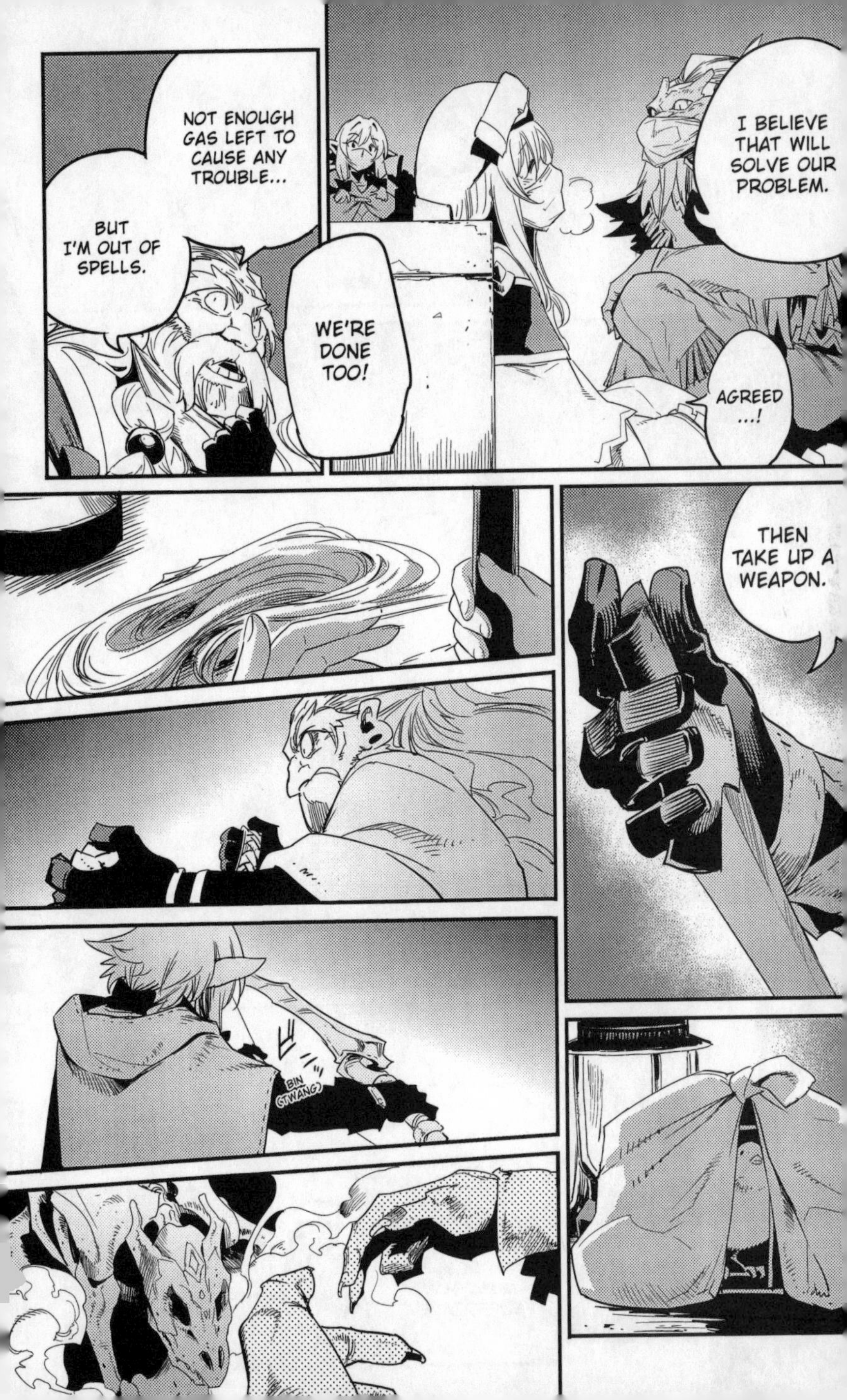
I BELIEVE THAT WILL SOLVE OUR PROBLEM.
AGREED ...!
NOT ENOUGH GAS LEFT TO CAUSE ANY TROUBLE...
BUT I'M OUT OF SPELLS.
WE'RE DONE TOO!
THEN TAKE UP A WEAPON.
BIN (TWANG)

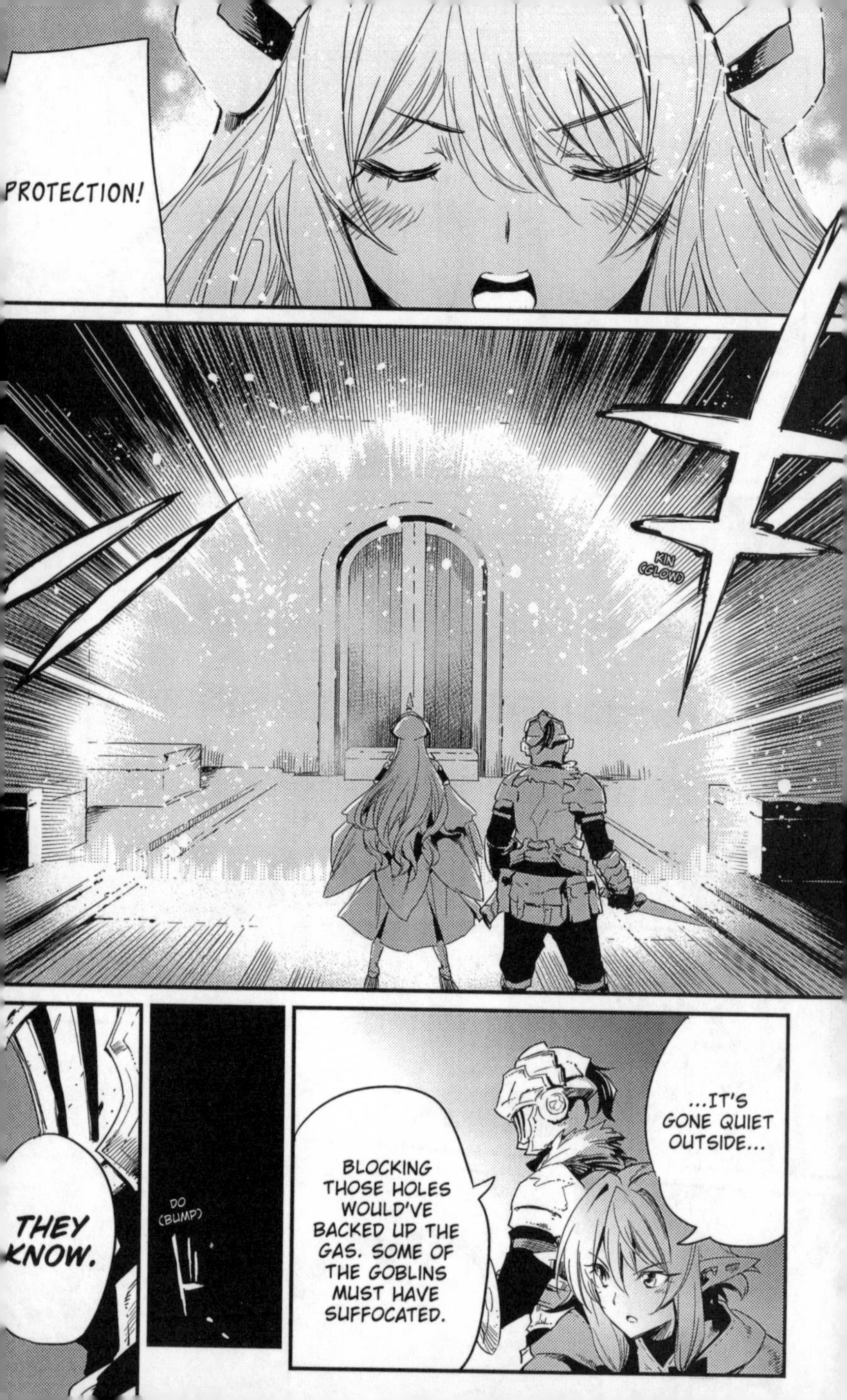
PROTECTION!
KIN (GLOW)
...IT'S GONE QUIET OUTSIDE...
BLOCKING THOSE HOLES WOULD'VE BACKED UP THE GAS. SOME OF THE GOBLINS MUST HAVE SUFFOCATED.
DO (BUMP)
THEY KNOW.

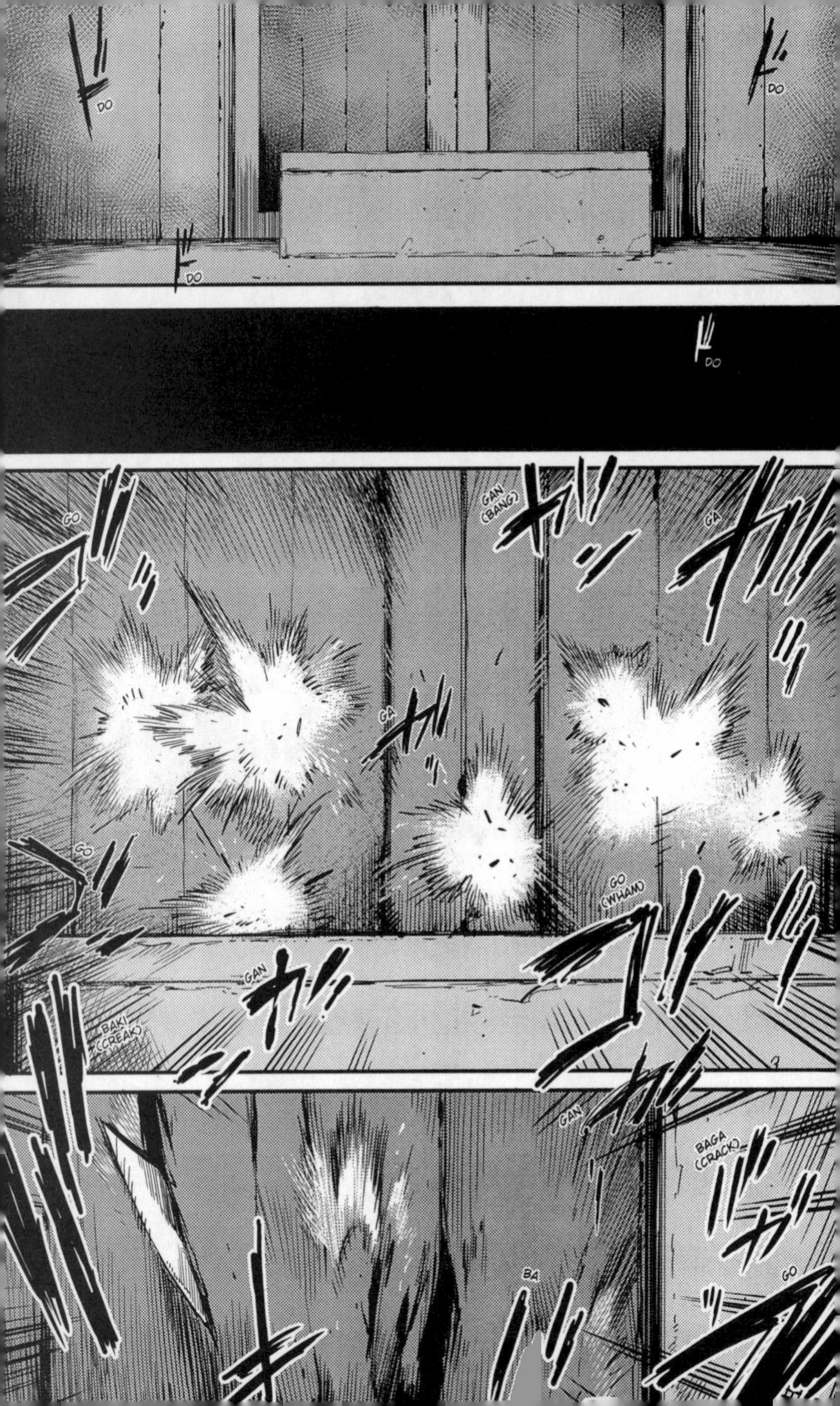
DO
DO
DO
DO
GA
GAN (BANG)
GO
GA
GO (WHAM)
GO
GAN
BAKI (CREAK)
BAGA (CRACK)
GAN
GO
BA

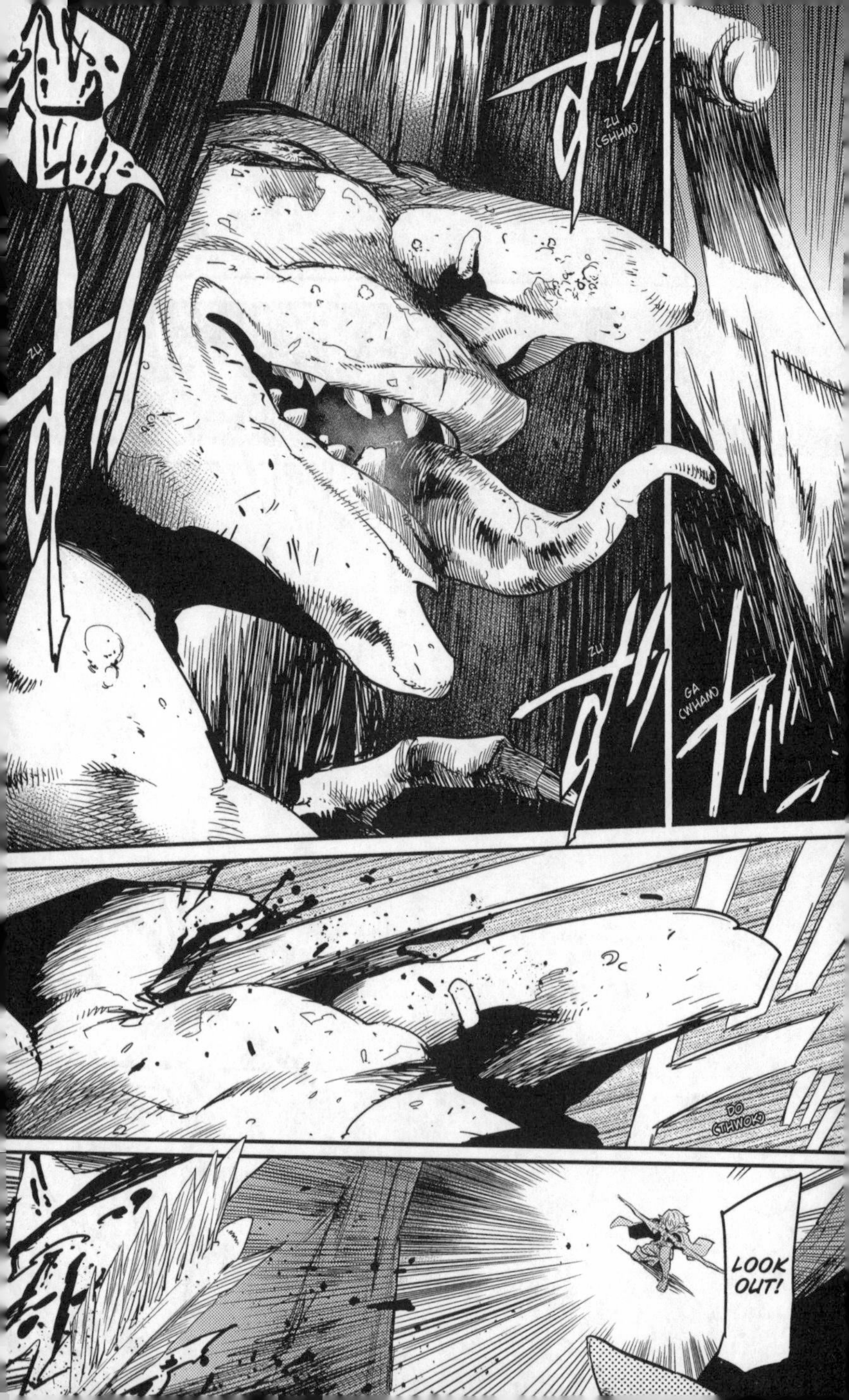
ZU (SHHM)
ZU
ZU
GA (WHAM)
DO (THWOK)
LOOK OUT!

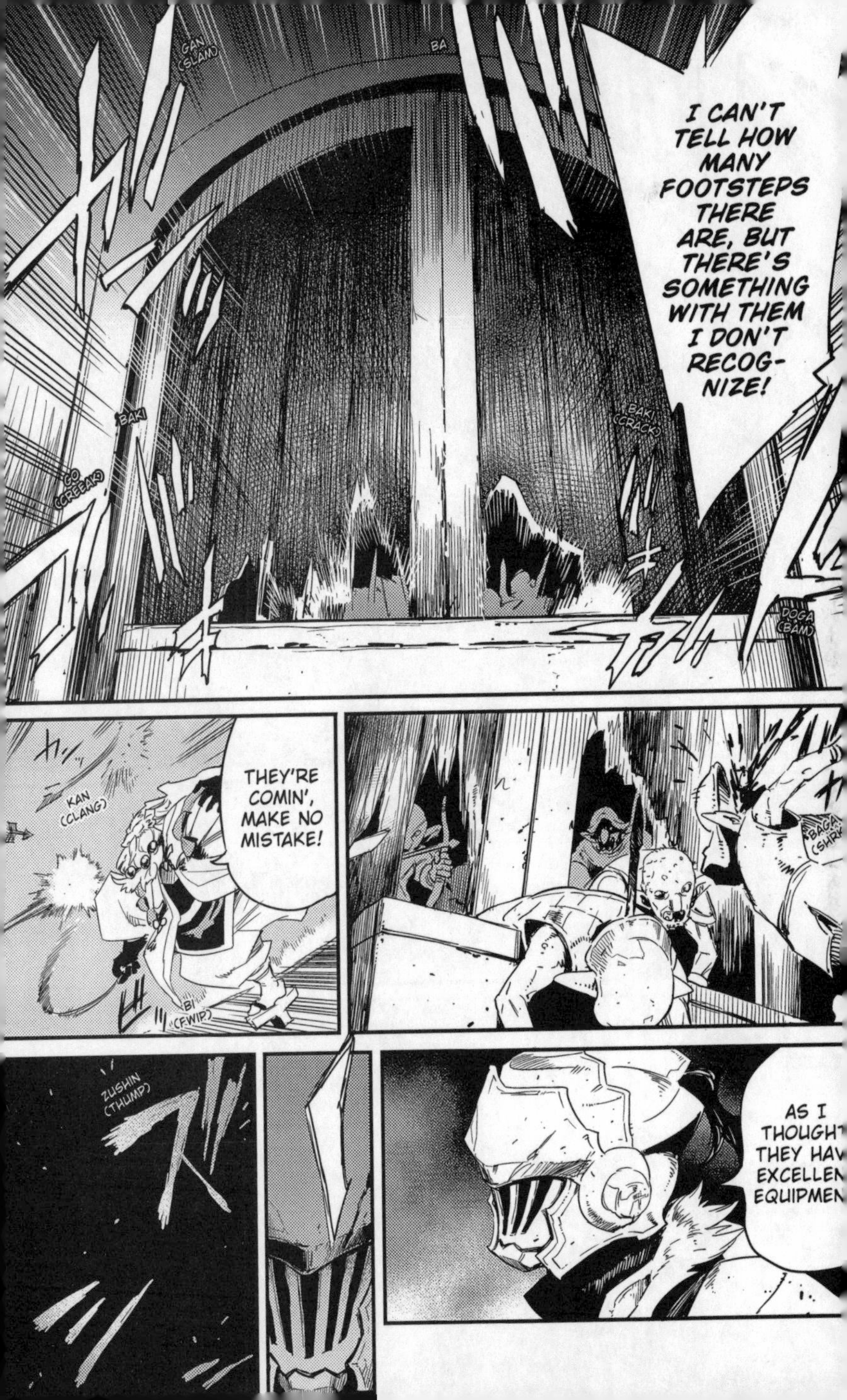
BA
I CAN'T TELL HOW MANY FOOTSTEPS THERE ARE, BUT THERE'S SOMETHING WITH THEM I DON'T RECOGNIZE!
GAN (SLAM)
BAKI (CRACK)
DOGA (BAM)
BAKI
GO (CREEAK)
BAGA (SHRK
THEY'RE COMIN', MAKE NO MISTAKE!
KAN (CLANG)
BI (FWIP)
AS I THOUGHT THEY HAV EXCELLEN EQUIPMEN
ZUSHIN (THUMP)

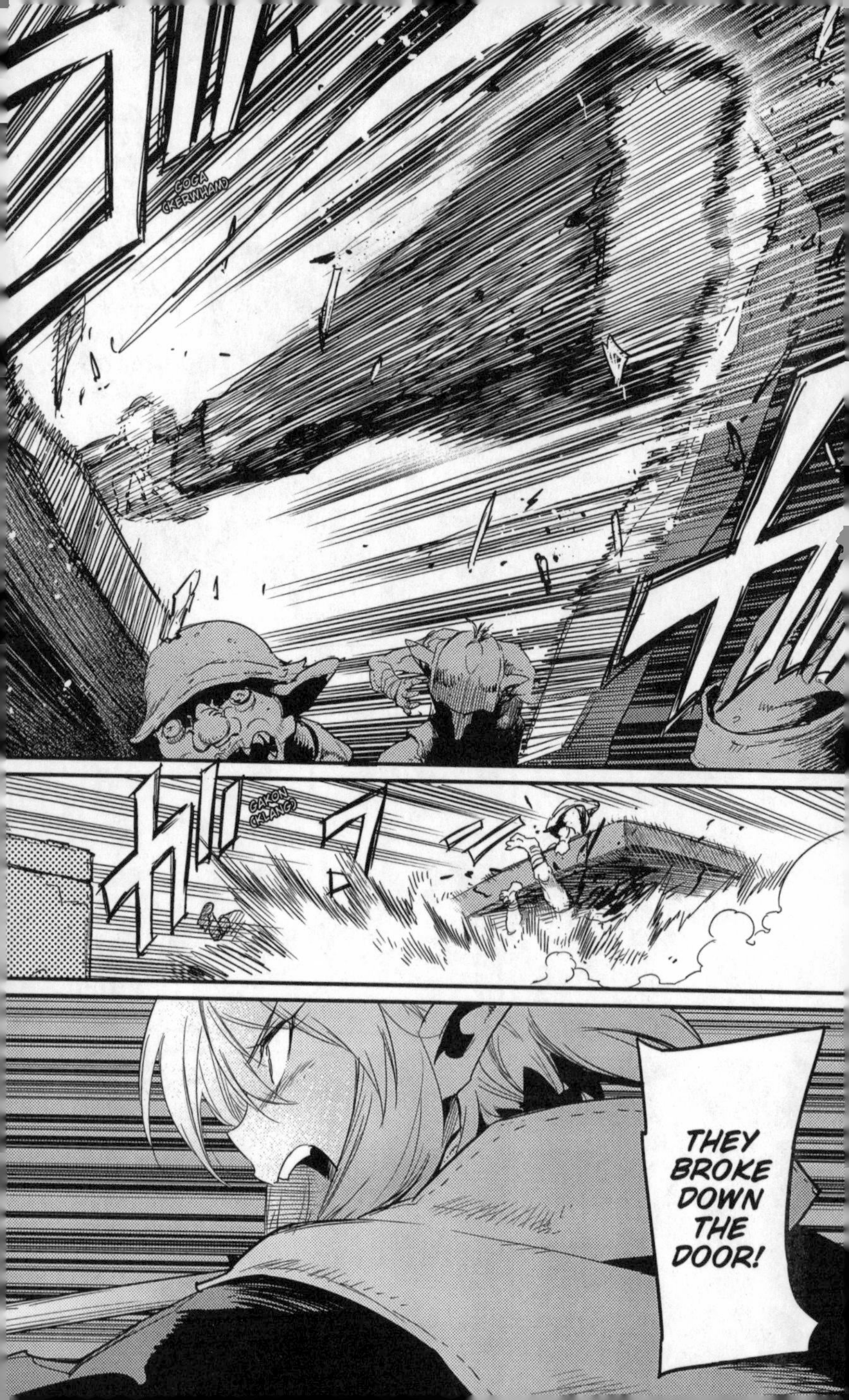
GOGA (KERWHAM)
GAKON (KLANG)
THEY BROKE DOWN THE DOOR!

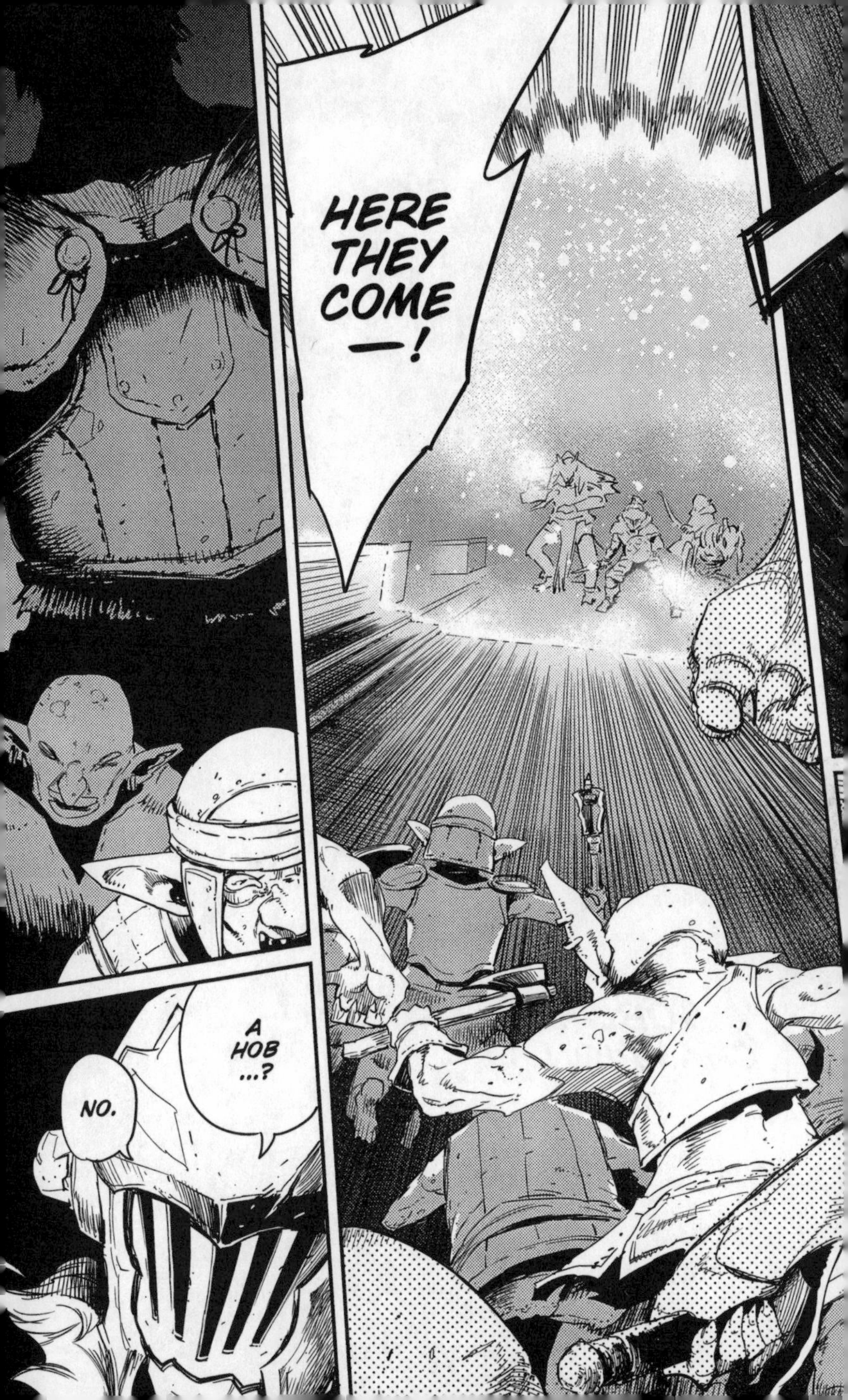
HERE THEY COME —!
A HOB ...?
NO.

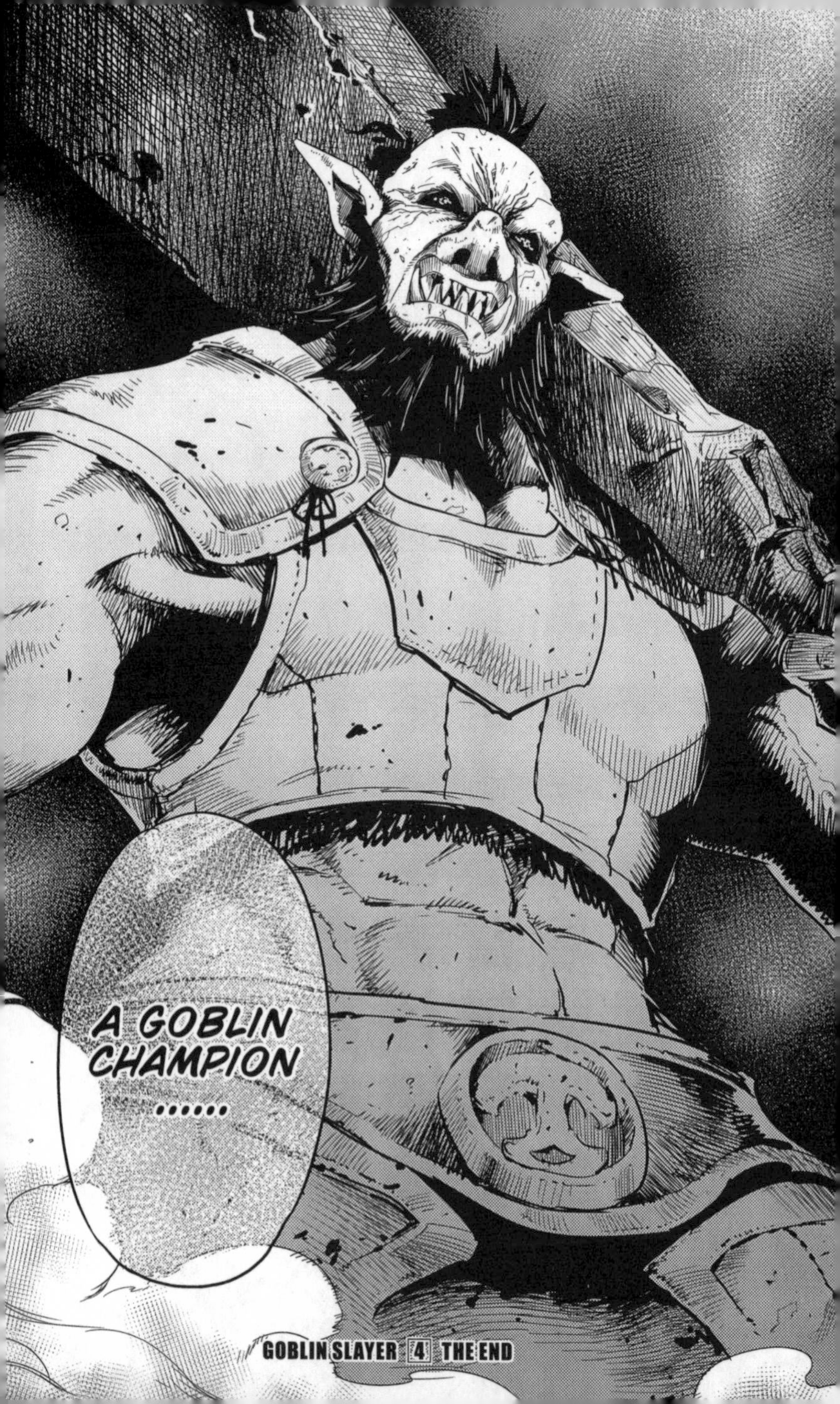
A GOBLIN CHAMPION ......
GOBLIN SLAYER 4 THE END

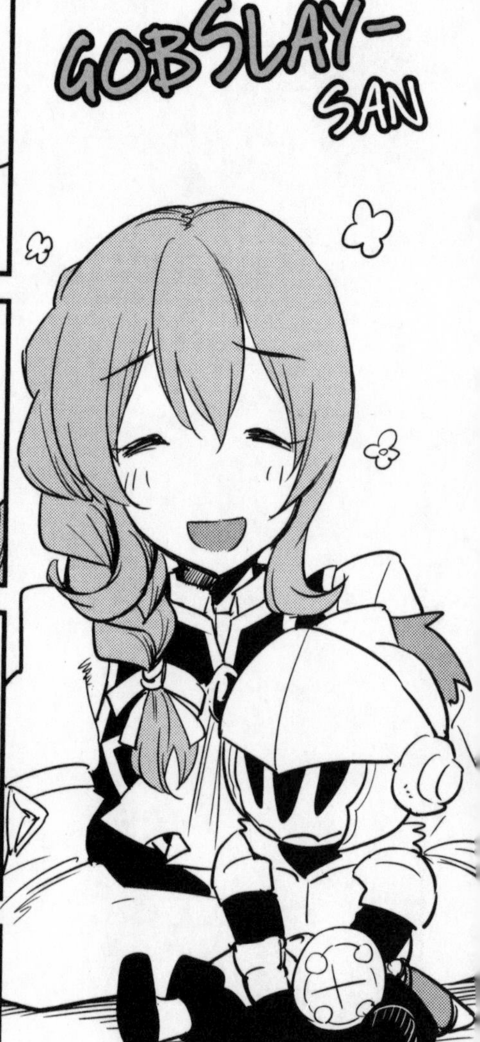
GOBSLAY-SAN

APPEALING REWARD

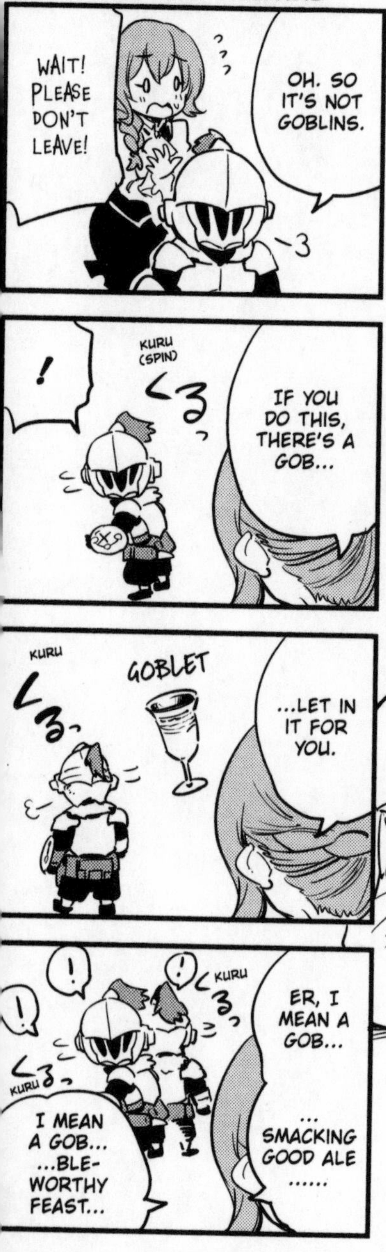
OH. SO IT'S NOT GOBLINS.
WAIT! PLEASE DON'T LEAVE!
IF YOU DO THIS, THERE'S A GOB...
KURU (SPIN)
!
...LET IN IT FOR YOU.
GOBLET
KURU
ER, I MEAN A GOB...
... SMACKING GOOD ALE ......
KURU
!
!
KURU
I MEAN A GOB... ...BLE-WORTHY FEAST...

A NEW WEAPON

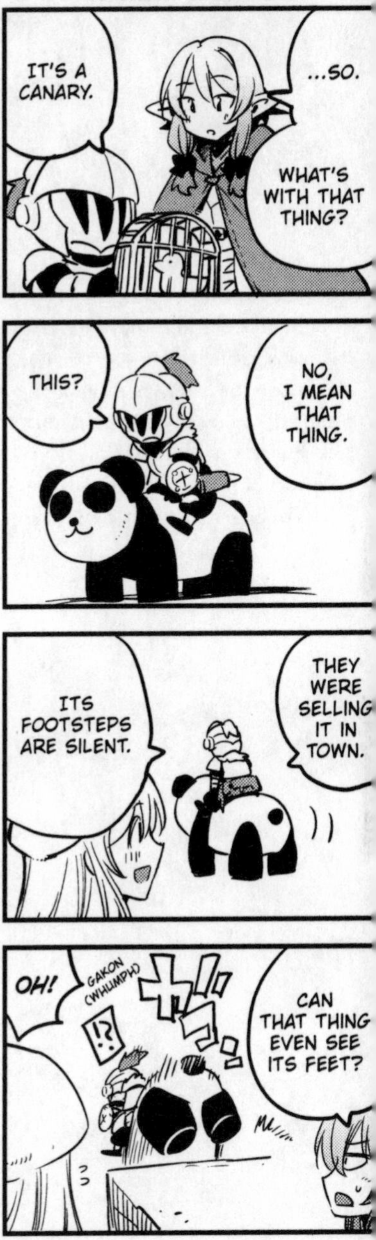
...SO. WHAT'S WITH THAT THING?
IT'S A CANARY.
NO, I MEAN THAT THING.
THIS?
THEY WERE SELLING IT IN TOWN.
ITS FOOTSTEPS ARE SILENT.
CAN THAT THING EVEN SEE ITS FEET?
GAKON (WHUMPH)
OH!
!?

EFFECTIVE

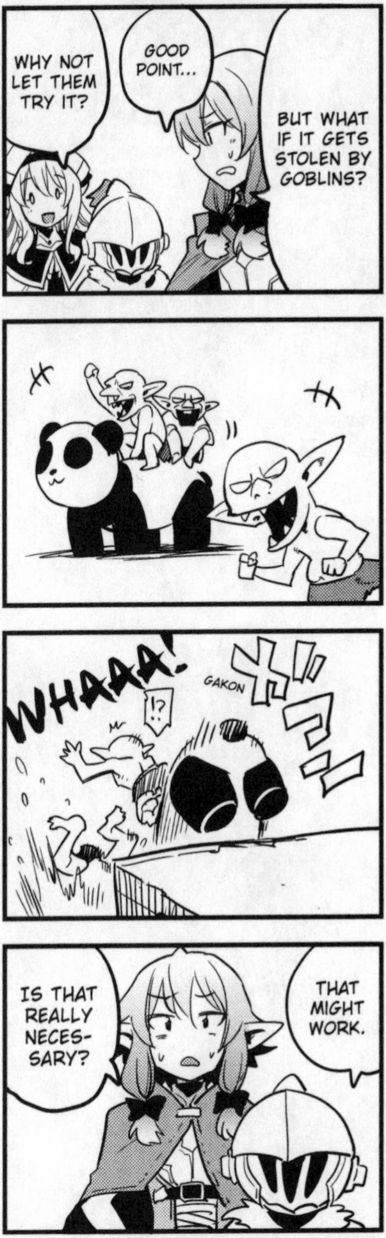
BUT WHAT IF IT GETS STOLEN BY GOBLINS?
GOOD POINT...
WHY NOT LET THEM TRY IT?
GAKON
!?
WHAAA!
THAT MIGHT WORK.
IS THAT REALLY NECES-SARY?

HE DOES NOT LET ANYONE ROLL THE DICE.

A young Priestess joins her first adventuring party, but blind to the dangers, they almost immediately find themselves in trouble. It's Goblin Slayer who comes to their rescue—a man who has dedicated his life to the extermination of all goblins by any means necessary. A dangerous, dirty, and thankless job, but he does it better than anyone. And when rumors of his feats begin to circulate, there's no telling who might come calling next...

Light Novel
V. 1-2
Available
Now!

Check out the simul-pub manga chapters every month!

www.yenpress.com

Turn to the back of the
book for a short story by
Kumo Kagyu!

GOBLIN
SLAYER

softly, "I'm going, then."

"Ah," Guild Girl said, a meaningless syllable. But the steel helmet turned to her.

"You will go back to work, won't you? I would not want to delay you for too long."

Guild Girl blinked. She almost felt as though, somewhere behind that visor, she could see a glowing red eye.

"Er, that's right," she said with a smile and a nod. "See you later, then."

"Yes. See you later."

Then Goblin Slayer stood slowly and began walking.

Guild Girl sat on the bench a moment longer, staring out at the scenery and the town and the firmament.

The sky was blue, the clouds were white, the sun was high, and the breeze was just a little bit chilly.

The road bustled with activity, and the smells of dozens of lunches floated between the comings and goings of people.

"Heh-heh!"

On her way back to the Guild, she skipped down the road, just a little.

some restaurant to eat, she might not have gotten to sit next to him like this.

She had to pick her poison. When it came down to it, Guild Girl wasn't quite sure what to talk about, so instead, she took a bite of her meal. Her nibbles were appropriately dainty, and she glanced to the side as she ate, allowing her to see him stuff his food through the visor of his helmet.

"What's wrong?"

The unexpected question evoked a scratchy little "Nothing!" from Guild Girl. She searched for something to say. She took in a breath, then let it out. "I was just thinking, back when we first met, I couldn't have imagined sharing a meal with you like this."

He didn't respond immediately. She had simply said what came to mind, but now that she thought about it, it was true.

It was a full five years now that this strange, serious adventurer had become a part of her daily life. Part of the daily life of this entire town.

"Everything changes," he said.

"That's true." She nodded and kept eating.

They didn't say anything. They didn't really have to. They simply sat and ate and watched the town go by.

What they were seeing was the result of Guild Girl's hard work, and certainly his, too. Consider a certain recent incident. If he hadn't been there—well, no. The goblin army would have been stopped even without him.

Yes, it would have, but surely what she was seeing now would be very different.

He finished eating. A little while later, he suddenly said

she didn't feel a twinge of jealousy at the idea. But the main feeling that welled up in her chest was a warmth at the thought of him in such a mundane setting.

"So do you...have any plans?" She tried to sound natural, to hide the racing of her heart.

His reply was as usual: First one word, "No." Then two more, "Not especially."

"Well, in that case..."

Guild Girl felt her chest growing tight; she forced herself to breathe. She struggled to keep her voice from squeaking.

Come on! This is no time to hesitate!

In lieu of giving herself an encouraging slap on the cheeks, she put on her famous smile and gave a little tilt of her head. "If you like...how about we have lunch together?"

§

"How about here, then?"

"Okay."

They sat down on a bench in one corner of the plaza. Nearby, they could smell the mingled aromas of oil and iron. Guild Girl fixed her eyes on the floor, just like she'd done the first time they had gone out together.

On her knees was the lunch she had just bought. It was a simple meal of bread sandwiching some lean meat. She didn't even need a plate.

Maybe I should've gone with something just a little more upscale...

She couldn't help the thought, but if they had gone to

"Well anyway, what are we going to do about lunch... hmm?"

Maybe that was why she so readily picked out the thing that didn't quite fit in with the otherwise normal scene.

Fluttering amid the crowd, she caught a glimpse of what seemed to be a piece of old cloth.

A cheap-looking steel helmet, grimy leather armor, a round shield tied to one arm, and a sword of a strange length at the hip.

She knew who it was immediately.

"Goblin Slayer, sir!"

"Hrm..."

Guild Girl suddenly blushed at how loud her own voice was. But the adventurer stopped walking and looked at her.

There was no turning back now. On impulse, she had called out to him, and now she trotted up to him quickly.

"Ahem," she said, looking for the words. "What brings you here? I thought today was your day off."

Wasn't it? she thought, reviewing his schedule in her mind.

"Yes," he answered even as she mulled it over. "That was my intention."

"*Was*"?

"However, I was chased out. Told I was getting in the way of the cleaning."

That made Guild Girl's eyes go wide, but then her expression softened.

Well, my goodness...

She imagined that girl on the farm having this rather domestic exchange with him, and it would be a lie to say town.

Having a meal was about more than the food. The location and the atmosphere mattered, too. (These reflections made her feel rather artisanal herself.)

Her braids bounced as she walked down the street. If you wanted to do your best work, you had to be constantly trying new things.

§

The sky was blue, the clouds were white, the sun was high, and the breeze was just a little bit chilly.

The road bustled with activity, and the smells of dozens of lunches floated between the comings and goings of people.

Guild Girl threaded her way through the crowd of pedestrians, each going to their own destination.

"Heh-heh."

She took a deep breath of the wondrously clear air and smiled. Her steps were as light as her heart, and only the impulse to act her age kept her from skipping along.

Guild Girl loved the smell of people at work.

There was no really special reason, but if she had to try and explain it, maybe it was because she was a civil servant herself. There were only so many jobs where you could see the fruits of your labor appear before your eyes, touch the product of the sweat of your brow.

I guess I'm just trying to justify it!

A giggle overflowed from her. She realized she had always loved this kind of weather, ever since she was little.

Interlude:
Of One Afternoon – by Kumo Kagyu

"Okay, I'm going to take my break, then."

"Sounds good. Have fun!"

Smiling as her colleague gave her a friendly wave, Guild Girl stood up smartly from her chair.

Back in the interior of the reception area, she moved her name tag from "present" to "on break."

It was noon exactly. They had mostly cleaned out the morning crop of adventurers, and no one would be back until evening. That left Guild Girl with some time on her hands, an opportunity she was not about to miss.

Hmmm. What to do today...?

She put a hand to her stomach (tight and fit thanks to her customary self-restraint) and let her thoughts drift.

The Guild had a tavern attached, and it would be easy enough to order lunch there. Yes, but...

"If I go there every day, I'm going to get bored with it."

Thankfully, the Rhea Chef was a veritable artisan. The dishes on the menu included seasonal and fresh ingredients, so the offerings changed regularly.

Still, having such fancy food every day didn't quite suit her, either...

"All right, then. I think I'll go out today."

The decision left her feeling lighthearted and easy, and Guild Girl eagerly went out onto the streets of the frontier

GOBLIN SLAYER 4

Original Story: Kumo Kagyu
Art: Kousuke Kurose
Character Design: Noboru Kannatuki

Translation: Kevin Steinbach ✢ Lettering: Bianca Pistillo

GOBLIN SLAYER Volume 4
©Kumo Kagyu / SB Creative Corp. Character Design: Noboru Kannatuki
©2018 Kousuke Kurose / SQUARE ENIX CO., LTD. First published in Japan in 2018 by SQUARE ENIX CO., LTD. English translation rights arranged with SQUARE ENIX CO., LTD. and YEN PRESS, LLC through Tuttle-Mori Agency, Inc., Tokyo.

English translation ©2018 by SQUARE ENIX CO., LTD.

Yen Press, LLC
150 West 30th Street, 19th Floor
New York, NY 10001

Visit us at yenpress.com
facebook.com/yenpress
twitter.com/yenpress
yenpress.tumblr.com
instagram.com/yenpress

First Yen Press Print Edition: November 2018
The chapters in this volume were originally published as ebooks by Yen Press.

Yen Press is an imprint of Yen Press, LLC.
The Yen Press name and logo are trademarks of Yen Press, LLC.

The publisher is not responsible for websites (or their content) that are not owned by the publisher.

Library of Congress Control Number: 2017954163

ISBNs: 978-1-9753-2806-1 (paperback)
        978-1-9753-2830-6 (ebook)

10 9 8 7 6 5

BVG

Printed in the United States of America